Abraham

Father of Many Nations

An Historical Novel based on the Holy Bible
and the Book of Jasher

By

WARREN K. JOHNSON, Th. D.

Christosoro Publishing
Post Office Box 1741
Santa Clarita, CA 91386-1741

Abraham

Father of Many Nations

An Historical Novel based on events described
In the Holy Bible and the Book of Jasher

Cover illustration by
Don Vernon

Library of Congress Catalog Control Number:
2001135703

ISBN Hard Cover Edition: 0-9715968-0-8
ISBN Soft Cover Edition: 0-9715968-1-6

Dedication

To my loyal wife Vera and sons Christian and Mathew,
this book "ABRAHAM Father of many Nations" is dedicated.
Their love and patience has endured over the years
to sustain confidence in my work.

W.K.J.

Contents of Abraham-Father of Many Nations

AUTHOR'S PREFACE

When studying any historical character it is important to know if the information at hand is authentic. It is especially important in the case of Abraham since many writers and teachers regard him as a legendary figure, more a product of fiction than fact. The Prologue that follows will present exciting scientific and Biblical evidence that you may not have heard before. It is sure to make a difference in your understanding of ancient times.

Evidence from the science of Archaeology and related fields removes Abraham and other Bible characters from a legendary realm to their rightful place as important historical figures. In this light, cities and civilizations of Biblical renown assume historical reality.

The personality of Abraham looms large on the horizon not long after the Bible record begins. The values of his character become woven into the fabric of his tribe, a tribe that develops into a nation, and company of nations, multiplying progeny and civilizing the world for four thousand years. Myths do not produce results such as this.

No attempt is made herein to interpret the Bible and fit its teachings into the pattern of any particular religious organization. This is not to be considered a religious book just because it boldly deals with a figure prominent in at least three major religions of today.

The purpose of this book is to bring Abraham to life with the license of a novelist, the evidence of science, and sacred literature as our guide. In an effort to glean as much information as possible about "Abraham's Family", I utilized information from a sacred source in addition to "The Holy Bible." Through this source, once lost, I have been able to add new life to old familiar characters.

There are a number of sacred scrolls named in the Old Testament which are classified as lost; books supposedly scattered or destroyed in the military conflicts that occurred in Judea. These writings, therefore, are not included in the Hebrew Canon. Among the several missing, I draw attention to one in particular.

The "Book of Jasher," referred to in Joshua and Second Samuel of the Bible, has been an object of curiosity for Bible scholars over a long period of time. Some contend that because these writings report the lives and acts of Abraham, Isaac, Jacob, and other

Patriarchs, who were upright in the eyes of God, the work is understandably titled: "Jasherim, the Just."

The translator, who put it into English from the Hebrew, renders the title: "The upright or correct record." This title was not known by scholars and became termed: "The Book of Jasher" (not to be confused as the book of a judge or prophet of Israel).

Why is "The Book of Jasher" important to the writing of this novel about Abraham? I call upon the translator's own words for my answer. *The important transactions which are narrated with so remarkable a brevity in the Bible, are, in Jasher, more circumstantially detailed.... The character of Abraham, for piety, true dignity and hospitality, appears to stand unrivaled... This book gives a particular account of the instruction received by Abraham, Isaac and Jacob, from Shem and Eber, through which they became so excellent in piety and wisdom, their tutors in learning having lived to so great an age....*

The roots of Abraham are an important part of his story. The Adamic family tree with its chosen branches (identified by different names as millenniums past by) were called Adamites, Aryans, Noahites, Semites, Hebrews, Seed of Abraham and Isaac. Subsequently they became known as Israelites on through David to Yahshua or Jesus. They have demonstrated God's selection and guidance of a family for purposes that ran contrary to all concurrent pagan religious practices.

Abraham was a world-renown historical figure. He was instrumental in eliminating horribly oppressive religious beliefs. Through faith in the Covenants offered by his God, he charted a new course of religious freedom for mankind. This became a critical turning point in man's civilizing development, for now man was no longer in bondage to religions and governments by extortion and fear.

This novel, written with no intention of being adequate or complete on the subject of Abraham's Family, intends to do much more for the reader, however, than just entertain. A new look at a vitally important religious/historical figure, his remarkable accomplishments, and world-shaping destiny, is certain to be educational.

Warren K. Johnson, Th.D.

PROLOGUE

CIVILIZATION

T he Bible's historical record has been substantiated by the uncovering of new information, time and time again, through archaeology. Sacred and scientific evidence allows us to put Abraham in a better perspective to understand his family heritage.

Were Abraham and his ancestors, from Adam forward, real people? Or were they legendary? Were Adam and Eve the first couple created on earth in its beginnings? Or were they the progenitors of a new family of man, from which civilization can be traced, starting only a few thousand years ago? What evidence is there to prove there was a Garden of Eden and Great Flood? Where did Noah, his three sons and their families settle?

How old is man's existence on earth? Scientists do not agree. Estimates range from 50,000 to one million years. In Jeremiah 4:23 we have a description of a destroyed society!

I beheld the earth, and lo, it was without form and void; and the heavens, and they had no light. I beheld the mountains, and lo, they trembled, and all the hills moved lightly. I beheld, and lo, there was no man, and all the birds of the heavens were fled. I beheld, and lo, the fruitful place was a wilderness, and all the cities thereof were broken down at the presence of the Lord, and by his fierce anger. For thus hath the Lord said, the whole land shall be desolate: yet I will not make a full end. (Authors underline.)

When translated properly the Scriptures of the Bible lend invaluable aid to a researcher looking for beginnings. In Genesis 1:26, the King James Translation reads in part: *Let us make man in our image, after our likeness; and let them have dominion over...all the earth.* Verse 27: *...male and female created He them.* Verse 28: *And God blessed them, and God said unto them, be fruitful, and multiply, and replenish (re-occupy) the earth, and subdue it...* (Author's underlines emphasize creation of men in the plural.

In the next chapter, Genesis 2, we find THE ADAM formed (in the singular) by God after resting from all other creations. The

Hebrew word 'aw-dawm' (rendered 'Adam' in English) is from a root word meaning 'To show blood in the face' or 'of a ruddy complexion', a word applicable only to the Caucasoid race and not to the Mongoloid and Negroid races or any mixture of these three primary races.

For many thousands of years before Adam, Man's existence remained unchanged with little sign of progressive improvement. But for the tools they fashioned roughly, pre-Adamites remained quite primitive and savage. They hunted for food, grew little, and fought enemies to survive or conquer. They had no alphabet and knew only primitive communication. We find the following supportive evidence in Genesis 2:20 of the Lamsa Bible:

> *And Adam gave names to all cattle, and to all fowl*
> *of the air, and to all wild beasts; but for Adam there*
> *was not found a helper who was equal to him.*

In Genesis 2:5 it says in part ...*and there was no man to till the soil.* It would appear that with Adam came the ability to reflect or think intelligently about complicated matters. A race of farmers, builders and administrators had begun.

Poor communication skills were a principle factor in the lack of civilizing development. When a new intelligence emerged, rooted in versatile language, civilization had dawned.

Annual flooding was tamed and irrigation on a large scale was effected through remarkable engineering. Expansive farming, animal husbandry, crafts, and manufacturing flourished. Trade grew and extended far beyond the borders of towns and city/states as exploration advanced with astronomy and navigation. Colonies were established and civilization spread.

The controversy of Creation versus Evolution is too huge to discuss in detail. Critical assessments, however, are important in understanding the foundation of civilization. The commonly taught theory that civilization, with all mankind, evolved from various species over a period covering millions of years is false.

After an important conference of some 150 specialists in evolution held in Chicago, Illinois, a report concluded: *Evolution is undergoing its broadest and deepest revolution in nearly 50 years. ...Exactly how evolution happened is now a matter of great controversy among biologists.... No clear resolution of the controversies was in sight.*

In their desire to find evidence of "ape-men", some scientists have been a part of outright fraud. For about 40 years the "Piltdown Man", discovered in 1912, was accepted as genuine by most of the evolutionary community. Finally, in 1953, the hoax was uncovered when modern techniques revealed that human and ape bones had been put together and artificially aged.

The oldest archaeological remains of Man, tested by carbon dating, reveal the presence of racial types other than Caucasian. Traces of the Caucasian, or Adamic Family, appear closer in time to the present, only about 6,000 years ago. Darwinian theories are not scientifically supported.

The Old Testament record, through Bible chronologies, trace patriarchal ancestries from Jesus Christ back to Adam. Adding the accumulated years of their lifetimes, the total amounts to about 4,000 years. By adding another 2,000 years from AD 1 to the present, we arrive at approximately 6,000 years as the time span from the forming of Adam to the present. The Adamic family, therefore, appeared at approximately 4000 BC This date is supported by science.

Considering the ample modern research by scholars into traditions and written records, it is safe to say that the very process of looking into the past, that is recording and preserving special events, has been going on for about 6000 years also. This is a hallmark of a civilized society.

In addition to contemporary libraries, ancient libraries, with many thousands of clay tablets in each, have been unearthed in various cities of Assyria, Elba, Mari, Sumer and Akaad. They all demonstrate a pattern in civilized administration to preserve the past.

In the cities of Mesopotamia, the craftsmen in metal possessed knowledge of metallurgy and a great technical skill. Artistic works with metal and jewels, rivaling those of today, were highly developed as early as 3000 BC

The contents of ancient tombs themselves illustrate a highly developed state of society. A society in which the architect was familiar with all the basic principles of construction known to us today. They commonly used not only the column, but the arch, the vault and the dome; architectural forms, which were not to find their way into the western world for hundreds of years.

Dr. W.W. Bell Dawson, a Canadian scientist has this to say in his book, "The Bible Confirmed by Science": *Neither in Egypt nor in Babylonia has any beginning of civilization been found. As far back as archaeology can take us, man is already civilized, building cities and temples, carving hard stone into artistic form, and even employing a system of picture writing. And of Egypt it may be said the older the country the more perfect it is found to be. The fact is a very remarkable one, in view of modern theories of development, and of the evolution of civilization out of barbarism. Such theories are not borne out by the discoveries of archaeology. Instead of the progress we should expect, we find retrogression and decay; where we look for the rude beginnings of art, we find an advanced society and artistic perfection. Evidence shows that the Biblical view is right after all, and the civilized man has been civilized from the outset.*

W. W. Prescott, in his book, "The Spade and the Bible," says, *Not a ruined city has been opened up that has given any comfort to unbelieving critics or evolutionists. Every find of archaeologists in Bible lands has gone to confirm Scripture and confound its enemies.*

God formed Adam as the first Patriarch (male head of a long family line) with his wife Eve, for the purpose of serving as an administrator, under the will of Yahvah to show how people should live.

It is through God's selected Patriarchs that justice and uprightness had any place in an opposing pagan world. An effort to maintain this standard, at least to some degree, was made during the development of civilization.

Survival as a family, as a tribe, and as a continuing race was very difficult for the Adamic Patriarchs, who tried to keep faithful to their high calling through belief in the one God Yahvah. Kingdoms and peoples, steeped in millenniums of primitive polytheism, pressed upon the Patriarchs their immoral sexual enticements and inhumane religion.

The polytheistic system was devoid of any redeeming values. God cleansed a portion of His earth by flooding away the Adamite undesirables who had mixed with the primitives and corrupted their high calling. God saved only a chosen remnant, Noah and his family, to start over and carry out His special mission for them. Through the leadership of His Patriarchs, they were to be an instrument of God and a light to the world in demonstrating higher civilizing values the world did not know.

In tracing the beginnings of civilization it is important to know where the Adamic family of man originated. Adam tended a garden or farm in Eden. But where was Eden? The renowned French Orientalist, M. Renan, believed the Pamir Plateau was the cradle of the Aryan Race. The region is located in that part of lower Russia protruding into northwest China, to the east of Afghanistan. It seems

X

that science and the Bible agree once again. This could have been the Paradise of Eden described in Genesis. It has the same four currents of water flowing from the one source in opposite directions.

Sir Gaston Maspero, late Director-General of Egyptian Antiquities, in his book "Ancient History of the Orient," also identifies the Pamir Plateau as the location of the Garden of Eden.

Professor Renan tells us the people of Asia consider this Plateau of Pamir to be the original Eden and the central part of the world. Orientalist scholar Professor Brunoff leads us to the same understanding. The Hindu traditions contained in the Mahabharata and the Purana converge to the same region as the source of Aryan roots.

The Pamir Plateau with the Tarim Basin is a very different place today, than it was six thousand years ago. At that time the whole of Asia was lower in elevation than it is today. A large inland sea covered the steppes of Southern Siberia, of which the Caspian Sea and the Aral Sea are now remnants. Over the steppes of Northern Siberia roamed the mammoth and the Saber-toothed tiger. All indications reveal that Northern Siberia then had a semi-tropical climate, and ideal conditions prevailed on the Pamir Plateau. It bears evidence of a heavily inhabited past.

Now the Plateau is uninhabitable. It covers an area 180 miles by 180 miles. It is at an altitude of fifteen thousand feet and upon it stand peaks ten thousand feet or higher.

The Tarim Basin is the greatest sinkhole in the world, although the highest mountain peaks in the world surround it. Its floor lies in many places below the level of the Indian Ocean, indicating that a great cataclysm tore the earth here in an ancient time.

The known geological structure shows that, in ancient times at least, beneath this desert, lay enormous underground natural reservoirs, caverns filled with water. These underground reservoirs were covered by waterproof layers of rock, which kept the waters beneath from overflowing out on the land surface above.

When Adam and Eve were driven from the Garden of Eden they traveled eastward to the Tarim Basin. It was in this mountain-rimmed basin, then a fertile, well-populated land, that Adam and Eve, or at least their descendants of a few generations later, settled.

In Genesis 6:5 it says:

And God saw that the wickedness of man was great in the earth, and that every imagination of the thoughts of his heart was only evil continually.

The word translated earth is the Hebrew word **eh-rets**, which means only the land, that particular land. The flood did cover the particular land where it occurred. That is, it was a local flood which covered one particular region, or land, not the whole earth as a planet.

More evidence is found in the high-water mark found in many places along the mountains, which rim the Tarim Basin, showing that at one time it was a lake, extending to a well-marked shoreline. The mountains which rim this valley were not fully covered, for many of them range from 16,000 to 25,000 feet in height, and one even rises over 28,000 feet. Within the basin, however, are several smaller mountains, which could be fully covered by a flood held in by the higher rim of the valley.

In Genesis 11:2 the Bible says that after the Flood, some of Noah's descendants *journeyed from the east* until they came to the land of Shinar, known today as Mesopotamia. They must have come from some place east of the Tigris and Euphrates Valleys. The only location where such a flood as the Bible describes could have occurred eastward from the Tigris and Euphrates Valleys, is this mountain basin in Sinkiang Province of China.

In Smith and Goodspeed's American Translation of Genesis 7:11-12 it says:

The fountains of the great abyss were all broken open, and the windows of the heavens were opened.

This indicates that a great earthquake broke up the waterproof layer of rock over an immense water-filled abyss or cavern beneath the Tarim Basin, causing the floor of the valley to settle. It allowed the enormous underground reservoir to overflow and submerge the valley floor. A great earthquake in the Himalaya Mountains in modern times produced similar effects.

The forty days of torrential rains added to the Great Flood. This filled the valley high enough to submerge the low mountains that were inside the valley.

And the ark rested in the seventh month, on the seventeenth day of the month, upon the mountains of Ararat. *Genesis 8:4*

Sometimes a failure to translate can be as misleading as mistranslation. Most people understand the verse to mean the Mount Ararat in the land once called Armenia, (now in eastern Turkey and western Russia) some 1600 miles west of the Tarim Basin. This not what the Bible really says. Note that the verse reads mountains in the plural. Mount Ararat in old Armenia is only a single peak. It was known until fairly recent times as 'Mount Massis'.

No one had ever heard it called Mount Ararat in Biblical times. The Hebrew word ararat means simply the tops of the hills. The correct translation of Genesis 8:4, therefore, says that the ark came to rest upon the top of the high hills which were within the valley of the mountainous Tarim Basin.

When Noah and his family moved onto the plains of Shinar and the story of the Flood was told, the people of that country, many years later, imagined that it was on the highest mountain to the north of them that the Ark rested. That is why they named it Mount Ararat.

The historic Euphrates River in Mesopotamia most likely derived its name from an eastern river of Eden, in the same way that English and Dutch settlers in America brought with them names from their fatherland.

The Shu-king, Chinese historical record, reveals that during the dynasty of King Yao (a time coincidental with Noah's Flood) the Hwang Ho River carried excessive floods for three generations. Drainage out of the Tarim Basin eastward would have been carried off in the Hwang Ho River and would account for this. Many historians consider a generation as forty years. If the Hwang Ho River carried excessive floods for a period nearly 120 years, it would be strong evidence that a great flood, as previously described, had occurred. The Shu-King continued the history of the Chinese-Turanian people through this flood period. The Egyptian records also show no interruption of their existence as a people by a global flood.

There were many legends current in Chinese Turkestan of the many cities there said to have been buried under a rain of "sand" as a Divine punishment for their inhabitants having ridiculed "a holy man" who had rebuked them for their sins. The Great Flood of Genesis was clearly the catastrophe that overwhelmed the "Forty Cities of the Takla Makan," according to ancient tradition.

The mighty seismic disturbances that caused the collapse of the Adamic "earth" also brought wondrous changes to the original Paradise, raising it into the highest plateau on earth, changing its climate.

Moses wrote under, Divine inspiration, that Noah's descendants went out into a world already populated by people who had lived right through the time of the Flood. Ferrar Fenton's Modern English Translation confirms this. In Genesis 10:1-5, we hear about the descendants of Noah's son, Japheth:

From these they spread themselves over the seacoasts of the countries of the nations, each with their language amongst the gentile tribes.

Three of Japheth's descendants are of particular interest: Gomer (darkness), Javan and Tarshish. The ancient Greek scholar Ptolemy, on his map of the world, has England named "Javan" This indicates that some of Javan's descendants settled there. The territory we know as Spain was named after Tarshish. Old Testament passages named various maritime possessions of Israel as "Tarshish." Genesis 10:20 tells us of the descendants of Noah's son, Ham: *These were the sons of Ham, in their tribes and languages in the regions of the heathen.*

Genesis 10:31-32 completes it:

These are the sons of Shem by their tribes and by their languages, in their countries among the heathen.

Various Orientalists, such as the noted scientist Lenormant, claim the Semetic People descended from Adam, and after originating in Central Asia, they migrated into Mesopotamia about 3500 BC. Here they discovered a population composed of a different race or races, which they quickly conquered, and built up the Babylonian Empire. This portrayal of a domineering race coming from Central Asia is correct. But they were not Semites; they were their ancestors, the Adamites. Shem did not come into existence until about 2400 BC

A historical name for these migrating Adamites comes from the title Arya, anglicized into Aryan, a descriptive name used as much as Caucasian. The world famous Dr. Huxley wrote a treatise in 1890 where he said: *There was and is an Aryan Race, that is to say the characteristic modes of speech termed Aryan were developed among the Blond Longheads alone, however much some of these may have been modified by the importation of Non-Aryan elements.*

Authorities adhere to the opinion that the Aryan influence was special in its importance to the progress of civilization. There are various monuments in India, the Middle East and Europe with inscriptions that show a predominantly Aryan character in their language. The Aryan personalities of the authors and their histories discovered in these writings assist experts in identifying the civilization from which ours has descended. From this it is possible to recover the lost history of the Aryan Race continuously back to the rise of civilization.

Doctor L.A. Waddell, a fellow of the Royal Anthropological

Institute and noted scholar of Oriental Studies, places great emphasis on the Sumerians as the oldest of all civilized peoples. He says their vast city ruins in Mesopotamia display magnificent inscribed and sculptured monuments, other works of art, libraries and treasures which prove conclusively that the Sumerians were Aryans in physical type, culture, religion, language and writing. They most likely had fair hair since their general term for the people they ruled was *the black-headed or black-haired people.*

The kings and officials usually wore the Goth-like horned headdress on state occasions. This is the same type of headgear worn by the ancient Britons and Vikings. This Aryan physical type of the Sumerians was confirmed in 1927 by Sir Arthur Keith's examination of several skulls unearthed from Sumerian cemeteries at Ur. Keith concluded that the Sumerians certainly belonged to the same racial division of mankind as the nations of Europe.

With the coming of the Adamic Flood survivors, Noah and his descendants, begins the history of the various kingdoms of Mesopotamia. The great archaeologist, W.F. Albright, concluded: *The Hebrews brought from Northwest Mesopotamia to the west, the Creation Epic of Genesis Chapter two, the story of Eden, the saga of the Patriarchs before the Great Flood, the Flood narrative itself, and the Tower of Babel story.*

All the most reliable evidence indicates that Shem, the patriarch of the Semetic peoples, migrated to the northern part of the Fertile Crescent known as Padam Aram (Field of Aram). The map shows it at the north end of the kingdom of Mari and includes the city of Haran. (A modern atlas shows the Syrian town of Abu Kamal seven miles from the ancient ruins of Mari.) The descended families of Aram, the fifth and last son of Shem occupied the area. It is likely that the Habor River (now Al-Khabur) was named after Heber, the namesake of the Hebrews.

A Tell Hariri archaeological dig, begun in 1933 by the French, uncovered the once magnificent ancient city of Mari. Among the many thousands of clay tablets uncovered in the Mari archives, some were found to reveal Biblical names preceding Abraham. Assyriologists found a whole series of familiar-sounding names from Biblical History in reports by Governors and district commissioners of the Mari Kingdom. The following names of towns or cities in the Padam area of Mari were uncovered: Peleg, Serug, Nahor, Terah, and Haran. In Genesis 11:17-26 the Bible reads in part:
...Peleg lived thirty years and begat Reu...
And Reu lived two and thirty years and begat Serug...

And Serug lived thirty years and begat Nahor...
And Nahor lived nine and twenty years and begat Terah...
And Terah lived seventy years and begat Abram, Nahor and Haran.

Haran became an important commercial city on the Belikh River, in the valley of the same name, sixty miles above its confluence with the Euphrates River (see map). Nahor, a neighboring sister city to the south, was also an important commercial trade junction.

Some critics believe the city of Haran should be recognized widely for its formative influence on the personality, faith and thought of the Hebrews. The evidence comes from the Nuzi, Mari, Hittite and Amarna Tablets. In comparing, they consider the experiences of the Hebrews at Ur as being, at the most, that of nomads who merely passed through the great southern culture but did not stay as residents. There is much archaeological evidence that links the customs of the Hebrew Patriarchs with the people of Northern Mesopotamia. In the 19th and 18th centuries BC the Padan Aram area was the homeland of Aram, Heber, and Terah with his sons, including Abraham.

After the Flood, Noah and his sons, with their families, migrated westward across Asia. They entered the Tigris/Euphrates Valley and settled first in Akkad. Shem crossed the land at the north of the Fertile Crescent leaving descendants principally in the Padan Aram area. He seems to have finished his migration in Southern Canaan. Sacred evidence indicates he became King of Salem, short for Urusalem, later anglicized to Jerusalem.

There are indicators in the Bible that Shem could have been Melchizedek (King of Righteousness). The book of Jasher refers to him as Adonaizedek, meaning God's King. Jesus Christ, who is believed by Christianity to become King of this world, was titled a "High Priest after the Order of Melchizedek."

Shem was most likely in regular communication with Heber, his grandson, the Patriarch of the Hebrews. Eber or Heber means "colonizer." The Hebrews were signified as those people whose origin was east of the Tigris and Euphrates Rivers (the Tarim Basin). Heber's descendants were also called Habiri, Abiri, Ibire, and Khapiru in other dialects of other lands where they became known.

The centuries following the Flood compose one of the most dynamic epochs of history. During that time there arose along the Tigris and Euphrates the Chaldean (from Akkadian 'Kaldu) civilization. It has baffled archaeologists, since it arose within such a short period, like that of the Egyptian during the pyramid age a few centuries earlier. The only explanation that can be given for the sudden development of both is that the Egyptian had its conception through the influx of the Adamite Pyramid builders before the Flood and the Chaldean through the influx of the sons of Noah after the Flood. This explains the advanced state of scientific achievement found in early Chaldea, particularly in mathematics and astronomy.

From the time of the Adamic Family, the first-born male of human families and animal flocks was expected to be dedicated to the Everliving God. This was accomplished literally or by paying Redemption Money. As minor as it may seem, this was an important civilizing factor. The earliest reference we have on the subject comes from an understanding of the Patriarch Shem.

The name Shem means Renown, and it was a name befitting this Patriarch's religious and historical contributions to mankind. Shem was the eldest of Noah's three sons and he received the birthright from his father. Monetarily the birthright involved inheritance, by the eldest son, of a double portion of the father's wealth.

More importantly, however, was the fundamental practice of training by the father and acceptance by the son, of divinely ordained law/standards of conduct helpful to the civilizing process. Noah promised Shem that the worship of the true God would continue among his descendants. *God shall...dwell in the tents of Shem.* This can also be construed as meaning: "Shem and his descendants were to enjoy the blessings that come from loyal adherence to the teachings handed down from Patriarch to Patriarch."

The Bible represents Shem as the ancestor of the Hebrews, Arameans, and Amorites, to name a few major racially Semitic groups. Semites or Shemites are names that have been applied, since the mid 1700's AD, to other peoples who speak the Semitic Languages. Therefore, all peoples speaking the Semitic Language do not constitute a racial unit, but rather a linguistic unit.

E. Renan, well-known orientalist, said: *The tent of the Patriarch Shem was the starting point of mankind's religious progress.*

The Scriptures tell us that Shem's ancestors; Enoch, Methuselah, and Noah were equally righteous in the eyes of their God. Their fidelity to God, and His civilizing standards, made these three Patriarchs worth emulating.

Religion has always been instrumental in the development of civilization. Biblical History demonstrates that righteous law and administration, the rich soil out of which civilization grows, were handed down in accompaniment to monotheism.

Both the Old and the New Testaments should be more accurately named "Covenants" because they denote agreements or promises between the one Everliving God Yahvah and His people for their improved conduct. The covenants progressed into a law-based standard of living providing humane justice. This law-based society, led by Yahvah through his Patriarchs, developed and grew. We can call this development "a schooling in rightness and justice," and see its civilizing effect on the early nation of Israel. They were supposed to set a proper example of an upright and equitable form of civilization for other nations to imitate.

The story of Noah is remembered most easily for his discrimination against ungodly practices prevalent in the land. All the remaining Patriarchs of the Bible, such as Abraham, Isaac, Jacob/Israel and their progeny, also had to discriminate if they were to maintain obedience to the righteous laws of their God. They were forbidden to be like other people around them. A good many of Yahvah's Prophets were persecuted, and some murdered, by Israelite kings thirsting after un-Godly forms and practices used by neighboring pagan kingdoms.

All over the world, governments and religious institutions deny their people the highest form of civilization possible. It is a civilization of peaceful, prosperous, and creative existence - a civilization based on the ideal that obedience to Godly Standards brings Godly Blessings. The Bible and its history is a witness to this declaration.

"Abraham" is the story of a most important civilizer. It is a story full of love and hate, war and lust, weakness and courage, abomination and inspiration, deception and heartfelt honesty, ignorance and wisdom. It is also the covenants the Everliving Yahvah made with Abraham that was to be repeated to his descendants. Yahvah promised Abraham that his seed, through Isaac, should become many nations who would be a blessing to the entire world. By enduring a testing of his patience and faith, Abraham proved his loyalty as a friend of the Everliving Yahvah. The story of his obedient good works is told to generation after generation of his (Caucasian) people, in nation after nation around the world, down the halls of time. It is no wonder that he is called:

ABRAHAM, Father of Many Nations

Chapter 1
Birth of a Patriarch

And Terah, the son of Nahor, prince of Nimrod's host, was in those days very great in the sight of the king and his subjects, and the king and princes loved him, and they elevated him very high.

And Terah took a wife, and her name was Amthelo the daughter of Cornebo; and the wife of Terah conceived and bare him a son in those days.

Terah was seventy years old when he begat him, and Terah called the name of his son that was born to him Abram, because the king had raised him in those days and dignified him above all his princes that were with him.

Book of Jasher Chapter 7, verses 49-51

Lush green fields of garden crops filled the landscape to the west, north and south. Irrigation canals, and narrow roads laced their access throughout the flat plain with a predictable pattern. Farming laborers trudged along narrow roads driving oxen before them. Having risen at dawn, they were returning home to hovels of mud brick after a day's work.

Rising up like a beacon amidst a sea of green, the walls and roof battlements reflected amber rays of a setting sun from their white surfaces. A palatial house, gardens, and stables with their surrounding wall, sprawled over two acres outside the city of Shinar. An unusual quiet hung within, like a shroud; a quiet filled with suspense.

Suddenly, a cry of pain tore the bucolic peace, followed by a moan - and a pause. Again the agony of a woman rent the air, followed by moans of residual pain - and a pause. For a time, longer than believed possible for endurance, this continued.

A shriek shattered the calm night. It was more severe than the others, stopping everyone within hearing distance to a standstill. Quiet followed. It seemed as though death had claimed another victory.

Only those in the room could hear soft moans turn to gentle sighs of relief.

A slap on wet flesh - and a new cry was heard; a baby gasping for the breath of life. His lungs full, a strapping, healthy, pink-skinned boy protested loudly.

The sweaty face of Mithra the midwife broke into a smile as she examined him thoroughly.

"He is perfectly formed, my lady, there are no defects nor blemishes. He has beautiful reddish-blond hair and he weighs a good amount for his size. He must be nearly a cubit long. See how I measure."

Amthelo watched as Mithra laid her forearm alongside the babe, with her elbow at his feet and her fingers along side his head. He was about four inches short of the 25-inch cubit.

"You see how long he is? And look at his chest and shoulders. He will surely make his father proud. Perhaps he will serve the great Nimrod as an officer or even a prince, just like his illustrious father."

"Perhaps, perhaps," Amthelo sighed weakly, her breathing shallow, "I am too tired to think about his future now. All I want is sleep, wonderful sleep."

"Yes, of course. You have labored long; the babe is large and he gave you much pain. I will be finished with you and the babe soon; then you may find the sleep you desire."

Shaking off fatigue as the midwife finished her duty, Amthelo ordered: "Tell my lord Terah of his good fortune. I am sure he will pay you well for delivering his son safely. He is concerned about our welfare, hearing the noise I made. Tell him... tell him I will rest and later make myself and his son presentable to him. Meanwhile we shall rest...my son is as tired as I am; he sleeps already at my breast...only a little sleep...."

"Yes, my lady, I shall do as you order. I will be at your call should you need me."

Mithra quietly issued orders to Amthelo's handmaids and left with one to give the good news to Lord Terah. She knew there would be great rejoicing in this house tonight!

And it was in the night that Abram was born, that all the servants of Terah, and all the wise men of Nimrod, and his conjurors came and ate and drank in the house of Terah, and they rejoiced with him on that night.

Book of Jasher Chapter 8, verse 1

T he estate of Prince Terah was alive with excitement. The cooks, the baker, the wine steward, the serving maids, the kitchen helpers, the servants to wash feet of arriving guests, the musicians, singers and dancers were called forth under the authority of the Ruler of the Feast, the Master of Ceremonies.

"Rab-Shalenak! Tend to the comforts of our illustrious guests," commanded Terah as he stood in the entry court, bowing and greeting palace dignitaries, officers, and friends.

As each person arrived their feet were washed and their hair anointed with perfumed oil. Terah's servants presented each with a fine linen robe to wear during the festivities. Ornamental wreaths were the final adornment provided; then guests were shown to their places for the feast.

The great court accommodated, on this occasion, an arrangement of tables in a 'U' pattern with the head table being the one at a right angle to the others. They were one cubit high by one cubit wide by four cubits long and covered with fine linen cloths.

Flat couches, without back, fanned out around the outside perimeter of the table. They were at the same height. Guests reclined two to a couch with a cushion under their left elbow, facing the table. Prior to eating, servants came with a pitcher of water and a bowl. Each guest washed their hands under the water poured into the bowl, and dried them with a towel provided.

Next, Servants came with wine and other liquors and continually refilled goblets. An ox had been slaughtered, dressed, and was roasting on a spit over an open fire in the kitchen area. Goats were slaughtered and dismembered; their meat cut off into smaller pieces. The bones were crushed and together they were boiled in a large cauldron of milk and water. The meat was served on platters from which guests helped themselves.

Platters of steamed vegetables were served in like manner. Fresh leeks and garlic added their pungent taste and aroma. Boiled beans and lentils were served with numerous loaves of bread. Platters of fresh fruit: grapes, dates, figs, and pomegranates came in the hands of a constant parade of serving men and women.

At the end of the great court, looking towards the head table, musicians played. The melodies of pipes and strings were accompanied by percussion instruments. While the guests arrived and were prepared for feasting, the music flowed lyrical and soft, dominated by the harp and the flute.

After food and drink had been placed before the guests, the Master of Ceremonies came to Lord Terah's couch. He waited for the appropriate moment, without intruding, and said: "Forgive this interruption, Lord Terah, but your wife Amthelo sends word that she is ready and anxious to present your newborn son. She awaits your permission to come before you."

"Ahh, very good Rab-Shalenak, her time of arrival is perfect. You may conduct her in personally."

"Thank you Lord Terah."

In a short time Rab-Shalenak re-appeared at the entrance, and looking to his master, nodded his head.

Terah, almost breathless with anticipation, arose from his couch and raised his arms for silence. The music stopped, and voices hushed to quiet as Terah turned to face the entrance. His arms outstretched in front of him, he announced in a booming voice: "Lords and Ladies, I present to you my lovely wife, Amthelo, and her gift of new life to me, A SON!"

Hearing this announcement, everyone at table arose and faced the same way. The servants and musicians ceased their activity and stood still.

Amthelo walked in slowly, followed by two handmaids and a nurse who carried the baby. Terah watched as every person bowed low and held the position until Amthelo stopped and bowed in acknowledgement.

She turned and took the child, cradling him in her arms. Continuing her slow procession, she passed between the tables as everyone looked, admired and complimented her on her good fortune.

"The gods have blessed you."

"The Goddess Ishtar has blessed you...."

"The gods, the gods, the gods... "she heard the repetition of credit to the gods and it disgusted her.

"I am the one who gave my son flesh and bone and blood," she thought as she smiled, hiding her true feelings. "Terah gave him form but I have carried him these many moons. I have suffered the long labor and the pain of birthing a large baby. Give ME honor, not the gods. Who are they but wood and stone? Can they give life as I have? No, by all that is good and right. This is my moment of honor. Give the tribute to me and to my husband, Lord Terah." The smile never left her mouth as she nodded acceptance of each bit of miss-directed praise

Finally she reached the head table and stood facing Terah. Her expression changed to one of pride and pleasure as she exclaimed for all to hear very clearly: "My lord husband, I gladly accepted your seed in my womb. I have nourished him most carefully through my body, taking nothing harmful to eat nor drink. See how strongly formed his is? How perfect his features are; his skin is without blemish. I have safeguarded him each day he grew inside me. I suffered a long labor and a painful birthing to bring him forth. All these things I have done to bring some small measure of honor and happiness to you. Now I give you your son. Name him well, great lord, husband and father."

Amthelo leaned forward slightly and Terah received the child. He examined him carefully near the lamplight and returned.

It is true what you say! He is strongly formed and his features are perfect. And, yes, his skin is without blemish, pink as a goat's udders. You have truly given me a great treasure, my wife. He shall grow tall and strong. He shall be mighty in force of arms to serve our King Nimrod and bring honor and distinction to my house."

Terah raised the child up for all to see and admire. "What name is fitting for a noble son such as he?"

Many names were suggested by the guests. Amthelo stood, waiting quietly until Terah heard every suggestion.

"What name do you offer, Amthelo? Surely you have given considerable thought to the possibilities."

Amthelo was ready. She had been ready with the name for three moons. She was that certain it was going to be a man-child.

"Why, yes, my husband, I have a name in mind that is most appropriate. I suggest you name him ABRAM because you are his MIGHTY FATHER in the court of Nimrod."

Amthelo watched Terah's face carefully as her words took their effect. His face and bearing were transformed. He arched his back as pride enveloped him. She knew he would pay many tributes to her after this day was completed.

"What say you all to the name 'Abram' suggested by my wife who honors me continually?" he called out to his guests.

"Yes, yes, yes...ABRAM, ABRAM!"

"His father is mighty in the court of Nimrod!"

"A perfect name for the son of so noble a lord."

"Yes, yes, ABRAM, ABRAM, ABRAM," they chanted.

"We salute you, great prince," shouted a guest.

"We toast your noble wife who honors you.

"We toast Abram, son of future greatness; son of Prince Terah, MIGHTY FATHER."

Abram was asleep when brought into the great court. He began fussing when handed to and examined by his father. By the time he was named, he was crying. The shouts of the guests, honoring him and his parents, was too much of a disturbance and now he cried and wailed his objections. He wanted the warmth and peace of his mother. He also wanted to be changed out of his wet clothing.

"Hear his voice, my friends, already he is giving orders."

There was an up-roar of laughter as Terah passed Abram back to his mother. Amthelo was exhausted but her victory was complete. All that she wanted now was to retire to her rooms.

"I beg your leave with reluctance, my husband, but I am tired," Amthelo sighed wearily.

"Yes, yes, of course Amthelo, by all means; give Abram all that he needs. And you rest well," Terah stammered.

"I shall send my handmaids for a meal in my rooms."

"As you wish, my wife. You gave me great honor this day, Amthelo. I shall make your name known throughout the kingdom of Shinar. Every house shall know of your great loyalty and blessings to Terah, Prince of Nimrod."

Terah turned to his guests and announced: "My honorable wife begs our leave to tend to the demands in hand...to Abram. What say you all?"

Laughing delightedly, everyone chanted and raised their goblets in time to "ABRAM, ABRAM, ABRAM, ABRAM, ABRAM, ABRAM!"

Amthelo could hear their voices well after she left the great court, through the entry hall and beyond. "...ABRAM, ABRAM, ABRAM!"

Her spirits had never been lifted higher. It was a time that would be remembered always, with a flush of pride.

The tempo of the music changed. It was now rhythmic. Dancers appeared when the ruler of the feast clapped his hands. Both entertainers and guests became more excited and enthusiastic in their mood. In the area between the tables, dancers seductively moved to the tempo.

Hoots and calls of enjoyment came from the male guests as intoxication increased from the never-ending service of wine and spirits. Laughter was contagious as it spread throughout the court. Terah was thoroughly enjoying the festivities as much as his guests.

The evening wore on late and Terah, stumbling drunk, was now in pursuit of the dancing girls. He lunged for one, then another, but they deftly eluded his grasp, laughing, twirling, and keeping up a rhythmic chatter with their castanets.

His guests, many of which were too drunk to stand, pointed at him and laughed hysterically as the tall, lumbering host missed his targets, stumbled, and fell. Each time, four servants at the command of the ruler of the feast, would rush to stand Terah on his rubbery legs. Once he was up, he proceeded to repeat his lusty quest. On each occasion he demanded a goblet of wine and drained it during the chase, sloshing it on himself and the floor as he staggered.

The most voluptuous dancer of all performed erotic, rotating bumps, grinds, and gestures that made Terah howl like an enraged bear.

"I want you...I must have you...the sweat glistening on your body is driving me mad with desire...if only I was not so full of wine...and if my legs would hold me firm...and if the floor would stop rocking...and...stand still you lusty bitch...you won't ... escape me...this...time, ARGHHH!"

He made a final lunge for the taunting girl who was confident she could dart out of his reach again, as she had many times before, to the delight of the crowd.

They encouraged her by shouting: "Tease him! Seduce him, but do not let him catch you!"

Shekels of silver were tossed on the floor at her feet each time she taunted him and escaped.

7

When she had begun her dancing she had several very delicate scarves or veils covering her. As she danced and teased, she removed them one by one, slowly, enticingly, seductively.

The court reverberated with chanting and the animal-like howling of the guests; then laughing and cheering for Terah and 'Salepha the Seductress'.

While Terah was staggering and spilling wine down his throat and chest, Salepha slipped around behind him. Undulating her body in snake-like movements, Saleph's beads and bracelets made a jangling noise.

"Look behind you for the snake, Lord Terah!" someone shouted.

"This time, my little charmer, you will not get away!" He spun around so fast he could not stand. His legs gave out, but his large hands reached out like huge grappling hooks and grabbed at Salepha's body.

She was too close this time. She had underestimated his quickness, even though he out drank any two men at the feast. His left hand clutched her beads and halter while his right hand grasped the veils covering her lower parts. As he fell he yanked!

Hundreds of beads flew everywhere in a flurry, rattling around the court. Her veiled halter came untied, and falling away it revealed Salepha's robust breasts. In the next split-second, Terah's right hand did its assignment in stripping off her lower covering.

The delectable Salepha gasped in mock surprise then squealed, putting on a small display of modesty by covering her lower parts with her hands. The ruler of the feast took his time ushering her out with some deference, as though she were an honored guest. He ordered a servant take her to a bedroom where she would await Lord Terah's pleasure.

The guests roared their approval: "The magnificent Lord Terah conquers once more; this time for Lord Terah, not for King Nimrod!"

"Hail Terah, conqueror of men AND women." "Hail Terah, hail Terah, hail Terah!" his guests lauded him as he staggered to his feet. He held Salepha's garments, as prizes, in each hand on outstretched arms and shuffled between the tables, full of pride for his conquest.

The laughter, the clapping, the praises and the pounding of tables diminished as Terah staggered away and out of the court to find his reward.

Chapter 2
Signs in the Heavens

> And when all the wise men and conjurors went out from the house of Terah, they lifted up their eyes toward heaven that night to look at the stars, and they saw, and behold one very large star came from the East and ran in the heavens from the four sides of the heavens.
>
> And all the wise men of the King and his conjurors were astonished at the sight, and the sages understood this matter, and they knew its import.
>
> And they said to each other, this only betokens the child that has been born to Terah this night, who will grow up and be fruitful, and multiply, and possess all the earth, he and his children forever, and he and his seed will slay great kings and inherit their lands.

Jasher 8:2-4

King Nimrod gave the wise men an audience at Mid-day in the throne room of the palace. It was a vast hall whose walls were 16 feet high and covered with paintings depicting Nimrod's victories over the earlier inhabitants of the land.

The king sat on his throne, elevated at least six feet up a flight of steps. The throne was high-backed and made of heavy plates of gold over a wood base. It glittered with inlays of such colorful gems as rubies, emeralds, lapis lazuli, onyx amethyst and crystal that displayed the finest workmanship in the craft of the goldsmith.

Thirty-six fierce warriors stood in groups of six at strategic locations inside the throne room. This was only a small segment of a force of six hundred palace guards. They were the elite corps of Nimrod's armed forces, specifically dedicated to his protection.

At both sides of, and facing the grand entrance, were huge wall carvings of a guardian image with the body of a bull, with great wings on the shoulders, and a man's bearded head wearing a turban.
Nimrod was magnificently dressed with a close fitting sleeveless white tunic made of finest quality lightweight linen, very elaborately embroidered in designs exquisitely expressed in gold, silver, scarlet, blue, and purple.

On his head the king wore a conical-shaped crown of heavy linen, bounded on the outside with a spiral of gold inlaid with diamonds, rubies, emeralds, and lapis lazuli.

Nimrod was a large man, six foot three inches tall, with great shoulders and arms of muscle and sinew. A fierce and ruthless warrior king, he bore the scars of previous battles on his face and arms.

The wise men came before Nimrod and at the steps to his throne, they all bowed down on their knees with their heads to the floor. "Long may the king live," they spoke in unison. "We come on a matter of great importance to you, O great king."

"And what could that be?" Nimrod questioned with a yawn."
"The night before last a son was born to Terah, prince of your host. We feasted with him in celebration and rejoiced in his good fortune. We all abstained from drunkenness in wine and liquors as is our duty while in your service, noble king."

"And?"

"Ah, well we... that is... when we, your servants went out of the house of Terah to go to our respective homes, we lifted up our eyes to the sky and saw a great star coming from the east. It flew with tremendous speed, and swallowed up four great stars from the four sides of the heavens. And your servants were astonished at the sight that we saw. We were greatly terrified. We made our judgement upon completion of the omen. We knew by our wisdom the proper interpretation of it."

There was a pause as the wise men looked at each other to confirm their agreement on the meaning of the omen, and their recommendations. They all swallowed hard, nodded their heads affirmatively, and their spokesman continued, stuttering with anxiety.

"O magnificent king...we tremble at the consequences of what we must say, for it concerns Abram, the new-born son of Prince Terah. We know of your love for him and how you have exalted him even above the other princes in your kingdom."

"Yes, that is true, and I am happy he has a robust son who may become as great and loyal a subject as his father. That is what Terah has informed me as of this morning through his steward. Haw, haw, haw...his master Terah was sleeping off the wine, I'll wager, and was unable to tell me himself. We have had many celebrations together, he and I, and owww, the mornings after...haw, haw, haw. I will hold a feast of my own for him soon, after he recovers," he laughed raucously. Looking at their somber faces, flushed and sweating, Nimrod growled: "Well, come on, say what you came to say and be finished with it!"

Once more the eight wise men trembled and jerked with fear! They looked at each other and realized there was no turning back; there could be no change in their interpretation of the omen.

"O great king, we know by our wisdom and understanding of the great mysteries that this omen foretells great evil that will come upon you from Abram, the newborn son of Terah. By our interpretation he will grow up and multiply in vast numbers. He will become most powerful, he and his seed thereafter, and they will kill all the kings of the earth, and inherit all their lands. And now, great lord, behold we have truly acquainted you with what we have seen concerning this child and his awful destiny."

Nimrod's demeanor changed from light-heartedness to worry. He rose up from his throne and began pacing the floor.

"The interpretation seems true," he admitted to himself. What else could it mean? If I ignore it and these things come to pass, I will have ignored the omen sent from the gods to me for my own protection. The consequences will surely cause me misery or death."

One of the conjurors sensed the difficulty Nimrod was having and ventured a suggestion.

"If it seems good to the king, give Terah value for this child, Abram. We will then slay him, before he grows up and increases against you and us to the extent that our children perish through his evil."

"That does sound like a fair solution," recommended an astrologer.

"Yes, it does," ventured another.

"The value must be very substantial, of course, your majesty," added another.

"I could give Terah a treasure in exchange; then there would be no dispute between us concerning the value of the child."

"You are most generous, O great king."

"Kretaken!"

11

"Yes, my king," answered the captain of the palace guards.

"Send for Terah! Tell him his king awaits."

"Right away, your majesty."

The captain barked orders and a squad of six men sprang into a jog that would not stop until they reached Terah's estate more than two miles away.

The doorman at Terah's house answered the pounding, looking out at six guardsmen dripping with sweat and parched with thirst. Before he could ask their purpose in coming, the leader spoke abruptly: "We are a squad of King Nimrod's personal guards sent to bring Prince Terah before his majesty, who awaits his attendance. Bring your master at once!"

"As you command," the doorkeeper answered yanking the cord on a bell that alerted the house's inhabitants. Shelesh, the chief steward, scurried to the entrance trailing other servants after him, and identified himself. The soldier repeated his message.

Turning to the doorkeeper, Shelesh ordered: "Go to the stable and have the stableman prepare Lord Terah's chariot!"

To another servant he ordered: "Get Harbona, the Prince's best driver, and have him drive the chariot here to the front!"

Shelesh then rushed to his master's quarters, knocked on the door, paused for permission to enter, and then proceeded inside.

"Lord Terah, forgive my intrusion, but I have been commanded by the leader of a squad of the King's guards to tell you that Nimrod awaits your presence, now. They look as though they ran all the way here."

"All right Shelesh, tend to my chariot and driver."

"Yes, my lord, I have anticipated your command and they await you at the front gate."

"Good, I shall be there as soon as I change into something befitting an audience with the king."

Terah donned his best attire, then commanded Shamgar his bodyguard to follow. They strode out to where the guardsmen awaited and stepped aboard the chariot.

The pair of onagers, somewhat larger than asses, stood abreast of each other. They were held in check by the strong hands and arms of Harbona, Terah's most skilled charioteer. The reins were looped around his back giving him the strength of his body as well as his arms in reining control of each animal. The reins were also secure in one hand while he applied the whip in the other, to speed the onagers forward.

12

"Haiee!" he shouted, and with a crack of the whip the chariot and its three occupants lurched forward and sped off towards the palace.

Terah was intuitive enough to think this audience might have something to do with the birth of his son, Abram.

"Perhaps the king, my friend, wishes to bestow a gift or an endowment for the child."

Terah was happy with his thoughts, and happy with his surmise, as the chariot rattled along at a bone-jarring speed, scattering pedestrians, animals, and carts out of the way.

When they arrived at the palace gates, Shamgar called to the palace guards outside the walls. His voice was heard inside as well, booming: "Make way for Terah, Prince of Nimrod's Host."

The guards saluted and called for the gatekeepers to open and admit Terah's chariot. The announcement was relayed from guard post to guard post, as the chariot and its occupants drove at a fast clip through the fortress defenses.

"Make way for Terah...make way for Terah," echoed the heralding of sentinels' through the passages.

Into a large open court the chariot appeared and Harbona applied pressure on the reins slowing the animals to a walk. In front of the palace steps he pulled up on the reins, calling the animals to a halt. Terah and Shamgar dismounted and started up the stairs. At the entrance they were joined by a squad of guards whose leader saluted Terah and asked him to please follow.

They walked briskly by a number of guard posts until they reached the throne room entrance. The doors were opened immediately at the command of the officer. Their stride continued uninterrupted as they marched into the great hall, and up to the steps before Nimrod, sitting on his throne. The officer commanded a halt and spoke: "Lord Terah, your majesty.

The front rank parted and Terah walked up to the steps, stooped and bowed low.

"O great king, I came on the wind, with my fastest chariot, upon receiving your orders."

"I appreciate your promptness, Terah. I have a matter of some import to talk to you about. Last evening, these wise men, which you see here, were feasting with you in celebration of the birth of your new son. After the feast, they observed an omen in the heavens. A large star from the east traveled to the four sides of the sky and consumed a star at each place. All eight of these men agree to the following interpretation."

The king paused and looked at each of his advisors with the lost hope that their interpretation would change. Finally, Nimrod continued.

"Their judgment is that this child of yours, Abram, will grow up and multiply greatly, and become powerful; so powerful that he will kill all the kings of the earth and inherit all their lands, he and all his seed forever. The gods have been merciful to me in revealing this omen, allowing me to prevent your son from carrying out his evil upon this kingdom. I therefore command you to give me the child, that we may slay him, before his evil springs up against us. In return, I will give you for his value, a treasure house full of silver and gold."

Terah was struck dumb with shock and fear. He came expecting congratulations, gifts, and blessings for the child, from a monarch who was his friend. He received, instead, a calamity.

"I already have ample wealth in gold and silver," Terah reasoned. The most important wealth to me, to any man, is his sons. Abram is a special son. He will be great in stature and leadership, a credit to me. I had publicly dedicated Abram to the king," Terah remembered, "and now Nimrod commands his destruction. I must find a way to save him; I must try...I must try!" he struggled inwardly.

"My lord," Terah answered, I have heard your words and this servant shall do all that my king desires. But, your majesty, I will tell you what happened to me the other day, in order that I may see what advice my king will give his servant, and then I will answer you."

"Speak," Nimrod answered.

"The other night, Ayon, son of Mored, came to me and said: 'Give to me the great and beautiful horse that the king gave you. I will give you silver and gold, straw and fodder for its value!

"I said to him: 'wait until I see the king concerning your offer and what ever the king says is right, I will do.' And now my lord, I have made this offer known to you. The advice you give to your servant, I will obey."

Nimrod's anger rose in him and he considered Terah as a fool.

"Are you really so silly, ignorant, or deficient in understanding to do this thing? To give your beautiful horse for silver and gold or even straw and fodder? Are you so short of silver and gold that you need to do this thing, because you cannot obtain straw and fodder to feed your horse? And what is silver and gold to you, or straw and fodder, that you would sell that fine horse which I gave you, especially when there is no other like him in all the land?"

EUPHI

CARCHEMISH

HARAN

KHALAB

PADAN-ARA

PHOENICIAN SHIPS SAILED FROM INDIA TO THE ISLES OF THE NORTH

UGARIT

HAMATH

TADMORE

M

BYBLOS

MEDITERRANEAN SEA

SIDON

DAN

DAMASCUS

TYRE

KARNAIM

HAZOR

ASHTAROTH

HAM

SHECHEM

JORDAN RIVER VALLEY

URUSALEM

DEAD SEA

EGYPTIAN SHIPS

HEBRON

KIRJATHAIM

GERAR

BETHEL

TANIS

GOSHEN

BEERSHEBA

VALLEY OF SIDDIM

KADESH

AR

MEMPHIS

ON

EZION-GEBER

SINAI

NILE RIVER VALLEY AND DELTA

RED SEA

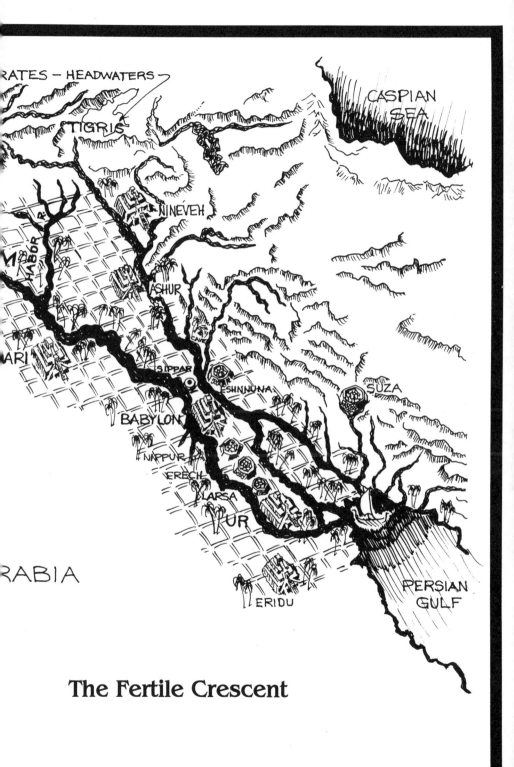

The Fertile Crescent

Terah drew up his courage and pleaded his cause. "My king has spoken similarly to me, his servant. I implore you, my lord - what is this which you demand of me, saying: 'give up your son that we may murder him, and I will give you silver and gold in return? Who shall inherit me? Surely, then, at my death, the silver and gold will return to my king who gave it!"

When Nimrod heard this reply, he became disturbed and his anger grew. "You dare to speak this way to your lord? Do you suggest I command this thing to merely profit from your lack of an heir? Do you take me for a fool that I do not know you have two older sons who will inherit your wealth?

Terah then realized his pathetic story had not only failed in changing the king's decision, but he was also dangerously close to losing more than Abram as a result of his attempt to shame Nimrod.

"I must think fast!" Terah urged himself, sweat pouring down his face. Quickly he offered: "All that I have is in your power. Whatever the king desires to do to his servant, let him do it. Yes, even to my son, for his life is in your power...without value in exchange. He, plus his two brothers that are older than he."

"No, but I will purchase your newborn son for a price, Nimrod declared, having calmed down substantially.

"I implore you, great king, to whom I owe all allegiance and life, let your servant ask a favor, and if it pleases you to grant it, my loyalty and dedication in serving you will be even greater than in the past."

Speak your wish, but do not trifle with me, I warn you."

"Yes, my king. All that I ask is this: Give me three days to consider this matter...that is, to prepare my poor wife before the child is taken from her." Terah pressed Nimrod with all the guile he could compose and the king finally gave him three days before Abram was to be brought to his execution.

When Terah arrived back at his estate, he told his family and his chief servants about the king's demand.

"Oh, my husband, surely you can do something. You are the king's most loved prince. He has given you more wealth and honors than any other of his noble men!" cried Amthelo.

"I have tried! I pressed the king until his agitation with me nearly destroyed all my sons! Those conjurors have convinced him completely that Abram will conquer all kings of the earth, including Nimrod. May the gods curse them! No, there is not a way I can think of to change the king's decision."

15

"Oh no, it cannot be! It cannot be! My baby! My baby! The flesh and blood of my body I suffered to bear for you. A perfect son, without blemish or fault whose very name signifies the magnificence of his father - you would allow his sacrifice?"

Before Terah could answer, Amthelo collapsed from shock as the weight of the terrible reality closed in on her. Her handmaids rushed to catch her as she fell.

"Here, let me carry her to the bed," Terah quickly slid his strong arms under her back and legs, lifting her easily. Gently he carried her to her bed and laid her down. Softly brushing her tear-stained cheeks with the edge of his big hand, he turned his head, heaved a big sigh, and walked out of the room.

When Amthelo came to, she struggled to her feet, ignoring the suggestions of rest offered by her handmaids. Leaving her room, she walked unsteadily through the expansive house looking for Terah. When she found him he was standing in the garden, looking depressed and defeated. Running to him, she clung to his tunic and slipped to her knees, pleading desperately.

"You must think of something, anything to save Abram!"

Terah could offer no consolation; only a terribly pained expression of hopelessness. Amthelo's pain and fear increased to anguish and hysteria as the picture of Abram's death at the hand of Nimrod, flooded her mind. The coming execution penetrated to the core of her emotions unbalancing her. She wailed the cry of the mourner so long and loud that she eventually became sick.

Amthelo was taken back to her room where she recovered enough to refresh herself and take Abram into her arms. From this time on, Abram was never more than an arm's length away from his mother.

The servants had never seen Lord Terah so fearful and agitated; nor had they seen him so continually drunk. The wine steward was ever present to pour the libations that provided Terah an escape from his tortured conscience. Amthelo's pleadings, his impotent, frustrated replies, followed by her cries of disappointment and dread, were repeated day and night. The house of celebration had fallen into mourning.

Chapter 3
Redemption

Soon after the time Shamgar and Shelesh first talked about trying to save Abram, a plot was hatched. Shamgar took instructions from his co-conspirator and then called together soldiers of Terah's guard who were most loyal. There were seven in all who swore an oath of secrecy and allegiance to their prince. They set out upon onagers riding in different directions to prescribed places. Shelesh and Shamgar could only wait and hope during the next few days.

On the third day at the prescribed hour, King Nimrod sent a squad of his guards to Terah's house with a message.

"I have orders to read it aloud to the Prince, in person," the officer in charge glared at Shelesh.

"Very well, captain, if you will be so kind as to wait until I prepare my lord's appearance?"

"Of course, chief steward," the officer replied.

When out of sight of the king's men, Shelesh hurried his steps, ordering servants about. Terah was deeply sleeping off his intoxication when Shelesh came to him. After several attempts to arouse his lord had failed, Shelesh took a bold approach. He ordered a servant to fill a pitcher with cold water and bring it to him. Shelesh gambled that his lord would forgive his effrontery in awakening him in this manner. He took the pitcher and heaved the entire contents into the face of his master.

Terah came out of his stupor, thrashing his arms wildly, sputtering, gasping and coughing. He choked on his first attempt to speak, gagging on the after effects of intoxication, combined with the water. In that instant he dreamed of drowning in a great deluge like the one in which Noah had survived with his family.

"A thousand pardons, I beg of you my lord," Shelesh trembled. "The king has sent a squad of soldiers to bring you and the baby Abram to him. I could not arouse you by ordinary means. I am sorry but this was absolutely necessary, under the present circumstances.

If I allowed you to continue sleeping, it could mean putting your entire house in jeopardy of the king's wrath. Even so, I deserve to be beaten, if that is your desire, my lord," Shelesh finished as he bowed on this knees.

"Terah sat on the edge of his couch in a state of confusion. He had a monumental hangover. His mind seemed to rebel against all the efforts to make it work. He had a pounding headache and he struggled to orient himself to the date, time, and present crisis that had been impending for the last three days. Gradually his reasoning ability returned and he groaned from a greater pain than that in his head. It was more than his stomach could take and he became sick.

Shelesh rose to his feet and called for Terah's servants. Under the chief steward's order they aided their master through his sickness. They prepared an herbal broth to stop his heaving, and eventually he stopped. They removed his clothing entirely, bathed and massaged him with perfumed oil, groomed and dressed him in princely garb. By the time he was ready to travel, he was also able to stand and walk, slowly by steadily.

"Prepare Abram to travel. When he is ready, bring him to me," Terah ordered with a husky voice. "It is time to leave."

"Yes, my lord," Shelesh answered and walked out of his master's room. His mind was racing. He ran through the house to find Shamgar and finally located him on the third floor lookout. "Has anyone returned?" he panted breathlessly.

"No."

"Can you see any riders coming?"

"No, I cannot."

"We have failed then," Shelesh sighed, the disappointment showing as he hung his head and his shoulders drooped.

"Perhaps Abram's God is not as powerful as those of the king."

"We have not lost until the moment comes when Nimrod destroys Abram," said Shamgar, "and the trip to the palace can be a slow one if arranged that way," answered Shamgar.

"Delay, steward, delay."

They hastily planned their final tactics and, after agreeing, Shelesh left to make the arrangements.

"Oh, captain, I humbly beg your apology but there is a delay in our preparations and I ask you to be patient for a little while. Meanwhile, please accept my lord's hospitality and wait in the shade and comfort of his garden. I will order pretty girls to serve you and your men whatever your body desires for satisfaction," Shelesh smiled and winked as he finished his invitation.

"Well, I do not know that we should..."

"These girls are the prettiest and friendliest in all Shinar." Shelesh insisted. It will not be long. I thought it hospitable to offer pleasantries while you wait, rather than let you and your men stand in the heat as you are. But if you insist, then..."

The squad of soldiers all heard and pressed forward eagerly to coax their captain to accept.

"Very well, I do not suppose it would be wrong...for a little while, that is."

"I thank you, captain," Shelesh said with a bow, "and I am sure your men thank you. Now please follow me," he asked, leading the way for the squad who followed him in a single file.

Shelesh was wise enough to know that time passes quickly when men are enjoying themselves. A little more than an hour had passed when the captain began to worry about the delay.

"Chief Steward!" He called out. There was no answer. The officer ordered his serving girl to find shelesh and bring him.

Shelesh was up in the lookout with Shamgar, peering into the distance, in different directions, for any rider headed towards the estate. "Curses! One of them should have returned by now," exclaimed Shamgar.

"I agree, something must have gone wrong. Perhaps we should have provided more silver?"

"Who knows, perhaps you are right. We could have taken more from the treasury, but then, giving too much wealth might draw suspicion upon our lord Terah. After all, how many lords would send a servant out with a small fortune in silver, trusting him to carry out such a mission?"

"How right you are, my friend, and how wise to have reasoned so properly," Shamgar complimented.

"But not wise enough, I am afraid. Our time is running out. The officer of the king's men must be looking for me even now. If he demands the child, I must comply. Our lord must bring him to the king."

"I understand. I shall remain here on lookout until they leave. Who knows...?"

The serving girl ran up breathing heavily, "The captain demands your presence!"

Shelesh sighed in resignation and walked away.

The officer was anxious about how he would answer to the king for the long delay and he pressed the chief steward for an immediate departure.

Very well, sir, but my lord Terah may not appreciate your forward attitude, especially after the hospitality he has shown you and your men. And when he tells the king..."

"Ah, please...chief steward...ah please, sir...I would rather he not do that. You see, ah, the king might look upon my...ah...permissiveness here as...ah...a dereliction of orders."

"Oh, is that so?" Shelesh acknowledged with raised eyebrows.

"Yes...so you see, we must leave right away. You do understand, do you not?" the captain urged, face flushed and streaming sweat.

"Mmm, yes by all means, I understand perfectly," Shelesh replied, turning and walking away with a slight smile forming on his lips.

It was some time before Terah appeared with Abram's nurse carrying the baby wrapped in soft cotton coverings. The staff of servants had lined up along the way out to demonstrate their respect and their sorrow at the departure of Abram. Tears flowed down their faces as he passed before them.

From within the recesses of the great house a heart-rending scream shattered the tense silence.

"My baby, my baby!" The cries of anguish grew louder as Amthelo ran to the entrance hall. "Abram, my baby! Oh Terah, I beg you, do not take my baby!" she pleaded.

"I...I have no choice...I...we must give him up." Terah stammered with embarrassment and regret.

"No! No! You cannot have him!" she shouted defiantly and threw herself upon the captain, clawing at his face with her hands in a mad frenzy.

Contain yourself, my lady!" shouted the officer as he grabbed her wrists to prevent further damage to his face. "Here, you servants! Help your mistress! Restrain her!"

On the third floor, Shamgar continued to scan the countryside for a rider. His eyes were tired and red from the daylong vigil, a vigil of disappointment. "Why am I still watching and waiting?" he asked himself. "They have taken Abram. He is on his way to die!" He hung his head in his hands, rubbing his eyes with the heels of his palms to be rid of their tiredness and irritation. "Oh, little Abram, whose future was to be so bright, like the evening star...would that your God had saved you."

He sighed a great mournful sigh and gazed tearfully at the sky. He wiped the moisture away with a swipe of the back of his huge hand and was about to walk downstairs when he caught sight of a rider coming fast. The man waved to him frantically, a sign of success! Shamgar could hardly believe his eyes and he raised both arms in a gesture of question. The rider waved again exuberantly, and Shamgar realized there may still be a chance to rescue Abram.

Taking the steps two at a time, he ran down the flights of stairs and through the house booming: "Shelesh! Shelesh! Where are you?!"

Shelesh was lying down, exhausted from the stress of the day's trials. He was sipping some wine to sedate himself and had managed to convince Amthelo she should do the same.

"Shelesh! A rider is coming from the northwest. He rides with the wind. There is still hope! There is still hope!" he shouted with emotion.

"But they left with Abram some time ago. Terah could be almost to the king's palace by now."

"Do not give up on me, Shelesh. Until Abram is in the king's hands, there is hope! Now think! What can we do?" Shamgar demanded.

Shelesh concentrated with all his effort, looking up with raised arms as if to draw inspiration from a source above. All at once it came to him. His eyes sparkled with excitement. He came off the couch, electrified into action, and began commanding servants with an authority seldom used. They sprang into motion, charged with the same energy that propelled their overseer.

"Shamgar, my friend, you have the difficult task. You must take the fastest chariot team to catch and stop our lord before he reaches the palace."

"And what shall I say if I am successful in doing that?"

"Let us not waste valuable time standing here. I will explain it to you on the way to the stables. Let us go quickly!"

Harbona was urging the stable men to hurry in hitching Terah's prized stallion with the king's powerful white mare to a chariot. They had been easily trained in harness together during short walks and mild runs. But they had not been put to a test such as the one they now faced. Harbona jumped on the chariot, grabbed the reins, and declared: "We are ready!"

Shamgar had his instructions from Shelesh and immediately hopped on board booming: "To the palace! We must ride like the wind of a storm!"

A crack of the lash sent the team off at a break-neck pace trailing a cloud of dust. Shamgar had never traveled so fast and the start nearly threw him out. His firm grip on the chariot side-rail saved him and he clung to it with both hands, bracing his feet for balance.

Breathless, Shelesh scurried into the house and up to the third floor lookout, his heart throbbing from the excitement as well as the exertion. Casting his eyes towards the king's palace, he caught sight of the chariot, a dark point at the head of a column of brownish gray dust. It was like a fire-arrow in slow motion, trailing smoke, flying towards its target, the king's palace.

Traffic on the road to Shinar was normally heavy this time of day with its assortment of travelers, rubbing shoulders, coming and going. Working people were accustomed to leaving the road to make way for the privileged who were in a hurry. Seldom had they seen the likes of this spectacle bearing down on them. Men, women, children, animals, carts with their burdens ran, jumped, and rolled out of the way as the chariot cut through traffic like the bow of a ship cutting through water, sending it to either side in a tumultuous, tumbling foam.

In the distance Shamgar saw the high fortifications that surrounded the palace. Approaching the west gate, about 300 yards from it, was Terah's palanquin rocking with the slow steady strides of the porters carrying it on their shoulders.

"Faster, Harbona, Faster!" growled Shamgar.

Harbona uncolied his lash and sent it snapping with great precision. The end of the lash hissed between the two striving horses, over their heads, and exploded with a crack! The team surged forward together as one and the chariot, with its occupants, careened down the road, scattering everyone in its path.

"Iieee-yah! Faster my beauties - fly! You have wings like great hawks!" he encouraged and flattered. Harbona spurred them on superbly with the lash lending emphasis to his urgings. He was careful to avoid striking them, knowing that if he did, a horse could bolt suddenly and break the team's stride.

On they raced with the wind at their backs. The chariot seemed to be flying, Shamgar thought, in the hands of divine ones in whose power the drama and fate of Abram's life rested. Both Shamgar and Harbona sensed it, exchanging brief glances. They smiled with awareness that their race, against great odds, was going to be close. When the objective came in sight, the gamble for success now held promise.

The promise then turned to a clear victory as they closed the distance, shouting with delight to congratulate themselves and gain the attention of the procession looming up ahead. And then they were there.

"Ho-o-old...hold my beauties!" Harbona called soothingly, reining in the magnificent pair and leaning his weight back slightly against the reins. The muscles in his powerful arms, shoulders and neck rippled from the tension they had endured.

"Hail Terah...wait! Stop!" Yelled Shamgar, vaulting out of the chariot and running up to the palanquin. "My lord Terah, I come on a most urgent cause!"

"Porters halt!" commanded Terah. "What is the matter, Shamgar?"

"I come with bad tidings, my lord. It is your wife, Amthelo."

"Yes, what about her?"

"She...she threatens to kill herself if she is not allowed to nurse the baby one more time. She says Abram was taken from her too suddenly at the time she was to feed him. I fear the spirits have entered her to encourage a desire for death.

Chapter 4
Young Abram

And the Lord was with Abram in the cave, and he grew up, and Abram was in the cave ten years, and the king and his princes, soothsayers and sages, thought that the king had killed Abram.

Jasher 8:36

Abram's little body grew strong and lean. In learning to walk he adapted to the rough, rocky terrain of the canyons in which he lived. His mind developed as rapidly as his body. He had six mentors that enjoyed answering the incessant questions and satisfying the curiosity of a growing child. Each one taught Abram useful functions they wanted him to learn.

At the age of three, he helped Bechorath plant and gather food, much to the delight of the manservant who knew farming quite well.

Eder, whose calling was animal husbandry, enjoyed Abram's help with the feeding and care of the goats, sheep, and camels.

Amthelo spent a little time each day teaching Abram the meanings of words, and the names of things with which he was familiar.

Bealoth taught him handwork in weaving goat hair and sewing.

Terah came once each month with extra provisions to meet their needs. It was on these occasions that Abram learned about hunting from his father who excelled with the bow and the spear.

With Shamgar, one of the most able warriors in all the Shinar Plain, Abram played at being a warrior, using sticks for swords and daggers.

Growing up in the wilderness instilled in Abram an understanding of his environment. He developed the ability to see game and approach it with the wind in his face so as to be undetected.

He could stalk animals for a long period with more than normal patience for a boy his age.

Abram's skill with the bow and arrow, and the spear improved rapidly for a young boy. At age nine Abram was proficient in the use of those weapons plus the sling. Eder had taught him how to sling rocks to drive off predators preying on their small flock of sheep and goats.

"Eder can bring down man or beast at thirty paces," Bechorath exclaimed once during Abram's instruction. "I have never seen better skill with the sling."

Eder passed off the complement as of no consequence by replying: "Well...I only use the sling seriously to protect the animals I am responsible for.

At age ten, Abram was making hunting kills on his own while Eder and Bechorath watched admiringly from a distance, ready to assist if needed.

After his kill, Abram bled and skinned the animal, with help from Eder and Bechorath. He learned how to treat the hide to make it soft and useable for clothes or bedding. Abram also learned from Eder how to kill and prepare goats for eating. His instruction included how to use other parts as bags for liquids such as water and milk.

Looking at her sleeping child, Amthelo laughed softly and remarked to Terah on his latest visit: "Abram has become fleet of foot and strong of body, my husband. As you already know, he has had foot-races over the years with Bechorath and Eder. Remember how they let him win in order to encourage him?

"Yes, I remember very well," Terah chuckled.

"They do not let him win anymore."

"Oh? Why not?"

"He wins without their help. He even gives them a head start advantage and still wins. Now they find he is too fast to lose, and they are too discouraged to race with him," Amthelo laughed gaily.

Terah broke out in laughter, slapping Shamgar on the shoulder. He guffawed, loudly, waking up Abram, but only for a moment. He jerked upright; his eyes opened and took in the scene around him. Lying down again, his eyes fluttered, and closed. With a sigh he was again fast asleep, seeing all was well: his parents were together, happy, laughing, looking lovingly at him, and Shamgar was protecting everyone....

On Abram's tenth birthday, Terah and Shamgar came from Shinar and presented him with gifts of clothing, sandals, a comb and a long dagger in a leather sheath. To Abram the clothing was nice, but not necessary out in the wilderness. The dagger, on the other hand, was special. It was like a short sword to him, because of its length. Made of the new gray metal, harder than bronze, and sharp as sharp can be, Abram fondled it like a mother caresses her child, with awe and appreciation for the beauty of it.

"Shamgar bought it from a trader who bought it from an armorer a great distance away, beyond the reaches of the Great Euphrates headwaters," Terah explained. "The trader also had two swords, made from the same hard metal. I tested one for balance, weight and strength against Shamgar's sword..."

"How was that done, father?" Abram interrupted, too impatient with curiosity.

"We had a mock fight...with some simple, slashing blocks and counter moves...lots of noise and dash...good fun of course; hardly worked up a sweat," Terah laughed.

"But that new sword, little Abram, Mmm-Mmm! It hacked my mighty Maralah like it was tin. Maralah! The invincible sword of more battles than I can count. By the gods, I, even I, Shamgar, mighty warrior of Akkad, would be of no account against common thieves with swords such as this."

"So you bought my sword," Abram blurted out.

"And two more: one for Shamgar and one for myself." Terah finished with a flourish drawing his sword.

"Shamgar, your sword!" Abram commanded, as if imitating his father.

In the blink of an eye Shamgar had his sword in hand.

"What say you, father?" Abram asked with his sword raised high.

"By the gods - with the three of us standing together in a fight, we are invincible!"

The ring of hard steel clanged as swords, big and small, saluted the bond just made, as though irrevocable, for life.

One month later Terah and Shamgar came as they normally did for their visit. Terah dismounted and greeted Abram, who ran into his arms nearly knocking him over.

"Oomph! Is this a little boy of ten who runs into my arms? Or is it an experienced hunter and warrior made of muscle, gut and iron?"

"A 'hunter/warrior' Abram growled back while throwing his arms around his father's neck and squeezing.

"What strength this warrior has! He squeezes the very life from me! Terah laughed, followed by the bellowing guffaws of Shamgar who always looked on with a fondness that moistened the giant's eyes.

Look at the lad!" Terah ordered, "I would wager his strength, and endurance are equal to, if not better than that of experienced desert travelers like us," he laughed again, beaming proudly.

An hour later, Amthelo was informing Terah about Abram's progress in her teaching him language.

"He is an eager, attentive student for any activity presented to him. I think you can see how well he speaks, for a ten-year-old boy.

"Yes, I have noticed his grasp of language and how clearly he speaks. It is important that he continue the good progress he is making. This should not prove too difficult. He has no children to play with, so he is likely to mature rapidly.

"Abram seems happiest in his mental activities when probing the mysteries of the world around him, my husband. He has an insatiable curiosity. The questions he asks now are beyond my humble knowledge to answer," Amthelo confessed. Perhaps he should have more knowledgeable teachers. Perhaps wise men from another city, like...Mari. Surely Abram would be out of Nimrod's reach there.

Mmmm, perhaps you are right, my wife; I shall give it some thought and let you know what I have decided when the time comes.

Nothing more was said about it during this visit. Instead, Terah and Amthelo listened while Abram, Shamgar, Bechorath and Eder played Abram's favorite game of stealth. They crept around in the dark of night somewhere near the cave. The warm campfire at the cave entrance was a welcome beacon providing direction. Abram knew almost every large rock, tree, bush, wadi and hole from memory. He did not need the firelight, but would have preferred to play without it being seen.

The person who could sneak up on the other, undiscovered, and poke him in a vital spot with a stick, won the game. As hard as Shamgar, Eder and Bechorath tried, they never won. One by one the men were eliminated, leaving Abram to deal with the last 'survivor'. Abram was as quiet and as quick as a chameleon. He blended into the inky landscape equally as well.

On this night, when Abram came in the victor, again, Terah put his arm around his son's shoulders and said: "My son, you are growing up so quickly, and so well. I am proud of you. Yes, by the gods, I am glad I spared your life ten years ago and rebelled against the command of my king.

"You are still a young boy, but in many ways you are a man already," Terah continued. "You can defend yourself quite well. You hunt like a man, better than many I have seen. Is that not true Shamgar?"

"What you say is true, my lord. Abram is quite at ease in this wilderness."

"Yes, Shamgar, but we must soon prepare his mind for manhood. I must give considerable thought to this and make some new arrangements."

Abram eagerly looked forward to his father's visits. He wished they could be more frequent. It had been two months since the last visit. Now on this occasion, after the sun had set, Abram listened intently as his father told him stories about the great patriarchs of his family. He started with old Noah who was still living with Shem, one of his three sons. Terah could not remember his ancestors beyond Noah, but the names he could recall he trained Abram to recite and commit to memory.

"You are a Shemite and a Hebrew, my son, destined for greatness. You are living here, separated from your true home and me, because of the jealousy of King Nimrod. He wanted you dead because...well, on the night of your birth, an omen appeared in the heavens foretelling your future."

Terah told him the story of the wise men's interpretation and Nimrod's slaughter of the baby, Terah had sold to the king in Abram's place.

A shudder of fear shook Abram and he clung to his father's waist.

Terah calmed him with the assurance that he had been safe here at the cave.

"I have made arrangements, however, to take you to your new home. You are fortunate, my son, to be accepted in the household of our Patriarchs, Shem and Noah. They will teach you more than I can about the heavens, and also about their mighty God, the Ever Living. I know nothing of these things. They are willing enough to have you; almost eager it seems, although they have never laid eyes on you. They are deep with wisdom, Abram. If anybody can truly understand the omen of your destiny, and help you fulfill it, they are the ones."

"Where do they live, father?"

"Shem is the king over Urusalem, in the land of Canaan. It is a long journey that will take many days, perhaps two moons."

"When do I have to go?"

"We will rise up, pack and leave here at the dawning of the next day's sun. Go to sleep now, Abram. The new day will be here soon enough and you must be rested for the long journey."

"Very well, father," Abram responded as he lay down next to Terah. He went to sleep still holding onto his father's hand, his mind full of questions about what lay ahead.

The early morning sky had a pink tint at the eastern horizon when everyone in the camp arose. They had a quick morning meal, packed their belongings on camels and proceeded west. Their first destination was the city of Sippar. After that they would proceed northwest on the caravan trail which paralleled the Euphrates River.

Abram had never been to an urban center. Sippar was only a minor city owing allegiance to Shinar with neither the size, the architecture, nor the industry of its capital. It held a fascination for Abram, however, who had never seen so many people, and living so close together. Terah postponed answering Abram's many questions. This was due to the need for haste to leave the city as soon as possible, out of the reach of Nimrod and his spies.

"Later, Abram, later we will come to the land of our fathers, Padan Aram. There lies the magnificent city called Mari. It is the capital of the Kingdom of Mari. We shall stop and visit that city on our way. Then we can show you everything that can dazzle your eyes, delight your stomach, and fascinate your mind. And...we shall then answer all the many questions you will ask."

Abram was disappointed and anxious; but he knew he should obey, so he kept quiet as he pointed with amazement to buildings, canals, bridges and other evidence of urban civilization.

Mari was located on the eastern side of the Euphrates, south of the Habor River. Like all capital cities of Mesopotamia, it had a number of towns spread out some distance from it as tributaries, forming an integral part of the kingdom. It was through these towns that Terah's small caravan traveled and camped.

Eventually they came to the great city itself and passed through its gates. This section of the city was choked with peddlers, beggars, entertainers, spectators, travelers, and city guards. Shamgar and Terah led the way through the crowds who gave way willingly for these towering, impressive visitors and their followers.

Abram had never seen so many people before. All the goings-on fascinated him, and he lagged along staring at everything that went on around him. Terah ordered Eder to tie a rope from his camel to Abram's, and from Abram's camel to that of Bechorath. Abram's animal was pulled and pushed along, in order to keep Abram from getting lost in the crowds. As they neared the heart of the city, the crowds diminished. Turning down a side street, off the central avenue, Terah's band found the bustling activity had lessened, and they made their way more easily.

Soon a caravanserai came in sight. The inn was a large, square building with no windows on the walls facing the street and a narrow walkway. The remaining two walls butted up to adjacent buildings. Terah stopped next to the large gate on the street side. Shamgar dismounted and pounded on the gate until the owner came and opened it enough to see out.

"Who is it that fairly breaks my door down with his impatience?"

"It is Shamgar, servant to Lord Terah and his family, little man. We desire lodging for ourselves and feed for our animals. Do you have rooms available? They must be clean, mind you!"

The man, although of substantial height and brawn, was fairly intimidated by the size and fierce appearance of Shamgar, who looked down on him as a lord looks upon a common man who has failed to be properly submissive.

"Why, a... yes, my lord," the man stuttered, noticing Terah sitting tall and looking splendid and rich. "Ah, please forgive my lapse of manners. Welcome to my humble caravanserai. Be assured my accommodations will meet with your approval, my lords."

"Then do not just stand there, man! Open the gate wide so that we may enter! Prepare your best rooms immediately! Provide ample water to cleanse and refresh! And...bring fresh fruit while we wait for the meal you shall prepare for us. Now hurry, before I become impatient," Shamgar ordered.

"As you command. Right away! Please enter my humble house. Wide swings the gate, and all that I possess is at your disposal."

As his guests were entering, the proprietor began shouting orders to servants, his wife and children. They, in turn, scurried to and fro. Rooms were swept, water drawn from the well near the center of the courtyard, and refreshments prepared and offered just in time to avoid an outburst of Shamgar's wrath. He stood watching everything with a keen eye, one hand resting on the hilt of his sword, and the hint of a smile on his lips.

An arcade occupied one side of the courtyard at ground level where the animals could rest with shelter. The camels knelt and their riders climbed down, glad for the chance to stand and stretch. Shamgar ordered the proprietor and his servants to assist Eder and Bechorath in carrying bundles to the assigned rooms. Packs were removed and the animals fed and watered.

The sleeping rooms were all located on what was called the first floor. They were situated above the arcade and ground floor rooms inhabited by the innkeeper and his family. A corner stairway on the ground floor led to a balcony that provided access to each room.

Terah grumbled over the stark, cramped lodgings, having become spoiled by the luxuries at his estate. Abram, on the other hand, was impressed by the architecture and experienced unending pleasure in running around the balcony, up and down the stairs, and drawing water from the covered well when he became thirsty.

In a short time, Abram found a stairway up onto the flat roof of the building. Stealthily he climbed the stairs, wary that he may be entering a forbidden part of the building. Up on the roof Abram discovered, much to his delight, sights that fascinated and occupied him for hours.

The city lay around and below him for as far as he could see: a maze of white structures surrounding taller, tapered constructions, the temples of minor deities that abounded in the city.

The king's palace, in all its height and splendor, was almost eclipsed by the gigantic magnificence of the multi-staged tower or ziggurat. Rising up out of the city, it was the focal center of Mari and dominated everything around it.

Around and around Abram walked the perimeter of the roof, stopping frequently to peer over the battlement and listen to the people below. It was hot on the roof but he ignored the discomfort. With the coming of dusk came a promise of relief. Darkness settled like a blanket blocking out the scorching rays of the sun. The only heat remaining was that rising from the ground and structures. The air was cooling and it could be felt on the rooftops first.

Shamgar came looking for Abram and upon realizing how comfortable it was above, returned to issue new orders to the innkeeper.

The household family members came with lamps and food. Following soon after were Terah, Amthelo, Bealoth, and Shamgar. Everyone sighed and breathed in the evening's cool air. Abram looked out across other rooftops and watched the city's occupants coming up for cooling relief. Roofs sparkled with the lights of many thousands of lamps and torches, dazzling Abram with its spectacle.

The innkeeper was a good host. He and his son provided mattresses for his guests to sit on while his two servants served wine, beer and food. After Terah was served, he flattered the innkeeper by inviting his family to join Terah's and sup with them. It was exciting for Abram. It was the first time he had ever talked to a boy or a girl. Slowly he began to realize what he had missed in not having youthful companionship.

That evening, Abram made three friends who felt honored to be with the son of a prince. But soon they liked him for his sincere, unspoiled attitude. They had a lot to share. Abram demonstrated his accuracy with those weapons he handled so well in the wilderness: the bow, the spear, and the knife. He explained how to stalk and kill game...or an enemy.

His young friends talked to Abram about how active life was in the city. There were so many exciting things to see and do. Strange people from distant lands came to trade everything imaginable. To the children, the market place was a wonderland where only seeing and touching was believing such things existed. They pointed out the huge tower rising above all other buildings, many times their height.

The evening ended, disappointingly too soon for Abram, when the adults retired to their sleeping rooms and insisted the children come to bed as well.

The next day Abram was taken on a tour of the city accompanied by his family and servants. It was a great adventure for him to see close up some of the sights he had seen from afar the day before. He was awestruck at the immensity of the king's palace. An officer of the guards, posted outside, was proud to describe its main features to this strange little boy who seemed so much in awe of everything around him.

"...and the palace alone covers more than six acres with more than three hundred rooms and courtyards. It has private living quarters, administrative offices, a royal chapel, a throne room, a reception hall, and a school for scribes. The walls are at least twenty feet tall and as thick as you are tall, young lad."

What impressed Abram most was the stupendous height of the temple tower, or ziggurat. Abram looked up at the monumental pyramiding platforms with the shrine at the top and was transfixed

The Caravanserai
in Mari at night

with wonder. It was about two hundred feet high, with each platform a contrasting color, and the shrine, a small room at the top, was glazed a brilliant blue. He had seen the tower at a distance but now, standing so near it, the stature of it overwhelmed him rendering him speechless; but only temporarily. When it was explained to Abram that the patron God Ninhursag lived in the shrine at the top, it seemed logical since the tower had such godly proportions.

City life was like a blur of motion to Abram. There was too much to see and understand before something new caught his attention and whirled his senses. His vision was adapted to the stillness of the open country where he could spot subtle movement in a still expanse and evaluate whether it was friend, foe, or food for hunting. The activity here made him dizzy.

Throughout their tour of the city, Terah purchased gifts that would be needed for the next segment of their journey. Abram watched his father barter at the stalls on various streets, some of which were named after the trades of the men doing business there. He bought bread in the street of the bakers that had a delicious aroma unlike any other street in the city. The most unpleasant street to walk along was the waterfront where fish vendors sold their catch.

Abram's curiosity was almost out of control in the bazaar of Mari. It was a street with a row of narrow shops or stalls down either side. Each one had a heavy cloth overhead, somewhat like a modern awning. Prosperous merchants had the most varied and colorfully dyed coverings. Those of the remaining traders were dirty, sun-faded, and colorless.

Persons of the same trade congregated together, offering a wider variety and convenience to shoppers. Open markets such as these were the center of city commerce. Products from all over the ancient world found their way here, for Mari was a magnificent city of trade.

Abram saw an endless variety of goods that he had never set eyes on before. It was another new experience as thrilling as everything else on the trip. He had countless questions about everything he saw. If Terah was too busy to answer him, he went to Amthelo, Shamgar, Bealoth, Eder, or Bechorath. His mind was like a sponge and his mouth like a bird's with its unceasing chatter.

Terah had very considerable wealth, but the practice of barter was a competition; a game of wits that gave meaning to the word shopping. He enjoyed the fawning attention lavished upon him and his family at every stall. Merchants were fascinated by the size and rich contents of his purse, but found this wealthy nobleman to be a worthy competitor in bartering prices. All along the street the mood of normal bickering and haggling changed to one of greater expectations. Terah was buying expensive items and news of it spread like a flash flood. Merchants un-wrapped their most valuable items, quickly polishing and enhancing their method of presentation while values and starting prices danced in their heads.

As Terah made each purchase Eder and Bechorath were ordered to secure them on the pack of the camels and guard them against potential thieves.

The practice of cutting a sack loose and running off was common in cities. While one thief was being chased by the victim, or the victim's servants, one or more collaborators would cut away more valuables or snatch the beast of burden if escape seemed feasible.

Terah was confident that with Shamgar keeping a sharp eye out for thieves, there would be no trouble. This allowed him to give his full attention to the enjoyment at hand.

For three days and nights they enjoyed the city's delights, mostly because Abram begged to stay longer. He had been living in a wilderness without young friends to play with, and without all these marvels. He yearned to stay and share life with his young friends, and know more about what Mari had to offer. But at the sun's rising on the fourth day, however, Terah awoke his family and servants, and prepared to leave. All the food, water, and gifts were packed onto the camels while Abram, Terah, and Amthelo said their farewells to the innkeeper and his family.

Abram had been given a small purse full of silver shekels and taught how to barter for gifts like Terah did. Looking now at the sad faces of his young friends, and not knowing how to say goodbye, he reached in and pulled out a shekel for each one and gave it to them. They were so delighted at his generosity that the two girls kissed him on each cheek and the boy grabbed abram's hand in both of his and squeezed.

"Come, Abram, we must go," Terah commanded gently.

Abram turned and wiped a tear from each eye and then mounted his camel. Glancing back, he noticed his friends were also teary-eyed.

"I wish we did not have to go...I really want to stay!" he cried unashamedly, his chin on his chest. On the way out of the city, everything was a blur to Abram, seen through tears of sadness.

Upon leaving Mari they followed, once again, the caravan route northwest along the Euphrates River. About two hundred miles from Mari they came to the Balikh River. Traveling through the Balikh River Valley, they continued to cross the Padan Aram region, until they arrived at the trading center where Haran, Abram's older brother, lived.

And Haran, the son of Terah, Abram's oldest brother, took a wife in those days.

Haran was thirty-nine years old when he took her; and the wife of Haran conceived and bare a son, and he called his name Lot.

And she conceived again and bare a daughter, and she called her name Milca; and she again conceived and bare a daughter, and she called her name Sarai.

Haran was forty-two years old when he begat Sarai, which was in the tenth year of the life of Abram; and in those days Abram and his mother and nurse went out from the cave, as the king and his subjects had forgotten the affair of Abram.

Jasher 9:1-4

Chapter 5
Iram and Abram, a Painful Lesson

T erah, his family and servants spent five nights with Haran and his family. They feasted and celebrated their reunion with emotional enthusiasm, telling and retelling stories of the past. Abram took pride in his heritage and put to memory as much of the lore as he could.

At sunrise of the seventh morning, Terah gave the command and his caravan departed amidst tears of emotion for their leaving. They traveled one day's journey to the east until they located the patriarch Heber and his families. Terah counted himself as the fifth generation from Heber and believed it important for Abram to know the Patriarch while opportunity allowed it. Heber and his tribe lived a reasonably short distance away. They were located along the Habor River (named after the Patriarch) in the northeastern portion of Padan Aram.

The reunion here was in grand proportions compared to the previous one. There were celebrations of music, feasting, and games of skill as families of Hebrews came some distance and gathered for the reunion of their kin. Every form of eastern hospitality was extended. Terah was honored and gifts were given to Amthelo and Abram as well. Terah reciprocated with expensive gifts purchased in Mari.

Abram played with the children during the day, demonstrating his hunting skills and talking about his life in the wilderness. He sat next to his father during the evenings absorbing everything possible from what he heard. Many were the fascinating stories about the traditions of their tribe. Abram made up his mind that he was going to be a prince like his father, when he grew up. The omen was prophetic and Abram believed in it; but Terah was his idol, his example that he would follow.

"No one is as important, nor as interesting, as father. I do not care if Heber is a Patriarch," Abram mumbled. "But I will be staying with the Patriarchs Noah and Shem," he remembered. The thought of being separated from Terah made Abram cling to him. Terah was embarrassed by this clinging affection when in the company of others.

"Abram!" he scolded. "A young prince does not cling to his father like a toddling child! You may stand or sit close by, but do not cling like a defenseless tot!"

Abram was wounded deeply. The words stabbed his heart and his emotions crumbled. He hung his head and covered it with his mantle to hide tears of disappointment from the stares of all the people.

On the morning of the seventh day with Heber, Terah and his small group prepared to join a caravan traveling south to Tadmor, Damascus, Hazor, Shechem and Urusalem on their way to Egypt.

"Guard yourselves well," Heber cautioned. "There are gangs of highwaymen that prey on weak caravans to rob and murder at will. They live in the mountains, in caves, and watch the trade routes for caravans or solitary travelers. You may be safe in joining a caravan, but I will not let you go without some added protection. I am sending seven good fighting men with you to make sure you and your family are well guarded."

"You are most thoughtful and generous, my lord Heber. I shall always remember your deeds and praise your name. Abram and his seed shall do the same. You will never be forgotten, even though countless generations shall pass; this I swear."

Abram joined his father in kneeling at the feet of the Patriarch, followed also by Shamgar and the other servants.

"When you reach Urusalem my men will present gifts to our Patriarchs Noah and Shem. And they will tell them for me and mine that we honor them at our campfires and in our homes. Now, rise up and go your way in safety."

"Many thanks, great father. I shall always remember your most kind hospitality and friendship." Terah rose to his feet, embraced Heber, turned and walked to his camel.

Abram stood up and held out his arms to embrace Heber. The Patriarch was so touched by the affection that he knelt and received Abram in his arms, kissing him on the neck. He held him longer than normal and when Heber released him he said: "I sense greatness in you, Abram. How great you shall become, in the eyes of your seed, I know not. But...here am I, a father over many, and yet, strangely enough, I do not feel out of place on my knees before you, my boy. I may be called sentimental...but this is not sentimentality I feel. Time will tell. My blessing upon you Abram."

Heber rose to his feet with some help from Abram.

"Ah...you are quite strong like your father, I see. Use your strength wisely my son. Be strong of mind and heart as well as body. Now go, but do not forget me."

"Never, great lord. I shall always remember you." Abram replied.

Two hundred miles south from the lands of Heber lay their next destination, Tadmore. This rich trade city developed out of an oasis on the northern edge of the great Arabian Steppe. Due to its strategic location, Tadmore had become an important link in the chain of trading centers. These cities, which were strung out along the rich river valleys from the Persian Gulf to the border of Egypt, gave birth to the title: 'Fertile Crescent'.

The journey out of the hill country down towards Tadmore was exciting to Abram. The caravan crossed several streams running down towards the Belikh River. They forded the river at a broad stretch where the water was shallow and sauntered over its slippery river-rock bed. Abram's keen eyes took in everything. Fish and game were in abundance, and the travelers never wanted for fresh food.

Iram, one of Heber's men, knew the territory well and was perhaps the best hunter in the caravan. He had heard Terah speak at length with a proud voice, about Abram's skills at hunting, for a boy of only eleven. It was time, he thought, to see if the reasons for a father's boastings were real or imaginary.

"Would you like to come and hunt with me, Abram?" he asked one night.

"Could I? Oh yes, lord Iram, it would make me very happy!"

"Good. Now, if your father permits it we shall leave before dawn. Let us ask him and then I will look at your bow and arrows."

Terah was pleased that Iram asked to take Abram hunting. He was confident about Abram's abilities. The smaller bow and arrows that he had custom made for Abram were of quality materials and workmanship. Abram's killing range was not as great as a more powerful man-sized bow, but his considerable stealth and ability for disguise allowed him to come quite close to his prey without being detected.

The next morning, Abram awoke as the sun gave a hint of its coming by turning the black night sky into a discernable blue. He ate some food set aside for a morning meal then prepared himself for hunting. He disguised his boy scent by applying oil from sheep fat to his body and wearing a sheepskin over his torso. All this and a skinned sheep's head for a hat fooled most animals who could smell better than they could see.

When Iram came for him, Abram was ready and anxious for a new adventure. He sheathed the knife he was honing to an even sharper edge, then slung the rawhide cord, holding a sheepskin case of arrows, over his head and shoulder so it rested high on his back.

Iram was also dressed in skins. His attire was from a goat and he smelled like a goat to Abram who smiled at seeing him. Their eyes met. Iram smiled, obviously surprised by what he saw, and nodded a silent approval in return.

Picking up his bow, Abram followed Iram out of the camp past the guards saying nothing; waiting to be spoken to before he spoke. Southward they walked in the semi-darkness, along the trail that the caravan would soon follow. When it became easier to see, Iram began an easy, loping run to gain distance from the camp. Looking back over his shoulder from time to time, Iram saw Abram running along close behind. After running non-stop for twenty minutes, Iram slowed to a walk. Not far behind, Abram caught up panting for breath.

In the early morning cold of the hills, Abram welcomed the run. Soon his shivering body was warm. His face was now wet with perspiration and his heaving chest glistened in the early morning glow.

Still Iram said nothing, but a smile formed on his quiet lips. That was enough communication for Abram, to believe he was not holding Iram back. Abram had no idea he was being tested. He merely wanted to please Iram; to do his part in the hunt for game and, of course, to bring honor to his father at all times.

"I will cross the river, hide and wait for an antelope to come and drink," Iram finally spoke. You will do the same on this side of the river. Do not expose yourself and do not speak. Do you understand?"

Abram nodded his head then watched Iram turn, walk to the bank and pick his way across the river. Soon he was out of sight, beginning his vigil hidden in brush caught in boulders along the river's edge.

Abram's first thought was to find a location similar to that in which Iram was hiding. He walked downstream looking here and there, but was dissatisfied. On the way he crossed a stream emptying into the river. Leaping over it he remembered a situation similar to this. It was not too many moons ago. While hunting near the Tigris River, he scouted the streams emptying into it. There he found prints left by various animals, and while hiding he spied his quarry, stalked and killed it.

"I will do the same here," he whispered to himself, and set off upstream. Looking carefully at the ground for animal tracks on both sides, Abram moved in a crouch, almost on all fours. Near the entrance to the river the first tracks he saw were that of a bear. A familiar feeling of fear gripped him, gnawing at his stomach, but he moved on more quietly and more cautiously than before.

Crawling along through the forest undergrowth, Abram managed to identify prints of the hare, antelope, panther, wild hog, wolf, fox, jackal, and hyena at the stream's edge.

"I have stumbled upon a popular watering place," he observed with anticipation. "Now to hide some place where I can see and be protected," he murmured.

Further upstream he saw a tree clinging to the edge of a bank. It had wide spreading limbs and plenty of foliage in its upper reaches where he could hide.

"Perfect!" he whispered excitedly.

A gentle morning breeze rustled its way through the forest, stirring brush and trees. The rushing sigh hid all sound and movement Abram may have made while he walked to the tree and climbed up. Settling himself as comfortably as possible, he waited...and watched....

From his vantage point Abram had an excellent view upstream and downstream for a hundred yards in both directions. Like a good hunter he waited patiently, motionless except for his eyes which moved from side to side looking for visitors to the stream. Two large hares eventually came to drink, sniffing the air and the ground, stopping frequently to listen with their big ears.

"They are only ten to twelve paces upstream," Abram calculated. "A small target...but at this distance I should not miss."

The hares were at the stream's edge, lapping water and bobbing their heads up to listen for a possible warning.

Carefully, quietly Abram armed his bow, drew the arrow back...back...sighting as he did so. "Slowly, slowly sight on target...allow for wind...distance...and...release!"

A quiet "thungg" of the bow's gut shot the arrow deadly accurate, impaling the larger of the two hares to the ground where it crouched. The other hare looked at her companion, bewildered. Nervously she jerked around looking in all directions to locate the danger. Sniffing and nudging her mate one moment, the next she held her head and ears high, listening. She stayed too long. Abram's

41

next arrow was on its way, a whisper above the wind. The female hare died quickly next to her mate.

Delighted with his success, Abram slipped the bow over his shoulder and began climbing down to claim his prizes. He had just dropped the last few feet, from the lowest hanging branch, and started towards his fallen game when he saw it. A large fox, who had been after the hares, rushed forward and claimed one of them. Clamping his jaws around the neck of the female, he attempted to drag it away. Abram's arrow had it staked to the ground, however, preventing the fox's theft.

Seeing this, Abram hastily drew another arrow to his bow, pulled and released...too quickly. The shaft missed...overhead. The fox hesitated, released his hold, looked up and around, seeing and smelling only a harmless sheep downstream. Reassured, the fox went back to his task.

"Take careful aim!" Abram scolded himself. Hunched down on his knees, without taking his eyes off the fox, Abram slowly drew another arrow, felt its feathered end seated onto the bowstring and brought it up to eye level. Gradually pulling...sighting... adjusting...then releasing....

Thungg...ssssss...thuckk! A short-lived shriek, a thrashing about, and again only the gentle sigh of the forest breeze.

Abram retrieved all of his arrows and washed their bloody shafts in the stream before returning them to their case. Untying a length of gut line from around his waist, he looped each end around the hind legs of the two hares. Hoisting the line over his shoulder, he carried his prizes back to the tree, climbed up and suspended them from a branch.

Climbing down again, he retrieved his bow, grabbed the dead fox by its long tail and dragged it back to the tree. Taking another length of gut line from his waist, Abram tied the fox's legs together with each end. Putting the line over his head, he rested the fox on one shoulder supporting the length of the animal across his back. Climbing the tree once again, Abram hung the fox on a branch stump, leaned back against the trunk, and panted from the exertion. His lean body was wet with sweat and stained red with the blood of his game. He was also a confusing variety of odors.

Sitting on a limb, Abram closed his eyes enjoying the breeze that wafted by cool and refreshing. A dream began forming in his mind as he relaxed. He could see his father and Shamgar boasting to Noah and Shem about the magnificent game he had killed all by himself. Included were a lion, a bear, a panther, and several antelope.

Abram had no awareness of how long he had sat there. He was deep in a reverie bordering sleep. Suddenly he jerked himself awake as he began to slip sideways and lose balance. With the quick reflexes of youth, he caught himself by clawing at the bark with one hand and catching a nearby limb with the other, letting out a cry of surprise as he did so.

Looking down to measure the fall he narrowly missed, he saw something that woke him instantly and struck terror in his heart. A large, black, panther was sniffing around the tree. The beast had come upon the blood of the animals Abram had slain and followed the scent of the fox Abram dragged to the tree. Abram's outcry called the panther's attention to a large feast roosting over-head, and the cat roared his intimidating approval. Trembling with fear from this danger, Abram clung to the tree and stared down with blinking eyes. Circling the tree a few times, the panther suddenly stood, front paws against the trunk, and roared in defiance up to the human who looked and smelled like a sheep.

Quickly Abram moved up higher and clung to a limb, too afraid to think. All he could do was stare down at the black, threatening menace.

The big cat must have been gauging the difficulty in climbing the tree, for he made one leaping attempt and failed to hold, slipping to the ground. Around and around he continued pacing...preparing himself.

Abram began to adjust to his fear. His mind started working again. Slowly he thought about solutions to his dilemma, forcing himself to reason with the possibilities.

"Give him one of the hares," he mumbled. "That might satisfy him. In fact, throw down both hares, and the fox too if necessary."

Abram started to climb down to the branch stub where his game hung when the big cat sprang onto the tree trunk clawing, holding, and lurching his way up. A trail of yellow scratches, deep in the smooth bark, was proof of the death dealing power in each claw.

Gaining position on the lowest limb, the panther hesitated and looked up at what awaited him.

Abram forced himself to look up and around to seek a further retreat. Quickly he realized there was no way to escape. An awful, paralyzing terror gripped him, blocking out possible solutions. He tried to scream but his throat was so dry only a whining sound issued forth.

A horrible picture of his lifeless, mutilated body came to mind and stomach bile rose in his throat gagging him. With eyes watering and blurring his vision, he thought of the terrible effect his death was going to have on his mother.

"Father and Shamgar will be sad, "he thought, "but mother, poor mother will wail and weep for days. Shamgar will ask father: 'Why did he not use his bow and arrows?' And father will answer...'he let the spirit of fear possess him and he did nothing except wait for death...such a waste. All he had to do was send shaft into the beast's vital place. Such a sad waste...a shaft...in a vital place...'"

These thoughts awakened Abram from his morbid death trance. Wiping the tears from his eyes, he struggled to control his shattered emotions. Taking deep breaths, a calming of his terror began to take effect.

The panther had moved up to where the two hares and the fox hung. To Abram's relief, for the moment, the cat was toying with the dead game, pawing, sniffing, and licking the blood.

This distraction gave Abram extra time, precious time, to pull himself together and become the hunter once again, instead of the hunted. Slowly, he drew an arrow, seated it in the gut string, and raised his bow. Drawing the string back slowly and carefully, he sighted down the shaft. His hands shook.

"I will miss! And then he will attack!" Abram shuddered. "Breathe in deeply and slowly breath out while you aim," he heard his father's instruction come back to mind. Just then the panther looked up, roared a vicious threat, and began to climb towards him.

Abram braced himself more securely and followed the panther's climb, sighting down the arrow's sharp copper tip.

Upward the big cat came, his fangs dripping saliva from anticipation of a large meal.

"Breathe deeply...slowly let it out..." Abram whispered.

Ever closer the beast climbed, slowly, snarling as he came.

Breathe deeply...hold very still...and pull..."

The panther crouched, ready to spring.

"Pull more...more..."

"Thung...hisssshhhtuck!" the arrow flew and struck home with deadly accuracy. The shaft flew the short distance, fast and true, penetrating deep through one eye and into the brain.

The black cat leaped up, roaring in outraged pain. With his sight gone, he missed his prey, clawing the air, wildly off balance. Hitting Abram's side a glancing swipe, the panther fell, crashing through branches and bouncing off large limbs. When it hit the ground with a great thump, Abram thought he felt the ground shudder from where he stood. Looking down with unbelieving eyes he fought off the bile that rose from his stomach. With death so close, his victory was unbelievable.

The light forest breeze continued to sigh through the trees as before, but to Abram it now had special significance. He was alive! Caressing his face and body, the gentle air was like the very breath of life to him. He breathed it in deeply, enjoying...relishing. "It is so good to be alive. Yes, I am really alive!" he shouted.

Abram looked around him at the quaking leaves all fluttering with life. They dazzled his eyes, sparkling from sunlight that seemed more intense than ever before. Gradually the tension in his body diminished, and his mind consciously returned to obeying Abram's will.

"My hares! My fox," he exclaimed. "They are still here! The panther never ate them!" Looking down at the dead cat Abram shouted: "And I have killed a panther...a huge panther at that! And...and with only one arrow! Only one arrow...and I really killed a giant panther!" his emotions soared.

The caravan had arrived and Amthelo was alarmed that Iram stood on the trail alone awaiting them. "Where is Abram?" she called out as soon as Iram was within hearing distance.

"Iram! Where is my son!" Terah demanded. "He was to be with you, in your care!"

Shamgar, Eder, and Bechorath rushed forward to hear the answer.

"If he is hurt or mauled, you will answer to me, son of Heber!" Shamgar threatened, his teeth clenched in a snarl.

"He went upstream instead of staying by the river as I did. Here is the antelope I killed. Look, it is enough meat for everyone in the caravan. I dared not leave it to look for Abram. Other beasts would have devoured it. Here help me gut and skin it. You shall have a large part of it," he offered nervously.

"Do it yourself!" Terah ordered. We are going to find Abram. If he is dead or maimed, I will return to gut and skin you...that I swear!"

"Find my son!" Amthelo pleaded. "Go now, please!"

Terah, Shamgar, Eder, and Bechorath headed up the stream Iram pointed out to them.

"Abram...Abram...?!" Terah shouted.

"Abram...Abram...Abram...?!" the other three called out. They had spread out several paces away from the stream on both sides. Looking around for a sign or evidence of Abram's presence, on they walked calling out his name.

Abram had been busy constructing a litter on which to drag his game back to the river. He began to hear shouting a long way off, so he paused from his work to listen.

"Abram...Abram...Abram!" he heard his name shouted by familiar voices, and he felt his heart pump harder. The voices grew louder...clearer.

"It is father, and Shamgar...and others.... Here father, here Shamgar...I am here. Bechorath, Eder...? Here I am!"

All four men came running towards the sound of his voice, and Abram also ran to meet them.

Up into Terah's arms he leaped, hugging his father's neck. For the first time in many years Terah, a cold, unemotional lord, shed a tear of happy emotion.

The three servants rushed up, surrounding the boy and his father, patting Abram's back and tousling his heavy mop of reddish blond hair in a display of affection. Terah shifted Abram's weight onto his hip, to easily support the boy's weight, and Abram let out a small cry of pain.

"What is it son? Are you hurt?" He asked letting Abram down.

"It is my side, father. The panther swiped me with his paw as I shot him with an arrow and..."

"A panther? What panther? What happened to you?

"It was huge and black with yellow eyes. Its fangs were as big as my fingers, dripping wet as he stalked me in the tree. And..."

"Tree? You were up in a tree with a panther and you sent an arrow into him? Is he dead?"

"Oh, yes, father, and I did it with only one arrow...in his eye...as he jumped at me...must have been blinded because he missed...except for this..." Under a ripped portion of his sheepskin covering, Abram proudly displayed claw marks, etched in blood, about five inches along the left side of his torso.

All four men gasped. Up to now they were not sure that Abram's panther was really a panther. The spread of the claw marks convinced them.

"Your sheepskin saved you from a bad wounding, my son. You were very fortunate. The gods were with you. Now, let us see this panther you have killed with one arrow."

Abram led the way upstream. When they came upon the dead panther, each man sucked air, marveled at the huge size and weight of the beast, and guessed at its age. Everyone agreed that he was a remarkable hunting trophy.

"A portent of Abram's future greatness as a lord, taking after his father," Shamgar offered.

Terah beamed with pride as his servants bowed their heads in tribute to Abram.

Abram took his father's hand and squeezed, while looking up at his face. "How good it is to be alive," he said softly. "How full of wonder life is. Yet..." feeling his side, "death is so close at hand. It can be swift. Is that not true father?"

Terah, amazed at his young son's wisdom, as well as his remarkable skill and bravery, agreed. "Yes, Abram, that is true. Now, let us be on our way back to the caravan, before they become too impatient and leave without us."

"Bechorath...Eder!"

"Yes, lord?"

"Finish that litter and drag the panther to the river. Hang him up by his hind legs for all to see and wonder how Abram killed the man-eater.

"Oh, yes, Lord Terah, as you command," Eder responded excitedly. "Come Bechorath, let us hurry. I can hardly wait to see their faces when the story is told."

"Gladly, Eder. I especially want to see Iram's expression when we show him this giant cat!"

"Let us be on our way, Abram," Terah ordered.

"Yes, father. Oh, I almost forgot...my game is still hanging up in the tree. Allow me to climb up and get it."

"No, my son, not with that wound of yours. Shamgar will get it for you."

"Up in the tree, Shamgar, fetch Abram's game."

"Ah...yes lord," Shamgar agreed with hesitation.

"And what game did you kill, Abram?" Terah asked.

"Just two hares and a fox."

"Just two hares and a fox?" Terah echoed with a smile turning the corners of his mouth, almost hidden by the large mustache and full beard. "Well, I want to see them."

"Come on Shamgar, up the tree; we do not have much time."

"Yes, lord...I am trying...but my weight...is too great...for this task...Ohhh, ouch! Curses!" Shamgar tried to shinny up the trunk and failed. Losing his grip, he slid down, hit the ground with a thump on his posterior, and rolled onto his back.

Terah and Abram laughed aloud, unable to contain themselves. Eder and Bechorath joined in, relishing this unique opportunity to laugh at a giant who was capable of killing anyone who dared laugh at him.

"I regret, my lord, I am not skilled at all in climbing a tree," Shamgar said meekly.

"It appears you are correct, Shamgar. Like me, you have put on too much weight. Not enough fighting, eh my friend?"

"Ah, yes my lord. Too much food and drink and women have softened me. What I need is a good fight now and then to get rid of this," he stood up, laughing, and held his stomach with both hands.

"Hmmm, perhaps you are right. You have given me an idea that should appeal to you as much as it does to me."

"Whatever you command, lord, I will gladly obey. Just release me from your order to climb this tree," the big man replied eagerly.

"Iram needs a lesson taught to him. Nothing requiring tools, mind you, just a lesson he will remember after being shown by your hands."

"Ahh, yesss!" Shamgar hissed his approval, glancing at Abram. "I understand completely, Lord Terah. You may trust me to carry out your lesson carefully."

"I would do this myself, you understand, except that being a prince I might offend Heber and risk losing the protection of his men."

"Yes, lord, of course; you honor me with this opportunity to serve in your place," Shamgar bowed with a broad smile on his beefy face.

"Good. Now let us be going. Eder...!"

"Yes lord?"

"Up the tree with you and bring down Abram's catch of game!"

As you command," Eder responded, then shinnied up with some difficulty.

"It seems, Abram, that you are the best tree climber of us all."

"It is because I am eleven, father, and you are all too old. I am young enough to climb trees, but you are not. Does that make you unhappy?"

"No, Abram, it does not make us unhappy," Terah laughed and was joined by Shamgar and Bechorath.

"That is good, because I want you all to share in my happiness. This has been a very exciting day for me."

"I am sure it has, Abram, I am sure it has. But now you look tired, my son."

"Ohh, maybe a little."

"Then you shall be carried, as befits a prince who has conquered his enemies."

"Shamgar!"

"Yes lord?"

"Carry the boy on your shoulders, and be careful of his wound."

"As you command, my lord, it is an honor," Shamgar replied and kneeled in front of Abram who climbed on his broad shoulders. Shamgar staggered to his feet with a grunt and started off a pace behind Terah. The even stride soon lulled Abram to sleep. Shamgar held the boy's hands to prevent him from falling as he slumped one way, then another.

Looking up at Abram with great satisfaction, Terah spoke softly to Shamgar. "To think that this, sleepy, young lad killed two hares, one fox, and a large panther in one morning. I am in awe. If he is this capable at age eleven, think what marvelous feats of accomplishment await him as a man."

"Ahhh, yes, master, he shall do wonderous things, perhaps more than we will ever know!"

"Time will tell...yes, only the passing of time will tell," Terah mused, thinking about the omen.

The caravan camped early that day. Terah called everyone to a celebration of Abram's hunting success. Wine was poured. Meat was plentiful, served with bread and vegetables. When everyone had eaten their fill, one of the men spoke up and asked Terah if he would tell the full story of Abram's very successful hunt. A rush of other voices echoed the request, the whole caravan being very curious about this marvel.

A silence fell upon the camp as the tall lord stood in their center and raised his arms for quiet. A loud murmur of approval was heard from everyone and then a complete silence. Only the sputtering of flames from torches could be heard as Terah, a masterful storyteller, began.

Like the stitching of a colorful embroidery, Terah wove the tale of Abram's adventure. Giving careful attention to every useful detail, he set the scene and played out the action. Lending an emphasis of emotion to each step of the drama, Terah led his audience through Abram's experience.

They "ahhh'd" with approval at Abram's hunting strategy and successes at shooting his game. They gasped and screamed in fright when the panther appeared. Bechorath, according to Terah's instructions, donned the panther's hide complete with head, claws and tail. He came on all fours growling and hissing an acceptable immitation. Trembling and perspiring, the audience saw the hugh black panther lick blood from the hares and fox on its way up the tree. Men and women moved away, moaning and howling, as the panther cast his yellow eye menacingly upon them and advanced.

Terah absorbed his audience completely into the drama. They were there as much as Abram was. The storyteller toyed with their emotions as a panther does with his prey; teasing with death...prolonging...relishing the conquest. His words held everyone in a wide-eyed trance, poised on the brink...waiting...waiting....

"And then the black beast leaped!" shouted Terah. The panther leaped at those nearest, with his jaws open and claws slashing at the air. "But Abram, my son, let fly his arrow straight and true! Into the beast's eye it shot, blinding and mortally wounding him! His hot breath covered Abram like the wind from the great desert to the south! The saliva from his mouth sprayed Abram like a rain. The giant cat was that close as he clawed at Abram in his great lunge!"

Many of the audience recoiled, falling over one another as they saw the panther attacking them.

"And a claw of the beast struck! He struck the side of Abram...clawing, tearing, ripping through his sheepskin covering and into the boy's tender flesh!"

Listeners felt their sides for the pain they imagined, and cried out, groaning with agony and fright!

"But Abram kept his hold on the tree and did not fall as the beast did. The panther howled in a fit of raging pain! Blinded, falling, hitting tree limbs, crushing bones...KA-THUMP! He smashed to the ground, shaking the earth and the tree rooted in it, upon which Abram clung."

Terah paused to let the story's action take its effect, then finished. "And so there we found Abram standing over his dead panther, a man-killer, time and times again the boy's size and weight and in the awesome power of dealing terrible death. Dead...dead with just one arrow from the bow of a mere boy."

Terah dropped his arms to the side, turned to Shamgar, and nodded his head. Shamgar took hold of Abram and lifted him easily onto his shoulder and paraded him around in a circle so that everyone might look up to him and remember. Their hands reached out to touch Abram, to take his hand in theirs, to be able to say: "I knew Prince Abram, the great hunter, son of Terah, a Heber-ew."

"Abram...Abram...Abram...little prince...great hunter...," the entire camp came forward to touch and give praise. And Iram, even Iram now believed in Abram as a hunter of considerable skill and bravery.

But Amthelo did not rejoice openly as all others did. The shock of Abram's brush with death stunned her terribly. His reward, a sizable fur trophy, would be more than a frequent reminder of her near loss. Looking up at Abram over the heads of everyone, Amthelo's memory recalled many of the events of his life. A young life, already filled with remarkable happenings.

"What will his future really be?" she thought. "Will he live to manhood? Will he have a wife, and children to comfort and amuse me in my old age? Or will the gods be jealous of his great lordship and cut him off? The Lord of Death seems to come as frequently as a trader with foreign goods, leaving tokens of his wares. How often will he be turned away? When will this 'black lord' insist on his due, having gone away empty-handed so often?"

A cold night breeze rustled tent shelters, and sputtered torches, threatening to extinguish them. Amthelo shivered then shook with a jerking shudder. "It is cold...the 'Lord of Death' has a cold breath. I feel him. He cuts a chill through my body to the bones!"

Happy, cheering praises diminished. A murmur of excited talk followed, then silence once again as Terah stood with up-raised arms calling for quiet attention. A hush fell. Everyone quickly seated themselves, eager for more excitement.

"Very early this morning," Terah began, "I entrusted my son to the care of Iram, the kin of Heber. Now, as you know, Abram is a skilled hunter for a lad of eleven," Terah paused waiting for a response.

As expected, the audience cheered their agreement.

51

"Now, Iram is renowned among his people as a remarkable hunter. Our thanks to Iram for the tasty antelope meat we ate tonight. Come stand with me Iram, so we may honor you."

Iram, quite astonished at this tribute, came forward uncertain of himself...and Terah.

"My lord honors me when I have done nothing to deserve it," Iram replied.

"Oh, but you have, you have! And we shall soon see what it is," Terah announced, turning again to his audience.

"My friends, look what a strong, able hunter and warrior he is. My Patriarch, Heber, chose him well to protect us, with his brothers, from our enemies the highwaymen."

The caravaners murmured their approval, and also their curiosity.

"But Lord Terah...," Iram started to question.

"Now do not be reluctant, Iram. Could it be our bold warrior hunter is a little shy? Who ever heard of a shy warrior hunter?" Turning to the gathering he laughed loudly, drawing laughter in return as an answer. "You, my protector, shall provide us all with a small demonstration of your skills."

"But Lord Terah..."

"Say no more, Iram. You will give your patriarch Heber a good report, when you return, of how I held you up before these people as an example."

"Very well, but I do not understand what..."

"It is really quite simple, Iram, just a little demonstration of hand-to-hand fighting. We all need to know how to handle ourselves if attacked. Besides, this is a festive occasion and a little entertainment is only proper. Am I not right everyone?"

"Yes! Yes" Lord Terah," the reply came shouting back from the audience.

"Very well, my lord," Iram agreed, "But who...?"

"I shall pick ... oh, just anyone from those here," Terah explained. Turning to the gathering again, Terah asked: "Is there anyone who wishes to learn a hand-to-hand fighting lesson from Iram?"

A few men stood up and answered. But Shamgar, who stood close by, stepped up and loudly volunteered.

"But Shamgar, you already know hand-to-hand fighting."

"Ah, yes lord, but perhaps the illustrious Iram can teach me a new trick...or I him... and everyone can benefit, hey?"

"Well... perhaps you are right, Shamgar. Very well, we have Iram's opponent, my friends. It should be a good match...er, ah, lesson that is. Now Eder, where are those mock swords I asked you to provide?"

Eder rushed forward with two sturdy staffs of wood. They were a little longer than the length of Shamgar's arm span, and blunt at both ends. He gave one to Iram, the other to Shamgar, and scurried out of the way.

The spectators gave way to form a large circle, buzzing with excitement over the prospect of a well-fought match.

"Let the lesson begin," Terah commanded.

Both men laid their real weapons aside and took up a staff. Advancing to the center, they took up a defensive posture with each staff outstretched or at the ready. The expressions on their faces were a marked contrast, one from the other. Iram looked worried and anxious, while Shamgar smiled, knowingly, mischievously.

The calm assurance of his opponent shook Iram's confidence; what little he may have had at the time he agreed to Terah's persuasion. This was apparent in the feeble thrust he made as the first offensive move.

Shamgar easily parried, then slashed, striking Iram on his sword arm. It was a quick blow that hurt but not sufficiently to prevent Iram from continuing. Shamgar was careful.

"Come teach me Iram," he teased, standing almost still while Iram circled him, gathering courage for another attempt. Shamgar lowered his staff as an invitation to strike.

Iram accepted it. Rushing forward he raised his staff and slashed diagonally, hard and fast.

Shamgar caught the strike on his staff blocking it effectively. Then, stepping in close, he hit Iram a blow to the jaw with his left fist. It staggered him and he rocked back on his heels.

"Ow! I am the one being taught a lesson, it seems," he moaned painfully. Then the logic of his own words struck his mind and he suddenly realized he was being punished by Terah. "How clever and devious a ruse," he thought. "Honor me before witnesses and then beat me until I am covered with welts. Very well, Lord Terah, your man is big and strong, but I am faster and I have a few tricks of my own. Lesson number one is about to begin."

Iram found a new determination fueled by a mixture of resentment and instinct for survival. Shamgar first became aware of it when the expression on Iram's face changed. The second time he was exposed to it occurred when Iram made some lightning fast movements.

Shamgar was caught off guard as Iram feinted a move to his opponent's right, faked a thrust to the left, went to one knee and ducked Shamgar's vicious slash at shoulder height. Iram brought his staff around with both hands, hard and fast. Its swishing sound preceded a resounding "thwack"!

Shamgar gasped with pain as the staff caught him on the side of his left knee. The blow staggered the big man and he hobbled away a few strides testing a leg that rebelled against his weight. He found a new respect for Iram as an adversary and when their eyes met again, the smile had changed faces.

"The insolence of this useless thorn," Shamgar whispered huskily. "I shall pluck him out and squash him underfoot. But I must be careful. He is fast with a trick or two, I have to admit. Ouch, this leg hurts like scorching fire. I need to even the score for that blow."

Iram should have pressed his advantage, but he did not. He was uncertain about how far this duel should go before Terah stopped it. "Perhaps I have not been punished enough?" he reasoned. "If my beating is the desired result, only that will end this contest; unless... I should somehow get the best of this overgrown hulk?"

Advancing on Shamgar, Iram judged him to be slower than ever, limping with each move. Shamgar never fought with any dexterity of feet like Iram, but stood like a fortress and fought tirelessly.

Iram tried every trick of feint, thrust, slash, swipe he could think of. Their staves rang out like cracks of a whip as Shamgar caught or deflected each blow expertly.

Iram's right arm felt weak and he panted from exhaustion.

The spectators were all on their feet shouting encouragement to their chosen favorite. Wagers were made. Excitement was rampant. Terah stood smiling. He saw that Shamgar had underestimated Iram in the beginning, but now he knew his victory was almost assured.

Then it happened. Countering another desperate effort to break through his defense, Shamgar stopped Iram's attack and engaged his own. His staff swung with brutal force from every direction as he limped an advance.

A quick, frightened look to either side proved there was no escape for Iram. The resolute force of Shamgar's arm delivered blow after powerful blow. Catching them on his staff, Iram was driven to his knees fearing the very next would hit his body. The thought of a blow to his head, and the resulting unconsciousness, was almost welcome; the ache in his hands, arms and shoulders was so great.

Then there was a different pain; it was in his chest. Shamgar was more agile than Iram believed. He never saw Shamgar's foot until it kicked hard, sending him sprawling on his back. The staff flew out of his hand. He lay doubled up on his side gasping for breath and writhing in pain.

Shamgar stood over Iram poised to strike again but a small figure ran up and stood in the way.

"No more Shamgar! NO MORE!" he commanded, holding his arms out to shield Iram. "You have won the contest, Shamgar, do not hurt him anymore!" Abram shouted up at a ferocious countenance he hardly recognized. Could it be the same gentle giant that always treated Abram with more care than his own father? Abram shuddered as a cold chill of fear overcame him.

Looking down at Abram, Shamgar withdrew from his rage and began to relax. Lowering his staff, he tossed it aside and wiped the sweat from his face with one downward swipe of his big hand.

"You would not hurt me, would you Shamgar?" Abram asked cautiously.

"I would sooner cut off my right hand than hurt you with a blow, my prince," Shamgar replied hanging his head."

"Are you still angry with Iram because he hit you in the leg?"

"Aww no, Abram. Why this Iram is a good fighter. He is very quick, and clever too. I got careless at first, when he hit my leg hard. I guess I became angry at myself as much as him...and... well, I fight better when I am angry. Say, I hope I have not hurt the poor man too much?"

Iram was still in misery. His six kinsmen ran up and stood ready to defend him against further injury. When they saw Shamgar toss his staff aside, they were relieved.

Everyone cheered both contestants after Shamgar complimented Iram's skills.

Terah stood smiling, satisfied with the outcome. One by one the spectators came and complimented him on a spectacular feast. They gave thanks for the many lessons learned about sword fighting and praised the contestants for their efforts.

When it was all over and the camp was quiet for the remainder of the night, Terah lay on his bed of skins reflecting on the evening's events. Out of the silence of the night could be heard a laugh and a snicker: "You sly fox, you have done it again," he congratulated himself.

Chapter 6
The Highwaymen

The caravan rested at Tadmore a few days and prepared for the next segment of its journey through dangerous lands.

Upon questioning a few merchants it was reported that somewhere between Tadmore and Damascus lurked sizeable bands of robbers that attacked almost any size caravan. In questioning the king's officers, Terah heard that only the largest caravans with ample fighting men did well in getting through. At first Terah was very disturbed by this bad news. He resolved, however, that this would not dissuade him from traveling on.

He carefully instructed his servants to spread the news that a strongly armed caravan would be leaving soon for Damascus. The caravan leader, a prince with several armed warriors, was accepting additional merchants with servants who could fight if necessary.

Within the same day fifty-five merchants approached Terah for permission to join him. He ordered Shamgar, Iram, and his kinsmen to test the fighting skills of these men and their servants. After qualifying their strength for defense in a battle, Terah accepted twenty-nine merchants. These had warriors, the most capable fighters, as guards. He knew that men, weak or unskilled in fighting, would be only a detriment to the safety of the caravan.

Terah gave orders for all members to make preparations to leave early in the morning in two days. Every merchant was required to have animal handlers in addition to their guards. Each man was to have ample weapons and provisions. Swords and daggers were to be sharpened, supplies of arrows increased, and shields procured.

The activity around Terah was electric; currents of motion flowed to and from him. He heard questions, gave answers or commands, and men promised compliance. Shamgar, Iram, and his men, became Terah's captains. They saw to it that his commands were carried out. A military unit was being composed, with Terah as its Lord Commander. There was no resentment by the merchants or their servants; to the contrary, every man was more secure in the knowledge of it and gladly complied with every order.

In good humor, Terah looked over at Shamgar and remarked: "We have yet to run from a fight, heh, my friend?"

Shamgar looked up, from testing the sharpness of his sword, and smiled knowingly. "We only run to fight, lord. We never run from our enemies. It has been some time since my sword has drawn blood, master, I am ready."

"Control your eagerness, Shamgar, this danger may not be as severe as reported to us. We could be completely bored for the remainder of our journey. But like you, I find my self restless and itching for excitement. It is the cursed rocking motion of the camels hour upon hour, day after day. I need something to get my blood up. A good fight, some blood spilled...yes, that would satisfy me too!" Terah exclaimed with a gleam of excitement brightening his lackluster eyes.

The distance from Tadmore to Damascus was about 175 miles, or almost ten days journey. The caravan had traveled seven days, wary and waiting for an attack that never came. It was now the morning of the eighth day. Just ahead lay the forested Anti-Lebanon Mountains. On the other side lay Damascus.

The caravaners relaxed their usual tense vigil, confident their strength of numbers had discouraged any potential attack. They started out just as the sun rose and set its golden sphere on the eastern horizon. Cumbersome weapons that had been kept at hand were packed away instead of carried. Alert eyes were more relaxed. Merchants began chattering about the profits they would be making on their goods and the many enticements this urban center could offer a traveling man.

While traveling up a mountain trail, Abram began noticing wild game running down from above.

"Iram, look there! A bevy of game birds flies down from somewhere up above, on the mountain. Have you noticed the animals coming this way?"

"Yes, Abram, I have a strong suspicion about their movements."

"What are your thoughts Iram? Are they the same as mine?"

"Perhaps, perhaps, brave hunter. I see you do have keen senses in the wilderness. Up ahead, somewhere, there waits one of two kinds of predators: animal or human."

"Yes, Iram. I think that perhaps robbers are up there waiting for us. Why do we not find out if it is so?"

"We? You and me?"

"Yes."

"You would trust me?"

"Can you move unseen and unheard, Iram?"

"As well as any man."

"Good, then let us tell my father and hear what he says."

"All right, but I doubt that he will agree."

Upon hearing the suspicions of Iram and Abram, Terah called for a halt and sent Shamgar with Abram to gather the caravaners for a council.

"My Lord Terah," Iram spoke privately, "Abram has suggested that he and I scout ahead, undetected. If there are robbers up there as we suspect, we would have an advantage if we knew their location, numbers and type of weapons."

"Well now, Abram suggested this did he? And you are willing to risk his life again?"

"NO, my lord, certainly not intentionally. I thought that with Abram's skill in moving unseen, he could protect my back while I sneak in close enough for a look. Your servants say he has no equal, even among men. Of course, if they only exaggerate with tall tales..."

"What they say is true! Abram is more skilled with the bow, at stalking, and running than most men."

"Then, where is the risk to his life, my lord?"

"There is always the odd chance that brings risk. I put it to you straight, Iram. My son's life is in your hands if you bring him with you. If his life is taken, I will take yours, personally! Is that understood?"

"Yes, I understand, my lord. My choice, therefore, is an obvious one. The boy does not come with me. I leave it to you to explain this to him. Now I shall prepare to leave," a stern-faced Iram concluded. Turning, he walked away.

Returning with all but the animal handlers, Abram and Shamgar talked excitedly about what parts they would have in the action that might lie ahead. They saw Terah standing in the shade of some trees and led the men there.

"Sit down, my friends, or stand if your prefer, but the reason I bring you here is an unpleasant one. I fear we may be in for some trouble up ahead."

Terah went on to explain the suspicions of Iram and Abram as if they were his own. A few men murmured dissenting opinions but were quickly silenced by a general agreement of the majority, who respected Terah's judgment and his authority over them.

"...And so my friends, go and prepare yourselves. Wait until Iram returns with a report. Then we shall make a decision as to where we travel."

Abram felt cheated when he found that Iram left to scout the trail without him "It was my idea to spy out the robbers as much as Iram's. Why did he not wait for me? I could ask father...but then, I think he would say: "It is too dangerous for you, a mere boy, to do a man's job. I forbid you to go!" If I go after Iram, without telling anyone, especially father, I would not be disobedient. Yes, that is the way to do it; just sneak away when no one is aware of it," Abram convinced himself.

It happened that while in the midst of preparations, Abram vanished in the direction Iram had reportedly taken.

"Abram! Abram!" Amthelo called out when his presence was missed. Again and again she shouted his name...without hearing a response.

"Terah, my husband, Abram does not come to my call. I fear he has left to go after Iram."

"Curse that boy's rash behavior! I try to protect him and look what he does."

Shamgar, Eder, and Bechorath looked at each other when Terah turned away to avoid Amthelo's pleading look. A slight smile formed on their lips and they swelled with pride. They had full confidence in Abram's ability to spy out the land ahead and return safely. "If he is seen by our enemy, Mistress Amthelo, Abram will run with the speed of a gazelle," Eder explained, consoling her.

"They could never catch him," Bechorath added.

"He killed a panther, mistress. He can kill a man with that same bow," Shamgar reasoned. "Do not worry about the boy. He has a destiny to fulfill as a man, and here he is still a boy. The gods will protect him."

Abram was hot. Running a wide-flanking route, parallel to the caravan trail up the mountain, sweat stung his eyes as he breathed in cadence to his steady pace. He had already taken off his mantle and hung it on a bush to mark the way back. Later he removed his tunic and did the same. Now, clothed only in a breech cloth and sandals, his tanned skin glistened with sweat.

He paused now and then, looking to his left for the presence of anyone watching for the caravan. Keeping very still, he scanned the area with the keen vision of a hawk. A light wind rustled and sighed its way across the mountain. Abram's movement submerged itself in this sound and motion. He uprooted a small bush, hacking at its roots with his knife. Camouflaging himself behind it, he moved forward almost on all fours.

Abram spotted the first robber lookout a hundred paces up and to his left. Continuing uphill, Abram saw the second man another hundred paces ahead. Creeping slowly forward another hundred and fifty paces, he saw Iram lying on the ground spying out a camp of men.

"We were right!" Abram whispered to himself. They are many, and they are waiting for us to walk into their ambush! I had better find out how many there are, if I can."

Abram managed to count thirty-six men that he could see. With the two lookouts, down the trail, they totaled about thirty-eight. While he watched, the leader, a big man answering to Beor, ordered one of those men, loafing, to go find out what was happening with the caravan. The man grumbled an agreement and started downhill at a jog to get a report from the lookouts. When he returned, the man reported: "There is no sight of the caravan moving yet, Beor."

"Hmmm, I wonder why they do not come?" the leader asked, not really expecting an answer. "This is the best place for an ambush. We will stay here a while longer and wait for them," he commanded.

Iram heard and saw what he came for. Backing away silently, he withdrew to a safer position, then began retracing his steps back to the caravan. Seeing Abram's garment on a bush, downhill, he held it at arm's length and saw it was a small tunic.

"Why...?" The question had hardly surfaced into words when Iram knew who the clothing belonged to and why it was there. Turning quickly, he looked carefully but could not see Abram anywhere. Replacing the tunic on the bush, Iram continued downhill. He spotted Abram's mantle next and changed direction, running toward the caravan.

Iram was parched with thirst when he returned. Taking a skin of water from one of Terah's packs, he raised it to his lips and let it trickle down his throat in small rapid gulps. Pouring a small quantity over his head, the evaporation began to cool him down so he could remember clearly what he had seen. Looking around for a shady place in which to sit and rest out of the sun, he was surprised to see a small figure beckon to him from the shade.

"Bring the water Iram, if you will. Like you, I am thirsty."

"Abram! How did you... when did you return?"

"Just now, Iram, and I am tired. The water, please?"

"Oh...yes, of course, here." Iram handed Abram the skin and watched him drink. "Do not drink too much. You can get an ache in the belly. Here let me cool you off a little."

Taking the waterskin back, Iram poured a liberal amount over the boy's head then tousled his curly crop of hair.

"Ahhh, that feels so good, Iram, thank you.

"Abram! Abram! There you are. Where have you been? I have been frightened terribly by your absence," Amthelo cried."

Terah, Shamgar, Eder, Bechorath, and some of the merchants came up quickly behind her. Taking charge of the questioning, Terah began: "Abram!"

"Yes, father?"

"You went after Iram, did you not?"

"Yes, but no one saw me...not even Iram."

"That is true," Iram concurred.

"Well...ah, you should have asked my permission before running off."

"Yes, father, I should have but, I believed it was important to help Iram, in case he needed me. I was never in any danger."

"The boy is invisible as the wind, and just as swift, my lord," Iram complimented. "I would be confident of his stalking skills if I were his father. Considering the danger we are in, I would also be grateful that Abram can shoot arrows strong enough to kill a man. His life, your life, Terah, or even your life, Shamgar, may be defended by him within the next hour."

"Why? What did you find?" Terah asked, putting Abram's adventure out of mind.

"Highwaymen, a large group of about forty waiting uphill on a rise."

"Aha! Just as I suspected," Terah claimed falsely. "Tell me what you saw."

"Yes, lord, as you command. But first Abram needs food to renew his strength. He has more service to give us," Iram said firmly, toying with Terah's authority. He greatly resented Terah's display of vanity. Normally he would have ignored this foolish behavior, long considered the privilege of lords, but the bruises and aches lingering from the "lesson" were reminders, of a painful sort, that he found hard to forget.

Without waiting any longer for Terah's order, Eder and Bechorath came forward, beaming smiles of pride. They served fruit to Abram and Iram, then cooled them with more water.

Amthelo yearned to comfort and caress Abram with motherly affection, as she had done so often before in the wilderness. But looking down at him, sitting near Iram and attended to by men servants, she realized he was no longer a boy needing a mother's affection. On this journey he had qualified himself as a young man. A young man sought praise from other men, not a cooing mother.

Terah sent Shamgar to gather all the men together for a council. As Shamgar called them, men came running, anxious to hear the report.

"Speak to us Iram; what did you find?"

Iram stood up and swept his stern gaze from man to man as he spoke. "A dangerous lot of forty men await us uphill, directly ahead. A big man answering to Beor seems to be their leader."

"Beor, the destroyer? Beor the burner? One of the merchants spoke out asking confirmation. "He is feared by all caravans. Many have been robbed and murdered by his bloody sword!"

An outcry of concern came forth as everyone expressed their fears aloud.

"Quiet!" Terah commanded. "Let us hear the full report witnessed by Iram and Abram. Then we shall form a plan of action."

Everyone stopped chattering and listened carefully as Iram resumed talking.

"Lookouts are hiding near the trail at intervals to give notice of our coming. Of the weapons I saw, most men were armed with spears and swords. A few had bows and arrows. Most had daggers at the waist for a second weapon."

"Only a few bow-men, Heh?" Terah commented. "That might indicate they are city people for the most part. Outside the city a man hunts with a bow. I would say these thieving murderers live in Damascus. They come out to meet caravans like us with their special type of greeting. Taking what they want, they go back and become absorbed into the city again, bartering stolen goods in their thieves market."

"I heard that if the caravans did not resist, all lives would be spared and only a portion of the goods would be taken," spoke a fat merchant, his voice quivering with anxiety.

"And if we fight them?" Terah asked.

"We, ah...we could all die; some quickly, some slowly, horribly as part of their celebration entertainment."

"Perhaps we should give in peacefully to their demands," said another merchant, too old to fight.

"I agree," remarked a prosperous fat trader. What value are my goods to me if I lose my life over them? I am of little importance in a fight. Let us appease these men and they will let us go on our way."

We could run from them," suggested another more practical trader. Why go this way? There are other trails through these mountains; we will simply go around the robbers."

"Yes, that is best," agreed several others.

"But will our enemies stay where they are while we attempt to find another way?" Terah questioned. "It could take days to find another route, if there is one. There is no surety that our enemy would not be there waiting for us again. They obviously know these mountains, and we do not. So what have we gained? Nothing! The fact is, we would lose our advantage and our strength in misdirected wandering. Here we have knowledge of our enemy's position, strength and the terrain. Also our enemy does not yet know that we are on to him. These are our strengths, my friends, and I intend to use them and save us all. I have a plan that will bring us victory and rid these mountains of Beor and his pack of wolves. We must act quickly, however.

"Iram, here is what you will do..."

Terah then gave orders to everyone, and the caravaners moved quickly to comply, especially when Shamgar reinforced the orders with loud commands of his own to hurry along any dissenters.

It was not until after everyone had dispersed, to do an assigned task, that Terah noticed Abram was missing, only his outer clothing remaining.

"That boy has done it again!" He shouted. "By the gods, he can make himself un-seeable! If I sent someone to bring him back, who could find and catch him? Hmmm, well, this day we shall all have to look to ourselves and give a good accounting of our fighting ability."

Iram looked down at Abram who walked quickly at his side. Abram must have sensed the attention, for he looked up and smiled back. In that brief glance a bond was established. Iram accepted Abram as a young brother who had proven himself worthy. Abram rejoiced within, having the friendship of a man he had come to like and admire. Abram felt no fear, only excitement. His energy had returned. The ground passed under his feet effortlessly and he felt more exhilarated than he could remember ever being.

Iram raised his free hand silently calling for a halt at a wet, marshy spot where a spring bubbled forth. Following their leader's example, Abram and Iram's six kinsmen drank to slake their thirst. Kneeling in the muddy mulch, Abram took a handful and smeared it in streaks diagonally across his entire body and face.

Iram's eyes opened wide with understanding. Nodding his head in agreement, he smiled and began applying the green/brown slime to his own body. His men also smiled, nodding their heads happily. Almost gaily they camouflaged their bodies, laughing silently, pushing each other over playfully in the muck.

Iram washed his hands and tousled Abram's hair in a playful gesture, then pushed him backwards so he sat down in the mud.

Abram grabbed a handful of mud and threw it at Iram splattering him in the side of his face. Everyone laughed quietly pointing at each other, thoroughly enjoying this marvelous interval of play and preparation. When Iram motioned them to move on, they were an almost inhuman sight, earth-colored from head to foot.

Upward they trekked, moving quickly until the position of the first robber lookout appeared in the distance. Now they moved slowly from bush to tree, unseen and unheard. Two men sat, their backs propped against trees, looking now and then down trail for the caravan.

"Ah, it is coming at last! Wake up you lazy oaf! We must go tell the others at the next lookout."

The sleeping man yawned, grunted a curse, and staggered to his feet. Still groggy with sleep, he stumbled after his companion. When his companion fell, several paces ahead, he only muttered: "Ha, you tripped! Serves you right for being in such a hurry."

When the arrow pierced him, the fire in his belly brought him wide awake. His eyes bulged and his mouth opened wide in an expression of disbelief over the shaft that stuck out near his naval. Final reality came when a second arrow silenced the outcry that formed in the man's throat. Feebly clutching at the arrow, protruding from both sides of his neck, he fell, kicked at death convulsively and lay still.

The mountain sighed its melancholy song as eight creatures of the forest advanced, unseen and unheard, towards their next objective.

The three lookouts were totally occupied with a game of chance. Iram and his men came and stood in plain sight no more than ten paces away. It was as though they were invisible. There was no recognition, no fright, and no alarm. A trio of arrows hissed deadly whispers and found their human targets. A small chorus of shock and pain issued from the men's lips. Mud clothed assassins rushed forward, drew daggers, and slashed their victim's throats, drowning the outcries in blood.

Abram had never seen a man killed. Now five had died in rapid succession right before his eyes. The sight and sound of death made him queasy at first, and then he was sick to his stomach. Turning away from his comrades, to avoid embarrassment, he vomited until nothing came but dry racking.

Patiently they waited, understanding. No one smiled. Each man remembered, only too well, when they were sick for the same reason. The men looked at each other, nodding sympathetically for their young friend, but they could not wait much longer. The caravan was coming and their work had only begun.

Iram stood Abram on his feet, kneeled with his back to the boy and drew him onto his back. Standing up, he began walking uphill towards their next objective.

Abram felt weak and ashamed of himself. He fought off the nausea, however, and began to regain confidence in himself. Strength began to return some as he breathed in deeply. The scent of Lebanon cedars smelled wonderful to him.

"Let me walk," he whispered in Iram's ear. His legs were a little shaky, but Abram concentrated hard so it would not show. More energy flowed through his veins and he knew he would be himself again soon.

Iram and his men exchanged glances. Now they smiled, a proud smile for Abram's quick recovery. Catching Abram's glance, Iram made a congratulatory gesture by clasping his hands together in front of his face. Abram managed a smile and underneath the mud and slime, his face took on an undetectable blush.

The sound of voices up ahead stopped them in their tracks and they dispersed to hide. Iram saw that little had changed in the enemy camp. The men were strung out parallel to the trail making it clear that they planned to attack the full length of the caravan all at once.

Iram cursed himself for not reporting this to Terah. He could only hope that Terah would prepare a good defense against a broadside attack.

"What would Terah do if he were me? What should I do next? Attack now? No we would be alone, a few against many. It would be a foolish sacrifice of seven men and a boy. Not just a boy, but a noble lad."

Suddenly it occurred to Iram that he held a strong brotherly affection for Abram. He vowed to himself that he would keep Abram safe by defending him with his life, if necessary.

By silent gestures, Iram instructed his men to wait and be ready to attack when he did.

"The caravan is coming! The caravan is coming... over the last rise! Pass the word. Get ready!" Beor, the robbers' leader, hissed in a shouted whisper to those nearest him. The band of highwaymen, shaken out of their lethargic wait by the un-warned arrival, readied themselves for an attack.

Abram recovered from his nausea. In place of it every muscle in his body was tense with anxiety. His stomach felt as though a fire was inside burning its way out. Iram knelt down next to him and said: "Stay here when the fighting starts, Abram, and you will be safe. You do not look well, my friend. Try to rest and do not worry. I have a plan that will help give us victory. I think we will be in less danger as well."

"But Iram...," Abram started to contradict.

"Shhh, not a word. Do as I say. I am in command!"

Abram caught the stern look of authority in Iram's eyes and hung his head in acquiescence.

The caravan approached.

Iram instructed his men and dispersed them with orders to pick their targets. Once they were in position his kinsmen watched Iram with side-glances while concentrating most of their attention on the targets.

The caravan began passing.

Tension mounted on both sides. Beor raised his sword as a sign for his band. Outlaws selected their probable victims. Blood ran hot in their veins as weapons were gripped tighter by hands slippery with perspiration.

Iram stood up and slowly advanced, arming his bow. All six of his men followed Iram's lead and moved forward. Arrows were strung and pulled....

The caravan was abreast of the robbers' position.

Beor's sword flashed downward accompanied by his mighty shout that catapulted the outlaws into action. Up they leaped from hiding places the length of the caravan.

Seven arrows split the air almost at once, imbedding themselves in the backs of their victims. Seven agonizing screams mingled with the shouting melee and little notice was given.

The caravan was ready. Terah had ordered the camels and asses to be roped together in a column so they would not run off. The attack came from one side and the defenders ducked behind their animals. This gave the outlaw bowmen little or no human targets. Wounding the animals would only remove the means of carrying away their stolen goods. The bowmen ran forward hoping to find a closer shot at the caravan defenders.

Suddenly, here, there, again, again, and again those bowmen fell, victims of their choice in weapons. Iram and his bowmen relentlessly pursued, shot and eliminated the enemy.

Abram ignored the way his stomach felt. He also ignored Iram's orders when the attack started. Following in Iram's footsteps, Abram ran and joined in the counter-attack.

The fighting was fierce now. Looking from one end of the caravan to the other, Abram saw men locked in mortal combat. Swords flailed, clattering and smashing against swords and shields. Some found their way to flesh and bone. Spearheads danced a different motion, thrusting death with a long reach. The brown earth was being splotched with a crimson stain.

Abram looked for his family and quickly spied Shamgar, then Terah as they were fighting off an attack by four men. Forgetting his own safety, Abram summoned up his strength, spurred with an overwhelming sense of duty to family and friends, and dashed around skirmishes in his way. Abram's bow was not as big as Iram's and he knew his arrows flew with less strength. When he approached within effective range, Abram halted, took careful aim, and shot an arrow with deadly accuracy, skewering the neck of a robber ready to thrust his spear into Terah. Advancing closer, Abram re-armed his bow, pulled, sighted, and let fly another arrow. The shaft penetrated deep into the side of a man raising his big sword for a deadly cut on Shamgar. The sword fell harmlessly out of his hand as he staggered and dropped to his knees gasping in disbelief. Slowly he lost strength and life...toppling over on his face as he died.

This outlaw was soon joined by a comrade. Shamgar's mighty sword arm over-powered that of his other combatant. The heavy blade caught him diagonally under the ear, severing the head clean from its body. Picking up the head by the heavy matted black hair, Shamgar heaved it at one of the men fighting Terah. It glanced off the man's shoulder hitting him in the side of his face. Stunned by the blow, he staggered backwards. Feeling the blood on his face, he looked at his hand, then the object on the ground that hit him. A grotesque face with an open-eyed stare looked back up at him. The man cried out in fright, turned and ran as fast as his wobbly legs could carry him.

Terah laughed mightily after him, joined by Shamgar. Turning their attention towards Abram, they saw a forest creature covered with mud and slime that might have been Abram, yet they were not sure. Realizing it was truly him, they laughed even louder. Regaining their composure, both men realized they owed their lives to this muddy little boy. It was his arrows that reduced the odds against them. Bowing their heads to Abram, they acknowledged their debt to him and gave thanks.

Downing the outlaws became easy sport to Iram and his men. They picked their targets with ease, waiting for openings to avoid hitting an ally, then sent their shafts flying.

Beor, who was smart enough to have survived other raids gone awry, hid himself apart from the fighting and Iram's arrows. Sneaking around to the other side of the caravan, Beor made an attempt to cut loose a camel packed with goods and make off with it.

Eder was not a fighting man. His task was to watch out for the animals. He had never hurt another man and had no knowledge of how to do so, except with a sling. There were occasions when he used it to ward off predators. Here was a human predator making off with one of his master's animals, and Eder made a determination to stop him.

Picking up a stone of the size his hand would fit around, he loaded his sling and whirled it around over his head. Concentrating his aim on Beor's head, Eder let the stone fly. It shot straight, hitting the bandit leader behind the ear. The blow knocked Beor out cold, sending him sprawling on his face in the dirt.

Bechorath, having seen the action, rushed up to Eder and congratulated him. "Marvelous shot, Eder, you put him away with only one stone."

"Let us truss him up so he cannot escape when he wakes up," Eder said hurriedly.

"If he ever wakes up, you mean. That is some lump on his head; bloody too. You may have put him to sleep permanently," Bechorath replied.

They stripped the big man of his weapons and clothes, then tied his hands and feet behind him so he could not move.

"By the gods!" exclaimed Terah. "Look at them fall! We are cutting them to pieces. Come Shamgar, this way. I see where we are needed!"

"Eayahh!" Shamgar roared into action, attacking two outlaws. He slashed them away from a fallen caravaner who clung desperately to the pack of goods he was defending. Shamgar's massive weight, size, and strength of arm bowled over the attackers, sending them sprawling in the dirt. A swipe of his giant blade cut through one man's up-raised sword arm at the wrist sending both sword and its owner's hand cartwheeling through the air.

The second man scrambled out of range, his face a mask of sheer terror as he saw his comrade kneel in a pool of his own blood from the fountain of his severed wrist. Uncertain about his escape from this bad fight, he stumbled backwards, then turned and saw Abram. "What is that awful looking boy doing in my way? I will have to cut him down if he does not move. Why the little demon has a bow and he is aiming an arrow at me...Arrgghh!"

Abram's arrow sunk into the outlaw's chest, stopping him in mid-stride. He dropped his sword and clutched at the shaft wedged between two ribs. His breath came in short agonizing gasps...his disbelieving eyes watched the ground come up hard as his legs collapsed under him, tripping him forward. The fall sent Abram's arrow through the man's body, its bloody shaft protruding out his back.

"Well done, Abram, well done!" Shamgar and Terah cheered.

"What a force we are! The invincibles, that is who we are!" Terah shouted. "Is there no one else who will fight us?" he laughed. "Where are all you thieving dogs?" Terah and Shamgar cried out, charging along the flank of the caravan.

Abram followed, exhilarated by the imminent victory as the remaining eight to ten bandits gave up the fight and began running for their lives. One was not quick enough to avoid Terah's spear. It was thrown with such force that it penetrated back to front, throwing the man to the ground, pinning him there.

Iram and his men ran after the robber remnant, shooting arrows at their backs. Three of them fell. The remaining five successfully dodged and outran their pursuers, escaping into the dense forest.

When Iram returned, Terah was taking stock of casualties and losses. Shamgar was busy at the grisly business of decapitating heads of the fallen bandits, while others gathered the heads and wrapped them in garments taken from the bodies.

Beor lay naked and trussed-up in the dust where he had fallen. Standing guard over him were Eder and Bechorath, enjoying their assignment. They kicked their captive when he cursed them for capturing him. Growling, he cursed them more for the kicks, so they kicked him harder. Straining and grunting to be free of his bonds, Beor spat at his captors.

"Aha! He tries to defile us with his spittle," declared Eder.

"I think his dirty mouth should look like it sounds. Do you not agree Eder?" Bechorath inquired, bending down to grab a handful of dirt from the dusty trail.

"By all means," Eder agreed as he stooped to pick up two handfuls. Standing up he threw the dirt onto Beor's sweaty face.

Bechorath took his handful and forced it into Beor's mouth while holding onto the bandit leader's beard.

Beor gagged, choked, and coughed out the dirt to the great amusement of his guards.

Abram and Iram had some difficulty recognizing Beor, but scraping the dirt off with a sharp-edged stone, Iram confirmed that it was indeed Beor, the bandit leader.

Abram shouted the news, repeating the message as he ran among the caravaners. They stopped what they were doing and ran to see for themselves.

Terah, delighted with this measure of good fortune, praised Eder and Bechorath, rewarding them each with a silver shekel.

"I have heard, my Lord Terah, that there is a reward to be paid for this bandit," remarked one of the merchants. I believe the King of Damascus will pay handsomely for him."

"Hmmm, yes, especially if we credit this battle to him, under his authority. And then...we will give Beor to the king as a present...for execution."

"But the king gave us no aid. Why should he take credit? He would reward us anyway, would he not?" challenged a merchant.

"Yes, what you say is true," Terah replied," but would you have, for your risk, a shekel or a mineh of silver?"

"Ahh, I see your wisdom, my lord, and bow to it."

"I understand your plan my Lord Terah. It is brilliant!" exclaimed another merchant. "The king will assume credit for our victory, we being his agents, and reward us handsomely for our loyal service."

"What is a little lie to share glory with a grateful monarch? A generous king, a king desperate for an achievement he can order chiseled into stone and written into clay?

Why should we not be rewarded as richly as possible? We have rid the king of a nasty scourge, that has surely reduced the wealth of taxable trade normally flowing into his city!"

I promise you, he will be generous, very generous!" Terah finished speaking and everyone cheered.

Wounds were forgotten. Depression over servants wounded and killed turned to rejoicing. The king of Damascus would pay for all their losses and they would be telling stories about this journey for a long time.

That night, around the campfires, caravaners heard in full all the details their comrades had to share. Toasts of tribute were generously applied to everyone for their bravery. But the highest tribute was extended to Abram, Iram and his kinsmen for their warning, and their slaughter, of more bandits than all the remaining caravan force combined.

Shamgar ambled over to Iram, sitting with his men, and slapped him on the shoulder. Iram jerked his head around to see Shamgar's big grinning face.

"You are a good fighter, Iram, better than I ever thought. And you took good care of Abram. That is good, very good! I like you. I do not want to hurt you again. I ..., I am sorry I hurt you before. We are friends, yes?"

Iram, relieved and grateful to have this giant as an ally, answered: "Why yes, of course Shamgar, we are friends. Thank you. I ah ... appreciate your friendship."

"Good, now we drink together and celebrate our victory. Here is my wineskin; I share it with you, and your men too. Drink. Drink up, my friends; let us be happy together!"

Abram was there, sharing Iram's fire, when Shamgar joined them. This was the Shamgar he knew best: friendly, sharing, and companionable. The smile on Abram's face revealed the gladness in his heart. His two friends had now become friends as well as allies. Abram sat between them, speaking very little; it was too exciting listening. After a while the fire made him drowsy and he leaned against Shamgar for support. The surrounding voices continued expounding exploits of the battle on into the late evening hours. They became only a distant murmuring as a blanket of sleep covered him. It had been a long, busy day for a boy of eleven.

Shamgar laid Abram's head in his lap. Looking down at him, the warrior ran his big fingers through Abram's curly reddish blond hair and encouraged him to sleep. "I used to do this when he was a little boy. He is no longer a little boy. A little man perhaps? Better still, a little prince."

"A little warrior, I would say," Iram stated."

"And brave as any man I have ever known," Shamgar added.

"Yes, I am sure we all understand just how brave he really is," Iram remarked as a prelude to telling how Abram became sick over the killing but left safety to join the counter attack.

"If he had not, Lord Terah and I both might be staining the soil with our life's blood, instead of celebrating," Shamgar added. "Who can doubt greatness in this young prince? Hear me now, you Hebrews: this lad who sleeps in my lap will one day become a patriarch of your race. He will defeat kings of the earth and be remembered through all time for his bravery and wisdom. Remember my words...remember...."

Chapter 7
Urusalem

And when Abram came out from the cave, he went to Noah and his son Shem, and he remained with them to learn the instruction of the Lord and his ways, and no man knew where Abram was, and Abram served Noah and Shem his son for a long time.

Jasher 9:5

"**W**ell done, well done my children!" exclaimed old Noah, caught up in the excitement of the story. "Go on, Terah, what happened at Damascus? Did old King Shashai Lim welcome your caravan and reward you as handsomely as you hoped?"

"Ah, dear Grandfather Noah, with an audience as eager as you, this humble teller of stories must quickly obey," Terah responded.

"Among the merchants traveling in the caravan to Damascus, was one by the name of Jattir. He was a frequent traveler to Damascus and was often a visitor to the king's palace. He dealt in only the finest quality jewelry, silver and gold objects. I instructed Jattir as to what he should do and say, as our spokesman before the king. His tongue was as golden as the objects he sold and Jattir was a welcome merchant among many kings for the stories he told. King Shashai Lim became fascinated in the tale of our victory over the bandits. Especially so when Jattir suggested the king accept recognition and public acclaim for authorizing the elimination of the notorious 'Bandits of Beor".

"When Jattir finished speaking, the king was excited and restless. Pacing back and forth near his throne, he began working out, in his mind, arrangements for a public acknowledgement of his great contribution to the merchants and people of Damascus.

"Jattir stood motionless, silent, waiting for the king to speak.

'By the gods, I can see profit in this for all of us!' he
exclaimed. 'I shall make a great public display over our success in
destroying the Band of Beor. Hmmm, yes - then I shall collect a
special tax from all merchants and traders in the city to pay the cost
of my special caravan. We shall have a celebration, a feast. Everyone
will enjoy themselves and forget I taxed them. Wine, women, food,
music, dancing, and contests...it will be a grand time...yes a very
grand time!'

'If it please my lord,' Jattir finally spoke again, 'we have Beor
alive! Perhaps you would consider arranging a proper welcome as he
enters your city?' the wily merchant suggested. 'We have also in our
possession the heads of all the slain outlaws, numbering thirty-eight.
They would make an impressive display to serve your purposes.'"

"'Oh ho! The entire city would gather to see Beor brought in
under the whip. And the heads from thirty-eight bandits! Ho, ho, ho
-- what a spectacle we shall have! And my scribes shall record it all!
You did well, Jattir, to bring this honor to me. I can afford to pay
well for such loyalty. You and your friends shall be my guests in the
palace and want for nothing. Now go quickly and bring your caravan
to the city. I am sending a troop of soldiers with you as an escort to
speed you on your way.'

Terah paused, allowing Noah and Shem time to capture the
scene and its dialogue in their minds. Then he continued.

"The caravan approached within sight of the city's gate,
preceded by its escort the troop of soldiers," Terah continued. "A
trump of the sentinel's horn sounded once, twice, three, and four
times alerting the city's inhabitants that a very special procession
was arriving. The king's soldiers were quick to maintain order and
prepare a route through the city, ending at the great square in front
of the king's palace.

"Through the city's gate we entered. After our escort walked
servants, single file, each carrying a bandit's head impaled on a pole.
The grisly death masks riding above the crowds drew gasps of horror
from the populace.

"Beor followed. His hands were tied behind him and a choke
rope around his neck was held on either side by Bechorath and Eder.
Repeatedly they shouted their boast: 'We captured Beor the bandit
leader, and slew his men.'

"Jattir, Amthelo and I followed on our camels, waving and
smiling. Behind us, also on camels rode Abram, Shamgar, and Iram.
They were followed by Iram's men on foot and the rest of the caravan.

75

All of the men brandished their weapons, pantomiming the battle they fought. This, of course, was to lend impact to the bloody evidence we displayed of our victory. The crowds seemed to react with an added measure of respect and enthusiasm. They followed after us eagerly as we made our way to see King Sashai.

"His majesty was just descending the palace steps with his scribes and ministers when the procession came to a halt. Taking in our spectacular appearance, with eager dancing eyes, Shashai took a deep breath, the excitement within intoxicating him.

"'Ah Jattir, it appears you and your friends have been successful with the mission I sent you on.'"

"'The brilliance of my king's plan was only outshone by the fierceness by which your servants carried it out. The noble Terah, son of Nahor, followed your commands to the letter, my king. He and his men shot through and cut to pieces the band of outlaws led by this thieving murderer, Beor, who we bring naked before you.'"

"'Ah ha! So this is the annoying pest, Beor, that has robbed so many caravans coming to our city. You have done well my servants, very well indeed. You shall be rewarded by a grateful king and his subjects for your valor and service. Let it be known that this day I, Shashai, King of Damascus hereby impose a special tax upon all who have a business dealing in goods. Now that they are free of Beor and his murderous thieves, their businesses will flourish.

"'Now hear this people of Damascus,' he commanded in a booming voice, 'I declare also that a celebration of feasting and entertainment shall begin immediately.'

"And so, my lords Noah and Shem, we enjoyed the king's hospitality for two days and left with his blessing. He was, just as I predicted, a generous king. Everyone of us were paid handsomely," Terah concluded.

"What a marvelous story," Noah complimented excitedly. For the next few days, Noah and Shem quizzed the adventurers about details.

On the morning of the eighth day, the awful truth of his parents departure struck Abram. He reacted as only a young child could.

"But why must I be so great a distance from you, father? And for so long a time?"

"You will be safe here, my son. And there are no greater teachers of wisdom than Noah and Shem, the greatest living patriarchs of our race."

"But how long must I stay, and when will I see you and mother again?"

"You must stay until Noah and Shem decide otherwise."

"But...but father...I...I want to learn from you; you and Shamgar...and ...and mother...and..."

"No Abram! It cannot be."

"But why not, father? Why?" Abram pleaded with tears flooding his eyes. "You don't love me! You don't even like me do you?!"

"Abram, Abram, don't say harsh things like that. Try to understand; it is my destiny to serve King Nimrod, your enemy. You have a different destiny, a destiny far greater than mine. It is one I dare not interfere in just...just because I love you."

"But surely you can come often and stay with me, can you not?" he reasoned tearfully.

"I have affairs of state that require my constant attention Abram. I will not lie to you. I do not see how I will be able to find the time to make the long trip here. I had great difficulty in getting away from the king for so long a time on this trip. I had to lie to him. I told him I was going to spy out the lands to the northwest and west disguised as a trader. I have to give him a detailed report on alliances, fortifications, troop strengths, weaknesses, and trade among the nations we have traveled to. It was the only way I could manage to bring you here. The king has spies everywhere. I cannot risk your life and mine until I am sure you are completely safe."

"Oh, father!" Abram cried as the full weight and impact of the terrible reality crushed his hopes. It was a cruel twist of fate. The father he had seen only periodically for his first ten years, had now spent more than a moon's time with him day and night without interruption...only to leave again...this time perhaps forever!

Abram's whole body was wracked with sobs of frustration, pain, and fear. He fell to his knees and clung to his father's legs. Tears streamed down his face wetting Terah's feet.

"But...but...I do not care...about ...living without you... father...,"he struggled to say with a broken heart.

"That is enough Abram!" Terah commanded with his princely voice of authority. He realized, then, that Abram was just a young boy clinging to those who are precious and necessary to him; those who said he could not be with them anymore.

77

"I will not allow you to cry and whimper like a baby, Abram. Now get up and stand on your feet like a man. You have hunted and fought in battle like a man. You want to be a prince like me? Start learning what it takes to become a prince. Sniveling, sobbing weaklings do not become princes in this world. You must be tough. You must be strong. You must be intelligent. I did not teach you how to hunt and survive only to simper like a woman because you are disappointed. A boy who wants to become a prince among men must be a man's man, full of courage and resolve. Now where would you be today if I did not have the courage and resolve to hide you from King Nimrod and deceive him...? Well? What do you say to that?"

"I...I would not be here at all, I guess?"

"That is exactly right, my son. The time we have had together has been good, has it not?"

"...Yes."

"Was there ever, at any time we were together, a moment when you were unhappy with your life?" Terah asked.

"Oh no, father, I loved every moment of every day! That is why..."

"Then remember them as precious, valuable moments. They will be your personal treasure... and mine. No one can take them from us. Keep them in your heart...your own treasure chest...and feed on them whenever you feel lonely and dejected. Do you understand, Abram?"

"Ah, I think I do, father," Abram admitted very softly, knowing full well what Terah meant. He always listened intently to every word his father said, out of respect and adoration. He was reluctant to admit to it now, but his emotions were getting in the way.

"It will not be so bad. I am leaving two servants with you. Your friends Bechorath and Eder will stay with you to cheer you up."

Terah issued a command and the two men came running up.

"Now, does that not make you feel better?" he asked, bending down and taking Abram's tear stained face in his big hands. He forced Abram to look up at him. "Did I hear you say yes?"

Looking into his father's commanding eyes he could not disobey. He lied and said: "Yes, father."

There was nothing else to say. Amthelo and Bealoth kissed Abram goodbye with tears running down their cheeks. Terah and Shamgar each knelt and hugged the boy, kissing his cheek. The tears streaming down Abram's face wet their beards and lips. The taste and feel of him in their arms was so emotional that the memory of this separation would last forty years.

Shem arranged for a company of his mounted soldiers to escort his departing guests to Ezion-Geber. This thriving seaport settlement lay at the head of the Gulf of Aqabah. The town was a transfer point in trade between India, Mesopotamia, Canaan, and Egypt.

Under orders from Shem, one of the king's ships took them aboard for their trip to Ur. It was to be an easier, though longer journey back. The days at sea would be long and listless. But they had their thoughts of Abram, however, and memories...many memories.

6.   And Abram was in Noah's house thirty-nine years, and Abram knew the Lord... and he went in the ways of the Lord until the day of his death, as Noah and his son Shem had taught him; and all the sons of the earth in those days greatly transgressed against the Lord, and they rebelled against him and they served other gods, and they forgot the Lord who had created them in the earth; and the inhabitants of the earth made unto themselves, at that time, every man his God; gods of wood and stone which could neither speak, hear, nor deliver, and the sons of men served them and they became their gods.

Jasher 9:6

Abram quickly adapted himself to the household of Noah and Shem. It had been quite some time since young children had stayed in the palace and been under the direct responsibility of Shem. Abram had never been in the company of men of such advanced age and importance. The arrangement was a new and challenging experience for all three. Abram was very responsible for a boy of eleven years. His experiences while living in the cave and traveling to Urusalem developed in him a mature attitude well beyond normal. It was a unique quality that prepared him to accept the mental, physical, and spiritual training he was about to undertake.

His first assignment was to sit at the feet of Noah, who was very aged, and run for things he wanted. Abram was with Noah day and night attending to his physical needs. Noah, in return, attended to the boy's questions. It was a fair exchange for both and they respected each other for value received. Gradually, a strong affection developed that bound them closer and closer. Abram made Noah feel younger and Noah gave wisdom in return that developed Abram's character.

Outdoor life was a part of Abram's nature and its call nagged at him regularly. When old Noah drifted off to sleep day or night, Abram ran through the palace and outside a city gate where he went to roam the surrounding hills and valleys. The tradesmen, caravaners, and storytellers at the gates attracted his attention as well. It was here that he would listen for news, rumors, and gossip about Padam Aram and Mari, Damascus, Shinar, and Ur.

It was the only news even remotely near to home and family. During the first weeks and months, Abram missed them with a heart that ached daily. Gradually the emotional trauma diminished. A young boy's action in new adventures and new responsibilities became the cure for melancholia

Abram served Noah responsibly for six years and had proven himself loyal, obedient, and receptive to instruction. One day Abram asked: "Where did your ancestors and mine come from, Lord Noah?"

"Ahh, now, Abram," the old patriarch sighed, shifting his position to get more comfortable before starting his long answer. "Our first ancestor on this earth was named Adam. Then the Everliving God, gave him a wife named Eve. She bore a son named Cain, which means 'metal smith' and another, Abel, which means 'breath'.

"Abel was like his father, Adam, in his responsibility to the Everliving God. Cain was like the father of lies, Lucifer, who in his angelic beauty and cunning intelligence seduced Eve to disobedience. Cain's offerings were unacceptable to the Everliving God and Cain became jealous of his brother, Abel, who had the favor of the Everliving God.

"Cain murdered his brother Abel. For punishment, Cain was cast out of the family to be a wanderer. Another son was born to Adam and Eve and they named him Seth, meaning 'another seed appointed' by the Everliving God.

"You will eventually memorize the names of all your ancestors, but for now remember these righteous patriarchs.

"Cainan, the son of Enosh, was forty years old and he became wise in the standards set forth by the Everliving. He turned men to the service of our god.

URUSALEM

"Enoch, a man of God, was king, wiseman and teacher. Also, importantly, he was knowledgeable of the heavenly bodies. Adam brought us a language and identification of all things, and Enoch carried forward the origin of our alphabet, the foundation of our language.

"Enoch bore Methuselah, the eldest of three sons and two daughters. Methuselah carried on the righteous works of his father. Enoch was my great-grandfather and Methuselah was my grandfather.

"Our righteous God chose me as Patriarch to safeguard a remnant of our race and the Divine Standards that guide it. I, in turn, chose Shem to receive the birthright of Patriarchal Authority over our people and the blessing of all my earthly estate.

"After Shem, Eber will have the authority and blessing. Each Patriarch of Righteousness has been the only light of the one creator. All other people in all places have lived in dark ignorance and savagery. In each and every choice, the Patriarchs have been the Everliving's singular remnant, preserving a continuing family heritage. It has been our responsibility to live as examples in obedience to the Divine Standards of the one true God which he first established with Adam and then repeated with all the others."

"But is it not true that in all kingdoms of this world many gods are worshipped?" Abram questioned. "My mother told me of the patron God of Ur, Nannar, and the gods Marduk of Shinar and Ashur of Assyria."

"Yes, many gods are worshipped in the kingdoms of this world."

"Forgive me, my lord, for questioning what you say, but I am confused."

"Do not be afraid to ask anything of me, Abram, I solicit all your questions and will answer them as completely as I am able. Now what is it that you are confused about?"

"You place so much authority and importance in one god only; a god that our people tend to ignore. It seems to me that the nations of the world worship many gods simply because the many are stronger at what they each do than a single god could ever be, doing all the same things. If this were not so, then why are all the people within those nations believing the way they do? Could so many be wrong and so few be right, such as you say?"

"What you question can best be resolved by an elaborate answer. It is an answer that traces 'religion' from its beginnings and

81

relates how religious authorities have managed to devise a religion that enslaves the minds of people and robs them of their prosperity.

"The earliest form of religion in the primitive world was a 'nature' religion. This was before the descendants of Adam and Eve peopled the world. When our people came to Shinar, the existing religion of that land was founded upon the worship of the vital forces of nature. They thought of these forces as spirits of generation and reproduction; that is to say male and female gods.

"A young male child god figure was always included to compare these gods with a human family. The child god possessed the powers and the characteristics of his father whom he tended to duplicate. The male child god was regarded as either son or lover of the goddess, depending on circumstances. Sometimes he was known as both at the same time.

"These all encompassing forces of nature became diluted by the creation of divinities with specific and limited functions. There were divinities of corn, forest, vine, stream, grain and cattle. There were spirits of the ground, stones, trees, seas, rivers, streams, and rain. People still worship household gods small and great. In addition, spirits of a lower order, called demons, were invented to account for the malignant forces of evil.

"Abram, this whole business of many gods can be very confusing. There are different names for the moon god, the sun god, and other gods worshipped by people from different lands. When one kingdom is conquered by another, the gods in each are blended together somehow. This accounts for the growth in numbers of gods and change in importance of some gods over others.

"This story about religion cannot ignore the number of women goddesses that have been worshipped. Ishtar, Ninharsag, Ninni or Inanna and a large number of other goddesses, all embody the principles of fertility and reproduction. Ishtar or Astarte has a very confused geneology. A list of her husbands would fill many tablets, because under one name or another she is the wife of the 'great god' in almost every city. She also represents the blending of two different characters in the person of one goddess: the lady of love and fertility, and the lady of battles.

Noah rose from his seat and stretched. With small, uneasy steps, he hobbled around the room to exercise his legs and ease his stiffness.

Abram followed on his heels anxious to learn more from this old man who seemed to be a spring from which one constantly desired to drink.

"It is sad indeed that the generations of my seed have ignored their God to pay tribute and extortion to the priests of a destructive religion. These priests grow fat and rich while the people who struggle for a living have to pay so many religious tributes. They pay offerings for water from the rivers and for rain from the sky without flooding. They pay offerings so that the sun will not burn their crops. They pay offerings so that the wind will not blow and destroy, the birds will not destroy, the locusts will not destroy! They pay offerings for victory over their enemies!

"All their solicitations fall on deaf ears, Abram, ears of stone and wood, without power for and without devotion to their supplicants. This way of life is only filled with hardship and misery. It is all so foolish and unnecessary to suffer and die when they could be blessed."

Noah's head drooped with an expression of extreme disappointment, and Abram noticed the Patriarch's eyes watered to the point of tears. Pausing respectfully, Abram interrupted the heavy silence with a question.

"What do you mean when you say blessed, my lord?"

Noah wiped his eyes with the edge of his forefinger, brushing the mist from his vision, and replied: "To have the Everliving's blessing is to have the most important thing in life. It is more important than life itself because - well, without it we ruin ourselves. We grow thorns and thistles and our enemies destroy us. The 'blessing' truly is the pleasant fruit of the Everliving's spirit."

"The diviners and sorcerers call upon their gods for their spirits too," Abram interrupted.

"Yes, but where there is no power, there is no spirit. When there is no spirit upon us from the Everliving, the only true God of power, there are no blessings. It is through seeking His favor only, and showing our obedience to his standards for life, that we open and keep open, the channel for his blessings to flow down to us. He can bless our crops with proper water and sun. He can bless the wombs of our wives for many children. He can bless the wombs of our animals that they multiply their kind. All our good works can be blessed...if we are obedient to the Everliving.

"As a people blessed by Him, we can multiply, grow strong, be prosperous, be happy, and protected from our enemies. We can be the envy of other peoples who, unable to conquer us, would eventually come under the influence and dominion of the one true God through us. The whole earth can become transformed, Abram. Prosperity and peace can be everywhere. The enemies of righteousness and our God can be of little consequence when our people live in harmony with His law. The whole earth can be fruitful and at peace. It can only come about under one king, ruling one kingdom, with the Everliving at its head."

"Will that ever be, Grandfather Noah?" Abram asked.

"Yes, in good time, my lad, when the Everliving is ready. Meanwhile, there is much that needs to be done, oh so much."

20. And King Nimrod reigned securely, and all the earth was under his control, and all the earth was of one tongue and words of union

Jasher 9:20

Chapter 8
Destination Ur

11. And Abram the son of Terah was waxing great in those days in the house of Noah, and no man knew it, and the Lord was with him.

12. And the Lord gave Abram an understanding heart, and he knew all the works of that generation were vain, and were of no avail.

Jasher 9:11 & 12

During the ensuing years Abram grew tall and strong. Those who ate at the royal table benefited from Abram's hunting skill. From his teen years on he relished the opportunity to leave the city for a few days to hunt and replenish the supply of meat.

In the beginning he took Eder and Bechorath with him for companionship. Abram's popularity grew among new friends his age, however, and before very long he acknowledged his leadership of a group of boys, all who were older than he was.

From time to time Abram would feel so closed in by the fortress walls that he would request permission to gather his friends and leave on a hunt. Old Noah preferred to keep Abram safe within Urusalem at all times but, he was wise concerning Abram's needs and not totally selfish for the boy's helpful companionship.

Abram saw Noah's mild reluctance couched in orders for caution and self-protection. After promising to heed his lord's commands and return safely in a few days, Abram gathered those friends who could come with him and left, ranging the countryside hunting together.

Ever faithful Bechorath and Eder followed a reasonable distance away, allowing Abram complete liberty. Abram appreciated their distance; knowing full well that Noah had sent them along to protect and serve their prince.

Abram shared both his skills and his knowledge with those that wanted them and expanded his leadership. At age 20 he began military training and learned the effective use of the sword, dagger and spear in combat. He was already one of the best bowmen in the kingdom, having proved it in several contests.

During his 25th year Abram was appointed captain over a hundred men, and he served King Shem in the palace guard. He had grown up to be a handsome figure of a man, over six feet tall, causing a number of maidens to turn their eyes toward him hoping for a match. Although Abram was attracted to one or two that he had the opportunity to meet, he was not in a position to make advances in a normal process of selecting a mate. He knew he had a special destiny to fulfill; marrying young was not a part of it.

Abram's hair was wavy and full, a reddish brown now. His strong blue eyes seemed to see through surface expressions and peer into the mind of anyone who faced him. It was an attribute that disconcerted all except those who were loyal to him.

The men in his command were all loyal, without question. They respected Abram personally as well as his ability to lead. There was no one stronger or more courageous than Abram when fighting an enemy. He had the bravado of Terah and the strength of Shamgar.

Over the following years Abram continued to absorb knowledge at the feet of Noah and serve Shem in the king's army. There were several battles fought with raiding nomad tribes who preyed on caravans, farmers, and shepherds. Abram customarily took punitive action against the marauders, with his company of warriors, since they were so effective. His fame grew, becoming fascinating material for the local storytellers.

When Abram realized he had been at Urusalem forty years, he came to a decision about something that had been nagging at his conscience for quite some time. Approaching Shem and Noah, he explained his feelings.

"I have turned age fifty, my lords, and my heart yearns greatly to see Terah and Amthelo, my parents. For several years I have controlled a burning passion; a passion to bring them out of bondage to idols and into the blessings of our God."

Abram's eyes watered with emotion as he drew a deep breath and continued.

"If I have found a small measure of favor in your eyes, my lords, release me from my service to you. Let me go to Ur."

"Noah and Shem looked at each other, passing a wordless message eye to eye, and smiled knowingly. Shem deferred to his father and Noah spoke.

"There is nothing more we can teach you, my son," old Noah replied. "You have served us well all these many years, Abram. Go with our blessings, but do not fail to serve your God as he commands. He will train you from now on and prepare you to do greater things than ever before, in His name and for His purposes. Be patient in all things. Endure all things to establish right living among our people."

"My mind and heart are no longer my own, Lord Noah, they belong to the Everliving, along with my body and my life. I am his servant from this day forward. Yet I shall hold you and Lord Shem in my memories each day until we are together again. Farewell...farewell...farewell...." Abram's voice trailed off in the distance as he left the fortress of Urusalem, escorted by a company of his own men.

13. And in the fiftieth year of the life of Abram son of Terah, Abram came forth from the house of Noah, and went to his father's house.

14. And Abram knew the Lord, and he went in His ways and instructions, and the Lord his God was with him.

15. And Terah his father was in those days still captain of the host of King Nimrod, and he still followed strange gods.

Jasher 11:13 - 15

The company of camels and onager-driven chariots traveled the two hundred miles from Urusalem to Ezion Geber in six days. Within the next two days Abram secured passage on a Phoenician ship sailing to Ur and Babylon around the great Arabian peninsula. Very early the next morning the ship set out with a high tide and headed south.

Through the length of the Gulf of Aqaba they sailed, and on into the Red Sea. Abram had never been on a ship before and the vastness of the sea filled him with wonder and excitement. The world was becoming a much larger place than he had ever thought it was.

Keeping within sight of the Arabian Peninsula, Abram's ship traveled the Red Sea's length. Passing through the strait of Bab el Mandeb they entered the Gulf of Aden and set course northeast until they entered the Arabian Sea. Continuing to skirt the coastline of the Arabian Peninsula, the ship sailed into the Gulf of Oman and circled north. Next they passed through the Strait of Hormuz and entered the Persian Gulf.

A few days later Abram stood in the bow of the ship looking north as the captain called out to him: "The city of Ur should come up on the horizon sometime today, if the wind holds as good as it is now."

"That is excellent, captain. I look forward to setting my feet down on something solid that does not constantly rock and pitch," Abram replied humorously.

The captain laughed heartily and remarked: "You have done well in not being sea-sick most of the journey, my lord. Most landmen are half dead with sickness of the stomach on such a trip as this."

"At age eleven I traveled by camel from Sippar to Urusalem. It was a great distance, taking more than a moon's cycle to get to our destination. The motion of a camel can be as difficult to endure as the motion of the sea. Mastering the rock and pitch of the 'ship of the desert' has prepared me to withstand the rigors of the sea, "Abram explained.

"So that is it! You would make a fine sea captain, if your calling led you to it, my lord."

"Thank you, captain, but I have been called to duties on land. Where do you sail to after Ur and Babylon?"

"I set course east to India, my lord. There is good trade of goods out of the vast Indus Valley. There are ports along the mouth of the Indus River. That is where we ship off to after leaving this river valley. Two moons from now, the gods willing, we will be back in Ezion Geber our return trip completed."

"A long journey, captain."

"A very long journey, my lord, very long," the sun-burnt sailor emphasized.

The sun was arcing westward when the captain caught sight of the northwest shoreline. He had piloted his ship within sight of the shores of Elam on the northern perimeter of the Gulf. This was the shortest route to the Rivers Tigris and Euphrates, after leaving the Gulf of Oman in the ship's wake.

"My lord!" The captain called out to Abram, who had fallen asleep from the monotonous motion of the ship. "My lord Abram! We are approaching the end of this almost endless sea and the mouths of the two great rivers will soon open for us."

Abram aroused himself, blinking away sleep and bright sparkles of sunlight on the water. The brilliance hurt so he pulled the mantle over his head to shield his eyes from the glare and extend his vision.

"Behold the delta of the Tigris River coming up far to your right," the captain exclaimed. A little while later he called out again: "Those small boats in the distance are fishermen working near the opening to the mighty Euphrates, life giver to the whole Plain of Shinar."

Excitement grew on board as both passengers and crew eagerly scanned landmarks and participants of a city's commerce at work. Water traffic increased as they left the Gulf and began tacking a zigzag course against the slow river current.

Gregarious with the excitement of making port, the captain began jabbering to Abram about this rich land they were entering.

"This is a prosperous farming delta, my lord. Ur has an elaborate system of irrigation canals and reservoirs, with extensive grazing lands bordering the edge of the Arabian Desert. They produce abundant yields of crops and large herds for export. Vessels of trade sail up and down the Euphrates River serving ports as far away as Carchemish above Padan Aram, Haran on the Belikh River, and settlements along the Habor River. Both the Belikh and the Habor feed into the great Euphrates, of course."

These names brought memories flooding into Abram's mind as the captain droned on.

"Changes in the river beds of the Tigris and Euphrates are caused by shifting silt on loose bottoms. This prevents seagoing vessels of deep draught, like mine, from navigating the greater part of their lengths.

"Those round basket-like boats you see are called coracles after the round baskets used by laborers for carrying earth and bricks on their heads."

"How do they manage to stay afloat?" Abram asked, showing polite interest.

"It is no mystery, even though they are only baskets made of plaited rushes. Their flat bottoms are usually covered with skins and caulked with oakum, hemp fiber, and scraps of wool. These are tightly compressed and mixed with fine earth and bitumen, making them watertight. As you can see, it takes some skill for two men sculling to propel a coracle forward without spinning in circles."

"Some of them are so fully loaded that their sides are less than a hand's width above the water," Abram remarked."

"Yes, my lord, and many of them travel great distances down river that way, and return.

"The rafts you see are called keleks. They are usually made of the best wood available locally, or from the strongest of the reeds that grow densely in the marshes. They are often tall enough to hide a man standing, even a man your size. Their buoyancy is increased by having inflated goatskins attached underneath. In this way keleks are capable of carrying a considerable weight.

"The loaded rafts are floated down river with the current, propelled and steered by a pole, until they reach some destination in southern Mesopotamia. After cargoes are unloaded, the keleks are dismantled, and the scarce wood sold. Goatskins are deflated, loaded on donkeys and the sailors, now caravan drivers, return to their starting point."

"And then what do they do?" Abram questioned, now engrossed in this fascinating story of river commerce.

"Why, they start all over again of course!" laughed the sun baked sailor.

From the eastern shore spectators saw the ship's square sail ablaze with the afternoon sun. She was beating up for the tricky channel across the bar, which every seasonal flood shifted and increased with its load of river mud. Soon she was in the lagoon, scattering the reed canoes of the delta fishermen from in front of the lordly surge of her high prow, the tall rushes along the shore nodding with her wash.

She swept past Eridu, with its towering ziggurat, its massive walls of coarse desert limestone, and its background of low cliffs. The city of the god, Ea, was declining; Ur had unseated her from her place of wealth, and river pilots shook their heads as they observed how, generation after generation, her quays had to be rebuilt to keep pace with the receding water.

Abram caught sight of Ur's profile against the skyline ahead. The city's most prominent feature, the ziggurat could be seen from miles away. White under scorching sun, the walls of Ur could be seen, set in a paradise of green. Her fields and gardens extended to the limit of those of Eridu, and were stopped only by a boundary canal. The ship glided between low banks nodding with barley ripe for harvesting or shadowed by orchards of pomegranate, fig or apple.

Here and there canals, their water funneled from up-stream beyond reach of the tides, wound through fields and meadows. At intervals, farming villages with clusters of domed mud huts surrounded by lofty date palms, dotted the valley. In the fields of stubble where grain had already been harvested, flocks of white and brown sheep, black goats and herds of fat cattle grazed.

On both sides of the Euphrates, beyond the cultivated land, stretched the summer-parched fringe of the steppe two hundred yards or more wide. The scattered goatskin tents of nomads were black against the brown of sparse grass.

Embowered in rows of palms, grapevines and fig trees between them, the capital city stood like a radiant pearl surrounded with living emerald. Along its Western Wall ran the Euphrates River. Inside its eastern wall a broad navigable canal led off from the river just above the city. Within the northern tip of the walled city was found the North Harbor serving both river and canal. On its western flank was located a second harbor, the remnant of a smaller canal that ran right through the city from the North Harbor in earlier times.

Abram gazed with wonder at the colossal brilliance of Ur. As the massive walls loomed before him his consciousness lapsed into a daydream and he traveled back in time forty years. He was riding a camel alongside his father as they approached the walls of Mari. He could even remember the questions he was asking as so much curiosity got the best of him. Memories of father...mother...Shamgar and Bealoth. Memories of living in the cave away from cities and villages...and the journey to Urusalem...

"There is the West Harbor entrance ahead, my lord; we will be putting in there," the captain explained, breaking into Abram's reverie.

"Get ready to make for the West Harbor!" he barked at his crew. "We will come about north of it mid-river, and swing in coming downstream. I will take the helm now; stand by to haul lines. When I tell you to, change sail angle and swing the boom to catch wind!"

Abram stood in the bow looking back, watching the execution of the captain's orders with a precision developed through years of sea-wary experience.

"Now trim sail! And hurry about it before we fly into half the ships in the harbor while docking!"

A few oaths were distributed to the crew by the captain while the ship maneuvered around harbor traffic and finally luffed into an opening and up to the quay. Seamen threw docking lines ashore to the attendant, who would be collecting the necessary fee, and the ship was secured for unloading.

Abram disembarked and began threading his way through sweating laborers off-loading various cargoes, scribes marking tally sheets, merchants, vendors, priests, and tradesmen. Harbor police were handy, keeping a wary eye out for trouble. Wending a path out of the waterfront activity, Abram made his way through the walled city. Stopping an officer, he asked directions to the house of Prince Terah. The policeman was courteous enough, being careful not to offend someone who could be a friend of Terah and equal in stature. With a vivid description and good directions, Abram wasted little time finding his way.

Just as in Shinar, Terah had a palatial estate outside the walled city. It was early evening when Abram saw the large two story house come into view. A setting sun bathed the white facade aglow with bright orange contrasting it sharply against a canopy of blue hues in the northeastern sky. Umber-toned mountains turned charcoal gray as the black shroud of night drew its darkness across heaven and earth.

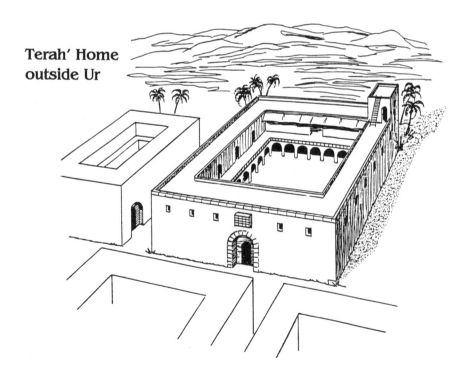

Terah' Home outside Ur

A loud knocking at the entrance door brought a servant running. He opened the door cautiously and asked: "Who is it that would come uninvited at this evening hour?"

"Tell your master it is Abram, son of Terah, who comes all the way from Urusalem in the Land of Canaan."

"Abram? From Urusalem in the Land of Canaan? Son of Lord Terah...?"

Shelesh, the chief steward, had heard the loud knocking and appeared at the entry in time to hear the servant stumble dumb founded through the introduction.

"Abram...?" "Abram, son of Terah? Is it really you?" the old man questioned in astonishment.

"Yes, indeed, I am Abram. And who do I have the pleasure of meeting, my lord?"

"Why Abram, I am your father's chief steward these many, many years; even before your birth. Do you know of me?"

"Know of you my lord? More than that noble servant - if my memory still serves me well, I owe my very life to you. You are Shelesh, Shelesh the wise, servant of the Most High God, who instructed you to save my life when I was a mere babe. I kiss your feet my lord!" Abram exclaimed falling prostrate at the feet of the chief steward, embracing his legs.

"Oh, no, my lord Abram, you must not! I am not worthy to be exalted so. I am but a servant to you and your father. You must rise and I must bow before you," he insisted stooping down to raise up Abram. As he did so Shelesh knelt facing him with tears of emotion welling out of his eyes.

"How can a man who owes his life to another be a master over him? It is I who am your servant, good Shelesh," Abram whispered tenderly, his cheeks wet with tears. He grasped the old man in his arms and held him with great affection.

Shelesh was astonished at the tribute given him with such gentleness, and by his master's son, a prince of the house of Terah.

"It is as true today, Abram, as it was fifty years ago; your God is with you. He must be a kind God, dispensing great mercies and love, if you are an example of his benefaction. Knowing you only these few minutes is proof enough to satisfy an old man's fifty years of curiosity about you. I can now see how it is possible that a great destiny lies ahead of you, Abram, for you demonstrate attributes that are non-existent in other leaders."

"And what are they, old friend?"

"Understanding and affection; not even the priests, to whom we give so much, have those qualities. No man could have filled your heart and mind with such instruction, my lord. In all the land there is no such understanding as I see in your eyes, hear from your lips, and feel in your heart."

"We are bound together, my friend, perhaps more than by circumstances."

"Yes, Abram, I feel it in my entire being. There is a good spirit with us."

"The Everliving God has his own power of spirit, Shelesh, and that is what you feel, nothing else. Where He is, there is no other spirit of the netherworld. You must believe this. The Everliving is the only God with power. All others are merely dumb as the wood, clay and stone they are made from. We will talk more about this later; now take me to my mother and father," he said raising the steward to his feet as he stood up.

"At once, wise lord, at once!" he exclaimed, his heart pounding with emotion, and his head light from the delightful, exhilarating uplift he had just experienced. Shelesh led Abram to the center of a large courtyard and asked him to please wait while he went to announce his presence. He shuffled off and Abram watched the old man, thinking: "Thank you, Everliving, for this loyal steward. May the remainder of his days be happy ones."

"Abram! Abram! Is it really you, my son?" A voice rang out from the first story balcony above and behind him. Abram turned and looked up to see his mother in the semi-darkness of flickering lamplight.

"Yes, good woman, oh yes! I am your son. Having lived the past forty years in Urusalem with the Patriarchs Noah and Shem, I have returned to rejoin my heart with yours. I have come to recapture forty years without you, my dear Amthelo, precious mother. And I have come to blend your tears of joy with mine as we embrace in reunion."

"Then come to me, Abram, my son, come quickly lest my heart burst and stop beating before my eyes feast upon you. Come quickly! Forty years of heartache and yearning to see you will now end. Every second you delay wrenches my heart that much more!"

Abram ran to the corner stairway he had seen Shelesh walk to. Up the stairs and around the balcony his sandled feet thundered. His chest was heaving, his heart pounding, not from the exertion but from anticipation of fulfilling a dream of forty years. He ran to within

94

a few paces of her and slowed to a walk, then went to his knees and embraced her with his arms. Amthelo took his head in her hands and raised it to see if she could find a boy of ten in the features of a man of fifty. Even with his beard, Amthelo knew this stranger was her son. She knew with an instinct exclusive to mothers; especially mothers like Amthelo who sacrificed to protect and preserve their children as she had done for Abram.

"Yes, you are my son Abram. I recognize something in your face, perhaps your blue eyes. Your blond hair is darker with age. Who else but Abram would kneel at the feet of his mother? Who else indeed would wet his beard with tears of joy from such a reunion? Only my son...only my son...," her voice broke and her body shook convulsively with sobs and moaning as she caressed his head and kissed his face repeatedly.

At the temple of Ishtar, located outside the Temenos but within the walled city, Terah amused himself in his usual manner.

"I drink to the glory of the Goddess Ishtar, Adna my pretty little priestess," Terah exclaimed, repeating the same toast he gave many times that evening.

Adna was in her twenties, clad only in a sheer, almost transparent gown, her face heavily made up with cosmetics. She had three different red tinting powders on her cheeks and forehead, blue over her eyes, and dark kohl on her brows and eyelashes. Adna's long black hair was neatly brushed, braided and coiled up on her head, held by ivory ornamented combs. Her graceful neck was inviting to Terah, who kissed and nuzzled her in between sips of wine. Adna's whole body beckoned him to explore with his hands and lips.

"You wish more wine, my lord Terah?" she asked, eager to increase his drunkenness.

"Mumm of course , you delicious little morsel; pour away, fill my cup. A little more libation while we enjoy each other, eh?"

"Why yes, great prince, I am but your servant to rule," Adna cooed softly, invitingly touching his hand to steady the cup.

"As long as I pay the price of course," he sneered.

"But surely you know the temple and its services must be supported and..."

"Yes, yes, I know," Terah drawled, bored with the usual explanation of expenses, when it came time to pay for his evening's pleasure. "I have heard it all before, many times. Now do not change your mood, my lovely. I am enjoying the wine and its relaxing effect. Soon I will take pleasure at its fullest...in you," he laughed lustily.

"Meanwhile entice me with your young body. Heat up my blood that runs slow and cold from boredom. Passion is what I want! Raw passion! Now, dance, girl! Dance!"

Responding to Terah's booming command, Adna put the wine pitcher down and picked up a set of castanets for each hand. Slowly she began clicking out a rhythm that guided her body. Undulating legs, hips, stomach, chest, shoulders and arms, her movements were sensual, erotic.

Terah, both amused and excited by what he saw, tapped his sandal on the floor in time with the rhythm and swilled wine until it was gone. Struggling to his feet, he staggered to the wine pitcher, picked it up in one hand and sloshed his cup full to overflowing. Wine ran to the floor forming a puddle on the tile.

Terah ignored the mess. Amusing himself, he attempted to imitate his hostess. Swaying, stumbling and spilling wine as he went, Terah suddenly felt the urge to catch and take the temptress. His senses dulled by the drunken fog, he made one lunge after another with his free hand. Clutched in the other hand, the goblet sloshed wine; some found its way in Terah's mouth.

The priestess knew how to play this game; she was no newcomer. Artfully dodging his grasp, Adna danced away, and then around him, to provide some challenge.

Terah laughed boisterously, enjoying the chase. "Aha, ho, ho, ho! You are a quick sprite. But I have played this game before, ha, ha, ho, ho, ho, and even drunk I catch my prize sooner or later.

Accepting the challenge in Terah's boast, Adna danced closer to him: taunting, teasing, then side stepped his clumsy lunge. Again she danced close. He lunged, missed and laughed raucously, voicing a mixture of obscenities. Terah thoroughly enjoyed this game of taunt and tease, knowing full well that whenever he wanted, he could catch her. He had played the game more times than he could remember. The night he celebrated Abram's birth came to mind, and thoughts of his son flooded his memory.

"Why am I thinking of Abram at a time like this? Do not get soft-hearted and ruin the fun you have started," he mumbled to himself. "Who knows when you will ever see him again? It has been a very long time. I wonder what he is like today?"

Adna watched Terah's mood change drastically. Suddenly he stopped lunging and laughing. Terah's face wore a blank, slack-jawed expression while his eyes saw what his mind remembered. Adna's sexual advances no longer held temptation; she did not even exist. In her place was the image of an eleven year old boy who moved and spoke.

"There he was, bare to his loin garment, smeared with mud, shooting arrows at murderous highwaymen."

"Terah! Lord Terah!" he seemed to shout.

"A warning...it was Abram's warning as he shot an arrow into the neck of the bandit that almost had me done for," Terah mumbled in his trance.

"Lord Terah!   What is the matter?   Have the demons possessed you? Terah...Lord Terah! They have possessed you, have they not?" Adna cried in fear. She had been with many men before but nothing like this had ever happened. Convinced that Terah was possessed,   Adna   ran   through   the   temple   halls   calling: "Shamgar...Shamgar?"

"What is it woman?" a husky voice answered from a chamber.

"Shamgar? Are you in there?" Adna questioned.

"Who else would answer to that name, priestess?   Curses! What is so urgent that you intrude upon my pleasure?"

"It is your master, Lord Terah. You must come at once!"

"What is the matter"

"He is in trouble."

"How? What...?"

"He is under the power of demons I think. He will not respond to me, yet I stand at his face and call to him. Come and take him away lest the demons make this temple their home and defile us all! Come now, quickly! Please!" Adna pleaded.

Shamgar clothed himself rapidly, picked up his sword and dagger, then ran with lumbering strides after the lithe priestess.

"Lord Terah!   Master, wake up!" Shamgar shouted and slapped him on the back with a wallop.

"What...? Shamgar?"

"Yes, lord."

"I was with Abram again. He saved my life, remember?"

"Yes, lord, I remember well. He saved my life too."

I miss him, Shamgar. All these many years... I still miss him, and wonder...."

"Yes, master, I feel the same."

"Suddenly I am weary...must be the wine...we will go now. Lend me your shoulder to lean on."

"Give me your arm, Lord, I will help you out to your palanquin."

"Good man, Shamgar; good, loyal servant," Terah drawled through his drunken haze. "Here, pay our offering to Ishtar, and her pretty maidens." Terah took a leather pouch out of his clothing and slapped it against Shamgar's chest.

Terah was conscious of being eased into his litter. The metalic sound of silver shekels changing hands reached his ears. Adna's response to his usual generosity was the last he heard, as sleep conquered him.

Porters adjusted the cadence of their steps to Terah's snoring, and Adna watched Shamgar lead them off into the dark night.

It was close to mid-day before Terah finally left his bed to face another day. He felt terrible. He had made attempts to get up earlier but failed; only to stagger a few steps and then retreat back to bed as an antidote for his sickness.

"Bad wine," he mumbled amidst curses. Eventually he was able to stand and tolerate his condition. He tried calling out in a loud voice for his manservant but his throat emitted an unintelligible raspy croak.

In anger he picked up a wine decanter, usually near at hand, and threw it against the door smashing it to pieces, raining wine everywhere. Goblets and other assorted breakables followed, until finally his servant opened the door cautiously, peered inside and asked:

"Do you command my attendance, lord?"

Terah nodded his head affirmatively and waved him in.

Abram had slept soundly until well after the sun was up. He and Amthelo had dined and talked far into the night. Shelesh had stood a short distance away, ostensibly to be of service. His presence was not required, but he remained out of a personal desire to hear and know as much as possible about this remarkable, sensitive man. Shelesh was a man of intelligence and he was fascinated by Abram's wisdom. It was not his place to question or even converse on equal terms with his master's family, but he was permitted to eavesdrop, and that he did with all the attention he could muster.

Today he maintained his standing-by position and ordered servants here and there to wait on Abram hand and foot. The returned son was bathed and rubbed with perfumed oil; his hair was washed and cut and his beard trimmed. Abram dined on the finest fruits, bread, cakes and numerous other delicacies such as he had never tasted before. Shelesh selected the finest linen and silk available from local merchants. He used Abram's tunic, taken for washing, as a pattern for size and put six servant girls to work cutting, and sewing new garments that were then embroidered with beautiful, colorful designs fit for a prince. The entire estate was a beehive of activity; all the servants worked with an energy unseen for quite some time.

Abram had never been treated this royally and he resisted it at first. He had just spent the past forty years serving two lords and he felt uncomfortable being attended to so lavishly.

"But Abram," his mother insisted, "you must allow Shelesh and me to shower you with attention. It is our way of giving affection to you. If you deny us our pleasure, you rebuke our love for you. Do you want that, my son?"

"Oh, no, mother! I do not want that. I cherish you both...and...it is just that I have such gratitude in my heart that I want to serve you...and Shelesh too."

"Abram, my son, my dear, dear son...who would suspect that within your tall, strong body lives a gentle, considerate man? You have no need to wait upon me, as a servant, in order to bring me satisfaction. I have more than enough servants. You bring great honor to your father and me by your wisdom, and by your purity of heart. These are rare values indeed and dispensed only occasionally, by a wise God, to one who is deserving of them.

"You have been chosen, Abram, to fulfill a great purpose on this earth. It becomes more and more understandable to me, a simple woman, that powerful forces of a great God are preparing you. I believe people will be drawn to you, as we are. The good spirits are with you, my son. So you see, there is no way that you can please me more or honor me more. I rejoice in the God's favor, allowing me to enjoy your presence."

Abram kissed his mother's feet and sat at the foot of her couch sharing his wisdom of the Everliving God.

Terah finally managed to make himself presentable and walked unsteadily out of his room. He was dazzled by the bright daylight. The mid-day sun was an adversary he usually raised his arm against to shield his eyes. Informed by Shelesh that Abram was in the house, having arrived the night before, Terah cursed his luck for being ill. He commanded Shelesh to send a servant to the temple of Ur-Nannar with a goat to be sacrificed in return for the healing incantations by a conjuror. The priests in most of the temples of Ur were familiar with Prince Terah's malady. In spite of many offerings for chants and incantations, his condition was never cured.

When Terah walked toward his wife and son, lounging in the shade of the court arcade, Amthelo looked up and said eagerly: "Ah, my lord husband has risen from his bed to join us Abram."

Abram leapt to his feet and ran to embrace him. "Father, father!" he exclaimed.

Terah was surprized at Abram's height, manliness, and his age. His memories were of a boy, and this stranger who hugged him was making him feel uncomfortable if not embarrassed.

"Abram, let me look at you. It is really you, is it not? I mean, you were only a sprout when last I saw you. How old were you?"

"Eleven years of age, father."

"And now you are...?"

"Fifty."

"So, in 39 years the sprout has grown into a tree; a tall, handsome and strong tree, I might add. Your body has the look of strength that I had in my youth from fighting battles. How did you come by your strength, Abram?"

"Through service, father."

"What do you mean, service?"

"I did my best in serving the Patriarchs well."

"Were you only a servant to them all these years?"

"They said, as I parted with them, 'You have been as a son to us all these years, serving devotedly'."

"But what did you do to make you as strong as you are?"

"Some hunting, some fighting. I was captain over a thousand before I left."

"And when you were young, in your prime?"

"At eighteen I started training in combat skills and strategy. I've never stopped training to some degree at least, since that time. I was just like all the other able-bodied men of Urusalem, serving to defend the city against conquerors and bandits. And like the rest, I helped strengthen the wall and fortifications with large rocks taken from the surrounding countryside."

"But that is common labor fit for slaves, not the son of a prince. You degraded yourself, Abram."

"Not so, Father. I wanted to prove my leadership by making wise decisions. I believe the way to become wise is to do the thing and learn from experience. My men labored and sweat more for me after I joined in and became an example to them. They stopped complaining and actually enjoyed a sense of accomplishment. I rewarded them with improved living conditions. Their morale became very high and they would fight an army ten or a hundred times their number in strength, if I ordered them."

"Ha! When I became a warrior leader, I struck terror in the hearts of my men by demonstration. I inflicted torture upon an enemy, or a dissident in my ranks, while everyone watched. I swore to do the same to any man unfaithful in his duties to me. And that included fighting an enemy to the death! Now that is the way to be a lord of hosts. King Nimrod showed me this unfailing method which is also used all over the world. Kingdoms are built by might and terror, Abram. I am surprised you do not know this. What did the Patriarchs teach you that cause you to be ignorant of this tactic?"

"To begin with, father, they taught me a concept called 'righteousness'."

"Righteousness? What is that?"

"It is doing things that are right or correct in the eyes of the Everliving God."

"You mean generously giving offerings to him through his priests, do you not?"

"No, father. Righteousness is right living according to a divine standard; the rules of conduct given to our first Patriarch, Adam. Those rules have been abandoned in favor of degrading human practices. As a result, our people have lost understanding of their purpose."

"Our purpose in life is to please the many gods and the king who sets forth laws according to his will," Terah asserted.

"But where every king enforces his own laws, if indeed they are laws of benefit beyond his own selfishness, where is righteousness for the good of the people?" Abram countered.

"The good of the people? Ha! The masses of common people, slaves and freemen, are created to serve many gods and try to keep them, and the genies, contented."

"And since kings of the world are their gods' rulers over the people, with priests and nobles such as yourself ruling under the same authority, the people have few mercies or comforts," Abram began to admonish. "They have only fear, toil, and pain as their lot in life to serve nobility such as yourself. Where are the joys and the blessings for them, that the Everliving God can provide for every man and woman?"

"What nonsense; complete nonsense!" Terah bellowed. "Joys? Blessings for the people? What are these things that you give such importance to?"

"Have you not known any joy in your life, father?"

"I have known many pleasures of mind and body, Abram, but joy? I know it not. And if these blessings you speak of are wealth and position? I am satisfied with my blessings."

"But they are not from the Everliving; they are from Nimrod, and they corrupt you in mind, body and heart. Do the people respect you and honor you for what you do?"

"They respect me out of fear and Nimrod honors me with position and wealth as long as I am proficient in my service to him. That is all that matters to me."

"And you care nothing at all for the people?"

"No, of course not, only how they can be used to good advantage. This is the way of the world. The strong govern the weak. Dominion will always be in the hands of the strong who rule through fear and force; taking what they want from those they govern."

"Not always, father, not always. We may not see a change in our lifetime but, the Everliving will have His way. Nothing can resist Him. His mercies to the people will be restored!"

It was as though the strength of Abram's God filled him. His eyes flashed with boldness. His voice boomed with authority and confidence. His body became pumped-up with power such as Terah had never seen before in anyone, not even Nimrod the Terrible. Shaken by his son's strange, and awesome, posture, Terah refrained from talking any further on this subject. He passed the remainder of the day talking, instead, about the old times when Abram was a boy. This was the Abram he knew. The man in front of him was a stranger to be feared.

Chapter 9
Ur

U r was, in all essentials, typical of the Sumerian city/state capitals from the Persian Gulf up to Mari. Ur consisted of three parts:

1. the Temenos or sacred area
2. the walled city that stood on a mound formed by ruins of successive buildings set up on the site of the original settlement.
3. The outer town

Ur was an irregular oval shape approximately three-quarters of a mile long and about half a mile wide. It was surrounded by a huge mud-brick rampart, about twenty-five feet high, with a steeply inclined outer face. Along the top of this slope King Ur-Nammu, of the third dynasty, built, in burnt brick, a huge wall of defense 'like a mountain'.

In the northwestern quarter of the city was the Temenos, the sacred palace/temple complex of Nannar, the moon god who was owner of the city. It was a rectangular enclosure measuring 270 yards by 190. Raised on an artificial terrace above the general ground level of the city, it was surrounded by a massive wall of mud-brick. In its west corner, on a higher terrace, also heavily walled, rose the ziggurat. Seventy feet high, it was capped by a shrine, a holy of holies, the dwelling place of Nannar. In front of the courtyard surrounded by storerooms and offices to which were brought offerings for sacrifice and rents due from tenants who farmed the god's lands. The rest of the Temenos was occupied by the palace.

This walled complex was the core of the city. The government of the city/state was a theocracy and the sacred area was the administrative center. Its terraces were planted with trees to give meaning to its name: 'the hill of heaven'. It dominated the entire city and could be seen twenty miles away across the flatness of the plain. Farmers looking up from their work in the fields saw the towering shrine as the actual dwelling place of the god, their master, and were continually aware of his divine presence.

UR – The Walled City

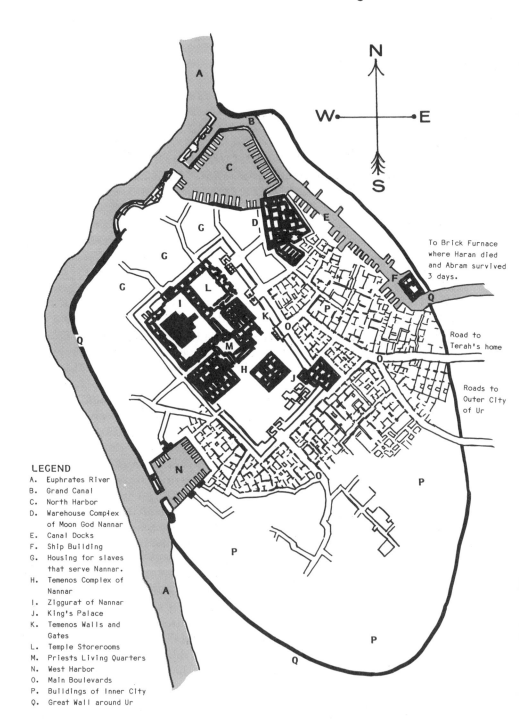

N
W • — • **E**
S

To Brick Furnace
where Haran died
and Abram survived
3 days.

Road to
Terah's home

Roads to
Outer City
of Ur

LEGEND
A. Euphrates River
B. Grand Canal
C. North Harbor
D. Warehouse Complex
   of Moon God Nannar
E. Canal Docks
F. Ship Building
G. Housing for slaves
   that serve Nannar.
H. Temenos Complex of
   Nannar
I. Ziggurat of Nannar
J. King's Palace
K. Temenos Walls and
   Gates
L. Temple Storerooms
M. Priests Living Quarters
N. West Harbor
O. Main Boulevards
P. Buildings of Inner City
Q. Great Wall around Ur

While the Temenos was strictly reserved for service to Nannar, other deities of the pantheon had temples set up in their honor both in the walled city and in the outer town. Some were large and imposing buildings, but they lacked the dignified seclusion of the Temenos because they were closely hemmed in by houses of the townspeople.

The streets of the residential district were unpaved, narrow and winding. Some were blind alleys leading to houses hidden away in a muddle of un-arranged buildings. All indications suggest that the city just sprouted and grew out of the status of a primitive village rather than having been laid out on any system of city planning. Houses large and small were jumbled together. Most of them were two stories high, some had one story and a few were three storied. Wedged in between the houses were little public chapels dedicated by pious citizens to the minor deities.

Ur, as an urban center, encompassed an area of approximately 1500 acres and had a population of about 380,000 people. Industry and commerce played a bigger part, and occupied a greater number of people than agriculture did.

Abraham toured the city, on one of the holidays, with his brothers Haran and Nahor, with Haran's son, Lot, and daughters Sarai and Milca. Abram explained how he had been instructed, by Shem and Noah, concerning the pantheon of gods worshipped in cities such as Ur. At one temple after another, Abram exposed the gods as evil, and called the worship of them a worthless endeavor. At the same time he expressed pity for the misled worshipers.

Sarai wondered at the intellectual and spiritual strengths of this brash prince. How was it that he dared to malign the gods? What strange power did he draw upon in standing opposed to all that went on around him? She feared for this magnificent man while being mysteriously drawn to him. Was he possessed by demons? Or was he wonderfully gifted by another god, a jealous god?

Nahor was alarmed at his brother's conduct and pleaded with him to be quiet, lest someone of importance overhear and report them to temple authorities as heretics.

Haran was concerned for the truth of Abram's criticism but also fearful of any condemnation and punishment that might come down on them.

Lot, respectful of his father's concern, said nothing. Inside, however, he felt drawn to Abram's wisdom. Milca knew little about the gods and cared less. She was bent on drawing Nahor to her, and that took all of her attention these days.

The day was drawing to a close and the dusky light of early evening was rapidly fading. Abram finished describing the religious practices of the temple priestesses of Ishtar at the very door of their establishment. He hesitated, trying to be discreet with his choice of words for the sake of Milca and Sarai. The group had only walked a dozen paces down the street when Abram and his brothers heard a voice familiar to all. They stopped and turned to look back.

Drunk or sober, in light or darkness, Terah was easily identifiable by his booming broadcast. In the semi-darkness Terah staggered directly into the temple without a moment of hesitation. The familiar greeting, Terah gave the young priestess who addressed him, carried out into the street before other conversation muffled and died at the close of the temple door.

Abram said nothing more the rest of the evening. He was too shocked and embarrassed. His father indulged himself of the very practices Abram condemned. It was also obvious that Terah was a frequent patron to the temple prostitutes. The vision of his father, that Abram had nurtured for forty years, was distorting more and more each day. Disappointment was compounding at an alarming rate.

Chapter 10
Measures of Faith

And Terah had twelve gods of large size, made of wood and stone, after the twelve months of the year, and he served each one monthly, and every month Terah would bring his meat offering and drink offering to his gods; thus did Terah all his days.

Jasher 9:8

Abram stood in a large room and looked at all the representations of gods carved from wood and hewn from stone. Twelve statues, each in their own temple, were arranged along three walls. Countless numbers of other smaller images filled the remaining wall and floor space. It appeared to be a collection of every conceivable icon made by the hands of carvers. As Abram stood there looking, an anger arose in him.

"My father, a collector of useless images, keeping in fashion by acquiring a representation of every god conceived by priests. My father, the prince of the host of Nimrod, an example for numerous thousands of subject peoples. I cannot accept nor can I submit to this evil! My Everliving God, I promise you this day, these images shall not remain in my father's house! Let my god break me in pieces if in three days time I fail to break all these!" he swore his oath with an arm raised and a fist clenched menacing the objects.

Abram found his father sitting in the court arcade with servants clustered around tending to his desires. Coming before Terah he sat and spoke what was on his mind.

"Father, tell me, where is the God who created heaven and earth, and all the sons of men upon earth? And who created you and me?"

Pleased with his son's question, posed as though seeking wisdom from him, Terah smiled condescendingly and answered.

"Why, Abram, my son, the gods who created us are all here with us in this very house."

107

"Father!" Abram's eyes were wide in mock amazement, if it please my lord, would you show them to me?"

"Very well, Abram, as you request." Terah stood up and walked to the chamber of the inner court where Abram had been earlier. They walked into the room and Terah proclaimed: "Behold - here are the gods which made all you see upon the earth; which created me and you and all mankind."

When he had finished speaking, Terah bowed down to them. In a moment he straightened up, turned and left with Abram following.

The next day, after Terah left the house, Abram went to his mother and sat with her in conversation. "My father has shown me those gods who made heaven and earth and all the sons of men. I must make obeisance to them. Go now and order that a goat kid be taken, slain, and cooked with herbs and spices to make it good to the taste. I will then bring it to my father's gods as an offering for them to eat."

Amthelo did as her son asked and brought him the savory meat after it had been prepared according to her recipe. Abram brought it to the room of his father's gods and placed it among them. For the remainder of the day he sat among the images in the room without his father knowing it.

The next day Abram gave directions to his mother again. She ordered three fine goat kids be purchased and slaughtered. She personally directed their preparation to produce the finest of savory meat. When it was ready, Abram took it to the chamber of the gods and again he placed it directly in front of each so they could eat. He sat in the room all day watching them to see, if by some magic, they might eat.

That evening he paced the courtyard and thought about his experience with the graven images over the past two days. The spirit of the Everliving was upon him and he called out: "Shame upon my father and this wicked generation! He found an ax, then returned to the chamber of the gods. A controlled rage burst forth from him in an explosion of swift movement and sound. His strong arms whirled with arcing strokes as the ax smashed and broke the images into pieces. Pausing for breath, he laughed at their impotence and their uselessness. Then he swore a holy war against them to his death.

"Swing...smash! Swipe...smash!" Abram's outer garment ruffled, and the sleeves spread like a giant bird, flapping for flight. Loud, gutteral sounding utterances issued from his throat like a warrior in battle. His motion was almost a blur as god after god was dismembered and beaten into rubble.

All during this foray Abram was careful to avoid one particular image, the 'great god' that was facing the others. With the destruction finished, Abram placed his ax in the hands of the 'great god' and left the room.

Terah was returning home when he heard the sound of metal crashing against stone and wood. He heard the frightening utterances of battle and was greatly alarmed. Rushing to the chamber of the gods he arrived just as Abram was leaving, his face glistening with beads of sweat. Their eyes met and Terah was shocked to see fierce anger kindling in his son's eyes. His whole body tensed with alarm, not knowing what to expect.

Abram, surprised by his father's sudden appearance, stopped momentarily and looked cautiously at him. What he saw was a tense old warrior, with questioning and a measure of fear darting from his eyes. Before Terah could speak, Abram turned from him and hurried away to avoid a confrontation.

Terah wrenched the door open and stepped inside. Staggering with shock, he saw all his gods smashed into pieces; the ax laid in the hands of the largest god which was the only one unbroken. Savory meat lay untouched in front of the remains of each god. Aghast at the scene of destruction scattered around the room, he became very angry. Whirling about, he ran out of the room shrieking his son's name.

"Abram, Abram! Where are you? You cannot hide from me!"

He found Abram in his room bathing the perspiration from his face and neck with a wet cloth.

"What is this evil work you have done to my gods?"

"Not so my lord. Abram answered. "I brought savory meat into their chamber and when I came close to them, they all at one stretched out their hand to eat before the great one had reached out his hand to eat. And as he watched them partaking without regard to him, his anger increased greatly. And he went and took the ax that was in the house, returned and broke them all. Look and you will see the ax is still in his hands."

"What kind of a tale is this you tell? It is nothing but a lie! Terah's neck muscles stood out, his face was flushed red, and he shook with rage, almost out of control as he spoke: "Is there in these gods spirit, mind, or power to do all that you have told me? Are they not wood and stone and have I not myself had them made? Can you now speak lies saying the large god smashed the smaller gods?" Without waiting for an answer, Terah charged: "It is you who destroyed them and placed the ax in his hands!"

"If it is as you say, father, how can you serve these idols in whom there is no power to do anything? Can those idols, in which you trust, deliver you? Can they hear your prayers when you call upon them? Can they deliver you from the hands of your enemies? Or will they fight your battles for you against your enemies? Surely you know that wood and stone cannot, nor can they even speak or hear.

"How can you forget the Everliving God, who made heaven and earth and who created you? Is it not true that our ancestors did the same abominations and the God of the universe brought waters of the flood upon them to destroy them? If you continue to serve gods of wood and stone you will incur the wrath of the Everliving upon you! Stop this foolish idol worship so that you will no longer bring evil upon yourself and those under your authority!"

Abram left the room hastily, passing by an enraged stuttering Terah, and returned to the chamber of the gods. Taking the ax from the hands of the largest idol, He smashed it into pieces with blows taking all his strength. Satisfied with all his work he left the room and hid himself from Terah's wrath.

Terah was insane with anger and frustration. His only thought was of revenge against Abram. He even regretted having saved him from Nimrod after he was born.

"That is it! I will go to the king and tell him what Abram has done. He will determine whose gods are most powerful. And he will punish Abram for his insolence!

Terah went to King Nimrod and bowed down before him.

"What is it that you want from me?" The king asked.

"A son was born to me fifty years ago. Hear, O King, the offense he has now committed against me and the gods."

Terah related the incident and Abram's confession of the destruction.

"And now, my lord and king, I pray you will send for him to come before you. Judge him according to your law, so we may be delivered from this evil."

Nimrod agreed to judge the matter and provide relief from Abram's heresy.

The next day, six of the King's guards brought Abram before the royal throne and forced him to his knees. The King's princes and servants were standing to each side of him; Terah was among them.

"What is this I hear that you have done to your father and his gods?" Nimrod demanded.

Abram answered the king with the same arguments he gave Terah.

"Do you imagine that these images can deliver anyone or do anything small or great that should warrant people serving them? Will you not serve the one Everliving God of the universe who created us all and who has the power to kill and to keep alive? You know full well your obligation to worship Him only as your god."

"It has served my purposes, as king over this domain, to carry on worship of the gods of my subject people. Besides, who gives you authority to speak in such a manner to me?"

"The Patriarchs of our race, my king. You, and nobles such as my father, enrich yourselves from the hard labor of the people while they wallow in sweat and fear, unable to rise above the status of a dumb ox in the field or a slave in chains. Why will you not be a leader of men rather than a leader of slaves? You were given the power, by the Everliving and you abuse it!"

Abram gazed into the king's eyes, burning his conscience with the truth, and continued.

"Is it not true, even today, O powerful king, that leaders of men preparing for battle say the following? 'Like God did to Nimrod, who was a mighty hunter in the earth, and who succeeded in battles wrought against him and his brothers, so may God strengthen us and deliver us this day?'"

Abram waited for a response, but there was none.

"Will you not cease your foolishness and embrace the one God to whom you owe your life and all you have?" Abram asked firmly.

Nimrod was stunned. He sat on his throne rigid with indecision. Sweat streamed down his face reddened with embarrassment. The truth of Abram's words bludgeoned him into deep reflection and he lost all ability to act decisively. It was as though the king had been entranced.

His advisors were alarmed and fearful that Abram was a sorcerer who had captured the king's mind. They conferred in a group and decided Abram should be removed immediately before his spell did any more harm.

"Captain of the guard! Take this man, Abram, and put him in prison until the king decides what to do with him!" commanded the high priest.

Abram was prodded with spears and ordered to walk out of the throne room. On his way he turned his head and warned the priests in a loud, commanding voice: "Your days are numbered! Your days are numbered, sorcerers!"

The next day Nimrod had Abram brought out of prison. He was suspicious, considering the advice of his priests, that Abram might have some special powers as a sorcerer. "How dare you speak to me and my priests as though you were a judge over us! Are you a conjurer with special powers?"

"No, my king, I am but a man chosen for a purpose and trained for that purpose by patriarchs of our race."

"What purpose?"

"To show the way of right living, my lord."

"As king, I am the only one who can say what is the way of right living, and I did not appoint you to speak for me. What you say, therefore, has no importance to me.

"Oh foolish, simple, and ignorant king, woe to you forever!" Abram shouted full of the Spirit of his God. "I thought you would teach your servants the upright way, but you have not done this. You have, instead, filled the whole land with your sins and the sins of your servants who have followed your ways. The same was done by our ancestors! The Eternal God brought the waters of the great flood upon them and destroyed them. Will you and your people continue in this evil and bring down the anger of the Everliving upon you and all the people?"

Abram's insolence and condemnation caused Nimrod to shake with rage. He clenched his hands so tight the knuckles were white and hatred burned in his eyes. His first impulse was to order Abram's death and watch him cut to pieces by the guards. A cautious judgment over-ruled his violent temper, however, and he ordered Abram taken back to prison until he could decide what should be done with him.

The king decreed that all his princes, sages, and the governors of the different provinces come before him in ten days.

On the tenth day they all sat before the king, in his grand throne-room, and he related to them how Abram destroyed his father's gods.

"This man, Abram, is resolute with condemnation of his father, his king, and all our gods. I have ordered you here to listen to your counsel in deciding what should be done with this man who destroys his father's gods and reviles your king."

The buzzing sound of many voices could be heard discussing the matter. Finally there was an agreement between principle authorities, and a spokesman addressed the king.

"The man who reviles the king should be hanged upon a tree. Having confessed to all the things that he did, however, and having despised our gods, he must be burned to death. That is the law."

Another governor added: "If it would please the king to do this, let him order his servants to burn a fire night and day in your brick furnace, and then we will throw this man into it."

Delighted that others had taken a hand in condemning Abram, Nimrod settled back on his throne and ordered: "Let it be so. Have my servants prepare a furnace for three days and three nights."

On the morning of the fourth day Nimrod commanded that Abram be brought up from the prison. Setting out through the east gate of the Temenos a procession started that was composed of all the governmental and priestly authorities, priests and priestesses of the major and minor temples, led by the king and his palace guards. Abram walked near the front, hemmed in between two groups of guards numbering forty soldiers in each.

Abram's hands were tied behind him. His legs were hobbled with rope, while another rope tied around his neck had long ends held in front and behind by guards.

"There is no way to escape," he admitted to himself as he hobbled along through the streets of the city. "Why do these people glare at me with such fear and hostility? What am I to them?"

Abram could not answer the questions. His mind and emotions were busy enough trying to cope with the dilemma he was in. Keeping his eyes down on the street, he moved his feet within the confines of their restraints as fast and as carefully as possible trying not to stumble and fall. He knew that if he fell he would be pulled to his feet by the rope around his neck. There was more he had to say, before he died, directly to the people, and he wanted his voice intact.

Praying silently to the Everliving for protection, Abram quietly gathered strength and a measure of comfort. The crushing fear of humiliation, pain, and death that he knew awaited him at the end of this march, was mysteriously lifted. In place of fear there was a strange feeling of satisfaction, even contentment about what he had done.

"The whole kingdom is against me, and although I am on the way to my death, I no longer have any fear. How can this be?" Soon the answer came to him. "It can only be the work of the Everliving God. Could this be a sign that I should trust in his deliverance? Surely anything is possible for Him to accomplish. Yes, I believe He wants me to trust in Him and have no fear! Noah trusted, and he with all his household were saved! What is fire, but an element under His control, just as water is. Believe in His saving power! That is it! Believe! Believe!"

The words flooded Abram's mind so completely that he was hardly aware of the waves of shouting crowds that had accumulated, like ripples in the water, and now trailed behind.

Starting from Royal Square, they proceeded through Sacred Way out to Church Lane passing by many chapels of minor deities. Coming to a junction with two other streets, the procession continued left on Broad Street and headed toward a gate through the eastern wall. This led to the outer town and the brick furnaces near a minor canal.

A bright sun had risen over the mountains to the east. Abram found a measure of satisfaction in its warmth; a soothing relief from the chilling, black depths of the king's dungeon.

Along the canal bank, Abram saw workmen dredging clay and mud and pouring it into brick molds of various sizes after the addition of dried grass or straw. Other workers were removing sun-dried bricks from long rows and carrying them to a large furnace.

Abram was jerked to a halt after passing through a crowd that had gathered a short distance from the furnace. Looking around he saw the king, his priests, conjurors, governors and princes sitting comfortably under the shade of a fabric pavilion, especially erected for this occasion.

More and more people gathered around, pressing against the king's soldiers who formed a protective barrier. The news had raced like a flash flood: "Abram, son of Prince Terah, is on his way to be burned alive at the brick furnaces!"

Shops were hastily closed. Farmers and canal laborers followed their overseers, running towards the city. Crowds of visitors were caught up in the flow. Temple priests and scribes turned away people who came to present offerings at the temples. Locking up storehouses and treasuries, they rushed to the scene pushing their way through the masses, insisting on an inside view. No one dared to object.

Up on the canal banks people stood, five or six feet above the ground level, with an excellent view of the proceedings. Children sat on their fathers' shoulders. Mothers held babies on their hips. Dogs dashed here and there in the streets, yapping and following at the heels of passers-by.

Nimrod talked at some length to those guests who shared his presence in the shade, giving the city's populace time to gather. Looking around at the multitude he smiled contentedly and then beckoned for Abram to be brought to within speaking distance.

Abram was moved to the center of the clearing, in front of the king, and clubbed to his knees by his guards.

A nod of the king's head at the high priest nearby brought the king's spokesman out into the sunlight. Pointing to Abram he announced: "This man is Abram, son of Terah, a lord of Nimrod's armed host. He has committed great crimes against his father and the king." With a booming voice the prosecutor read from a clay tablet describing Abram's law breaking acts, dramatizing each one to emphasize its seriousness and its punishment. Next he paused, raised his eyes, scanned the faces of the crowd and asked: "What would you have us do with him, people of Ur?"

Instantly the crowds became electrified. "Kill him! Burn him! Burn him in the oven!" they shouted in their lust for blood and punishment. The son of Prince Terah being the offender made this event even more exciting and dramatic.

"Is there anyone here who will stand up for the accused and defend him?" asked the prosecutor dryly.

There was a roar of laughter from the crowd that lasted some minutes as if a great joke had been shared, then retold again and again. The king and his authorities also laughed with delight encouraging the joke until Nimrod raised his staff for silence.

The noise faded and stopped and the prosecutor again spoke turning toward Abram.

"It seems there is no one in the entire city who has a good word to say for you. Do you wish to speak in your own defense?"

Abram rose to his feet, turned his back to the king and slowly swept his gaze over the masses. At first there was a great cacophony of jeers and taunts; their final insult to an enemy of the state before he was silenced forever. Gradually, however, the tumult waned as their curiosity was aroused by this light-haired, robust man who gave no appearance of fear.

"Let it be known that I, Abram, son of Prince Terah am not possessed by evil spirits. That which I am accused of doing, I admit to, having a sound mind and body. I have chosen freedom from the slavery that binds all men, from king to servant. The Everliving God condemns the corrupting practices of the priests, who rob you of your abundance and deny you your blessings from the one true God. I have come to reveal these things to you, my people. Do not condemn me! Think on what I say! My God is merciful and generous, with great powers to protect you."

"Oh, is that so?" yelled the crowd. "Let us see how he protects you from the fire. The fire! The fire! The fire," they chanted until the prosecutor raised his arms signaling them to stop.

Abram listened as his sentence of death by fire was repeated, but it did not destroy the confidence he had found. Retreating within his consciousness to another state of being, the imminent prospect of death by burning failed to shatter his determination to meet and accept it calmly.

Standing in front of the king, Abram spoke no more. He raised his head and scanned the cloudless sky, wondering if there would be a sign. Finding none, he stood proudly with chest out, shoulders squared back, feet apart, ready. His eyes were penetrating...looking through and beyond...perhaps the suggestion of a smile barely recognizable on his lips.

There was a murmur of voices among the priests and one of the sages cried out to the king.

"Our sovereign Lord, surely this is the babe Abram grown to a man that we warned you about fifty years ago. We declared to you, at that time, the omen of the heavens where the great star from the east swallowed the four stars, forecasting his threat to you and other kingdoms in the four parts of the earth. Behold, now it is clear that his father disobeyed your command and mocked you by bringing a different child, which you killed."

Nimrod became very angry upon hearing this. "Bring Terah before me!" he screamed.

"Lord Terah had no stomach for his son's execution, my king. He waits at your palace with his body guard," an officer of the king's guards advised.

"Go there in my chariot and return in haste with Terah only. I do not want any trouble with that monstrous old warrior, Shamgar. Put him in the dungeon if you have to."

"As you command, my king, right away," the officer replied, saluting, then backed away. "Back to the palace!" he ordered the king's charioteer, stepping on board.

The crowds quickly opened a path before they were run down, and the chariot raced towards the walled city.

Arriving at the palace the officer ran inside and confronted Terah as he paced about nervously.

"The king commands you to leave your bodyguard here and come with me to appear before the king!"

"Why? For what reason?" Terah pried.

"It is not for me to say, my lord, I am under strict orders to bring you immediately! Any further delay can only make the king more impatient."

Terah's curiosity turned to unreasoning fear and a knot formed in his stomach. He knew it was useless and foolish to resist Nimrod's command or even delay any longer, so he reluctantly ordered Shamgar to remain at the palace. Collecting himself, mentally, he turned and left with the officer.

Traveling through the city, Terah was startled by its emptiness. The streets were almost deserted. Merchants' shops and stalls were locked or empty. Only women and young children appeared here and there. They stared at the three men curiously, as the chariot thundered by.

"Make way, make way for the king's chariot," the officer shouted, coming to the site of the furnaces. The masses of people gathered in the way were more numerous now than before.

Terah dismounted, elbowed his way through those in his way and approached the king. Bowing before Nimrod, Terah spoke, with an effort to maintain his normal composure. "My king, you summoned and I willingly came."

Nimrod looked sternly at Terah searching his facial expression and his eyes for signs of guilt. "Hear what my wise men revealed to me concerning this son of yours called Abram; this same Abram who destroyed your household gods and whom we have condemned to the fire on your account. Listen to them Terah: they speak of YOUR TREASON!"

"Treason, my king? Surely not I, your loyal servant all these many years?" Terah implored defensively.

"Treachery! Deceit! Defrauding your king who has been so generous with wealth and prestige."

"But I ..."

"Quiet now and hear what has been hidden for fifty years and is now revealed!"

Terah broke out in a sweat that drenched his body, salting his taste and stinging his eyes. Fear gripped him like a strong man and he struggled against it with all the reason he possessed. The truth of Abram's redemption as a baby was fully exposed. Looking aside at the furnace, he could almost feel the heat burning his flesh.

"Surely I am condemned," he thought. "I will join Abram in the flames and all will be for nothing."

The words of the wise men penetrated him like arrows, mortally convicting him.

"You have heard the report; now tell me if it is true and I may show leniency," Nimrod demanded.

Terah saw such anger in the king's face that he knew there was no way out but to confess. "My lord and king, what the sages report is true. You heard it correctly," he confirmed dropping to his knees and hanging his head remorsefully.

Nimrod looked at Terah with disappointment, his anger subsided. The king's curiosity about an old dependable friend's treachery was stronger now than his anger.

"How could you do this thing? How could you transgress my edict and give me a child other than this Abram who now embarrasses us both? And you took value for him besides. Great value I recall. What is your answer to all this treachery?"

"I had tender feelings for my son at that time, my lord, feelings very strong," Terah shuddered with vibrant passion. "I purchased a child and brought him to my king as a substitute."

"Who advised you to do this? Tell me!" Nimrod roared. "Do not hide anything from me and I may spare your life."

Terah was greatly terrified by the king's threat. Again he looked at the furnace and the thought of being burned alive crushed the last ounce of courage he may have had. But he sensed that the king wanted to save his life, and his mind raced with cunning speed to evaluate his alternatives. His first impulse was to tell the truth and lay all the blame upon Shelesh, even Shamgar if necessary. "But the king would hold me up to ridicule before his court, the priests, and the people as a lord prince who was ruled by his servants. And he would most assuredly have to kill me, whether he believed such a ridiculous story or not. No, I must put the blame upon someone else," he reasoned, "but who? Think! Think! Oh why did I let Amthelo talk me into this deception, a deception that now threatens my life? What free man of standing can I accuse that the king would accept as a substitute for me? And who would accept the blame for me? No one, Terah, you fool, no one! But... who do I have dominion over that could have advised me, and is important enough to me for the king to believe was responsible? One of my family perhaps...a male child...he would have to be close...important to me...Haran, my eldest son? To save your life? Yes! Yes! Are not sons to protect their fathers? Even the eldest? Yes, even the eldest!"

"You dare to keep your king waiting? Who advised you to do this?" Nimrod shouted.

"It was Haran, my eldest son, who advised me." Terah lied as convincingly as he knew how.

Nimrod looked at him with eyes that penetrated to his heart. "I know he is lying," the king reasoned, "but this is a way to save his life. I must also minimize the embarrassment he has become to me, for my own sake. He has been a loyal noble in all other respects...and as such he is more valuable to me alive than dead. If I spare his life he will be more devoted than ever, through fear."

Standing up Nimrod declared: "I hereby command that Haran, your son who advised you to trick me, shall die in the fire with Abram. My sentence of death is upon him for having rebelled against the king's desire!"

Haran was among those watching and waiting. The king's guards sought him out and returned in quick time throwing him prostrate before Nimrod. Haran was paralyzed with fear and stammered a garbled speech full of questions. As the king's servants grabbed him and began stripping his garments off, he shouted: "Father! Father! Why me? What have I done? I do not deserve to die! I have done nothing wrong! Please, please have mercy! Please...oh please ...I do not want to die!" Haran pleaded and fell on his knees, stripped of everything except a cloth undergarment.

The king's servants disrobed Abram of all his clothing in the same manner. As they did so he looked down on Haran and his heart was full of pity.

"Believe in the Everliving God, Haran, my brother."

The king's men bound both victims' hands and feet with linen cords, preparing them for the fire. Haran's mind raced in desperation to find understanding of his dilemma. He reflected on Abram's teaching, the destruction of Terah's gods and his imminent death without cause. Earlier he had developed a love for Abram and was inclined to follow his ways, but kept it to himself. He had reasoned: "The king has seized Abram on account of heresy. If Abram should prevail over the king, I will follow him. But if the king prevails, I will go after the king."

But now here he was along side of his brother, doomed to the same fate. Haran watched, horrified as temple priests took Abram in their grasp.

Abram's resolve was slipping away from him. The terror of death gripped him. But his mind was still working and he said to himself: "Give me courage, Everliving God, for I have lost all that I once had. Let me be an example of your power over this kingdom. Preserve me from the burning fire which is yours to control."

On a signal, the priests lifted Abram horizontally and heaved him through the mouth of the brick furnace into the intense fire.

"My Everliving God, accept your servant!" were his last words.

The crowd was disappointed that Abram went so quietly, without the pleading and groveling hysteria usually exhibited by those about to be executed.

Haran provided another opportunity to satisfy their cruel, blood-lusting appetites. Priests toyed with him, to please the crowd; his agonizing fear progressed into screaming hysteria... then wild madness.

Terah tried to leave and avoid seeing his sons die but Nimrod commanded him to stay and witness everything without turning his head nor closing his eyes. The king threatened Terah with death by fire if he failed to obey in every respect.

When Abram was thrown into the furnace, a shudder ran through Terah's body. Now, as he watched his oldest son humiliated and driven insane with fear, the knot in his stomach exploded. Terah vomited until he fell on his knees.

Thousands of voices laughed and jeered raucously. Through a haze and swirl of moving figures, he forced himself to watch the screaming, writhing and, kicking Haran. Sweat glistened Haran's trembling body. His eyes rolled around in his head and he foamed saliva from his mouth amidst crazed utterances.

Terah was sicker than he had ever been. Through his agony he mustered the strength to shout his loudest: "Burn him! Burn him! Burn him! Burn him!"

The crowd began to take up the chant: "Burn him! Burn him! Burn him! The volume of chanting grew into an immense wave of sound building louder and broader, more and more expansive as if the entire world cried out the order for the grand, final act of this command performance.

Nimrod waved his staff of authority. Twelve servants grabbed Haran and threw him into the furnace, stopping his agony forever.

Immediately, great tongues of flame belched out of the oven, engulfing the priests, swirling, and licking with deadly heat. Cries of shock and agony were quickly stilled as twelve charred bodies lie strewn near the furnace.

The crowd was awe-struck by this phenomenon. The king, however, was unmoved by the retribution and prepared to return to the palace. He and his guests were satisfied that justice had been properly administered.

The death that ended Haran's screams was an act of mercy for him and a release for Terah as his strength gave out completely and he collapsed face forward in his own vomit.

The Everliving God loved Abram. His spirit of protection enfolded Abram and prevented the fire from touching or hurting him. The servants who fed the fire saw him alive, and finally found the courage to report this miracle to the king.

"O great king, we have watched the furnace where Abram was cast these three days and nights, and our eyes show us an unnatural sight. He...he walks about in the fire! He does not appear to be burned, nor is his undergarment, yet the cords that bound him are burned off."

"Impossible! The heat plays tricks with your eyes!" Nimrod reacted with shock. His heart pounded heavily and sweat ran down his face and body. He would not allow himself to believe them, so he ordered some faithful nobles to look and report to him just what they saw.

A short time later they returned and revealed that it was just as the servants had said.

It cannot be! No one can live in a fiery furnace for even three minutes! It must be an illusion - a spell that sorcerer Abram left for all who look for him. I shall go see for myself. Have my chariot ready; we leave at once.

Arriving at the site Nimrod strained his eyes, staring into the furnace from a safe distance. He remembered the fate of his twelve servants burned to death near its opening.

"What...? It cannot be! My eyes deceive me. I must be cursed by the spell also. I, too, see what appears to be the man Abram walking about, unhurt. Yet there are only ashes of Haran's body! This is truly a great mystery!"

Consulting with his priests and conjurers he found no competent explanation except that Abram was empowered by his God to survive.

"He must come out of the furnace! If he stays there he will become a god to the people and turn them away from us. They may even revolt against us and our gods...and worship Abram and his God. Bring him out! Now!"

Approaching the furnace, Nimrod's servants were repelled by an amazing fire that surrounded it and extended towards them as they came near. They ran from it and drew the king's rebuke.

"Hurry and bring Abram out of the fire, you cowards, or you will die by my command!"

Eight men again approached the fire with water vessels hoping to douse the fire. Flames lashed out engulfing them setting their clothing ablaze. Their blood curdling screams hung on the air: resounding, eerie, and foreboding.

Nimrod finally realized his servants could not bring Abram out. Desperate for a way, he tried it himself, by another method.

"Abram! Abram! Abram, O servant of the Everliving God...come forth from the fire and stand before me!" Nimrod ordered loudly.

Abram heard the king's command and he came out of the furnace to stand before him. His body was all aglow and there was no evidence that the fire affected him at all. Nimrod, with all his priestly advisors and nobles, watched Abram reappear unharmed and they fell back in fear and astonishment.

"How is it that you were not burned in the fire?" they asked.

"The Everliving, God of Heaven and Earth, in whom I trust, has all things under his control. He delivered me from the fire as an example of his powers to save and to destroy. Now it is proven that I speak not of my own authority, but with that of the Everliving God!"

37. And Haran was eighty-two years old when he died in the fire of Casdim (Ur). And the king, princes and inhabitants of the land, seeing that Abram was delivered from the fire, they came and bowed down to Abram.

38. And Abram said to them, do not bow down to me but bow

down to the god of the world who made you, and serve Him and go in His ways for it is He who delivered me from out of this fire, and it is He who created the souls and spirits of all men, and formed the world, and it is He who will deliver those who trust in him, from all pain.

39. And this thing seemed very wonderful in the eyes of the king and princes, that Abram was saved from the fire and that Haran was burned; and the king gave Abram many presents and he gave him his two head servants from the king's house; the name of one was Oni and the name of the other was Eliezer.

40. And all the kings, princes and servants gave Abram many gifts of silver and gold and pearl, and the king and his princes sent him away, and he went in peace.

Jasher 12:37-40

Chapter 11
SARAI: Courtship and Marriage

Abram returned to his father's house, after his victory over Nimrod and the furnace, with three hundred men eager to serve him. It was a responsibility he did not expect, but was prepared to receive. He gave each man the freedom to pursue his own trade as before but set forth rules of conduct and worship for all to follow. For many days he taught men and corrected their old ways. During his busy ministry, he found little time for personal pursuits.

Abram's brother, Nahor, courted Milca after the death of her father and they married.

Abram's courtship of Sarai took more time. The demands of ministering to three hundred men and their families was considerable. Sometimes he would not be able to find any spare time for weeks on end. But when the time came and his yearning to be with her was too compelling to resist, he went to her.

Abram's visits were properly chaperoned by Sarai's mother but there were always times when the couple could be completely alone for a few minutes. On one occasion they were strolling about the house, out of sight of Sarai's mother for the time being, when Sarai stopped and turned to face him. Abram construed this as an invitation for an embrace and with a sigh in his voice, he spoke her name softly and kissed her lightly on the mouth.

"Abram...," she whispered affectionately, encouragingly.

"Sarai...how sweet you taste," he replied softly and kissed her longer. Putting his arms around her, he drew her to him gently.

"Abram... you are my lord: lord of my mind, my heart and my body!" she sighed fervently. Reaching up with her arms, she encircled his neck and drew herself full length against him. She sensed he was afraid to hold her too tightly. "I am not a fragile clay figure, my love. You will not break me with your embrace," she pressed against him, pulling up with her arms and feeling his strength against her.

Confident, now, that he was not overstepping his bounds as a suitor, Abram accepted Sarai's invitation for more amorous attention. He enveloped her in his arms pressing her soft swells against him, and kissed her harder, longer until they were both gasping for breath.

"I love you Abram...I love you...I adore you...," she panted between kisses.

"And I, too, am full of love for you, Sarai. With each visit I am tortured by having only a taste of you. A small morsel ...tantalizing ...tempting ...filling my empty void with only desire for more of you.

"Oh my love, my prince, I wilt like a flower without water when you leave, and I thirst for your return."

"Then we shall become as one so that I may nourish you all your remaining years. I shall taste your sweet nectar, smell your bouquet, and be enhanced by your beauty every day."

"Make the arrangements soon, O staff of my life...very soon," she pleaded then kissed him hard, pressing against him with a promise of fulfillment.

"He is coming, Sarai, he is coming!" shouted the young messenger. " And his train, that follows, numbers far too many men for me to count. And he rides tall upon a large camel arrayed as those rarely seen except carrying great princes or kings."

"And Abram, boy, how is my husband-to-be dressed? What is his appearance?

"Oh my lady, he is magnificently dressed from the jeweled turban upon his head, to his sandals. The richly embroidered tunic he wears with an outer mantle also embroidered...he is truly the personage of a great prince."

"My heart yearns to see him. How fortunate I am to be the bride of a great teacher chosen by the Living God. Men bow low before him. King Nimrod even bowed down to Abram after he survived the fire. I am truly blessed among women."

"You are a beautiful woman, Sarai, deserving of a prince or even a king," Milca complimented as she finished sewing a last touch to Sarai's finery.

"But am I really worthy? Perhaps he marries me only out of loyalty to his brother's family? He was very generous with my dowry...and the gift to mother, as well, was very generous. Perhaps that was because he is my father's younger brother. Oh Milca, will I be sufficient for such a noble lord? Am I attractive enough? Tell me

'Yes?' I want to be beautiful for him. I want him to desire me. But what if he is so godly that he has no desires for love?

"Calm your fears and cease your useless questioning, Sarai. I can assure you that Abram and you are perfect for each other. And as for his appetite for love...how can he resist the tempting delights you offer?" Milca giggled. "I only wish I were as physically endowed as you, my sister. No man can resist you. Just be sure to hold your chin up and arch your back."

Sarai blushed and burst out laughing; a perfect antidote for her feelings of inferiority.

Milca laughed along with her and the two women spent some exciting, joyful minutes sharing thoughts about activities in the marriage bed.

"Come you, Sarai, out to meet him!" came the call from one of Abram's men.

"Oh, Milca!" Sarai exclaimed, surprised that the moment was at hand.

"Yes, my sister, he has come for you. Be of good cheer. Show him he has chosen a happy bride as well as a beautiful one. Now go to him."

Abram looked at the house and watched Sarai appear in the doorway. She stopped there, framed in her beauty, and the sight of her caught Abram's breath.

"You are breath-taking, my bride; words fail me in describing your loveliness. My eyes shall not leave you as we ride to my house; such is your beauty, it entrances me."

Abram was true to his word. He could not keep from staring at Sarai atop her camel during the ride back. The light of the setting sun caught the gold of Sarai's hair and the pink/white of her skin. To his eyes she was aglow with light from her white bridal attire. She rocked with the camel's easy stride. Her posture erect, her smile tantalizing, Sarai acknowledged Abram's stare that whispered intimacies, an overflow of a burning passion.

"Yes, he is a man not a god," she admitted to herself.

Torches were lit as darkness descended and bearers walked ahead to light the way. When Sarai looked back to those following, the trailing procession stretched out a long distance punctuated by a myriad of torches.

Musicians with instruments set the tempo and the lead for hundreds of voices that started singing in celebration.

Dancing began and oral expressions of joy were heard, heightening the mood and activity of the participants. The people in the once calm, sedate procession transformed it into a high-spirited festival, dancing and singing as they passed through the darkness.

The wedding ceremony itself was a simple rite. Sarai, with a veil over her face, stood facing Abram in the court of his home, surrounded by guests. As they watched, Abram reached up and slowly lifted the veil as if to look at her face for the first time. He uttered a joyful cry of surprise, exclaiming: "Oh what beauty!"

The expression was imitated by the groom's brother, Nahor, to the guests nearby. They in turn repeated the groom's delight in his bride until everyone inside and outside the house was satisfied that the groom was pleased with his bride.

Abram raised his arms for quiet so that everyone could hear what he said next. Then he declared: "In the name of the Everliving God, I Abram, son of Terah, enjoin Sarai to me as one flesh. I will love her only and protect her as I do my own body."

"And I, Sarai, cleave to Abram, my husband and my lord. In all things shall I be his helpmate."

Abram took the edge of his mantle and drew it over her so that it covered both of them. This was the seal of their pledge, and he drew her tightly against him.

The excitement of this caress surged through them both and they wanted each other more than ever before. There were other obligations, however, that they knew must come first. The festivities were only beginning and would go on for as long as seven days, maybe longer since there were so many guests.

An eye-squinting bright sun rose on the merrymakers whose festive spirit had hardly diminished. The newlyweds had a private celebration in mind, however, and they met by plan at a particular room on the first floor.

"Were you seen coming here?" Abram asked.

"I do not know," Sarai giggled like a girl delighting in a game of hiding. "I gave excuses to some and went in different directions among the throng until I stole away up here."

"Good," laughed Abram huskily. "Let me bolt the door so we will not be disturbed."

"Hurry Abram! My yearning for you is overflowing!"

Abram threw the bolt, turned and absorbed her in his arms. He kissed her lips, her cheeks, her neck and down the cleavage of her breasts. His left hand supported her back and his right hand caressed the outer garment over her breasts. He was tender with her and cautious. His urges were almost uncontrollable, but this was the first time for both of them and he knew it would be remembered all of their lives as the time that was most special.

"If my husband would be so kind as to turn his back while I undress and lay under the bed clothes? No man has seen me without clothes...and ...I am shy...this first time."

"Very well, my wife, but only on one condition."

"Yes, Abram, what is the condition?"

"No woman has seen me without clothes...and...I am shy...this first time." His eyes lowered for effect and then raised to meet hers. His expression displayed timidity at first, but then...it changed as he smiled...then laughed.

Sarah understood the humor as much as Abram understood that this shyness was only the accepted tradition of all brides who are about to lose their virginity to their husband. Never-the-less Abram turned his back to her and she to him as they disrobed on either side of the bed. He heard the rustle of bedding as she slipped underneath a light sheet of white linen. It felt luxurious against her skin and she could not resist the need to stretch.

Abram turned and watched Sarai's generous breasts swell under the sheet as her body arched. His desire for her welled up to his throat and he could hear his own heart pounding in his ears. Slowly he laid down and turned to face her.

"Love me, Abram, love me...and do not stop," she whispered as he came to her.

During the weeks that followed their wedding, Abram and Sarai were almost inseparable. Sarai took charge of the household servants and saw to it that her planning of home affairs was carried out properly, but she often found time to be near Abram. When he instructed and counseled, Sarai would, if proper, place herself within hearing distance. It was in this way that she shared him with others while being close enough to adore him.

Her adoration was fed by more than his attractive physical appearance and the frequent pang of sexual desire she experienced. That in itself was ample reason to be satisfied; but watching and listening to Abram added a new dimension to him that Sarai found exciting and fulfilling to her intellect. She never interfered nor made herself noticed while he was engaged with others. She waited until she was alone with him, after hours, and then they conversed at length on many facets of life.

Abram was surprised, at first, and a little amused at Sarai's interest in subjects usually reserved for conversations among men. But her mind was bright and she kept him alert, honing his powers of reasoning with her questions.

"Why is it you question so many mysteries, my love?"

"My lord husband is a veritable fountain of wisdom from which I gratefully drink. I delight in feeding from you, to partake of your mental and godly self. In this way I may become more as one with you. This is my pleasure and my ambition," she explained while they were alone one evening.

Abram took Sarai's hands in his and looked into the deep blue pools of her eyes, as if to fathom the mysterious depth of this remarkable woman.

"You are stimulating to my whole being, Sarai, a princess of exceptional beauty, gifted with intelligence, and a heart open to the Everliving's spirit."

He kissed the palms of her hands and placed them against his heart drawing her close to him.

"This is a blessing from our God, Sarai, that we may find shelter, comfort, and joy in each other. I am truly blessed more than any man living for the delight you bring me. You are food for my life. I hunger to feed upon you daily as needful as my lungs feed upon the air that brings me life and energy. I am no longer Abram, alone. I am now Abram/Sarai... a completed man... twice the person I was before I joined you to me. This is a mystery that Lord Noah explained to me. When the Everliving formed Adam, then Eve from Adam, He established marriage.

For the Everliving said: 'It is not good that Adam should be alone; I will make him a helper who is of the same kind.

'But there was not to be found a helper equal to him among the people outside the garden. So the Everliving caused a deep sleep to fall upon Adam, and he slept. The Everliving took one of Adam's ribs, and of that rib, the Everliving made a woman and brought her to Adam.

"And Adam said, 'this is now bone of my bones, and flesh of my flesh. She shall be called Woman because she was taken out of Adam Man. Therefore shall a man of my family leave his father and his mother, and shall cleave to his wife, and they shall be one flesh.'"

"I pray that you will cleave only to me and have no other wives," Sarai remarked timidly. "I wish to share you with no other woman."

Abram drew her to him with an embrace, a long tender kiss, and answered softly: "Worry not over such an impossible thing, Sarai. You shall be my only wife as long as you live. No one could ever be the same as you, my love."

They undressed slowly and caressed tenderly as their mutual compliments were expressed, nurturing yet relishing each other. When their hunger was too great to restrain, he gave himself to her completely. Sarai received him, asking...urgently....

The months went by pleasantly, even blissfully for Abram and Sarai. She lived each day to please him, giving special attention to their nights. Each month, however, brought its time of disappointment. Sarai's womb, empty of a new life conception, broke down its tissue and carried it away in blood.

The months went by bringing only blighted hope for a pregnancy as her cycles repeated their red defeat.

Two years from the time Abram came out of the furnace, Sarai was still without child. She wanted desperately to have children for Abram, especially a large number of sons.

"Oh, how I envy you, sister!" Sarai confessed to Milca with a great sigh. "Already you have one son and another child is being formed in your womb. Your husband, Nahor, is so proud of you."

"Yes, Sarai, it is true, but Abram loves you no less because you have not produced a child. Have you not told me, in secret, how affectionate, yes, how loving he is towards you? Be patient, Sarai, and always be ready and most willing to give him your love."

"Oh, yes, my sister, I am ready and I shall try to be patient," responded Sarai.

Chapter 12
Flight

PART ONE

Two years from the day Abram came out of the furnace, Nimrod was reigning from his throne in Babylon. One night he had a very disturbing dream. He woke up screaming with fright and sat bolt upright in bed. Afraid to return to sleep he paced the floor, then summoned his priests and conjurers. When they were before him he related his dream.

"I was standing with my hosts of warriors in a valley opposite the brick furnaces at Ur. I lifted my head to see a man, in the likeness of Abram, coming out of the furnace. He came and stood before me with a sword in his hand. All of a sudden, he sprang towards me brandishing the sword, but I fled from him, terrified. While I ran, the man threw an egg upon my head, and the egg became a great river. Then I saw that all my warriors sank in that river and died."

Nimrod paused, reflecting on the words that would most accurately recount the next events of the dream.

"I ran, and running ahead of me were three men who escaped with me. I looked at the men and they were clothed in the raiment of kings. Then while we were running, the river again turned into an egg before me. There came, bursting forth from the egg, a young bird which flew at my head and plucked out my eye. I woke up at this moment with a terrified scream, drenched with sweat. What is the import of this dream?" he demanded.

"This is nothing else than the evil of Abram and his seed that will spring up against my lord king in the latter days," replied a conjurer named Anuki. "Behold, the day will come when Abram and his seed, the children of his household, will war with my king, and they will smite all the king's armed host."

"Aha! It is as I suspected. And what of the three men dressed as kings?"

"By running away, you and three other kings will escape death in battle. And the river you saw turn into an egg, out of which came the young bird who plucked out your eye... this means that the seed of Abram will rise up and slay you in the latter days. This is my king's dream and I have given the interpretation. The dream is a forecast and the interpretation which thy servant has given you is true."

"But how can this come to pass? I was very generous to Abram with gifts. I even bowed down before him when he came out of the furnace. Why should he have conflict with me?

Consider, my king, it has been fifty-two years since the birth of Abram when your sages saw this evil was to come. If my king allows Abram to continue living it will be to your injury and that of your kingdom all the days that he lives. All this was known formerly at his birth. Why is it that my king will not slay him so that his evil will be kept from you in the latter days?"

Nimrod became convinced that Anuki's advice was good, so he ordered a troop of his warriors to travel in secret to Ur and seize Abram without giving notice as to who sent them. They were to bring him back to Babylon to suffer death secretly by the king's hand.

Abram was aware that Nimrod was not to be trusted. For that reason he ordered Eliezer, the servant given to him by the king, to remain in the king's court with ears and eyes open to treachery against Abram. Eliezer overheard the king's plot and he immediately set out to warn Abram. He ran to a stable where two camels awaited him day and night, ready for just such a contingency. Supplies of food and water were packed, and off he rode leading the relief camel on a long tether.

It was a distance of more than two hundred miles from Babylon to Ur. Eliezer started before the king's servants and he knew he must stay well ahead in order to warn Abram in time. Realizing that a good, steady pace was best, Eliezer alternated camels every few hours, stopping only after it was too dark and dangerous to continue.

At the first light of dawn each morning, Eliezer was up on one of the camels making a fast pace south.

In the early hours of the fourth day, before a hint of the rising sun could be seen, he came to Abram's house and aroused the household.

Abram came running and asked: "What is it Eliezer? What brings you here at such an hour?"

"It is the king, my lord. He had a terrible dream and Anuki, one his wise men, interpreted it against you." In panicked breaths Eliezer continued. "He warned that the dream represented death to the king, and all his host of warriors, at the hands of you and your seed."

"But I have said nor done nothing against the king. Why would he have such thoughts in his sleep?"

"The priests are jealous and fearful of you, my lord, and the one God you represent. They fear their loss of power over the people and the wealth they enjoy.

"Yes, Eliezer, I understand, but it saddens me. We must flee from here. May the Everliving bless you for your loyalty.

"I am yours to command, my lord. You own my heart as well as my body. I too believe in your God. But let us hasten and leave before the king's men arrive!"

Abram instructed Sarai and a few servants to quickly pack only the valuable and necessary possessions on asses and camels. Within two hours they left, going east from their location at the outer fringe of the city, towards the foothills of the mountains.

By afternoon they approached their destination. It was a large fortified house on a promontory with only one access, a narrow trail wide enough to allow only a single file. A heavy wood gate reinforced with copper, strong enough to withstand a battering ram, was the only entrance through a six-foot thick wall. Abram pounded on a metal striking plate with a stone to announce his presence.

Soon a gruff voice from behind the gate snapped: "Who is there?"

"It is Abram, son of Terah, with Sarai, his wife and their household servants. I am the servant of Lords Noah and Shem, and their Everliving God."

A peekhole opened, a man looked out, and Abram heard the sound of gate bolts releasing and bars sliding free of their locks. Slowly the heavy gate creaked open wide.

"Ah, my lord Abram, please come in. It is an honor to have you here. Please forgive my precaution."

"You did your duty well Ebronah."

"Thank you my lord, I shall announce your presence to the steward."

The huge man picked up a club and hit a large piece of copper plating one time. The reverberation signaled servants of the household that guests had arrived.

This small fort had been built by the servants of Shem many years before. There were times when Shem had stayed here after journeying to Ur on missions of establishing trade. Abram had been here on a few occasions to visit and share his experiences. The staff on duty were instructed by Shem to receive Abram at any time and serve all his needs.

Shem's steward, an elderly man almost as tall as Abram and very thin, came walking quickly to meet him and bowed low.

"Lord Abram, how good it is to see you again. We are honored by your visit. It is by good fortune that Lords Noah and Shem are both here. They will be delighted to know you have come. I shall direct you to your rooms and then inform my lords that you will come to them in the room for dining. Food and drink will be ready for you there."

"Thank you, Shemachiah, I shall compliment you to our lords for your efficient hospitality."

"You are most gracious, Prince Abram. I am just eager to serve my righteous lords as is only my duty."

And Abram hearkened to the voice of Eliezer, and Abram hastened and ran for safety to the house of Noah and his son, Shem, and he concealed himself there and found a place of safety; and the king's servants came to Abram's house to seek him, but they could not find him, and they searched throughout the country and he was not found, and he was not to be met with.

Jasher 12:61

Abram had been at the fortified house of Noah and Shem one month when he sent Eliezer to Terah. On the morning of the second day, three riders on camels left Prince Terah's house. The sky was scorching bright when the trio reached the gate and pounded to arouse the gatekeeper.

A peek-hole opened and Ebronah challenged the men to identify themselves.

"It is Eliezer with Lord Terah, father of Abram. His bodyguard, Shamgar, attends him. Let us in Ebronah; your lords are expecting us."

Later, Terah was sitting in the company of Abram, Noah, and Shem. They had been discussing the conditions of life in the land under the rule of Nimrod. Abram related the story of the king's dream, the interpretation of it by Anuki, and the men sent to bring Abram to his death at the direction of Nimrod.

"Are you not aware, father, that your king's constant desire is to rid my name from the earth? The priests poison him against me because of the power I received from the Everliving at the furnace. They hate me because I exposed their corruption and their useless images. They will never change; their greed is too great. It is now clear to me that I must leave this land and go to a place where my family and I will be safe."

"Where will you go?"

"To the Land of Canaan...to Urusalem, the City of Peace. Our Patriarchs offer us their protection. We shall be free of Nimrod."

Abram caught his father's eyes with an expression of entreaty: "Come with me, father!?"

"But Abram, as a prince of Ur I have so much wealth, comfort and prestige. Why should I give it all up to be with you?"

"Nahor and his family are going with us. If you stay, you and mother will have no family around you; no grandchildren to tell your stories to. What else do you really have that you can depend on in your old age? Nimrod does not give you your wealth, comfort and prestige out of fondness for you.

"Consider the torture and death of Haran. Also remember your embarrassment, all for the king's amusement. It is only for his benefit that he bestows wealth upon you. You administrate for him through fear of him. You have displeased him in the past and you will possibly do so again.

"You can be replaced by a better, younger puppet administrator any time the king chooses. When that happens you will be dispossessed of all your wealth and prestige. You will have no comfort in your old age. You will die lonely, poor and without your loved ones nearby to tend your needs. But if Nimrod continues to honor you as prince over his host, surely the wealth and prestige are only vanities of no consequence, and they cannot avail you at all in the time of the Everliving's anger and punishment.

"Now, therefore, weigh carefully what I have said. You can have a new life of security ahead of you. Let us, as a family, arise and go to the Land of Canaan, out of reach of injury from Nimrod. There we will be free to serve the God who created us, and it will be well with us. Cast away all the vain things that you pursue. Release them; they are nothing to you."

When Abram stopped speaking on this subject, Noah and Shem spoke.

"True are the words that Abram speaks. We confirm them. Think well before you refuse him Terah."

And Terah hearkened to the voice of his son Abram, and Terah did all that Abram said, for this was from the Lord, that the king should not cause Abram's death.

Jasher 12:70

PART TWO

And Terah took his son Abram and his grandson Lot, the son of Haran, and Sarai his daughter-in-law, the wife of his son Abram, and all the souls of his household and went with them from Ur of Casdim to go to the land of Canaan. And when they came as far as the land of Haran they remained there, for it was exceeding good land for pasture, and of sufficient extent for those who accompanied them.

Jasher 13:1

"And how shall we travel undetected, with all our families, servants, animals and goods?" Terah asked.

"We shall pose as a nomadic tribe, traveling to the lands of Haran to find better feeding grounds for our flocks and herds."

"But with all of ours combined we do not own a sufficient quantity of animals."

"That is true, but we shall. We will have a number of our servants buy them from different nomads and bring them to a place bordering the desert. We will look and act like just another tribe of Heber-ew nomads."

"But we have no tents, Abram!"

"We will make them just like our wandering brothers do, out of goat hair."

"My servants know nothing about this sort of thing!"

"We will have help father, much help," Abram responded confidently. " We will pay to have our servants learn how it is done. There is much more for them to learn."

"But who could we trust not to betray us?" Terah asked with a challenge.

"Numerous men have come to me since I was saved from the fiery furnace. Most of them are Heber-ew nomads. I will be working with them to make the necessary arrangements in our transition from princes to nomads. They shall not betray me, I am certain, for several will be coming along."

"How much time will pass before you leave?"

"We will be ready to leave one moon cycle from now. Everything will be arranged slowly enough to be undetectable by Nimrod's spies. Nahor and I will be living unnoticed in tents with our families. You and mother will join us on the day we move slowly with our flocks and herds towards the northwest. It will be a pleasant journey, father, and we shall be safe."

Terah paced the floor and stopped to gaze out a window. The white maze of Ur sprawled out in the distance. Terah's thoughts went there weighing and measuring his past, present and future. Abram's words filled his mind, overflowing into a conscience unused for many years. He was getting old and tired. Nimrod could easily cast him off like an old garment. He had not thought about it before now, but Abram was right, his future was insecure.

The lure of young flesh, on temple love couches, was no longer tempting to him. His ability to perform was greatly diminished. Alcohol had reduced him to a staggering eunuch and contemptible glances were his reward for futile efforts.

His life had become miserable after the death of Haran. Jokes abounded regarding Terah because of his disgrace at the furnace. He seemed to be the laughingstock of Ur. The city held no pleasures for him any more, only bad memories and embarrassment. "Abram is right; it is time to leave," he thought.

Finally, turning back to face his son, he answered. "Very well, Abram, I shall join you. My heart has been softened and your planning seems sound enough. But as for a safe journey...well, we shall see, we shall see."

Early the next morning, Terah set out to return to Ur. Accompanying him was Abram, Sarai, and their servants. They stayed with Terah at his house and put their elaborate plans into motion.

The next day Abram met with his loyal followers and told them what his needs were. "You will be paid for your services from my treasury, but you shall report to my chief steward with an accounting before payment is made. I will owe no man for his labor, goods, or animals. Everyone will be paid a fair price.

"I shall measure your progress each day through reports of my servants who will be dealing with you in my behalf. When the time is appropriate, I will come to you again and inform you of the purpose for these preparations. Meanwhile, say nothing about me or our business to anyone else, even your family members."

The remaining fifty-eight men, all Heber-ew nomads, swore allegiance to Abram and pledged their secrecy.

Servants from Abram, Terah, and Nahor were assigned to live and work with the nomads to try and learn their way of life. Abram knew it would not be an easy transition. Servants used to the comforts and conveniences of city life would have a difficult adjustment to austere transient living. His confidence never wavered, however, and he pressed forward with a positive determination that conquered all obstacles.

The work went as Abram planned. Loyal Heber-ew nomads worked to help produce the shelters, furnishings, food and transportation required for the expanded community.

Cloth for the tents was manufactured from coarse hair of goats and camels; the black or brown color was preferred. Money was no object of concern, therefore the cloth was of good quality, impervious to the rain and a protection from the sun's rays. (It was superior to material commonly used for tents in modern times.)

After being woven into cloth of the required width, the material was stitched together and provided with cords and loops, then the tent-cloth was spread over poles of about the height of a tall man, and securely fastened to the ground by tent pins. The size of the tents varied according to the taste and requirements of those who occupied them.

Some tents were round in form, but most were rectangular. When spread, they had the appearance of the hull of a ship turned up side down. The sides of the tents were covered by either the same material or with mats.

Interiors were divided into separate apartments, generally two or three, by means of curtains fastened to the parallel rows of poles holding up the tent. One portion would be assigned to the men, another to the women, and where there was a third, it would be set apart for the servants.

Terah and Abram, being of the highest stations were given separate tents for their servants as a mark of wealth.

Furniture for the tents was a drastic departure from that which the city dwellers were used to. It was very simple and portable, composed mostly of mats and skins. In the tents of Terah and Abram there were rugs of fine quality. These ground covers would serve as chairs and tables. Couches would be made with the addition of skins. Other articles found within the tents were: sacks for grain, pack saddles and tack, a hammer for driving tent pins, a hand mill for grinding grains, a few copper pans, and oil lamps. Also included was a cooking stove, shaped like a large inverted pot, for baking bread. Distended skins containing water and curd, leather buckets for drawing water, and bowls for receiving milk were other indispensable items.

Abram visited each of the trusted families, every few days, to praise and encourage them for their efforts. Work progressed well and at the end of the fourth week, the new tents were ready to be occupied.

Gathering the fifty-eight Heber-ew men together, Abram spoke to them.

"I have asked you here first to compliment you on the very satisfactory way you all labored to furnish the items I asked of you. There is no doubt you have wondered why I commissioned you to produce all these things."

There was a murmur of agreement among the men, and then silence as they hushed to hear the reason they had patiently waited for.

"The king sent his men, some moons ago, to capture, and bring me to Babylon so that I could be slain by his own sword."

The men reacted with shock, considering Abram was treated with great respect and honor by the king.

"As you can see," Abram continued, "his men failed to find me. They may still seek me; although my servants have asked people here and there, about the city, for the past few weeks and no one inquires about me with silver in his palm.

"I shall move my family and the families of my father and brother away from Ur as soon as possible. We will live and travel as Heber-ew nomads, avoiding possible detection by the king's spies."

"If I may be so bold, master, I and my family would like to join you, if you would permit it," spoke one of Abram's disciples.

"May the Everliving's blessings of wealth and many sons be upon your head, Uzal," Abram declared so that all might hear."

The memory of Abram's miracle in the furnace was still vivid. The remaining men began to realize that Abram, representative of the powerful Everliving God, was freely giving a blessing of wealth and many sons to any man who would travel with him. Surely his God would protect them all from the king. What was there to worry about?

The camp buzzed with conversation as each man discussed this marvelous opportunity with his neighbor. Out of the din came requests from each and every one of them urging Abram to allow them to join with him.

Satisfied with the reactions of the men, Abram raised his hands for quiet. With their attention riveted on him, he spoke.

"My friends, I welcome you all to my side. The condition I must impose, however, is this. I must be accepted as your chieftain with the power of life and death over you, as is due any lord. My word must not be challenged, nor my law refused. I will be your goel, your protector, and you shall be my people. As I am blessed by my God, the Everliving, you will be blessed as well. There is no other way. Those of you who will not accept this arrangement shall stay at this encampment when we leave and nothing further will be said. Those who accept me will prepare to leave in a few days."

Abram left them and went to instruct his father, brother, nephew and their families concerning their new homes and their kin now allied to them.

During the next day, servants began leading asses carrying bundles of rugs, clothing, and other portable possessions out of the city from the houses of Terah, Nahor, and Lot.

Very early the following morning, Abram and all the family members except Terah, left the city behind them for the last time.

When they arrived at the nomad encampment, they found all the tents were staked down in a circle as an enclosure for the protection of numerous flocks and herds at night.

Abram assigned Nahor, Lot, and Eliezer, with their families, to their tents. Nomad neighbors on either side were ordered to assist them in adjusting to the ways of tent living.

Two days later Abram was satisfied that all was in readiness for the move northward. He sent Eliezer's sons with a message to Terah. He was to leave lamp lights on in his house and come with the boys at dusk. The encampment would move the next morning.

Terah arrived laden with wealth he refused to leave behind and was shown to his tent. Abram came, shortly afterward, and pointed out the unique features of nomadic living. Terah's tent had the most luxurious furnishings of all; Abram made sure of it. He knew Terah was vain and un-predictable, and it would take some time for him to accept that Abram, and not he, was chief of this tribe. Abram realized, however, he must defer to his father for advice, weigh it against his own opinions, and then direct the people according to his own conscience.

The next morning Abram arose early and went to his father's tent. Terah was reluctant to rise from his bed. Seldom did he ever awake until the sun had risen fairly high in the sky. Abram's insistence eventually won out and Terah showed himself at the tent door, grumbling and swearing about the rights of a lord. Abram ignored this effrontery by endeavoring to distract him with prospects of delicious food being prepared for the morning meal.

"It is good for our people to see their lords up early, especially when there is so much to do this day. Join me now; together we shall inspect the encampment. You will notice, father, that the people are well provisioned with food, transportation, weapons and all necessary articles for living on the move."

A feeling of satisfaction welled up in him as he walked from tent to tent, proving to his father that the promise he made a month ago had been fulfilled.

Outside Nahor's tent a servant girl was mixing dough in an earthenware kneading trough. At Lot's tent another servant girl was churning butter in a sheepskin bag, hung like a cradle from a tripod of three sticks. She pulled on a cord, attached to the bag, with short, quick movements until the cream, flavored with scented herbs to give it a bouquet, began to bubble. Moving on they approached the door of Uzal's tent from which an appetizing aroma escaped. Terah's nostrils twitched, then sniffed, again and again.

"Mmmm, what is that delicious aroma?" he asked.

"Let us find out," Abram replied with a smile on his lips. They approached a girl on her knees in front of a strange cooking device. The girl looked up from her work when the two men approached and at the sight of Abram she bowed her head to the ground.

"It is a good morning, when two men see an attractive girl, cooking," Abram commented to his father.

"Especially when the food smells so tempting to the taste, and a lord's stomach is so empty," Terah added.

"Rise girl," Abram ordered mildly. "What is it you are cooking that smells so good in the morning air?"

"Barley cakes, my lord. Would you honor this tent and its servant by accepting some cakes?"

"Indeed we would," Terah answered. "Look Abram, that upside-down looking pot is actually an oven. Those notches in the walls feed air to a fire within; how clever."

Terah watched, genuinely interested, as the girl plastered dough on the heated sides. They cooked evenly, held on by rims over the notches. When the cakes were baked on one side they fell away into the girl's hands. She turned them over and reapplied them to bake on the other side.

Abram smiled broadly at Terah's concentrated attention on this simple cooking chore that was repeated daily.

"May I serve you some in cream, my lords?"

"Just one or two for the taste," Abram replied.

"Ahh... my stomach would appreciate more than a taste," Terah added almost eagerly.

The cakes were freshly hot, crumbly and delicious with the cream. Both men were enjoying their portions when Uzal and his wife returned.

Seeing the lords at their tent they hurried along and then stopped before them bowing low.

"I commend you for your fine hospitality, Uzal. Your servant honors you with fine cooking and generous service," Abram complimented.

Terah belched, and added: "Good, very good. You must teach my servants how this is done."

"My lords are indeed most gracious with your praise. We are but your humble servants who give thanks to be in your service. Please, have more cakes and enjoy them if it pleases you!" Uzal exclaimed. He laid down the fire's fuel he had been carrying and ordered his servant to hurry. Abram refused, politely, but Terah held out his bowl for more, still licking the remnants of the first bowl from his lips.

For most of the day Abram inspected the camp with his father. Terah was not interested in how the nomads lived or made things. His chief steward and servants always tended to those details. He enjoyed once again, however, the respect of people for his lordship. All around him people bowed with great respect and were quick to serve at his beckoning.

"Maybe Abram was right," he mused. "Mmm, the head of my own tribe; this could serve my needs quite nicely. Maybe Abram really does have a special purpose after all: to serve my needs in old age, to build a nation of our own? Who is to know?"

Completing their inspection and Terah's familiarization, they returned to Abram's tent in the afternoon. Sarai was supervising servants in the evening meal preparation. She had ordered a lamb slaughtered earlier and now it was skewered on a spit, rotated over heated rocks by a servant. While turning it he basted the meat with herbs in oil. Animal fat, combined with oil, sizzled and smoked, flavoring the meat.

The smell made Terah's mouth water and Abram's belly growl with hunger.

"Meat is not a part of the ordinary diet of our nomad brothers, like it is commonly found at your table father. Today is a special day, however, because it is the last we will spend in Ur; tomorrow we leave. Tonight we celebrate with a feast! We share this meat with you and mother, as well as the families of Nahor, Lot, Uzal, and our servants.

A short time later the families of Nahor, Lot, and Uzal arrived with bread, butter, vegetables, nuts and dates, and cakes and cream for the best meal they would have for some time.

"I cannot remember when I have eaten so much tasty food," Abram sighed patting his stomach. "I wonder if it is because I am living out in the open once again? My thoughts travel back in time forty-three years when I lived in a cave." For almost an hour he relived his experiences and stopped telling stories only when he noticed Terah had nodded off to sleep.

Once again Abram praised the food, as well as Sarai and the servants who prepared it. He was a contented husband and chieftain, pleased that his planning had gone so well. The sun was setting and the crimson glare in the west flooded the land with rapidly fading glory.

"Look at the sky," he gestured with a sweep of his hand. "This is a beautiful closing to a perfect day. The Everliving smiles down on us with his goodness."

Chapter 13
To the City of Haran

The next morning, tent pins were pulled, tents folded, utensils, furnishings, clothing and food were packed onto asses and camels. Here and there complaints and curses could be heard as men struggled to heap their belongings on the back of animals who balked and whined their reluctance to be so burdened.

Asses pawed the ground, staggering, kicking up dust, bucking and hee-hawing to shake off their unbalanced loads. Camels refused to rise up. When they were forced to, the unfortunate beasts staggered as if drunk or drugged and soon collapsed with a great bellow of protest throwing their riders like sacks of grain.

Looking around him, Abram realized that the tribe might never leave unless he found a solution to the problems at hand. He went to Uzal, who seemed most knowledgeable about this way of life, and sought his assistance.

"What can we do about this, Uzal?"

"Lord Abram, I suggest the servants of your families come among those of us who are experienced at packing and loading animals. We will show them how to do it properly and how much weight the animals will be able to accept," he said with a smile.

It was obvious to Abram that Uzal and his people were finding the spectacle quite entertaining. He had to admit, that from their point of view, the sight of city dwellers packing up like nomads must be quite a humorous sight. Unfortunately, he could not allow himself to share in their humor, for the situation was serious. He knew they would be fording canals and the great Euphrates River itself.

If the animals were poorly packed and overburdened, a family's food, shelter and belongings were in jeopardy. Any loss to one family would be a loss to all, since all would have to give up something to make up for what was lost.

"Uzal, I will call an assembly of the men immediately," Abram replied. "Gather your experienced men to you and join me in the center of the camp."

"As you command, lord," Uzal responded with respect, the smile disappearing from his face.

Abram took his ram's horn and blew one long call for assembly. The men came to him, some sweating and red-faced with frustration. He stood in the center of their gathering and assuaged their declarations of defeat.

"I have ordered Uzal to bring experienced men forward who will direct you how to pack your animals properly. You will listen to them and do as they suggest so that you will not lose your possessions. He who refuses out of pride and embarrasses himself on route, by losing his food and shelter, will answer to me and pay a high price! Now come forward with your difficulty. It is no shortcoming to be inexperienced. It is a matter of disobedience, however, to ignore my command. The penalty may be hunger and exposure. I have spoken." Abram turned a deaf ear to complaints and walked away to inspect his own packing.

Sarah rode on a camel next in line behind Abram. Following in single file behind Sarai's camel were all the other camels and asses...connected one to another by ropes that swayed in rhythm to the measured pace. Some had riders and the rest carried other burdens. This long procession formed what might be called the backbone of the caravan.

On both sides of it, like a torso, were herds of cattle and flocks of sheep, moved and guarded by drovers and their dogs. The oxen led, followed by cows with calves, then goats and sheep. They meandered along, diligently chewing anything left growing since preceding herds had come this way.

Abram looked back now and then to confirm the well being of the procession. Small children were put into baskets that were tied together with rope, and hung on both sides of the backs of asses like saddlebags. Abram smiled as he watched their inquisitive heads peer over the rims. Children who were a little older sat either in front of or behind their mothers astride asses.

Older boys and girls walked and ran along the caravan file vying with each other by throwing clods of dirt at birds and poking into bushes in search of eggs. And so the hours of the day passed, harmlessly, with the monotonous rhythm of hoof beats lulling many to sleep under the hot sun. Then the time came when Abram sounded off two blasts on his ram's horn and waved a circle in the air.

The sun was low in the west and only an hour of sunlight remained in which to set up camp.

The backbone of the caravan began curving into a circle that encompassed the herds and flocks on its western side within its perimeter. Those on the eastern side were driven around Abram, who was slowly arcing the head of the column to join full circle with the tail.

"Ahh, what a marvelous sight," he sighed. The working together of a tribe, its men and animals preparing for night camp under the golden heavens."

Abram thought about the importance of every person cooperating in doing their part, and doing it well. "The actions of one affects all others in our community. I must remember that," he observed.

The selection of halting places was governed by availability of water. Abram had turned inland from the river to avoid being seen by anyone in passing who might recognize him. In summertime the numerous wadis were dry courses striping across the land, but at this season they still retained some moisture. When the need arose, men and boys dug a shallow well in a dry bed. After awhile it would fill with water oozing up from under the surface. Each evening, when the caravan stopped for the night, a number of these shallow wells would be dug; by morning they would be full enough for the people and all the animals to drink from.

Abram had detected no sign of discovery by the king's spies since he came out of hiding. And so he allowed the caravan to travel unhurriedly so the cattle and sheep grazed as they meandered along. Abram had taken a course farther to the west than normally done by nomads, in order to avoid cultivated fields and people. Ahead, in the distance, he spied a lone figure riding his way. Even though he could not identify the rider, Abram knew who it was. He had sent this man off on other scouting trips to locate the best overnight sites, and here he was reporting back.

"Greetings Uzal! Blessings be upon you."

"Thank you, gracious lord, I have good news. I have found a large, abandoned stock pen in the midst of cleared ground suitable for our encampment. I believe water is also available there not far below the surface. It is only about two hours travel from here."

"Excellent, excellent. Take the lead; I will spread the good news."

146

From time to time Uzal discovered old stock folds, which were capable of accommodating the herds. The surrounding grounds were a suitable place for the tribe to bed down for a night.

Now that a campsite had been selected, the caravan's pace quickened measurably. One-fourth the time was removed from Uzal's estimate. The herds sensed that another day's travel was coming to a close. With heads up, their eating only sparse, they bunched up for the last segment and surged ahead.

Arriving at the grounds, drovers and dogs directed the herds into a large yard that was walled with rocks on three sides. Drovers closed the remaining open side with thorn bushes to form a removable barrier.

Guards were posted and relieved twice during the night. They talked and shouted to one another to keep awake and to testify to their watchfulness. The noise also discouraged wild animals from attacking.

Looking at these stone enclosures, Abram reasoned they were evidence that the caravan was moving along an ancient track made by nomad tribes. Turning his thoughts to the past, he reflected upon the people of past generations who had laboriously collected the many rocks and built these shelters for generations to come. Perhaps his own forefathers had a hand in it.

Forty-five days had passed since their departure from Ur. Abram dozed lightly, lulled by his camel's steady rocking pace, as the afternoon sun scorched the Arabian Steppe.

"Lord Abram! Lord Abram!"

The shouts woke Abram with a start, jerking him erect.
"What? Who calls?"

"It is Zaccur, servant of Terah. Your father sent me to beckon you to him. He says it is a matter of great importance!"

Abram ordered Zaccur to assume the lead, and rode back to see his father who was looking out with keen interest at the surrounding territory. Abram reined in his camel and with worry written on his face he asked:

"What is wrong, father? Do you sense that we are in some danger?"

"Possibly, Abram, just possibly.... We will soon be approaching a place where the twin rivers Tigris and Euphrates, come so close that perhaps a day's journey is all it takes from one to the other. Nimrod's border army often patrols this region, even out into the desert. It may well be the king's best chance to discover us

...and his last. Beyond the border, Assyrians dwell. Later we will come to the territory of Padam Aram and be among our Aramean relations. Only there shall we be in total safety, beyond the power and control of Nimrod. Yes, it will be on this side of the border that we may come under attack. Here we can be easily found."

"Ah, my lord father is wise. I shall prepare our people immediately," Abram responded.

Raising a horn to his lips and blowing a signal, Abram called the caravan to halt. A second call was blown. Every man armed himself with battle weapons and stood ready.

Upon Abram's command, flocks and herds were driven into a condensed pack.

Riders closed up the distance between themselves.

All of those who walked and played came close to the riders. Young boys armed their slings and little girls looked for stones as ammunition.

Abram watched approvingly as his tribe of shepherds mobilized into a small army; even its youth were ready to defend the tribe.

"What more loyalty could a chieftain want", he said enthusiastically. "Who ever comes against us, we will meet them bravely. I pray for the might of the Everliving in every sword, spear, arrow, and stone, to vanquish our enemies!"

Terah armed himself and watched Abram exercise his authority over the tribe. An electric tingle of fatherly pride ran up his back and over his scalp, covering him like a pleasant dip in a pool. Inhaling a deep breath he sighed with resignation. A little jealous of Abram's strength and authority, Terah realized he was diminished to the role of merely a counselor to a tribal chieftain. Terah's fatherly pride won a battle over his self-centeredness. This was the first time he truly realized he was growing old - too old especially to compete with his own son.

The temperature was extremely hot as Abram guided the caravan through the open expanse of shadeless country. A sluggish stillness lay over the land as they pushed along, tense and on guard. The hours dragged on suspensefully as every man, woman, and child strained their eyes against the haze of heat, alert for any approaching group.

The sun was sinking below the western horizon when they stopped and formed their encircling camp for the night. Abram banned all open fires except those used for cooking. He did not want their presence discovered by Nimrod's border army through an abundance of open campfires.

The number of guards on watch was doubled. Everyone else slept fully clothed and armed, prepared to leap for the defense of the tribe.

A yelping of jackals pierced the night's silent shroud, followed by a worried bleating of sheep and lowing of cattle. The men on guard laughed, as was their custom, over this common night sound. They sensed no real threat. Their light-heartedness calmed the flocks and herds...and the night wore on...uneventfully.

Sarai, and other women under her authority, were up at the first hint of the new day. Working in the dim light they prepared a morning meal. The smell of freshly baked cakes awoke Abram's appetite and then his consciousness.

"So, my husband is awake," Sarai cooed softly.

"What a delicious way you have of raising me out of bed, my sweet wife. Most of me aches to sleep on, but my nose and my stomach have an alliance with my mind. They overcome this tired body, and now my whole being is under the power of yearning to eat...to taste what has conquered me."

"Last night you gave orders that everyone in the tribe was to rise at the first hint of daybreak," Sarai reminded. Now how would it look for your people to see you still sleeping when they are ready to travel on?" Without waiting for an answer she added: "And I want you full of strength and your mind on the battle, if we should come to it, and not on your empty stomach," Sarai smiled hiding her inner fears.

"How right you are, good and loyal wife," Abram smiled briefly in return. As the burden of a chieftain's responsibility returned to his awareness, his expression became serious.

The cold night air still had a nip to it, causing Abram to shiver when he rose from his bed. Temperatures dipped to 45 degrees at night and increased to 105 degrees during afternoons. In the regions of Padam Aram temperatures would be even more extreme.

Sarai served her husband hot bread of fine meal, butter and cheese, along with a bowl of grain that had been hulled, boiled, drained and served hot with honey and milk.

"Ahh, the food warms me and gratifies the hunger in my greedy stomach. Sarai, how good it is to have a diligent wife," Abram complimented.

The eastern sky was tinged with only a hint of warmth. Abram's people and flocks and herds moved as black silhouettes in the dim umber of early morning light as the caravan resumed its travel. The sun rose, climbed the eastern mountains and blazed its arcing course through a cloudless sky parching the Shinar Plain.

The caravan was casting long afternoon shadows when Abram saw the tiny outlines of a substantial body of men in the distance. He watched and waited as the distance lessened somewhat... then he determined they were coming towards the caravan from the northeast. Pulling a horn from his pack, he blew warning signals, ordering his people to close up the column and prepare themselves for battle.

Shielding his eyes to see as clearly as possible, he strained to discern the enemy's numerical strength. As the moments flew by he estimated but could not yet see well enough to count.

Copper, conical headpieces could now be seen, reflecting sunlight like the sparkle of many signal fires. Bronze weapons flashed a warning as the cutting edges of spears, swords and axes caught the amber glow.

Terah and Shamgar rode up next to Abram and he felt grateful for their presence. Looking towards the oncoming threat, Terah diligently strained to see details of their uniforms that would reveal just who they were.

"Unless these old eyes are deceiving me, those are not Nimrod's soldiers," he remarked almost casually.

"They are not?" Abram replied both astonished and greatly relieved. "But, then, who are they? And what do they want with us?"

"They are Assyrian border guards, my son, and if we wave and smile at them like friendly cousins, they will believe we are simply the nomads we appear to be."

The strong hands and muscular arms of professional soldiers flexed in ominous readiness as they approached the 'nomads'. The Assyrian detachment filed alongside the slow-moving travelers, eyeing appreciatively their affluence and their women. The commander had orders to be friendly to all caravans but to be wary of sneak incursions by Babylonian troops. He separated himself from his main force and with two subordinates strode up to confront Abram, Terah, and Shamgar.

Abram first signaled for a halt and then followed Terah's example of holding his right arm up, empty-handed with fingers spread.

"Peace, commander," Terah bellowed in a passable Assyrian dialect.

"Peace to you in return," replied the Assyrian. "What brings you to the territory of the God Asshur?"

"We are only humble nomads, my lord, seeking pasture for our flocks and trade with our neighbors," answered Terah disarming the officer with a deep bow of respect, carried out in unison with Abram and Shamgar.

The officer acknowledged their deference to him with a bow that was little more than a nod of his head. He sensed, with an ability acquired through years of experience in dealing with people, that these were not the usual nomadic leaders he was accustomed to dealing with.

"Their bearing, speech and fine linen attire sets them apart," he thought. "There is extreme confidence written in the features of the older one. His attitude has a hint of haughtiness usually displayed more fully by kings, priests and noblemen. The savage features on the huge one bears the awesome stature of a protector, despite his many years. The younger one has the eyes of a wise man that see into a man's inner thoughts and strip him bare of all secrets. A strange threesome, strange indeed. But trouble is not what I want with nomads, so I will give none. And I will keep my head where it should remain by watching what I say and do. Judging from the looks of these three and every man with them, we would not fare very well in a battle with them."

Addressing himself to Terah the commander asked: "What city or town do you come from?"

"No city or town, my lord, we roam the land wherever grass grows at the desert's edge," answered Terah, suspicious of the officer.

"It appears that you travel from the southwest through the lands of Nimrod, King of Babylon and Ur."

"Ah, you may be right, commander," agreed Terah.

"Have you been confronted by Babylonian soldiers in your travel across their border?"

"No, my lord, we have met with no soldiers at all, save your troop. We are a peaceful tribe; respectful of property rights and honest in our trade."

"Yes, yes, but how did your caravan get through Babylonian territory without being challenged and taxed in leaving?"

ABRAHAM Father of Many Nations

"The gods are with us, my lord. The gods are with us," Terah replied.

"Apparently so, apparently so," the officer mimicked, aware that he would have little success in getting information from these nomads who were friends of no one and a society unto themselves.

After an exchange of courtesies, the officer returned to his troop and marched them southward, passing by the length of the caravan.

Now that they were out of danger, Abram called for Uzal to join him. Riding alongside, Uzal saluted Abram and asked: "How may I serve my lord?"

"Uzal, are you familiar with the best route to Mari?"

"Why, yes, lord, and Vashti, my beautiful one who drinks, knows the way better than I," he said patting the camel's neck.

"Very well then, I give the lead position to you and Vashti," Abram ordered.

"I...that is, we are honored my lord."

Uzal took the lead and immediately began a one-way conversation that Abram found both amusing and informative.

"Vashti, oh queen of camels, you know the way to our northern home where the grass is green, the water cool and fresh, fruits you can eat...all you can eat and drink Vashti. Take us there, my pet, and you may rest in the cool shade feasting on your favorite foods. You remember your way do you not? Now be good and make straight the way. Do as Uzal commands and I will give you delicious sweet treats at the end of each day. Yes, Vashti, sweet treats you love so well and will do anything to get. Sweet treats reserved for only you."

"Abram listened to this odd communication between two seasoned travelers. The master talked and his camel reacted. Abram was not as experienced and capable with animals as Uzal, but he was open-minded and intuitive. He watched the camel carefully and was amazed to see what he thought were reactions that indicated understanding of what was expected, and the rewards for good guidance.

"Mari, my lord, Mari!" Uzal exclaimed.

Peering across miles of sun-hazed desert, Abram strained his eyes to see what his guide pointed to.

"You have eyes like a hawk, Uzal. I see nothing but waves of heat."

"It is a faint white line on the horizon ahead and to the right. The ziggurat stands tall as a limestone mountain."

As the hours dragged on, the city's skyline gradually took on more and more shape before Abram's eyes. He tried to remember Mari as it was to him, as a boy of eleven, forty-two years ago, and wondered if it would be the same. What had become of the children he played with at the caravanserai?

An uneasiness was building among the animals. It started when the scent of water was first detected by Vashti. Her grunts of recognition and quickening of pace were picked up by other camels in the column, then by the herds and flocks.

The caravan stretched out, from its surging forward members, and expanded to twice its normal length.

"Uzal!" Abram called out from his position behind the lead camel.

"Yes, my lord?"

"Move ahead with speed and locate a good place to pitch our tents with access to water."

"As you command, Lord Abram," Uzal responded, untying the rope from his pack-rack. Handing the loose end to Abram he turned and urged: "On Vashti! Aieee! On to Mari!"

The camel shot forward like a lizard racing for a hiding place.

"It is only right that we drink first, heh, Vashti? After all, we led them here, is that not so? Ho, ho, ho, you surprise me old girl, I did not think you had this much energy left in you. Aieee ya!"

Coming abreast of the city of Mari, Abram ordered encampment just beyond its rich cultivated fields. Grass was plentiful and water easily available. To the east Mari sprawled like a great multi-faceted jewel bedecking a green setting of the Plain. In the fading afternoon sunlight it changed from a brilliant white to yellow during the time it took to set up the caravan's encampment.

Before tents were erected, Abram ordered six drovers to a canal. They beat the reeds at the water's edge, with their long sticks, and blew horns to scare off any possible predator that might be lurking in the dense cover there.

Terrified by this disturbance, waterfowl left their sanctuary. Squawking and flapping their wings, they took flight, circling overhead, uncertain where to go. Balancing on air currents in the zenith high above, falcons and hawks were hovering...waiting. Now their waiting was over and they plummeted like dark stones out of the sky, hitting their prey with deadly accuracy.

Men and boys from every family came to the canal's cleared space and filled skins and bladders with water for drinking, cooking, and washing.

Mari was now glowing an evening orange when herdsmen drove the animals, bulls first, towards the water. Next came cows and calves, then heifers. Goats and sheep followed at the end.

By the time all animals were driven back into camp, the rapidly fading glory of a crimson sun cast a purple hue over the Plain.

Cooking fires sprang alive from hot coals and embers carried in pots, protected and nourished all day. For a woman to beg embers from another was to admit gross neglect. A servant could be whipped, a wife embarrassed.

The land turned gray and cold. Jackals, the first harbingers of night, yapped in the growth outside the camp. Dogs of the tribe answered with angry barks.

Bats flitted swiftly and quietly around the tents. Cattle, sheep and goats, their thirst satiated, voiced routine sounds then quieted down for a night's rest.

"Ah, Sarai," Abram sighed, "life in a tent on the Shinar Plain, with my tribe around me is far more beautiful and joyous than life in a city."

"It is not so joyous for the women who must tolerate dirt on their bodies and in their food, clothing, and bedding. Cleanliness is impossible, my husband. Bathing is forbidden, for water is too scarce in the desert. Water is plentiful here. Let us bathe tomorrow, my lord. Let all the woman bathe and wash the desert out of our clothes and bedding."

Abram was embarrassed by Sarai's request because it was almost a plea. He mentally condemned himself for not considering his wife's needs. A bit of advice given him at his wedding feast now came to mind. 'A contented wife is a soothing balm rubbed on a tired body. A discontented wife is a burr on a man's seat.'

"It shall be as you desire, Sarai. I will order it after the morning meal when the heat of day will warm you and dry the washed clothing. More than that, after the women are done, I shall command every man and boy to follow me into the water and bathe as well. The next day we shall visit the city and trade for goods, weapons, and fresh food. It shall not be said by city dwellers that the tribe of Abram is an unclean people."

Sarai became both proud and grateful for her husband's wisdom. He had sensed the tribe needed a diversion from the dulling effects of a long, sustained journey. On alternating days, he allowed portions of his people to visit the city. It was exciting for them to see its sights, trade in its markets, and listen to storytellers weave tales of adventure, heroism, fate, justice, conquest, victory and defeat.

The camp buzzed with excitement in conversation, laughter, music and dancing. Spirits soared. Children played gaily. Husbands and wives frolicked. Romance was in the air and new alliances were formed. It was a time of contentment for everyone.

Seven days after they arrived, Abram's people folded their tents, packed up and started towards Haran.

Chapter 14
The Covenant

When Abram and Terah arrived in Haran with their very substantial caravan, they were a cause for celebration among the relations of Heber. The newcomers were an impressive, worthwhile addition to the community of Heberews. Presents were exchanged. Feasting and celebrating carried on as news reached more and more kin about the arrival of Prince Terah and Prince Abram. Everyone was most anxious to see for themselves the friend of the Everliving, this Abram, who by his God's power miraculously survived three days and nights in the intensive fire of King Nimrod's furnace.

People came and examined Abram. Crowds listened with wonder as he spoke of the truth and power of the Everliving God to create, to save, and to bless. They found that Abram was upright with men because his God expected this quality of conduct from all who worshipped the Everliving. It was clear that Almighty God was with Abram in all that he did. Some of the Heberews were touched in the heart by the spirit in Abram's instruction and they joined him.

Terah, Abram, Nahor, Lot and their families had resided in the land of Aram for three years when something extraordinary happened to Abram very early one morning. He had been peacefully asleep through the night when before dawn a voice spoke to him.

"ABRAM! ABRAM, SON OF TERAH, LISTEN TO MY VOICE!"

"What? Who calls me...?" Abram called out in his vision, a dream very real and intense, yet he was unaware of who addressed him. He opened his eyes wide and blinked, probing the darkness for the man who called him.

Suddenly, a blinding white light appeared. It was so bright that Abram shielded his eyes, half-blind, straining to see who or what was causing such a miraculous phenomenon. It was very frightening, even to Abram, a brave and educated man not given to believing in evil genies or the like.

"Who are you?" he cried out. "What do you want of me?"

"BE NOT AFRAID, ABRAM, 1 AM YAHVAH, THE EVERLIVING GOD WHO DELIVERED YOU FROM THE FIRE AND ALL YOUR ENEMIES. 1 BROUGHT YOU OUT OF UR AND PROVIDED SAFE PASSAGE FOR YOUR PEOPLE. NOW, THEREFORE, IF YOU WILL HEARKEN TO MY VOICE AND KEEP MY COMMANDMENTS AND MY LAWS, THEN 1 WILL CAUSE YOUR ENEMIES TO FALL BEFORE YOU. 1 WILL MULTIPLY YOUR SEED LIKE THE STARS OF HEAVEN, AND 1 WILL SEND MY BLESSING UPON ALL THE WORKS OF YOUR HANDS AND YOU WILL LACK NOTHING.

"ARISE NOW. TAKE YOUR WIFE AND ALL THAT YOU HAVE BELONGING TO YOU AND GO TO THE LAND OF CANAAN AND REMAIN THERE. 1 WILL BE THERE TO BLESS YOU AS YOUR GOD."

The voice stopped speaking. The light departed in a swift upward flight and Abram sat up quickly, fully awake.

"Was it a dream? How could it be? It was so real! That voice...the voice of the Everliving...sounded like a multitude of kings...speaking as one, with the utmost authority! And his form...too holy to be seen, emanating light too bright for human eyes. Yet I, Abram son of Terah, have heard and I have seen that which is impossible to be heard and seen... the Everliving God, YAHVAH...creator of the heavens and earth! Yes, He spoke to me...ME, in a vision! And the covenant He offers me...such promises...such promises! My descendants shall be multiplied as numerous as the stars of heaven!

With that thought in mind, he leaped to his feet and ran out of the tent. The clear black night displayed a dazzling multitude of heavenly bodies, twinkling with light. Abram looked up and scanned the sky from one horizon to the other, covering the four parts of heaven. The impact of the holy covenant struck him with such awe that his legs shook, and he went to his knees.

"The Everliving promised me...he promised me..." His voice breaking with emotion, he pounded his chest with clenched fists for emphasis. The physical effect imparted a reality to the vision he had experienced.

"He will cause my enemies to fall before me...He will send His blessing upon all the works of my hands...and I will lack nothing...if I will listen to His voice and obey His commandments and his laws...obey Him..."

Abram stayed there on his knees savoring the ecstasy of his godly encounter until the pale light of dawn outlined black tribal tents against the eastern sky. Then he rose to his feet full of determination and a new, greater spirit of authority and purpose.

Abram went to Sarai, in her separate chamber of his tent, and awakened her: "Sarai ... Sarai!"

She awoke with a start, surprised to see her husband kneeling at her side in the semi-darkness. "What...what is it?"

"I have received a visit from the Everliving God, the almighty whose name is YAHVAH, and whose voice is more magnificent than the voices of a hundred kings speaking as one."

Sitting bolt upright, Sarai's eyes widened, startled and shocked. "Am I awake? Is it really my husband who tells me this? Or am I still asleep having a dream so real I am unable to know the difference?"

"You are awake, my wife. Here, let me prove it to you."

Reaching out with his strong hands, Abram gently took Sarai by the shoulders and brought her against him in an embrace. He kissed her boldly on the lips, holding until she gasped for breath.

"Now do you believe you are awake?"

"Ohh! Yes, yes!" she panted. Now tell me, what message did you receive from the Everliving whose name is Yahvah?"

"We must leave this place and go to the Land of Canaan. He has made great promises to me, if I obey Him. The greatest of them all is this: He said, **'I will multiply your seed like the stars of heaven...'**. Do you understand what that means?"

"I will no longer be barren?"

"Yes, Sarai, yes!"

"Ohh, Abram, if it is only possible?"

"Believe it Sarai, believe it."

"I shall, Abram, oh I shall!"

"Good, now let us reveal this vision to my tribe and then make preparations to leave."

Abram sent messengers to the houses of Terah, Nahor, and Lot, asking them to come immediately on an urgent matter. Next he called for an assembly of his tribesmen and sent for all the free men who pledged allegiance to him through his ministry.

Abram's male servants were ordered to begin rounding up his flock and herd. Women cooked a morning meal very quickly for their families, preparing them to do their assignments with some food in their stomachs.

A warm sun had risen to replace the cold darkness. Outside Abram's tent all the men who were free or servants to him sat in a semi-circle waiting. When Terah, Nahor and Lot arrived they were seated in front as was proper.

Abram came out of his tent and stood before his tribe. Sweeping his gaze over every face, he wondered how they would accept his revelation. Would his family come with him? Or would they stay here where they were comfortable. Would those free men who pledged allegiance to him and his God be willing to give up this homeland and move to a strange land under his authority? This departure would be a test for everyone. Raising his arms Abram spoke.

"Listen, O my people! I have assembled you all to hear my testimony of the visitation of the EVERLIVING, the ALMIGHTY GOD whose name is YAHVAH! He came to me a few hours ago in a vision. There are no words that can recapture the experience of being in His presence. He is too wondrous for this humble servant to describe. But I can say this much. He is brighter than the sun... with a voice speaking as a multitude of kings.

"Yahvah God revealed that as much as He saved me from the fire, He also protected us in our travel from Ur to Haran. He saved us from our enemies.

"Now the Everliving has made a covenant with me to multiply my seed, to make my enemies fall before me, and to send blessings upon all the works of my hands so I will lack nothing.

"This covenant is conditional. The conditions are that I obey his laws and commandments... and that I leave here today."

The hushed silence turned into a great hubbub spawned by the rush of anxiety from hundreds of curious voices.

Terah finally ventured the question: "Where is it that you must go, my son?"

"To the Land of Canaan, father, to the Land of Canaan."

"But the living conditions in Haran are good and we are secure here."

"Haran is not the place where my God wishes me to settle, father. I must go wherever He sends me. I am compelled to go; the choice is not mine. Come with me, father, we will want for nothing."

"Nooo, Abram, I think not. This is your God and your destiny He delivers you into. My destiny will end here. Thanks to you I have found a new life, a life of peace. I shall enjoy my last years in comfort among our kin. Your greatness is only beginning, whereas mine is ending. It is not proper that my faded glory should diminish the brightness of yours. Go with your God; let your brightness shine."

Terah arose and embraced Abram. Turning his face so that Abram would not see the moisture in his eyes, he walked away and did not look back. Amthelo, his mother, stood in back of the crowd of men, hidden by their height. Her sigh of shock and disappointment blended with those around her. Tears streamed down her face as she turned to follow Terah. Nahor and Lot also rose, embraced Abram, and after a few sentiments were exchanged, they also returned to their homes.

Some of the free men came forward with heads hung low. They too expressed regret for deciding to stay. After each apology, Abram embraced and excused them with a blessing. He bid them good bye, promising to return.

"With the feel of your embrace in my arms and the kinship of our race in my heart, I shall never forget you.

"Those of you who choose to share my destiny and enjoy blessings from the Everliving...you are my people and I am your goel. We have but one God. It is YAHVAH who leads us. Now pack your belongings; we leave today!"

Abram was fifty-five years old when he left Haran to return to Urusalem in the Land of Canaan. It was there that he taught men the Divine Standard for living.

Three years had elapsed since they arrived. One day Abram was out in the hills sitting under a tree and watching his sheep. He was enjoying the peaceful serenity of the pastoral scene that lay before him.

"The grass is ample and my flock is multiplying. How good it is to be a free man bound only by the law of a righteous God."

Gradually Abram's eyes closed and sleep overtook him. With no awareness of time lapsed, he heard:

"ABRAM ... ABRAM, SON OF TERAH ... HEARKEN TO MY VOICE!"

Invading Abram's sleep, the sound of the Everliving's unmistakable presence seemed to resound among the hills and valleys like rolling thunder. Opening his eyes slightly from a deep sleep he observed:

"It is strange that the sheep are unaffected by the sound and go on nibbling grass as though their ears were stopped. The mid-day sun overhead is like polished brass in the cloudless sky."

Suddenly Abram saw a light, more intense than the sun, descending through the branches he sat under. It turned the entire tree into a torch so bright that Abram drew his mantle over his eyes. Yet the tree did not burn; it merely surrendered its form and substance to the majesty of the godly light-force enveloping it.

Abram remembered the first time the Everliving had appeared to him in his tent as a blinding light. Now that Abram was aware of God's divine presence, his shock and fear were less paralyzing at this visitation. He was no less in awe as he laid himself prostrate, trembling.

"ABRAM...THIS IS THE LAND THAT 1 HAVE GIVEN TO YOU AND TO YOUR SEED AFTER YOU, FOREVER. 1 WILL MAKE YOUR SEED LIKE THE STARS OF HEAVEN, AND 1 WILL GIVE TO YOUR SEED ALL THE LANDS THAT YOU SEE, FOR AN INHERITANCE. REMAIN FAITHFUL TO ME AND TEACH MEN CONCERNING MY MERCIES. HAVE NO FEAR, FOR 1 AM WITH YOU... 1 AM WITH YOU...AND YOUR SEED...." The light rose and its heavenly voice trailed off, leaving Abram once again in the shade of the branches, seemingly midnight dark.

Abram blinked and gasped for breath. With heart pounding and emotions surging, his ears still retained the godly voice with its message.

"Thank you Yahvah for your presence...and... thank you for your promise! I will not forget our covenant! I WILL NOT FORGET!" he ran out into the open shouting up to the heavens.

The gentle waft of a cooling breeze passed over him, and then the normal heat of mid-day returned. Abram smiled at this, assured it was a divine gesture.

For the rest of the day and night Abram thought a great deal about the Holy Covenant. Keeping to himself he weighed and considered his relationship with the Everliving. One after another, Abram asked himself questions and reasoned the answers.

"Yahvah comes to reassure me by confirming again his promise. In return I must show my loyalty with a sign. But what? A monument? An image of manly form to represent the Everliving? No! That image would become a corruption, worshipped as an idol. There are already too many idols of wood, clay, and stone in the world, representing concoctions of men. My God must be worshipped by men through examples of obedience to His word. By what action can it be seen that men submit, if they do not submit to an image? In the kingdoms of this world, sacrifices are made before idols. Some are animal sacrifices, but many are human. Many daughters are brought under the knife or destroyed on altars of fire. Eldest sons are even killed in time of desperation. All this to appease vengeful gods. The Everliving is not vengeful against His people. He is protective. He is our friend from on high. But people remember the old ways. Would they respect Yahvah through obedience, without paying some price for disobedience? The payment of a sacrifice is a very old custom, one that everyone accepts. Perhaps an altar for animal sacrifices is appropriate? To give up an animal in sacrifice to God is to give back a portion of a man's wealth, only a small portion, depending on his wealth. To most men their wealth is their substance of life. Requiring a man to give up a portion of it to recompense his disobedience is a valid exchange...a fair practice. Yes, that is the answer! Let it begin with me."

Abram raised an altar with his own hands. It was constructed simply by means of piling natural rocks without shaping them by tools or securing them with mortar. In this way no man made shape or imagery could be contrived.

The altar was built at the location where Yahvah appeared to Abram. A lamb was sacrificed by Abram in the presence of all his tribe and he called upon Yahvah, to accept it. Following this ritual, which he ordained henceforth, Abram taught great truths to his people.

This particular evening was typical of many others over the past months since Abram committed the sacrifice. The men of his tribe gathered around Abram, sitting in the light of torches that flickered and sputtered in a breeze sweeping the hills. He stood looking up at the sky bejeweled with countless millions of heavenly lights, and was inspired again by God's covenant. The spirit of wisdom entered his mind and he began to speak.

"How are we to know our higher purpose in life, my brothers? I talk of a purpose beyond caring for your family and serving your goel"

All of those assembled turned one to another and shrugged, expressing uncertainty about how to answer the question.

"The answer comes to men by knowing the will of the Everliving," Abram declared, satisfying their curiosity. "Yahvah reveals His wisdom to those who seek to know Him. He has given a jewel of knowledge to me, which I shall now teach you. Within this gift of great worth lay an understanding of our purpose and a message for every man and woman of our tribe.

"This world was created to be God's domain. We were created as His servant race with a responsibility to exercise dominion over the earth and to replace evil with good. We can only understand our individual nature and purpose in life in terms of this responsibility. But what is this dominion and how are we to obtain it?

"The task was first assigned to Adam, and it had two aspects. First, he had to rule over the territory called The Garden of Eden. Second, he was required to name the creatures, by description, that were created under his dominion. This meant he had to understand all creatures in order to name them. Third, he had to be obedient to the Everliving's commands.

"We are called forth, therefore, by work, knowledge, and obedience, to subdue the earth, develop its potential, and multiply our numbers as servants of our God. We are to cover the earth with knowledge and fruitfulness as our numbers increase. Our purpose is to establish God's kingdom on earth with Yahvah's principles in every man's heart.

"Let it be known that any vocation is a holy calling whereby a man extends his dominion under respect for God's Standard. The opinion that says: 'a calling into the ranks of a priesthood is the only way to be found worthy of God,' is nonsense!

"The Kingdom of God is not a religious order. It requires the fruitful expansion of knowledge within a God-given lawful society. We and our seed after us shall extend the frontiers of our knowledge. We may learn more about the nature of things and their usefulness. We should be creative or useful with our endeavors so the community will benefit. Through this we can find exaltation in a task well done or in knowledge gained. It is in this way that we are obedient to Yahvah as His dominion is extended.

"You all know I have made a covenant with the Everliving in which He promises me blessings greater than I could ever hope for. All that is required of me is obedience to his law-order. Great blessings will be yours as well if you respect my words and conform yourselves to them. Just as I am a covenant man with God, you may also be a covenant people.

"Now go to your tents. Cast out your images and forget the foolishness of the priests. Know that we are called to a magnificent destiny if we keep faith in Yahvah.

Chapter 15
Farewell Noah

At the end of Abram's third year in Canaan, Shem sent a platoon of his guards to find and bring back their former commander. They ranged the hill country southeast of Urusalem where Abram and his tribe were last reported to be. On the fourth day of their search Abram welcomed them into his camp.

The officer in charge gave his regrets in not accepting Abram's festive hospitality, but the urgency of their mission prevented a lingering reunion. Hearing the reason for their haste, Abram gave instructions to Eliezer and Sarai to facilitate his own rapid departure. A hasty meal was provided and provisions packed for the journey to Urusalem.

Abram said little on the way. His thoughts were steeped in the past and he rode on his camel staring into space. Memories of a grand old man he loved more than words could relate, flooded his mind. Glimpses of Abram's life with this patriarch brought smiles, and watery eyes. Abram had known this time would have to come one day. Yet, somehow, Noah seemed immortal, and indispensable.

Abram was trained to be knowledgeable about many things concerning life, and death. He was also a sensitive man when it came to family. Noah was very special to him, and Abram knew Noah felt the same towards him. He sensed that his mentor/grandfather had postponed death so that Abram could be there to provide a measure of comfort at the end.

When Abram rode into the city he sensed a great depression in the mood of the people of Urusalem. Hurrying his pace, he arrived at the heavy gate of the fortress.

There was no question, by the guards posted, as to who this big man was that rode towards them.

"Abram is here! Commander Abram is here! Open the gates! Open up quickly!

From within, bars were withdrawn and bolts thrown open. The gates creaked as men struggled to swing them wide.

When there was scarcely enough room Abram charged his camel through disregarding the troop that had escorted him. Shouts of permission, from the gate sentries to other guards in series, barely preceded Abram as he whipped his camel through narrow death-trap passages. Archers, behind high battlements, withdrew their aim as Abram heard his name heralded again and again above the echoing rhythm of his gallop.

Out into the open, Abram entered into a large court. Reining his animal to a halt he vaulted off without waiting for it to kneel. A grand concourse of stairs ascended toward the royal quarters. Taking the steps in leaping bounds, he ran past door sentries, through well-known corridors, and past saluting guards and friends keeping a vigil. Servants opened doors in advance of his approach as heralds announced: "Prince Abram comes... Prince Abram comes!"

"King Shem awaits you, my lord," a familiar servant announced.

Abram walked into the king's private quarters with only a slight hesitation.

Shem had risen from his seat in anticipation and held out open arms to receive Abram as a father greets a beloved son.

"Abram, how good it is that you are here. I embrace you with the love of a father for his eldest son."

My king, my patriarch, my father...," Abram replied clasping Shem then slipping to his knees. Taking Shem's hands in his, Abram kissed one, then the other, and placed them alongside his face in an act of devotion.

"Rise Abram, my son, friend of the Everliving God.

We must put aside our reunion for now. Father Noah is dying and even he cannot keep death waiting much longer. He waits for you, Abram. It is very important for him to see you again and have you kiss him farewell. He loves you as a favorite grandson. Rush to him now. I will follow."

Abram ran to Noah's room. Of all the rooms in the fortress it was the most familiar to him. He found his way as though he had left only yesterday. Slowing his steps, Abram entered the room quietly and came to where Noah was sleeping. He sat alongside the bed and looked at the wrinkled face of the man who had been more of a father to him than Terah.

"My thoughts go back to when I was a frightened boy of eleven, Grandfather," he spoke very softly. "I remember with fondness how you soothed my fears and loneliness away. You have been loving, kind and generous of yourself with me. You are, indeed, a most noble example of the righteous man; a patriarch to be known and respected through all passages of time."

"Abram...? Is it you I hear?"

"Yes, my Abi (father/progenitor)".

Noah feebly raised his hand to receive Abram.

Abram reached over and took the thin, wrinkled hand gently in his. Palm against his cheek, he brushed it around his face kissing as it passed his lips.

"I...I am glad you are here...so glad," Noah sighed deeply.

"I have come to stay with you and comfort you, grandfather. I will run and get what you need. I will care for you. I will talk to you and report the news. It shall be as it was when I was a young boy and you were a father to me - a loving, wonderful father whom I honor above all that live."

"Abram, Abram...my beloved Abram....the Everliving gave you to me as a gift... to delight me in my old age. Oh how I have thought about those thirty-nine years you lived with us. You blessed us with your glowing countenance and your zest for life and knowledge. You needed love and tenderness, as all children do. And so, when we gave, you gave in return, abundantly...eagerly."

Noah paused, for breath and for strength; his frail body shuddered from the effort.

"Please rest, my Abi; I will remain here as long as you need me."

"No more rest until I bless you, Abram. I am determined to continue... until all is said that needs to be said. Now help me to sit up a little so that I may see you better."

Abram gathered some fur wraps together. Slowly lifting Noah at the shoulders Abram stuffed the furs behind and settled him down.

"Ahh, that is better. I can see that you are still big and strong, as before you left us. You have aged well Abram...that is good. You will need three kinds of strength in this world...physical, mental, and strength of faith in the Everliving. Ahh, but I have already taught you this, have I not?"

"Your words are like cool water to a man parched from the desert. They are familiar but most refreshing, my lord. Quench my thirst for your wisdom, if it please you."

"Ohh, if only I could, if only I could...but...ohh...I am afraid... my time is near. Abram?"

"Yes, lord?"

"Next to Shem you have been my most valuable reward in the late years of my life. Now...now I will depart from you and join my fathers – but not without my blessing upon you.

"Shem? Shem are you near?"

"Yes, father, I am here." Shem came and knelt down on the right side of Noah, and took hold of his cold hand.

"I have given you my birthright and my blessing. Beloved Shem...all that I possess is yours... and the blessing of the Everliving is yours. There is nothing more in this life that you could want. Yet...because of my love for you...I give you in your old age the same gift that our God gave to me. Abram?"

"Yes, Grandfather?"

"Behold your Abi. Shem?"

"Yes, father?"

"Behold your new son."

Both men looked up, their eyes met forming a bond, and they nodded their commitment to it.

That subtle pledge was the last thing Noah saw. The great man took his last breath and went to his final rest.

10. And Abram dwelt in the land of Canaan, he, his wife, and all belonging to him, together with those that joined him from the people of the land....

Jasher 13:10

Chapter 16
East and West

I

In the fifth year of Abram's dwelling in the land of Canaan the people of Sodom and Gomorrah and all the cities of the plain revolted from the power of Chedorlaomer, King of Elam: for all the kings of the cities of the plain had served Chedorlaomer for twelve years, and given him a yearly tax, but in those days in the thirteenth year, they rebelled against him.

Jasher 13:11

It was during Abram's tenth year of residence in Canaan, that a war broke out between Nimrod, King of Shinar (Babylon) and Chedorlaomer, King of Elam. Years before, Chedorlaomer was appointed governor over the city/state of Elam by Nimrod and eventually rebelled against his overlord.

Chedorlaomer enlarged his domains by conquering the five cities of the Plain of Siddim, near the Dead Sea. He exacted tribute from them for twelve years; then they rebelled and refused to pay any longer.

Sometime afterward, Nimrod heard of this rebellion and saw an opportunity for punishing his former prince's rebellion against him. He mustered his forces and full of pride and anger marched to war against Chedorlaomer. Nimrod was confident that his superior army would win. He assembled all his princes and subjects, numbering about 700,000 men, and prepared for war in the valley of Babel.

All the forces of the two kings fought in that valley which lay between Elam and Shinar. It was a massive battle that resulted in huge losses of life. As many as 600,000 men of Nimrod's army fell and died. Mardon, King Nimrod's son, was included among them. Nimrod fled from the scene and returned in shame to Shinar.

From that time on, Nimrod was under subjugation to Chedorlaomer. This victorious king sent princes of his armies to the kings that dwelt around him and made a covenant with them. They all agreed to obey his commands. Chedorlaomer's domains were enlarged and strengthened as a result.

II

While Chedorlaomer rose in power to the east, Abram maintained a peaceful co-existence with his neighbors in the land of Canaan to the west. He enjoyed the pleasant pastoral life and attracted increasing numbers of Heber-ew families by the wisdom he taught. They too wanted the peace and security possessed by this tribe.

Abram frequently taught his people useful personal and community lessons. While sitting on the hillsides, watching their flocks or gathering around a campfire at night, they had plenty of time to think about and discuss the applications to their simple life style. It was in this way that their understanding grew, along with their loyalty to a prince who was so wise.

The tribe's prosperity grew also, since there was no longer a need to mollify many gods and demons with offerings. Men were now able to enjoy the fruits of their labors for the first time.

Families grew along with the growth in prosperity. Children, an indicator of a family's well being, were needed to help with the added work and bring credit to a man's name. Although Abram prospered in wealth, he was destitute for lack of even one heir. Sarai continued to be barren.

Abram was now seventy years old and had been living in the land of Canaan fifteen years when, one night as he was sleeping, the Everliving appeared to him in a vision of blinding light. The thunderous voice exclaimed:

"LISTEN TO ME, ABRAM, I AM THE EVERLIVING YAHVAH, WHO BROUGHT YOU OUT OF UR TO GIVE YOU THIS LAND FOR AN INHERITANCE. WALK BEFORE ME, BE PERFECT AND KEEP MY COMMANDMENTS. I WILL GIVE TO YOU AND YOUR DESCENDANTS THIS LAND FROM THE RIVER MITZRAIM TO THE RIVER EUPHRATES. IT SHALL COME TO PASS THAT YOU GO TO YOUR FATHERS IN PEACE

AND IN GOOD AGE. THE FOURTH GENERATION OF YOUR SEED SHALL RETURN HERE TO THIS LAND AND INHERIT IT FOREVER."

The words penetrated Abram's soul and gave him support for the convictions he demonstrated to his people. But underneath, deep in the recesses of his mind, Abram had nagging doubts.

"How can this covenant be true?" he asked himself. "I have no heir! Nor is there any hope for children. I will not put Sarai away because she is barren; I love her too much for that."

Abram kept these questions to himself, holding onto the only hope open to him: a faith in God's power to create life even in a barren womb.

Abram built an altar, again without tools or mortar. He made animal sacrifices to Yahvah and called upon His name frequently to hear Abram's plea for fertility.

III

For quite some time Abram yearned to be with his mother, father, and other family members. Missing them greatly, he wanted them to be with him in Canaan. Finally the day came when Abram decided he must leave for Haran; the thought of reuniting with his family became overwhelming.

Abram arrived in Haran with all those in his household, and a grand reunion took place. The celebration lasted several days and Abram's heart was at peace. He felt at home.

Days turned into months. Months became years, and Abram, too, became comfortable in his surroundings, not wanting to leave, and eventually not even considering returning to the Land of Canaan. During the first year of his visit Abram tried on many occasions to convince Terah, Nahor, and Lot they should return with him to Canaan. "Why leave when we are prospering here at Haran? No, we shall stay here awhile longer," Terah answered.

Abram waited and tried again with new reasoning but the result was always the same.

Five years elapsed since Abram had returned to Haran. All during that time he taught many of the Hebrew people to worship the one true God, to refrain from worshipping idols, and to understand the God's instructions.

One night the Everliving again appeared to Abram in a vision. The heavenly voice boomed:

"BEHOLD, I HAVE SPOKEN TO YOU FOR THE PAST TWENTY YEARS SAYING: 'GO FORTH FROM YOUR BIRTH-PLACE AND FROM YOUR FATHER'S HOUSE, TO THE LAND THAT I HAVE SHOWN YOU, TO GIVE IT TO YOU AND YOUR CHILDREN. I WILL BLESS YOU THERE AND MAKE FROM YOU A GREAT NATION. I WILL MAKE YOUR NAME GREAT, AND THROUGH YOU SHALL THE FAMILIES OF THE EARTH BE BLESSED.'

"NOW, THEREFORE, ARISE AND GO FROM THIS PLACE. TAKE YOUR WIFE, EVERYONE BORN IN YOUR HOUSE, ALL THE SOULS YOU HAVE BROUGHT TO ME THROUGH YOUR INSTRUCTION, AND ALL THAT YOU OWN, AND RETURN TO THE LAND OF CANAAN."

Abram awoke shivering. It was not from the chill of the mountain air, but rather from realization that he had been soundly chastised by his God. A sense of guilt welled up in him and Abram knew, at last, that obedience to God came before even the strongest family ties. At that very moment he determined that in the future he would be more faithful and not allow his personal feelings to interfere with the Everliving's instructions.

"I am leaving Haran this day," Abram told Nahor, Lot, and Terah. "Yahvah, The Everliving God has come to me in a vision and commanded that I return to Canaan. Although it saddens me to leave you, I am convicted by my negligence of His covenant with me. This is my last appeal to you. Come with me; be a part of God's covenant people. There is so much good that we can do. Join with me now. Let the scribes record your names with mine for the good works that we shall do under the protection of Yahvah."

Lot was moved by Abram's entreaty. This was not the first time. Back when Abram returned to Haran, Lot was one of the first men converted to believe in the Everliving God. He sat at Abram's feet more than any other and developed a strong loyalty to his uncle. That loyalty was now going to take him into adventures beyond the limits of his imagination.

Terah and Nahor refused Abram. They were staying in Haran where they had a secure home and lucrative trade.

The departure was a sad one, with weeping by men as well as women and children. Abram gathered together all those of his household plus the new souls believing in Yahvah, and they left for the Land of Canaan. Abram was 75 years old when his tribe arrived at the Plain of Mamre and settled themselves there.

IV

And in that year there was a heavy famine throughout the land of Canaan, and the inhabitants of the land could not remain on account of the famine for it was very grievous.

Jasher 15:1

Abram, Sarai, members of their household, and all those attached to him packed their belongings and traveled southwest towards Egypt to find relief from the famine. When they had come as far as the Brook Mitzraim, near the border of Egypt, they remained there some time to rest.

One day Abram walked along the tree-shaded edge of the stream with Sarai, and he spoke openly to her about how beautiful she was.

"The outdoor life has been kind to you, my wife. I love your fine even features. Your pretty straight nose," he caressed her face with the tips of two fingers. "Your eyes are as blue as a morning sky and your hair is a golden wheat that takes men's breath away. At the time of our marriage, your hair was almost the color of bright new gold. Now, as age changes it, your golden hair has a trace of silver, only enhancing your maturing beauty."

Stopping, he turned to her with a look of embarrassment. Dropping his eyes, he paused and sighed. Taking her hands in his, Abram continued his praise.

"Sarai...like other Shemitic women, you are gifted with ample breasts. Unlike other married women, however, your breasts have not lost their attractiveness by giving suck to babies. You still have your youthful appearance I knew at the time of our wedding. It has not been changed, like other women, by having children. Even when in a crowd of women, your attractiveness sets you apart. Many, many times, over the years, I have congratulated myself on choosing you as my wife because of your beauty. But now I am worried - very worried!"

Sarai, red-faced with embarrassment, answered: "I would gladly lose all my attractive appearance for the sake of bearing children for you, my husband."

"I have accepted God's promise for many seed. Your beauty was never a condition; do not regard it as such."

"My adoring husband praises my appearance and is worried? Why, my love? What is it that concerns you?"

Abram found it difficult to come to the point directly.

"Our God has created you with such beauty that the heads of all men turn their eyes to behold you and uplift themselves by your loveliness."

"I am grateful that God made me pleasing enough to men's eyes that they honor you with praise."

"Yes, among our own people where we are safe, I can enjoy the tribute that your exquisite face and form brings. Now, however, I am afraid of the Egyptians. If they see you they will desire you and take you from me by force. I may die in the struggle and you will become an Egyptian's wife or concubine. A respect for our God does not exist in the land of Mitzraim, and that which I now fear will most likely come about!"

"I could not bear life without you, my husband, especially in the arms of a Hamite. What shall I do? Shall I hide myself?"

"But what if you are discovered? You will most certainly be taken. Here, then, is what you shall do. To all who ask you, say you are my sister. I shall order all the people with us to say the same."

And so Abram issued his command to his nephew, Lot, and all the others in his camp before they resumed travel. As they approached the border, however, Abram became fearful. Placing Sarai in a large chest, he concealed it among the other forms of luggage.

They had just entered a gate into the city of Sile when guards came up to them and demanded: "Give ten percent of what you have to the king! Only then can you come into the city."

Abram and his men obeyed the order and prepared to give the tithe. In the process of accounting for all the property, the chest holding Sarai was included among other baggage. Abram tried to sneak it by without being opened, but one of the king's servants observed the act and challenged Abram.

"What do you have there in that chest? We have not seen what is inside. Open it now and give to the king the tithe of what it contains!"

"This one chest I will not open, but I will pay any demand you put upon it," Abram replied as a last resort to keep Sarai hidden.

"Very well," said the king's officer-in-charge, "the chest is full of precious stones. Give us the tenth part of their value."

Abram was very agitated. Sweat ran down his face forming droplets in his beard. He squeezed his hands together in frustration and fear as he answered: "I will give all that you demand, but you must not open that chest!"

Abram tried to be calm and show no anxiety, but the situation was very dangerous. His thoughts focused on Sarai, Lot, and all the others traveling with him.

"We have traveled all this distance to escape death by hunger," he reasoned. "I must avoid armed conflict with the Egyptians. Death by the sword would be no better solution."

The Egyptian officer looked at Abram carefully and sensed there could be trouble so he called for reinforcements. In little time a contingent of armed soldiers ran up and encircled Abram's caravan with their spears poised for battle.

All of the men with Abram laid their hands on weapons and awaited his command. It was a desperate situation and Abram knew he could do nothing but watch as the king's officers approached.

Soldiers pushed Abram aside while two officers drew their swords and hacked at the leather straps holding the chest closed. Opening the lid they were startled by their discovery. Instead of rare gems, gold, or silver, they found a woman of rare beauty and form.

"Ohh? And what kind of a creature do we have here huddled in a chest and shaking with fear?" asked one of the officers. Reaching down he took Sarai by the wrists and gently lifted her to a standing position. Releasing her, the officer stepped back a pace and admired his find.

"Please, my lord, be kind..."

"Have no fear, woman, no harm shall come to you."

The second officer was struck speechless not just because a woman came from the chest, but that she was the most attractive woman he had ever seen.

A rush of sighs from the Egyptian soldiers demonstrated their agreement.

Sarai found herself the center of a great controversy between a large group of alien admirers and her tribe. She was still standing in the chest when a war chariot, drawn by two magnificent black Arabian horses, pulled up nearby. A man with the bearing of a nobleman stepped down followed by his bodyguard. His driver checked the reins and calmed the anxious steeds.

The nobleman advanced with the stride of a man confident of his authority. The encircling rank of Egyptian soldiers gave way quickly for him to pass through. He appeared to be a man of considerable experience. Scrutinizing the scene, he rapidly drew his own conclusions. Fastening his eyes on Sarai for an uncomfortably long time, he ignored the impending drama beyond this center.

The officer in charge of the gate came up to the nobleman and started to report the incident at hand. He was silenced as the prince raised his staff of authority, cutting off the report in mid-sentence.

"Who is this beautiful woman?"

"I do not know, my lord, I was about to find out. You see, this man..."

"Yes, yes, I know. They tried to smuggle her by your men to avoid discovery. They must be fearful that she will be taken from them and put among the concubines of a prince," he smirked with a leering smile, his gaze still fixed on Sarai.

"Or a king," said the officer. His mind conceived there could be recognition and reward from a grateful king.

"Heh? What? Oh yes, Mmm." Giving his full attention to Sarai he asked: "Who are you, lovely lady?"

"My name is Sarai, my lord. I am the sister of Prince Abram, the chief of this tribe."

"So, you are a princess, my lady. Permit me to introduce myself to you. I am Prince Amidhotep, at your service. I shall take pleasure in sheltering you from any further discomfort and embarrassment. Here, take my hand and step out of that ridiculous chest. This is certainly not the way for a lovely princess to arrive in our fair city. You must be in need of rest and refreshment. Please allow me the privilege of providing it for you."

Before Sarai could reply, the prince gently but forcefully walked her to his chariot. Helping her step up on it he commanded his driver to leave. Horses pawed the earth as a whip cracked at their ears. Stirring up a flurry of dust, the chariot rumbled off at considerable speed.

Abram looked after the abduction of Sarai with impotent weakness. The terrified expression on Sarai's face made his emotions surge and her shrill cry of: "Abram!," almost smothered by the sound of the chariot, stirred him into action, futile action. He dodged

Egyptian spears, knocked soldiers out of his way and ran after Sarai's cry. On he ran, choking in the trailing dust, until he was exhausted. Stumbling on, Abram tripped and fell face down. As he lay there in the dirt, gasping for breath, the officers and soldiers broke into derisive laughter, ridiculing 'the Prince of Canaan.'

Lot and the men of Abram's house were stunned and defeated by this embarrassment of their leader and the abduction of his wife. Their threat to the Egyptians dissipated and they paid the tithe without further incident.

Chapter 17

A Present for Pharaoh

I

And when the officers of the king beheld Sarai they were struck with admiration at her beauty, and all the princes and servants of Pharaoh assembled to see Sarai, for she was beautiful. And the king's officers ran and told Pharaoh all that they had seen, and they praised Sarai to the king; and Pharaoh ordered her to be brought, and the woman came before the king.

And Pharaoh beheld Sarai and she pleased him exceedingly, and he was struck with her beauty, and the king rejoiced greatly on her account, and made presents to those who brought him the tidings concerning her.

Jasher 15:14,15

"I know it would be foolish to bring Sarai to my own house, even long enough to prepare her as a gift for the king. Jealous officers would surely get word to Pharaoh that I wanted her for myself and I might bring the king's wrath down upon my head," Prince Amidhotep reasoned to himself as he rode along the dusty road towards the king's palace.

The chariot driver pulled in his reins and the Arabians thundered to a halt at the entrance to the palace fortifications, pawing the ground, snorting, and shaking the harness that controlled them.

"I am Prince Amidhotep, here on personal business for the king," he announced himself.

An officer of the guards relayed his identification and he was admitted. Once inside, he stated his purpose in coming to the chief officer.

The gruff man, in mid-life, had several years of service and high responsibility behind him. With the king's safety in his hands, he was careful about who entered and why. Peering at Prince Amidhotep, he recognized this noble visitor. He had memorized his face just as he had memorized the faces of many other guests. It was a few uncomfortable moments, then:

"Ahh, yes, Prince Amidhotep, welcome," the chief officer admitted finally with a smile. "What is the nature of your personal business with the king, my lord? Ah, that is, how may I serve you?" he was quick to add, not wanting to offend any friend of the king.

"I have a rare gift for his majesty," the Prince replied gesturing towards Sarai.

It was as though Sarai had been invisible until now. The chief officer reacted with mild surprise. He had seen many beautiful women come and go but this one was exceptional and all he could do was stare at her.

"I shall present this gift to his highness only after she has been washed, perfumed, clothed, and bejeweled properly. For that I need the services of harem servants and a number of merchants. Now if you will detain me no longer I shall be about this important business?"

"Oh, why yes, of course, my lord, right away. I shall conduct you to the harem quarters myself. Please follow me," he asked eagerly.

Prince Amidhotep was escorted to a room and asked to wait. In no time at all, a middle-aged woman entered, accompanied by a giant eunuch. The woman bowed but the eunuch stood in the doorway with a palm resting on the handle of his sword.

"What is it that I, Shemsa, may do for you, my lord?"

I am Prince Amidhotep, good woman, and friend of Pharaoh. Here with me is a gift for the king, a rare beauty from the Land of Canaan. I require the assistance of the chief beautician and fashion designer who wait upon the king's harem."

"They are here under my authority to serve. Command and we shall obey, my lord." The woman was quick to recognize a matter of great consequence to the king. Her life might improve with a great reward, or it might end, depending on how well she and her staff applied themselves. She shot a stern glance at the eunuch and forced the lines of her mouth into a smile.

The eunuch knew what that communication meant and smiled in return, along with a small bow.

"I put this woman named Sarai into your hands," Amidhotep said sharply. "See to it that she is bathed and rubbed with oil and myrrh. I shall go now. When I return it will be with merchants and their servants burdened with fine garments and proper jewelry to adorn her. You will have her ready, will you not?"

"Oh, yes, my lord, she will be ready for you...as if my life depended upon it."

"I am glad you value your life, Shemsa, do not disappoint me," he hissed through clenched teeth.

Shemsa looked into cold, humorless eyes that struck terror into her heart. She shuddered involuntarily as he turned on his heels and walked out, pushing the eunuch aside.

During the chariot ride Sarai had tried desperately to have Prince Amidhotep return her to her people. His answer was always the same. "You have nothing to fear, Sarai. You will be treated royally as never before." Amidst tears of despair she acquiesced to her abduction.

Now in the palace harem, Sarai listened in stunned silence as the weight of her predicament pressed upon her. She was guided to a corner of a large room where several women languished about, partially or totally naked.

"Disrobe," ordered Shemsa.

Sarai's eyes widened in shock. She tried to resist but soon realized how futile her efforts were, out-numbered as she was.

"I am a princess, a Heber-ew," she declared. "I will not lower myself to disrobe for you or anyone else."

"Since my life depends on preparing you for the king, you will part with your garments, now!" she shouted.

The word became action. The strong arms and hands of the eunuch quickly encircled Sarai, grasping her wrists and preventing struggle. Arms of giggling, women servants, held her legs securely to prevent any kicking. Sarai's eyes widened in fright as she watched Shemsa draw a small but very sharp dagger, from a sheath at her waist, and approach menacingly.

"What are you going to do to me?" she cried.

"Hold still and it will be very painless, my Heber-ew princess. If you squirm and kick, who knows...this dagger may slip and cut that milky white skin of yours," Shemsa warned with a sadistic look in her eyes.

Sarai strained to free herself but was powerless to do so. She fought the indecency the only way left open to her. Screaming hysterically, Sarai called: "Abram! Abram! Abram!" over and over again.

"I will scratch out your eyes if you touch me, you...you wart hog!" she threatened.

"Wart hog am I? It is a good thing for you that you are of value to the king. If not, I would love to cut pictures into your white flesh," the ugly matron seethed with a tightly controlled anger.

"Ohh, I must find relief from this terror, before I go mad," Sarai moaned in desperation. I must think of something else...something that might save me."

Sarai tried to retreat within herself as Shemsa began cutting her garments apart and yanking them off. She strained with closed eyes to avoid the embarrassment, but its reality was so frightening she had to scream.

Shemsa cut the last of Sarai's undergarment and pulled it away. A naked servant girl scooped up the pieces of Sarai's clothing and disposed of them, leaving Sarai naked to the gaze of unfriendly faces.

Strong hands released her body and stood back to stare at what would soon be the King's pleasure. Sarai covered her breasts with one arm and the golden V at the apex of her legs with the other hand. This measure of modesty was soon aborted. More naked servant girls came forward with cleansing ingredients. Gently but forcefully, they moved her hands out of the way as they swabbed her from head to toes with water and cleansing powder. To her hair they applied ashes from burnt plants, combined with plant juices, as a cleanser. Bending her over, a servant poured water from a pitcher over the back of Sarai's head as a rinse.

"Your hair is so golden and your skin is very fair," a young brown skinned girl remarked, as she dried and combed out Sarai's long hair. "I have never seen a woman with beauty such as yours. You are most fortunate, my lady, I envy you."

Another servant proceeded to massage oil into Sarai's skin, working it to the smooth velvety luster of a youthful woman. The perfumed oil of myrrh was applied afterward, giving her whole body a provocative scent.

Sarai was hardly conscious of the servant's ministrations. She could feel the brushes stroking her hair but it seemed to be someone else sitting there surrounded by attendants. She had closed her eyes and relaxed, shutting out the scene around her. A measure of peace had come at last.

The full length of Sarai's long hair cascaded around her shoulders and breasts with the brilliant luster of a golden cape. She kept silent, saying nothing in answer to questions and comments from the Pharaoh's wives and concubines who came close to examine her. Getting no satisfaction from their efforts, they retreated to their former state of repose. Each one began reflecting on their future diminished status. Sarai would surely become the favorite of Pharaoh because of her unusual beauty.

Prince Amidhotep returned with merchants and their assistants following, their arms filled with bolts of cloth, garments, footwear and an abundance of exquisite feminine adornments. The chief cosmetician and chief fashion designer came scurrying in upon Shemsa's order and bowed before Prince Amidhotep.

"And Sarai? Where is she?" he demanded.

"Step through that doorway, my lord, and you will be satisfied," Shemsa replied.

Bristling with anticipation, Amidhotep barged through. Sarai stood facing him, naked, but surrounded by four naked servant girls. Her fair skin and golden hair shown like the flame in the center of a clay lamp.

"By the gods!" exclaimed Amidhotep, returning to the outer waiting room, "She takes my breath away. If the king reacts similarly we shall all profit greatly. Now dress her like a queen; a queen that even Pharaoh cannot resist for his passion.

A process of garment style and fabric selection began, accompanied by suggestions for makeup and hairstyle. Both women were experts at what they did and knew what would please the Pharaoh. They made several trips between the waiting room and the harem anti-room, where Sarai stood like a queen bee around which worker bees fussed.

Amidhotep lounged on a couch, refreshing himself with fruit brought by a servant. He tried to imagine how Sarai would look when she entered the waiting room. His thoughts rambled on and he pictured himself being rewarded richly by his grateful king.

His reverie was interrupted as the chief beautician and fashion designer entered the room and announced: "Queen Sarai! A gift fit for a king."

Amidhotep sat up, and then stood in respect. "A love goddess stands before me. I can only bow to pay homage, since humble words fail to give sufficient praise."

A fine white silk tunic closely fitted Sarai's body contours. It displayed her voluptuous figure, tantalizingly exposing one bare breast as the garment partially covered her torso. The material was supported by her left shoulder and clung diagonally around her chest and back.

"This is the current fashion among the rich and noble of Egypt, Prince Amidhotep. The style may not be considered uncommon nor original, but Pharaoh likes it," the fashion designer stated confidently.

"Mmm yes...and I understand why. One of Sarai's jewels is exposed enough to reveal the quality but not the whole substance of her treasure. I am an admirer of Pharaoh's taste in fashion and I compliment you on your skill in clothing her with seductive appeal."

"Thank you, my lord. Your words are most comforting since my only desire is to serve Pharaoh for his pleasure."

"Yes, of course, I too have the same calling. Now, if I may make a suggestion...?"

"Please do, my lord. A man of your experience honors me with your opinion," the woman replied.

"First, place appropriate jewelry around her neck."

Amidhotep clapped his hands twice and two merchants scurried forward to display their array of the finest, most expensive jewelry in the city.

"A necklace, I think, of rare gems in a delicate setting. A complement, not a contrast, to Sarai's natural beauty...perhaps something to match her eyes."

Both merchants insisted that various items they offered were most appropriate. The prince finally selected an exquisite necklace that enhanced her exposed flesh. Like fine, golden lace it bridged the change in color from Sarai's suntanned face and neck to her creamy breast. It was composed of four rows of very thin gold filigree, with the clearest lapiz lazuli in gold settings regularly spaced like the folds of a fan across her chest. While accenting Sarai's form and beauty, it also brought out the blue of her eyes.

"If my lord will permit a suggestion?" asked a disappointed merchant, anxious to equal his competitor in a large sale.

"Yes, if it is valid," replied Amidhotep quite pleased with the effect his own selection had created.

"A head piece of royal quality for a royal beauty..." Very delicately he unwrapped the black silk covering and held up to eye level a stunning tiara/crown of silver set with pearls and lapis lazuli.

On the front and sides were suspended delicate silver chains with small clips from which a veil could be attached.

Prince Amidhotep took the crown and placed it delicately on Sarai's head. He stepped back to look at her and called for a pale blue veil, never taking his eyes off her face.

A flurry of hands by cloth merchants produced an assortment of possibilities, and one was selected.

"May I suggest also a seductively thin mantle of almost transparent white silk, my lord? The reason is to allow only Pharaoh the privilege of revealing Sarai's naked beauty publicly or privately as he wishes. Exclusivity of beautiful objects is one of his desires, I have heard," confided the fashion designer.

"Excellent recommendation! Yes, I agree. Our prized package must be wrapped very properly. And white is the proper color: the color of purity."

Busy hands quickly started work on the mantle, fashioned from a very delicate white silk whose radiance matched that of Sarai's golden hair. The length of the veil was increased so that it lay upon her breasts and hinted at a lover's desire that swelled beneath. When the mantle was finished, it was draped over Sarai's head and shoulders, ending at her thighs.

"Beautician!"

"Yes, lord?"

"Apply a small amount of cosmetics."

The woman removed the veil and made a thin outline of black around Sarai's eyes with a touch of light blue shadow on her eyelids.

"Do you wish tattooing of any kind on her face or body, my lord?"

"No, you fool! She is Heber-ew, not Egyptian. To mark her would ruin her appearance and make our gift imperfect. Now move away from her so my view is unobstructed.

Ahh, yes, yes," sighed Prince Amidhotep. "The effect is perfect. She is the fulfillment of every man's desire, even a king's, for a fair-skinned, golden-haired goddess. And by the gods, I am enticed to feast upon her myself - more than I have ever been tempted. But such is not to be. I am a servant to my king; an ambitious one, I should add," he smiled at Shemsa.

"Fit her with sandals proper for a wife of Pharaoh."

Amidhotep paid the merchants and gave instructions to Shemsa.

"I will go now to seek an audience with Pharaoh where I can present this gift to him. Have our precious lady ready to come at his command."

II

During Sarai's adornment, she ignored those who prepared her, and thought about the day of her wedding to Abram. Her mind wandered far away, in time and distance, in a retreat from the present. Servants had bathed, oiled and perfumed her body that morning. Her clothing had been far less disclosing and her jewelry of less value. These memories were so comforting, however, that she drifted into a reverie and experienced them once more.

Her oblivion was ended when a new, commanding voice intruded and demanded her full attention.

"Is she ready for the king? Pharaoh wants her brought to him immediately," ordered Pharaoh's minister.

"Yes, she is as ready as we can prepare her to be. If she stays in her present state of mind, however, I doubt that Pharaoh will have much pleasure from her. Beauty is not everything desirable in a woman," replied Shemsa.

"Hmm, you may be right. Sarai? You are about to give yourself to the king for his entertainment. If I were you, I would make the most of your situation and give him great satisfaction. He can be very generous with gifts to the women he enjoys the most."

"And if I do not please him?"

"Ohh, I do not want to think about that, and you do not want to know the consequences."

"Yes, I must know; please tell me."

"I doubt that the king would harm you; you are too beautiful. The people you came with, however, they are of no use to Pharaoh, except as slaves. And if the men resisted the king's soldiers...they would all surely die. The women would, of course, become concubines and your tribe would no longer exist. So you see, to resist the king would be very foolish."

Sarai was so stunned by the import of the minister's words, that she became totally defeated with no will to resist. Obediently following the king's minister, she came out into a large shaded garden court with a rectangular pool of water at the center. A large variety of flowering plants, small trees and shrubs provided color, comfort and the luxuriant atmosphere of a delightful oasis.

She caught sight of Prince Amidhotep reclining on a couch within easy conversation distance of another man. He, too, was reclining on a couch but it was situated on a dais two feet higher than the floor of the garden. She noticed that his head was shaved, in the fashion of the nobility, for relief from the heat. Wigs were worn only when formality required it.

Both men, and the servants that fanned and attended them with food and drink, were under the shade of overhead lattice works that were interwoven with flowering vines. The sweet fragrances, splashes of color, and coolness of the garden would have been enchanting to Sarai under normal circumstances for it was the most beautiful garden she had ever seen.

Naked, tan-skinned women were all about, in and out of the shallow pool. Some were playfully splashing, some lounged sleepily, and others, attracting attention by their movement, walked about the garden exposing themselves to the wandering eyes of the two noblemen.

A motion of his hand, by Pharaoh, silenced Prince Amidhotep in the middle of a sentence. Pharaoh raised himself to a sitting position as Sarai, the vision of a goddess, entered the garden. She stood under a shaft of sunlight, as directed by the minister, and the heat began melting a small lump of perfumed fat that was placed within the crown on her head. The fragrance was exotic and she felt slightly dizzy from the heat as she stood waiting for permission to approach.

"My lord king, the lady Sarai awaits your pleasure," announced the minister.

Pharaoh was now on his feet staring at the dazzling spectacle. Sarai was so mystically beautiful the effect shortened his breathing. The minister waved Sarai forward but his lord shouted: "No! Stay where you are! I am only a king and what stands before me must surely be a goddess!"

He walked slowly towards her, peering at her glowing presence as the sunlight flared from the white of her garments. Standing before her he said nothing but held up his hand to command silence from all at hand. His eyes slowly took in every detail of her then, curious about the hidden beauty beckoning him, he slowly removed her featherweight mantle, letting it fall to the floor.

The sun's light dazzled his eyes as it reflected a gold and silver brilliance from Sarai's hair and crown. Reaching out like a man blinded, he felt the gold of her hair cascading down around her back and shoulders.

186

"Such hair, so golden, long and beautiful. Never have I seen the like of it, although I have heard of the light-haired Heber-ews. You may well be the prettiest example of your race, my dear. I desire to see your face and prove myself right or wrong," he remarked eagerly.

Reaching up, Pharaoh carefully removed the long veil and stood back. His eyes traced a course from Sarai's face down her neck to the blue stones in the necklace, and were struck by the color comparison in her blue eyes. He gasped then crowed with childish glee: "I am right! I am right! She is a goddess!" His eyes darted back at Prince Amidhotep.

He gaped longingly at Sarai's pert, naked breast and a little moan of desire escaped from his throat. Recovering his composure, he rasped: "Come out of the sun, my dear. Join me where it is cooler." Clearing his throat he remarked superficially: "You must forgive my keeping you standing in the heat of the sun; it was rude of me. Your beauty distracted me so that I forgot my manners."

Taking Sarai by the hand, he walked with his head turned to watch her movements. He gazed compulsively at her curves, swells and valleys undulating beneath the close fitting tunic that reached to her ankles.

Sarai flushed pink from the heat of the sun and Pharaoh's lustful stare. The thin silk became semi-transparent as the perspiration on her body made the gown cling to her crevices and strain over every contour.

"Come stand by my couch so that I may feast my eyes on you. Ah, here we are. Now to cool you a bit...Fans!" he snapped.

Four servants with large fans, constructed from woven reeds, moved the tepid air around the threesome.

"Ahh, now that is better, is it not?" Pharaoh asked.

Sarai was so fearful she began to tremble and her flesh was raised from the chilling prospect of the tan-skinned stranger sexually assaulting her. She never felt the gentle wafting of air across her body.

To Pharaoh, who kept his eyes trained on Sarai, it appeared the fans were cooling, for her nipples became erect and tight beads formed in the pink circles at the summits of her breasts.

"I am so delighted that you and your people have come to visit my kingdom, Lady Sarai. You shall be my personal guest here. I hope that pleases you?"

Sarai remained mute. She was afraid to say anything for fear the king might be offended and bring harm to her husband's tribe.

"I cannot understand your sadness, Sarai. Look about you," Pharaoh declared with a sweep of his arm. "Do any of these lovely women appear to be unhappy? They have all that a woman could ever desire. Servants provide everything to make their lives comfortable and trouble free. They make me content and I keep them in comfort. It is a generous exchange for the honor of my attentions. There is not a woman in all Mizeraim, married or not, that would not give up all she possessed to live here with me and enjoy my generosity. Is that not so, Prince Amidhotep?"

"Oh, yes. That is quite true, my lord, quite true. I thought this would apply especially to a woman who was confined to a trunk while traveling," he snickered sarcastically.

"Yes, I would certainly think so," agreed Pharaoh. "Tell me Sarai, what is your relationship to the man that brought you to our land?"

"He is my brother," she lied, remembering Abram's fear and the minister's warning.

"Ah, good - then it is incumbent upon me to make him prominent in wealth and position. I shall elevate him and do for him all the good that you will command of me. Now, does that make you feel better?"

"Yes, my lord," Sarai uttered softly, "I was fearful for him. But now that I know you intend only to honor him with a dowry...you must have honorable intentions towards me as well."

"Uh, why yes, of course my dear lady. And to show you proof, I shall have your brother showered with gifts, and then brought here as my guest so that we may seal the arrangement for you to become my wife."

III

It had been two days since Sarai was abducted. From the moment Abram ordered an encampment, he had gone into his tent for seclusion and had refused to see anyone. His grief was so intense that he ripped his tunic off and poured ashes over himself from head to foot. Day and night he could be heard moaning and cursing intermittently. He neither ate nor drank, welcoming the additional punishment of hunger.

Lot was grieving also, but there were responsibilities of leadership he reluctantly assumed for Abram.

It was late in the morning of Sarai's third day in Pharaoh's palace when the captain of the camp guards came running up to Lot, who was sitting in the shade at the opening of his tent.

"Lot! Lot! A column approaches! Men leading camels and mules burdened with goods... men and women slaves, and large flocks of sheep and goats! They are escorted by the king's soldiers. Two of Pharaoh's chariots lead them...and they are coming here!"

Lot had no experience as the chief of a tribe. He had a difficult enough time managing his own family. Now with the burden of Abram and the tribe weighing upon him, he needed time to think of a solution. Abram was in no condition to meet the king's representatives. Of that he was certain.

"Oh, why must I be the one to make such difficult decisions?" He complained while pacing back and forth in front of his tent, his eyes on the ground. "The Everliving God gave wisdom to Abram! He even talked directly to him in visions, not me. Abram must find a way to stop grieving and take command again. But how?"

Lot stopped his pacing and looked ahead. Raising his eyes to the sky he seemed to find some inspiration and shouted for the guard captain: "Sorek!"

"Yes?"

"I will meet the Egyptians in the name of Abram, who is away from our camp. Do you understand?"

"Yes, lord. I shall so inform the men of our camp."

Lot watched the Egyptian column stop as the officer in charge held up his arm commanding a halt. Another, older man spoke. Looking at his attire, Lot guessed he was a person of considerable importance.

"I come seeking the Heber-ew called Abram."

"Who is it that seeks him, and for what purpose?" Lot challenged.

"I am Iknahten, the king's minister. He has charged me to bring all these gifts to Abram, the brother of Sarai, and command him to appear before the king this evening."

"Very well, minister. I am Lot, the nephew of Prince Abram. My uncle is out of the camp looking over your fair land for acceptable grazing by our animals. I will accept these gifts for my uncle and tell him, when he returns to camp, of the order to appear before Pharaoh this evening."

"That is unacceptable!" Iknahten exclaimed. "I must deliver these gifts only to Abram. If he is not here, I will withdraw a short distance and wait until he returns. You will come and tell me at that time." He made a motion to leave, then added: "And Lot, as Pharoah's representative, I do not want to wait very long!"

Lot watched as Iknahten issued commands to his driver. Reins slapped the rumps of two horses and the chariot whirled with precision. An officer in the second chariot commanded his driver and they turned in unison. The column turned and followed the vehicles until they stopped about two hundred paces away and settled down to wait for Abram.

"Abram! Abram! My lord prince, you must listen to me!" Lot implored.

Stepping into the tent, Lot saw an unrecognizable dirt covered figure sitting on the bare ground. He had never seen such a sight before. Was this miserable wretch truly Abram?

"I am stunned," he gasped.

"Go away Lot, can you not see that I grieve for Sarai, your sister?"

"Yes, my lord, but the king of all Mizeraim sends his minister to you and only you! He comes with a caravan bearing mules burdened with precious gifts, male and female slaves, and large flocks of sheep and goats. They are all for you!"

Abram howled with frustration, his face distorted with emotional fear and frustration.

"He sends a large dowry to me as the head of Sarai's family - her brother!"

Lot's heart was broken to see his uncle in such a painful condition. Comforting Abram he said: "Beloved uncle, my lord, my teacher...grieve no more. There is a way through this tragedy; there must be! It is time to stop blaming yourself. You must regain your strength and your wisdom. Let us pray to our God. We shall ask Him to restore you and deliver Sarai back to us."

Lot grasped Abram's hands and together they kneeled facing each other. They prayed, openly, taking turn until words failed. And still they knelt... waiting...hoping. Tears of submission trailed down their faces and bodies. Two strong men, made weak, looked for strength and deliverance from the authority who could grant it...if only asked.

They were still kneeling, exhausted from their outpouring of emotional appeal, when the tent filled with heavenly glory. A male figure emanating light, appeared and spoke commandingly in a voice of authority that startled the supplicants, especially Lot, who was frozen with fright.

"I am a messenger sent by the Everliving God Yahvah who bids me to say: 'Take heart. Grieve no more, for I have heard your prayers. Sarai is protected from Pharaoh and will return safely with honor.'"

The divine messenger stopped speaking and disappeared as the two men watched in awe.

Lot shook his head with a shudder, amazed at what he had seen. Remembering the divine message, his heart was uplifted greatly and he exclaimed: "Did you hear that?"

"I have been a fool, nephew," Abram uttered morosely. I should have had faith. I should have come to my God right away with my problem, instead of relying only on myself. I realize now that I am nothing without trusting in Him and the covenant he made with me. I know now that it is everlasting, and not dependent on the endurance of my faith."

"Does this mean that you will be yourself again and take command of the tribe?" Lot asked eagerly.

"Yes, nephew. I will straighten up and be what I was before I lost my faith, hopefully more. Now, order servants to bring water in abundance, that I may wash off all signs of my misery! And order food for me to eat! There are things to be done and I must have my strength back. Sarai shall be returned; Yahvah the Everliving has said so! We must be ready to do our part, as His servants, to help bring it to pass! Hurry, nephew, hurry!"

"As you command, lord, as you command!"

Lot scurried out and ordered servants to bring water enough for bathing and place it at the tent opening. Bringing it inside, he poured water over Abram's head and body, and helped wash off the dirt and ashes. Once Abram was clean and dressed in his finest attire, Lot called in a servant who was expert in grooming his master. After combing and trimming Abram's hair and beard, he looked and felt once more like Prince Abram, friend of God and full of authority among men.

"Where is that food? I am starved!" Abram bellowed with a smile on his face.

Lot was happy to see that the tribe was under the control of Abram's authority again. He jumped with delight and answered: "Right away, lord, right away!"

Very shortly, a parade of women brought food of all kinds to the door of Abram's tent where a carpet had been spread. Abram ate his fill and began to feel like a prince again. His strength was returning and along with it his good judgment.

Picking up his ram's horn, Abram signaled all the men to assemble in front of his tent. Upon their arrival, he formed them into two ranks and spoke to them with a power they had never witnessed before.

"I have been ordered by Pharaoh, King of all Mizeraim, to accompany his minister back to their palace. I require seven men to accompany me now as security against Egyptian treachery. Although I have the protection of our God, I will need experienced fighting men, brave and strong, to be the Everliving's battle weapons."

"I will go with you, lord!" everyone answered without hesitation.

"I commend the bravery of you all, but I only need seven men. This small contingent will merely represent the normal amount of guards for a prince being escorted to an alien or rival monarch. It may prevent a contrived accident from occurring en route that could cause me harm or death. Seven men will not be considered a threat or a danger to Pharaoh.

"I have no knowledge of who among you are the most able warriors. It will be decided, therefore, by contest without weapons. You men in the front rank will wrestle a man behind you until one of you is thrown on your back, or surrenders."

The smallest men were eliminated first. Abram sat watching the match as he ate. The rest of the tribe also watched as the victors stood and formed two ranks. They chose off and began to wrestle again. Eventually the victors narrowed down to seven and Abram had his seven strong men.

"Wash yourselves, then dress for battle with a king. Bring spear, sword and dagger. Women, attend to your men's needs!"

"Uncle Abram...with your permission, I shall inform the king's minister that you have returned and await his attendance."

"Yes, Lot, you may do just that, but first there is one important thing I must do."

"As you wish, my lord, but what is so important that we keep Pharaoh's minister, his troops and slaves waiting longer still?"

"You, nephew. You are more important than them all." Abram put his big hands on Lot's shoulders and looking into his eyes he said: "May Yahvah the Everliving bless you as much as he blesses me. May you prosper and multiply your seed to be the father of a nation. You have my affection and my loyalty, always! Whatever you need of me, I shall give it to you. I shall protect you as your goel for as long as I live."

Abram embraced Lot, kissed him on the neck, and said quietly: "Now you may go to the king's minister and tell him I wait impatiently."

Lot saw the slight smile on Abram's lips and acknowledged the order with a smile of his own and a small bow. Turning, he walked to his camel and mounted.

Abram watched with pride and satisfaction as Lot rode off towards the royal caravan.

Iknahten and his royal caravan returned to the Heber-ew camp. Abram received Pharaoh's many gifts with the dignity befitting a prince and assigned them to the care of Lot. He agreed to return with Iknahten to the palace as commanded by the king. Calling for his seven guards to come forward on their camels, Abram turned to Lot and ordered:

"Nephew, I place you in charge of the camp while I am gone. I shall return late tonight, God be willing."

"Be ever cautious, my lord," Lot advised.

"Our God is with us; who can withstand Him?" Abram replied.

"After our experience with Him today? No one, no one at all," Lot smiled confidently.

Abram, surrounded by his guards, fell in with the king's escort and began the ride towards the Pharaoh's royal summer palace at Lake Balah, south of the fortress of Sile.

"I feel a new spirit of confidence," Abram sighed to himself, believing that in some way Sarai would be returned to him, and soon. "I have placed the matter in the hands of Yahvah the Everliving, and now I must trust that Sarai's release will be accomplished," he thought as he rode erect and proud. He looked at the land around him for the first time since entering Egypt, and he discovered its natural splendor.

The sky above was a vivid blue and the landscape around him a bright picture in raw artists' colors. The great Pilusiac, or eastern branch of the Nile, cut its eastward course from where it began north of the City of On down to the Mediterranean Sea one hundred fifty miles to the northeast. It passed through the Land of Goshen and nourished the richest farms in the nation. The water was reddish brown with the silt carried down from the heart of Africa. On both sides the waters spread out, islanded with towns and villages, and criss-crossed by dikes that marked the banks of canals.

Here and there Abram could see the living green of olive groves, date palms and fruit trees, vineyards, and fields of produce or grain. The river was alive with craft that crowded its broad reaches. Sails of red or white flashed their square and triangular shapes. Papyrus skiffs, their prows curved into graceful necks and spread in imitation of the lotus flower, scurried from bank to bank. Some of these, of quality workmanship, bore nobles and their friends or families for the recreation of sailing, fishing, or shooting arrows at waterfowl overhead.

In some craft, noblemen's wives were painted and bejeweled, while in others, naked children laughed, splashing water on the broad backs of oarsmen. Down from the first cataract came enormous barges, floating with the current, water up to their gunwales from their loads of granite blocks. Up river came large ships laden with logs from Lebanon and copper from mines in Canaan.

The earth underfoot was black/rich with silt and the normally thick vegetation was worn away from constant travel over this route. Now and then they passed by groups of laborers trudging southward. Their destination, Abusir between Gizeh and Memphis, was adjacent to the Nile but well above its flood level. For twenty years 100,000 men worked there just to provide a tomb for Pharaoh.

Masons worked year 'round at the quarries of Aswan, cutting huge blocks of granite according to a master architect's specifications. Laborers dragged stones on sledges to waiting barges at the water's edge. The barges were rowed down river, aided by the slow-moving current. Unloaded at a quay onto sledges, they were hauled up a causeway to the building site. Unlike the serfs, all free men, such as artisans, were paid for their services. Their wages were meat, grain, linen, dyed cloth, and rings of copper.

The wealth of the nation, collected ruthlessly by the king's tax collectors was spent on Pharaoh's monumental vanity, the pyramid.

While 100,000 laborers worked at Abusir for twenty years, thousands more men died fighting Nubians, so that the flow of gold from the southern mines to the workshops of Pharaoh's goldsmiths would continue uninterrupted. Others sweltered and died in the Sinai mines to provide copper for tools and tomb utensils.

Peasants sweated out their lives tilling the farmlands to feed this huge mass of workers who could have been engaged in more functional labor within the nation's economy.

Pharaoh's sons feared that so much would be spent on their father's pyramid tomb that too little would remain to pay for theirs. The country was being ruined by this unending extravagance, repeated by every Pharaoh on a grander scale than the one preceding.

There existed a real risk that the fields, left without men to cultivate them, would become non-producing. Eventually famine would follow and in its wake, pestilence.

Pharaoh's summer palace and its fortifications occupied a prime location at the northwestern side of Lake Balah, a pleasure lake excavated by Pharaoh. On either side of it ranged villas of the nobles, gleaming white from their painted brick and wood. Wherever Pharaoh resided, his society of nobles relocated with him to give favors and seek favors in return.

Abram was impressed with the architectural design of the palace fortress as it loomed ever closer. A stone-paved road greeted visitors at quite some distance away from the only gateway through the palace's fortified wall. The gate was only large enough to allow passage of the king's litter or a team of horses drawing a chariot. It was defended by towers on either side from which defenders could rain down arrows on attackers.

Crenellated walls extended to the left and the right of the gate. The water of a thirty-foot-wide moat, connected to the lake by a canal, surrounded the palace grounds. Block walls were resplendent with scenes of Pharaoh's exploits carved into the granite.

The minister ordered a halt a short distance from the guards at the gate, raised his staff of office and identified himself. The soldiers saluted him, opened the gates and stood aside to watch the procession pass through.

Once inside the walls, Abram and his men were guided into a white wing of a large building. They passed through corridors flashing with colored relieves.

Entering a great court, Abram saw a row of columns carved with a papyrus motif. The ceiling was a star-studded blue, representing the sky. Walls were carved with pure, flowing lines and painted in the colors of life depicting fields being tilled by naked serfs. Men and women were graphically recorded threshing grain, trampling grapes in vats, grinding grain into flour, and kneading bread. Servants, so faithfully drawn that they seemed alive and moving, bore platters on their heads, heaped with fruits.

Abram and his men remained standing just inside the doorway while Iknahten made his way around the several guests lounging comfortably about the court. Coming before the raised dais at the opposite end of the room, he bowed low and waited for permission to speak.

Pharaoh delayed acknowledging his presence, and the arrival of Abram, until he had finished an ongoing conversation punctuated by a sip of wine from his goblet. Turning his attention at last to the minister, Pharaoh said casually: "You may speak, Iknahten."

"I have done as you commanded, my lord. Your bride money and gifts have been delivered to the Heber-ew Chieftain, Abram. He has placed them in the charge of his servants and has returned with me. He now stands at the entrance with his body guards, awaiting the hospitality you proffered."

"Ah, yes, the brother of my new...wife. Bring him before me and announce him to my guests."

"As you command, my lord," the minister responded. Backing away so as to avoid showing his back to the king, Iknahten eventually turned sideways and stopped. Tapping his staff on the tile floor to get everyone's attention, he announced: "Presenting to his holiness, the king, nobles and ladies...Abram, son of Terah, Prince among the Heber-ews."

Abram ordered his guards to remain where they were, then approached Pharaoh.

"Prince Abram, how good of you to come," the king uttered facetiously.

"Your invitation is a command to me, great king," Abram responded in like manner.

"We are honored by your visit to our land, noble Abram, and especially that of your sister, Sarai. She is a remarkably attractive woman whose beauty of form and face I find irresistible. It pleased me to send you gifts as compensation for her. Would you agree that the payment is adequate?"

"You are most generous, my lord, and I am honored by this contract," Abram lied, desiring to rush forward and lop off the man's head with a swift cut from his sword. He smiled as he asked: "And is my sister available? I desire to embrace her and give my blessing to your marriage. This happened quite unexpectedly, you realize."

"Ah, yes. The poor woman was rather concerned about her welfare, and yours too, considering the unfortunate way you entered our country."

Abram felt embarrassed and angry at Pharaoh's snide remark and his smirking expression. Knowing he would have to answer for that failure, Abram steeled himself to overcome the effrontery without reacting to it. He said nothing more to encourage further discussion of the matter. It was almost more than he could stand, enduring the remarks of a pot-bellied, debauched, glutton. Looking at the king, he saw a wanton ruler who could never be satisfied...nor trusted.

"Yes, noble Abram, I will present Sarai to you and this illustrious gathering, but first I must prepare them for her."

Turning his attention to his courtiers Pharaoh began: "Nobles and ladies...a very remarkable incident happened recently..." Pharaoh delighted in the telling, languorously hanging onto certain details and creating emphasis for entertainment value. The intrigue and the humor of Abram's futile attempt to smuggle Sarai into the country were the beginning. Then Pharaoh described Sarai's mystical appearance in the garden court, and her feminine attributes. He was drooling with lust by the time he finished telling his experience. Keeping the audience fascinated by his command over them, Pharaoh changed his expression and took on an attitude of sincerity.

"In keeping with Sarai's value as a goddess of love, my goddess of love exclusively, I have given the following wealth to Abram in exchange for her as my wife."

Clapping his hands, the king ordered a scribe to come forward and read off the items from a scroll of parchment.

At the conclusion, a servant brought Abram a robe of finest silk, singling him out as a special guest.

"Now hear me; your king commands. All of you will treat Abram with dignity, so that he may be honored by all while he stays in Mizeraim for as long as he desires.

"Pharaoh, my lord, you play with us," a nobleman spoke up. "How long must we wait for a look at this woman you pay a king's ransom to have?"

"Patience, Snefutep, patience," Pharaoh teased. "Must you cajole your king to reveal his new treasure before the proper time?" He chastened with a smile, enjoying this new game that kept everyone in suspense.

"It is time for a change of surroundings and a taste of the feast I have ordered prepared for this celebration. Come now everyone," he gestured with a flourish, "the coolness of the early evening breeze from the lake wafts through the garden and the lowering sun shall deliver us a goddess before it retires for the night."

In the garden, rich carpets were spread to form a continuous ground cover between blooming shrubs. On the carpets were placed stools and finely carved chairs of hard woods. The cooling air was fresh and pleasant, perfumed with the scent of flowers.

Pharaoh sat on a raised dais with an empty chair next to him. His guests sat below him in a double line. There were no tables. A swarm of naked, tan and brown skinned girls stood ready to move among the rows of guests. With bowls heaped high with food, they served each guest a portion and then placed the vessels on stools where they could be easily reached.

Fruits were served first in gold and silver bowls. The guests ate, talking and laughing without constraint. Fowls were roasted within sight on copper braziers set between ornamental columns supporting vine-covered trellises.

Next on the menu would come boiled meats and steamed vegetables: peas, onions and papyrus shoots. Following this would come roast ox, roast geese, and wine.

Sarai had been waiting in a private witness chamber by the king's order. Watching, she saw Abram, handsome and fearless, stride into Pharaoh's court with his men. Her heart pounding in her breast, Sarai pressed her face to the reed lattice, attempting to see Abram clearly. She yearned to call out his name and run to him...to be held and comforted by him.

Rising above her desperation, with some new, hidden strength, she realized she must trust in the promise made by the Everliving's messenger and wait upon His deliverance. Listening carefully, Sarai heard all that Pharaoh said, and knew he had delivered to Abram the compensation for her that he had promised. She was amazed at the circumstances unfolding and still feared the outcome.

It happened as they ate. Some gasped; some choked and coughed on food or wine. Others sighed, and the remainder stared in slack-jawed awe. Sarai appeared from a doorway as the gentle lilt of a harp announced her entrance. Again, the bright sun spawned its goddess in a dazzling display of brilliance. From the gold of her hair, the cream of her exposed flesh, and the white of her dress, Sarai was the most radiantly beautiful women ever seen in Egypt.

"Come to me Sarai, my goddess, my wife," Pharaoh commanded, flushed and puffed up with pride as he watched the faces of his guests.

Sarai walked slowly, from the far end of the garden, anxiously looking for Abram amongst the strange faces. When she saw him near Pharaoh, her heart leapt under her breast. She could not hold back her anxiety any longer. The yearning for his protection burst her self-restraint and she hurried her steps until she halted in his arms.

"Nobles and ladies, I present to you: Sarai!

"Abram - behold your sister with her honor preserved," Pharaoh spoke loudly, happily. Delighted with himself and the way the evening was unfolding according to plan, he tolerated the lingering embrace of Abram and Sarai, scanning the garden and memorizing expressions on the faces of specific individuals for future reference.

"Fear not, my love, the Everliving sent his messenger to me and promised your deliverance. Everything is in his hands," Abram comforted Sarai.

"Oh, yes, Abram, He answered my prayers and assured my release."

"Has Pharaoh violated you?"

"No, my lord, I have been kept safe, but I fear that tonight will be the test."

"Hold to your faith for protection. That is your connection with our God. Remember that when you are in jeopardy."

"Sarai - come to me! Your husband and lord calls. It is time to give up fealty to your brother and rejoice over your future as my wife.

"Wine everyone! Let us celebrate the good fortune Sarai and I have found in each other. Will not one of you raise his cup and give tribute to my bride?"

The response from his guests was just what Pharaoh expected. They almost fought for the opportunity to be heard first. But the noble Amidhotep, less stunned than the rest and more prepared, stood first to get the recognition he justly deserved.

"I, Amidhotep, take privilege of being the first to pay homage to Pharaoh and his bride Sarai, a lovely goddess fit for our god/king. For it was this servant who rescued Sarai, a rare jewel of the desert, from a life of menial chores and harsh climate. And it was this servant who presented her to Pharaoh as you see her now. Live forever, Pharaoh and Sarai!"

"Live forever!" echoed the gathering.

"Let it be known that your king is generous to his loyal subjects who seek to please him. I hereby reward noble Amidhotep for his service."

Pharaoh clapped his hands and a middle-aged man came forward bowing low. "My lord?"

"Read aloud to my guests the list of rewards."

"As you command, my king."

Pharaoh watched, intently, the expressions on faces looking up at him. Amidhotep was gloating, puffed up with self-pride, that his venture had proved so successful and so very rewarding. He also saw jealousy in the eyes of men around him. The tight lines of their mouths, as everyone shifted their gaze back and forth between Pharaoh and him, were additional proof.

Abram and Sarai found in this an opportunity to steal loving glances at each other, hoping that Pharaoh would not intercept them. They risked his suspicion by displaying a desire for each other in their expressions of longing.

"Everyone drink! Be happy! This is a celebration!" Pharaoh commanded, smiling.

"Everything has been perfect, so far, but the best is yet to come," he mused looking hungrily at Sarai.

Naked slave girls staggered with diorite and alabaster vases filled with wine. Each bore the flagon upon her right shoulder, clasping the neck with hands raised above her head. Standing beside the guests, they went down on one knee and poured from the shoulder into cups of gold for the men and into delicate pottery, glazed with bright enamels, for the women.

Music of harps and flutes filled the air. The low chanting of singers, hidden among the shrubbery, added dimension. Little naked girls ran in and lay lotus flower wreaths around the necks of the guests. As the wine began taking effect, they laughed joyfully, for mirth loving Egyptians rejoiced with intoxication.

Suddenly, in rushed troops of dancers: slender, lithe girls of Upper Egypt and supple acrobats of Syria. Each in turn danced fast or slow to the rhythm of flute and harp.

Tumblers received the most applause, breaking the swift, rhythmic movement of their feet to stretch their bodies backward in an arc from straining toes to fingertips touching the ground. They crawled about this way, then reversed their position with backsides up.

Other dancers followed, their long hair weighted at the end with two light balls that twirled an added emphasis to the motion of their bodies.

Later came wrestlers: first men and then women - thick waisted, muscular women with short kilts and bare breasts. Guests laid bets on them while commenting on their muscular arms and shoulders, and their sturdy legs. Shouts of encouragement, curses of disappointment, and boisterous laughs of ridicule filled the garden as one, then another wrestler slipped in a pool of wine and went down awkwardly.

The hour grew late and palm torches cast their light on a mass of drunken male and female figures lying back amidst cushions, indulging themselves. Here and there groups of three or more were expending extra lusty desires in orgies.

The scene going on about him revolted Abram. Never before had he been exposed to such unbridled lust of the flesh. An almost constant parade of naked slaves approached Abram with lewd gestures and invitations.

Sarai was forced to watch the drunken orgy spread out before her, and the tempting of her beloved Abram. Her fear of the king was replaced by loathing, especially when she realized all this was calculated to excite her and Pharaoh in preparation for their wedding night.

Pharaoh called for his concubines, one or two at a time, and engaged in lascivious gestures and foreplay with the naked women. He forced Sarai to watch his disgusting display in spite of her blushing embarrassment. In fact, the king was amused by her reaction, interpreting her pink-flushed appearance as sexual desire for him.

Satisfied with his preparations he stood, commanding Sarai to take his arm and come along with him. Staggering slightly from the wine's effect, he smiled down at Abram, gave a low sneering chuckle and turned to exit.

A naked wine bearer was at Abram's side during the entire evening, constantly refilling his cup. Sarai's heart sank as she saw her husband drunk like the other guests, and feared what would happen next. She almost gave up hope. Then she remembered his comforting words, and her courage returned. 'Hold to your faith for protection. That is your connection with our God. Remember that when you are in jeopardy.'

Abram watched his beloved Sarai leave with Pharaoh and his faith was tested to the utmost. He fought within to keep from rising up and slaughtering the debauched monarch. When they were out of sight he stood up, gaining sobriety remarkably fast, and went to his men who were sprawled in drunken postures around the palatial garden. He called them individually, by name, and they too recovered instantly. Each man had drained his cup into the ground unseen, as instructed by their chieftain

Adjusting their clothing and arms to what they were earlier, Abram's guards fell in behind him and marched out of the palace. Mounting their camels they rode to the gate, past sleepy guards who were surprised to see a distinguished guest leave at this time of night. Seeing Pharaoh's gift robe on Abram, they saluted him as he passed by.

Outside the walls, Abram looked at the nightscape around him and discovered how brightly lit it was by a moon, close to its fullness.

"A perfect robber's moon; an ambush could be waiting for us on our way back," Abram thought. "I wonder if Pharaoh is as dishonorable as I suspect he is? Why would a self-indulgent, debauched king be so generous to a tribal chieftain under his authority? Pharaoh's servants were obviously instructed to make sure my men and I became drunk and dissipated. Of course everyone else had satisfied themselves to that extent. Am I unduly suspicious? The king is a very wealthy monarch. Remember how he rewarded Amidhotep for bringing Sarai to him? Curse that pig! I could cut him to pieces for that!"

Abram became submerged in bitter thoughts, unaware that they were distracting him from his suspicions. Without being aware of it he found himself passing through acres and acres of grape vineyards.

"Look ahead, Abram!" a voice commanded.

Shaken out of his submersion, Abram focused his hunter's vision on the road ahead and caught the slightest reflection of moonlight on metal. His skin prickled with alarm and a shudder of fear ran through his body. Raising his arm he silently ordered his men to halt. Dismounting, his men did the same and gathered close to hear his whispered commands.

"If it is as I suspect, an attack will come upon us as we pass between the vineyards up ahead. We will not run! We will stand and fight, squaring off against them, as I have taught you for a defense of the tribe. Now form up with the animals on our outside and memorize where your brothers are around you. Yahvah protect us, we pray. Strengthen our arms and weaken our enemies."

"So be it," the seven men agreed and they walked ahead in unison.

As many as two dozen armed men hunched themselves down, out of sight behind vineyard rows, waiting for eight hapless victims to meander by. They had been waiting for some time, confident of their superiority over a supposedly weakened handful of shepherds, inexperienced in combat. The king's soldiers, disguised as highwaymen, had been drinking for some time, bored as they were with the long wait. Many had fallen asleep, and those who had not were weak from their indulgence.

The captain of Pharaoh's bandits readied his men by whispered commands as he caught sight of Abram's party advancing toward his position. Within a few minutes they were passing through. The captain screamed at his men to jolt them into action.

"Kill! Kill! Kill!"

Twenty-four men stood up, staggering and attempting to run. Awkwardly they charged in from both sides meeting unexpected opposition. Abram's animals bolted, knocking over attackers and weakening the force of the Egyptian charge.

"Now!" Abram shouted.

His men formed a tight square with him, two men to a side. They held their shields and spears ready in defense to impale the onrushers. The Egyptians surrounded and rushed upon them screaming terror. The Heber-ews parried, blocked and stabbed. Each defender had consistent strength and agility to meet the groups of assailants as they threw themselves upon the unbreakable square. Eight Heber-ews fought as a fierce, precise death-dealing machine, each man assisting and defending the other next to him.

The Egyptians, although more numerous, were no match for them as the Heber-ew defense held tight. Each time the Egyptians attacked their strength failed and they fell, mortally cut.

Abram's combat square undulated as its eight elements moved to defend, to kill and form again to its leader. The first wave's slaughter lay around them and the second wave began falling in the same manner.

The Egyptian captain then began to realize the seriousness of his situation. He was losing a fight that was supposed to be an easy ambush of a few drunken shepherds. It was clear that he had to kill

Abram as ordered or die in the attempt. Pharaoh would not accept his failure.

"Form on me!" he yelled, and the remainder of his men, only half of the original twenty-four, came together in a disciplined military formation. "Kill Abram, their leader! Kill him or your souls are lost."

The rank of twelve Egyptians charged with swords waving, but the sounds of their howling battle cries were soon cut off in anguished gurgles of blood. The Heber-ews met the onslaught with a phalanx of seven men and Abram at the rear. The wedge cut through the soft Egyptian line like a knife through warm cheese. Abram slashed any attacker who managed to out-flank his men and come at them from the rear.

Sounds of battle rang out in the still night. The once peaceful moon-lit landscape lost its serenity and became a life and death struggle with the cacophony of weapons clashing, lips cursing and crying in agony as men fell bloodied and dying.

The battle wedge reformed again into a square, moving with its leader like an eight-legged spider, thrusting death at its enemy and walking over those that fell before it.

"Spare their leader and capture him!" Abram commanded his men. The sides were even in numbers now, eight against eight.

The Egyptian officer rallied the remnant of his command and tried desperately to concentrate their attack on Abram.

The Heber-ews formed their fighting wedge and, calling upon the Everliving to strengthen their arms, they pierced and slashed in a blur of motion until the only enemy left alive was the officer. Quickly Abram's men surrounded the officer who stood splashed with the blood of his fallen soldiers. He was disarmed by a blow to his arm, his sword falling away. More blows to his legs by spear butts drove him to his knees. Guarded by seven blades poised nearby, he heard Abram question.

"How is it you know me, captain? And why have you and your men set upon us to murder me? Speak the truth and I will spare your life. Lie to me and I will have my men cut out your tongue, blind your eyes and deliver your naked body to Pharaoh tied across an ass."

"In my humbled position, I salute you Abram. You and your men fought remarkably well. As for me...I am a captain of Pharaoh's soldiers whom you have conquered with amazing strength and ability. My name is of no importance since I am about to join my fallen comrades in arms."

In the next instant he drew a long dagger, placed the sharp point against his stomach and fell forward on it. His weight drove the blade clear through his stomach with the tip protruding out his back. Falling on his side, he screamed and jerked in the agony of dying.

Abram felt pity for his hapless adversary. Ending the Egyptian's suffering with a great swing of his sword, Abram separated the captain's head from his body.

"Drive three of their spears into the ground in a row, a distance of one cubit," he commanded.

Removing the fine robe Pharaoh had presented to him, Abram slipped it over the shafts so that it hung to the ground. Next, he took the Egyptian's head and impaled it on the end of the spear in the center so that it faced the king's palace. He opened the mouth and stuck out the tongue as a final touch. Stepping back to appreciate the effect, he turned towards the palace and shouted at his loudest: "Your captain awaits you with a message, Pharaoh!"

Abram's men laughed raucously, slapping each other in playful comradeship, their wounds forgotten. Then leaving the killing field strewn with men's bodies, they gathered up their camels, remounted and rode towards camp with vigor.

Abram had taken a count of the Egyptian dead before leaving. Looking at his men now, he was more proud of them than he had been of any other command. They had survived a night ambush and killed a professional enemy three times their number.

Abram wondered how Pharoah would react to this embarrassment. "Will he come after me with an army to take back his compensation and destroy me? Can he prevent his embarrassment from becoming known? What will become of us in this wicked land?"

While his men boasted to each other the wonders of their fighting prowess, Abram was silent during their ride to camp.

Back at the Heber-ew encampment, the sun's dawning light revealed to a sentry a group of men in the distance coming his way. He could not make out their number or identity. Taking no chance he called out to another guard, one of four patrolling the four sides of the camp. When the second guard responded, he was ordered to arouse Lot from his sleep.

"What...what is it? Is there some danger?" Lot asked.

"A company of riders approach, lord. I cannot be sure who they are, but they seem to be few in number."

Lot jumped up, threw on a mantle to ward off the cold, and went with the sentry. At the camp perimeter Lot strained his sleepy eyes to see, but was no help in the identification.

"I believe there are six or seven riders."

"Oh Lord Yahvah, let it be Abram returning safely!" Lot exclaimed.

"There are eight riders...yes eight!" yelled the sharp-eyed sentry.

Soon Lot heard a mighty voice shout in the distance: "Hello in the camp. It is Abram and his men who approach!"

"Welcome, brothers," Lot shouted in reply, his voice cracking from emotional excitement.

"Go quickly! Rouse the camp from their sleep. Tell everyone that Abram returns!" Lot commanded the sentries.

The tribe awoke and bustled with the excitement of curiosity. While the men gathered to greet their lord and his guards, women hastened to start preparations for a morning meal. Fires were started up from banked embers.

Dismounting at the perimeter of the camp, Abram's men formed a wedge behind him with spears upright and hard leather shields across their torsos. Each man fell in step with Abram's confident stride and they marched into camp like a crack military unit on parade. Men, women and children swarmed around them, shouting praises and welcoming them back. The strong seven chanted with each cadence: "A-bram, A-bram, A-bram, A-bram..."

Wives of the seven warriors fussed over their men with the utmost care and affection. The ambush battle was described by each man with particular attention to detail regarding how their own wounds were received. Everyone in the camp knew it was a marvelous victory that would become legend among Heber-ews for generations.

Abram looked at the scene of his united tribe with strong emotions. The day before he was a defeated wretch of a man, his clothes torn, and his body covered with ashes in misery over the loss of Sarai to Pharaoh. Now, having trusted in the aid of his God, he was the military leader and hero of his people, in addition to being their chief.

"Oh Sarai, my love, how I wish you were here tending my wounds, caressing me, and hearing my story," Abram sighed unhappily.

Chapter 18
Deliverance

And the Lord hearkened to the voice of Sarai, and the Lord sent an angel to deliver Sarai from the power of Pharaoh.

And the king came and sat before Sarai, and behold an angel of the Lord was standing over them, and he appeared to Sarai and said to her, do not fear for the Lord has heard thy prayer.

Jasher 15:19-20

P haraoh was in high spirits as he led Sarai away from the festivities in the garden.

"Abram and his drunken bodyguards will be slaughtered like sheep by my soldiers posing as highwaymen," he snickered silently. "I will have my gifts returned and the demoralized Heber-ews will become my slaves. Sarai, the prized flower of Canaan, for whom I have been hungrily lusting, will now open herself to me."

Dismissing his servants, the king stood with Sarai next to his large bed. He gawked at her entire body from head to foot mentally preparing for delicious foreplay. Slowly he removed her semi-transparent mantle and let it slide off to the floor. His eyes darted back and forth from Sarai's bare shoulder and heaving breasts, to her eyes and hair, then returned to her exposed breast.

Saliva trickled from the sides of his mouth as his hunger increased. Reaching up to her left shoulder, he un-did her tunic. Holding onto it at the front with one hand, he slowly lowered it, the fine silk gliding down seductively. The sight of Sarai's pink/white voluptuousness was staggering. Pharaoh let the gown fall to the floor and scanned her beauty until the temptation of his lust for her became unbearable.

His groin ached with a throbbing and his heart pumped with such intensity he felt it in his ears.

"I am hot...so hot!" he sighed with desire. Tearing at his clothes to remove them, Pharaoh advanced to take hold of Sarai.

"Eeeyow!!" he cried out in pain. Suddenly he was repelled by a powerful, unseen and unknown force that threw him to the floor. He laid there in shock, disbelieving such a thing could happen. Looking up at Sarai, he saw her standing motionless. She had not moved at all. Her face bore the same expressionless mask.

"She is a goddess!" Pharaoh murmured his heart pounding harder than before as he gazed up at her.

The beauty of her tortured him. The longer he looked at her, the more he desired her, almost forgetting his previous experience. Staggering to his feet, he approached Sarai very slowly. Standing at arm's length in front of her, Pharaoh slowly reached out to touch her. His fingers inched forward to within the space of a hand span. He hesitated, afraid to touch, his eyes staring hypnotically at the rise and fall of Sarai's breasts as she breathed.

"I am Pharaoh, God/king of all Mizeraim," he declared. "No harm can befall me. I hold the power of life and death over all my subjects, including all demons! Now, I shall have this woman, as is my right and privilege!"

Before he could move to touch Sarai, a blinding white light hit him full-bodied, sending him flying backwards to land painfully on his back.

"What is this that you are doing to me?" he shrieked. "What is this power you have to both seduce and strike me so terribly? Such agony you bring me. Are you a goddess come to torture me with unfulfilled desire, and then kill me with blows?"

Sarai stood unmoving, statuesque, saying nothing.

Pharaoh thought he was having a bad dream and shook himself to be sure that he was awake.

"Yes, I am awake! But why is this happening to me? Could it be a curse put upon me by the great gods?"

Looking at Sarai with disbelief, he saw only her beauty attracting him like a moth to a flame. His lust for her was driving him insane. She had become an all-consuming impassioned goal for him.

"I must have her! If she is a goddess, perhaps I may become immortal by consuming myself in her! Ah yes, yes...Sarai is worth suffering for, perhaps dying for, if only to be reborn a greater god."

Struggling to his feet, the king made a lunge at Sarai with all his weight behind him in a do or die effort. In spite of his momentum, he never touched her. The angel of God struck him again with such force that the stunned Pharaoh rolled over three times and lay jerking with pain, whimpering like an injured dog.

When he recovered his senses, the king realized he would never be able to have Sarai. Almost out of his mind with anger, frustration, and embarrassment, Pharaoh struggled to his knees and dragged himself to where he could summon his guards. He screamed for them hysterically as if he were being assaulted.

"Get more men! I want a hundred or more of my strongest guards!" he ordered the officer.

Big, strong warriors, the elite of Pharaoh's army, came running through the halls. A clapping thunder of leather sandals violated the early morning silence of a sleeping palace. Shields, spears, and swords clanked and rattled as they were drawn, ready for action.

The king's chambers filled with men who were startled at seeing their lord bruised and beaten with his clothing torn.

"Where are those who attacked you, my lord?" an officer questioned. "I see no one except...except your wife, Sarai."

"She is not my wife!" Pharaoh screamed. "She is an evil enchantress, come to drive me insane and destroy me with blows by an unseen power! But, If I cannot have her, I give her to you and your men! Now take her by force! Have your way with her! Ravish her! I command it!"

Slowly, at first, the bewildered men accepted this strangest of orders laying down their weapons and shields. They were stunned by Saria's beauty and stance. Standing straight and unafraid, in every respect a goddess, she looked through them as though they did not exist.

"Rush upon her! Do it! Do it!" Pharaoh shouted in frenzy for revenge.

Jolted into action, the king's men surrounded Sarai and began to close in. Suddenly, every one of them cried out in agony, holding the palms of their hands against the excruciating pain in their eyes. They reeled about the room, writhing, stumbling, and falling over each other in heaps...totally blind. Not one man touched Sarai. Those who came close were knocked away with blows that rendered them unconscious.

Pharaoh backed into a corner looking on in horror. Shaking with fear, he watched Sarai finally move to dress herself. Fully clothed, she walked out from among the fallen, wailing men into another part of the palace, away from the awful scene.

Pharaoh gathered his courage and cautiously followed her at a considerable distance, still terrified by her power. Speaking timidly and soothingly he hoped to discover why this misfortune had come upon him.

"Tell me truly Sarai...I implore you...who are you?" What are you to this man Abram who you came with?"

There was a silence...a heavy, heavy silence as Sarai pondered her answer. Finding courage and security from the protection around her, she decided to reveal the truth.

"Abram is my husband."

"Your husband? But...but why did you tell us he was your brother?"

"We were afraid that you would put him to death after taking me. As my brother, we felt you might spare him."

Pharaoh was speechless. He could only ponder the possible consequences that might come upon him for ordering the murder of Abram by ambush. A cold sweat covered him and he shivered with fear.

"He must be a sorcerer. Yes...yes, it must be so! That fool Amidhotep has brought me the wife of a sorcerer! Perhaps he did it to kill me and take over my throne. Yes, of course! He is an ambitious man."

While Sarai walked off to find a place where she could rest undisturbed, Pharaoh remained agitated for hours, unable to sleep.

It was dawn and the rays of morning streamed into the palace courts and gardens heralding a new day.

"Where is that captain? He was ordered to report to me this morning!" The king demanded of his minister.

"The captain has not reported back, my lord. I know not where he is."

"I wonder if he lost any men against the sorcerer? Is Abram really dead? Was he too drunk to save himself?"

The king's impatience became unbearable and he gave orders to his minister.

"Ride towards the Hebrews' camp until you meet the captain and his soldiers. They must be returning by now! Take a chariot and speed you away. Hurry!"

"Iknahten ran to the palace stables and ordered a chariot made ready in haste. He aroused a sleeping driver, pulled him out of bed and pushed him into the chariot. Instinctively the driver took reins in hand and guided his team through various turns on their way out of the palatial grounds. Through the open gates and over the moat bridge the chariot glided at an easy trot. Once they were on the road Iknahten ordered the driver to increase the pace.

"Faster! Faster! On towards the Heber-ew camp!

The wind in his face helped wake up the driver. He needed all his faculties alert to prevent the chariot from going into an irrigation ditch as they whipped around curves and negotiated ruts and holes.

It was a teeth-chattering, bone-jarring ride. Seeing anything clearly in the distance was very difficult. Iknahten peered ahead into the bright sunlight for any sign of marching men. There was nothing...not even a dust cloud from their feet scuffing the dirt. He was worried. He should have met them by now.

"Look! Ahead, where the road passes between those vineyards.... What is that? Is it a man?" The driver asked.

"I am not sure," Iknahten replied.

The chariot raced on, closer and closer.

"Yes, it is a man...but... By the gods! It is a severed head skewered on a spear!" the minister exclaimed. "What... who are all those men scattered about on the ground?"

Wary of the approaching chariot, vultures scurried off a short distance, anxious to return and resume their unfinished meal. The sight was gruesome and the king's men had no stomach for their task. It was necessary, however, to remember and report the details to Pharaoh.

They turned over each corpse to establish whether it was Egyptian or Heberew. When this grizzly detail was completed, they removed the impaled head and robe from the spears and the captain's dagger from his body. Wrapping them in Abram's robe Iknahten put them aboard the chariot and raced back towards the palace.

Pharaoh heard the detailed report from Iknahten and the chariot driver, who added his testimony to the accounting. The king asked questions until there was no further information available. He ordered a discreet burial of his dead soldiers in a mass grave to be left unmarked. The whole matter was to be kept secret.

Dismissing his servants, Pharaoh crawled into his bed to find some sense of security, somewhat the way of a child. He lay there unable to sleep. Shivering with fear he muttered: "He knows! He knows! I gave him that robe and he left it with the captain's head! Twenty-four men ambushed eight drunken shepherds and only the shepherds live! The God of Sarai protected her husband as well. I, even I, Pharaoh, king of all Mizeraim, have no authority over those who call upon the power of a God who is so mighty and so terrible in His deeds."

Fearful of Abram as a sorcerer who might conjure up more evil upon him, Pharaoh aroused Iknahten from his dozing and gave explicit orders.

"You will go immediately to the camp of the Heber-ews and give the following message to Abram, their chieftain. 'Sarai, your wife, awaits you. Come in peace; I shall return her to you."

"Abram! Abram! Wake up! The king's minister is here! He has come with a message from Pharaoh for you to hear directly."

Lot's voice became part of a dream Abram was struggling with and he awoke with difficulty. The rigors of battle, fought after late sleepless hours, caught up with him when he returned from the palace. It seemed as though he had just fallen asleep, but when he shuffled out of his tent, the position of the afternoon sun indicated he had been asleep for about ten hours.

"I am tired, very tired," he mumbled, "but the message must be important. Bring the minister here, nephew."

"As you command, lord."

Abram received Pharaoh's communication with exultation.

"Lot, did you hear? The king is releasing Sarai!"

"Yes, lord, I heard; but what if it is another trap?"

"I will pray again for The Everliving's protection. He was our shield, our sword and our strength of arms last night. He will not fail me."

"Yes, of course, but I will hold this minister of the king here as security until you return safely," Lot replied.

"Very well, nephew, if it pleases you. Now gather to me my strong seven. Prepare nine camels; we leave at once!"

On the way to the palace, Abram and his men rode over the ambush ground. How different the area looked from the first time they rode through the day before. Although the bodies of the dead were gone, there were signs of life and death struggles, and blood had stained the earth red. The strong seven looked at each other with great pride and began chanting: "A-bram, A-bram, A-bram..."

Abram smiled broadly, full of confidence that with the almighty God protecting them, even Pharaoh was impotent.

"How quickly the king found and buried his mistake," Abram remarked to his men. "We shall soon know if he has changed from the offensive profligate of last night. His insults to me were his only reward. With the Everliving's blessing we found our satisfaction by taking the lives of twenty-four of the king's men. Perhaps our God has taught him some additional manners in preserving Sarai's honor."

Abram raised his hand calling for a halt before the moat bridge. "I am Abram, prince of the Heber-ews, returning at the command of Pharaoh!" he called out to the guards atop the fortifications. "Tell your king I await his presence, here," he added as an extra precaution.

"If Pharaoh is still bent on my murder, he will be using the promise of Sarai's release as a deception. Lot's warning should be heeded. We will need the advantage of this ground position. The bridge is too narrow for the king's men to easily overwhelm us. If they do attack, one of you will ride back and warn our people to prepare for the worst," Abram instructed his strong seven.

"If it please my lord," spoke Telah, whose name meant strength, "I believe I speak for my brothers in arms in saying you, and only you, should be the one to return if Egyptian treachery greets us. We could stall them long enough for you to prepare the tribe for battle or escape."

"Your thoughts are commendable, Telah. I am committed, as a patriarch of the almighty God, to neither hide nor run any more. Here I shall stand as his instrument, should it be for instruction or for battle. We shall not cower nor experience fear should the entire army of Mizeraim come against us! Only Pharaoh shall tremble at the presence of the Everlivng in our midst. Now, dismount and form two ranks across the bridge with spears ready.

"Prince Abram! Prince Abram...er...ah...what is this that you have done to me?" Pharaoh questioned in an emotionally disturbed, hesitant voice. "Why did you say that Sarai was your sister, when she is really your wife?"

"I feared your power, oh great king. I believed Sarai to be so fair and beautiful that you would kill me and take her for a wife." Abram paused to lend emphasis to his wily explanation. "It is due to her beauty, therefore, that I said she was my sister.

"It is plain to me, especially now, that you are a just king, my lord." Again Abram paused to watch Pharaoh squirm as he stood on the battlement over the gate.

"How appropriate I listened to Lot's caution and chose this place to meet the king," Abram mused.

"You are a just king, my lord," Abram repeated to impose on Pharaoh's mind a sensible solution. "I can clearly see how wrong I was to fear injustice from you," he exclaimed facetiously. The people of your land and mine shall praise you for your wisdom, mercy and generosity," Abram lied to avoid the possibility of Pharaoh's wrath being loosed.

"Now return to me Sarai, my wife, I pray. The punishment that has come upon your household will cease. Let us dwell in your land in peace until the famine in Canaan is over."

"How could Abram know what awesome punishment took place in my bed chambers last night?" Pharaoh cried within. "He must be a sorcerer that knows all and sees all. Look at him standing there with only a few bodyguards, as bold and secure as a king at the head of a victorious army. I could summon a thousand men at arms to challenge him. But what assurance do I have that he would not strike them blind? My servants would kill each other without a blow from a Heber-ew."

"Yes, yes, it is my will that your wife return to you. Here...here she is...Sarai!" Pharaoh capitulated.

"Open the gate! Hurry, you fools, before we all die on her account!" Pharaoh shouted down to the guards, his voice quivering with agitation.

There was a rattling of bolts and bars and then the gate doors swung slowly open.

Abram saw her standing alone in the court, framed in the gate opening. His heart leaped. Her hair gleamed in the sunlight like a signal beacon.

"Sarai, come to me!" he commanded with a detectable sense of urgency.

"Abram! Abram!" she cried in answer. Picking up the hem of her tunic, she ran through the fortifications with her sight fixed on Abram's face. She was confused about the conversation between her husband and the king, but it did not matter. She was being freed...freed!

The strong seven parted ranks to let Sarai through, and closed again as Abram took his wife into his arms and kissed her longingly, thankful to have her back.

"Abram? Prince Abram?" the king called out. "It is my pleasure to give you more gifts, in addition to the rich dowry I have already given to you ... if you will leave Mizeraim ... perhaps tomorrow? Er...ah...tomorrow I will have more gifts awaiting you outside the gates of my border city. This will...ah...further demonstrate my generosity and mercy as you travel back to your land.

"A land of famine. You are withdrawing your hospitality, after we have paid the tithe, O noble swine?" Abram murmured for Sarai's ears only.

"You are most kind, noble king!" Abram called out in reply. "We shall accede to your wishes and leave tomorrow morning."

There was an exuberant celebration that night in the Heberew camp. Princess Sarai was returned with honor. She told her story of victory leaving out one important part. Relating her nakedness would embarrass Abram before his tribe. He was angered enough against Pharaoh. If her embarrassment were made public, Abram might be compelled to seek some revenge. This, in turn could endanger the whole tribe. That was too high a price to pay for avenging her embarrassment.

The next morning Abram paid careful attention to the arrangements for travel. When all the packing was completed, he commanded his men to be ready to do battle in case of Egyptian treachery.

At the gate out of the city of Sile, Iknahten's familiar figure greeted Abram.

"Salutations, Prince Abram and Princess Sarai!"

"How good to see you again, noble minister. Your presence, with a small armed escort, indicates the king has sent you to fulfill his covenant with me."

"You are all knowing, my lord Abram. Pharaoh sends me with bounteous gifts to you. If you will accompany me through the gate, I will present you with more cattle, servants, silver and gold."

Abram commanded his strong seven to accompany him as he led the tribe through the gate. A short distance beyond the entrance, they met a small troop of the king's men waiting in the shade of the great wall surrounding the city.

Iknahten showed Abram the new contributions to his wealth with the flourish of a merchant selling his wares.

"And finally, my lord Abram, Pharaoh gives to you this quite attractive, virgin maiden. She is the king's very own daughter, by one of his concubines."

"I have no desire for a second wife," Abram remarked, raising both hands in a gesture, declining this special gift.

"She will become your concubine then."

"I have no desire for a concubine."

"Then surely a handmaiden for your wife Sarai."

"I have no desire to offend the king by refusing his generous gift. I accept his pretty daughter to serve my wife. What is the maiden's name?"

"Hagar, my lord, Hagar is her name."

And the king said to his daughter, it is better for thee my daughter to be a handmaid in this man's house than to be a mistress in my house, after we have beheld the evil that befell us on account of this woman.

And Abram arose, and he and all belonging to him went away from Egypt; and Pharoah ordered some of his men to accompany him and all that went with him.

Jasher 15:32 & 33

Chapter 19

Separation

And he went on his journeys from the south even to Beth-el unto the place where his tent had been at the beginning, between Beth-el and Hai;

Unto the place of the altar, which he had made there at the first; and there Abram called on the name of the Lord.

King James Bible: Genesis 13:3,4

After their departure from Egypt, it developed that Abram and Lot waxed wealthier as they resided close by one another. Lot possessed a large stock of cattle, flocks of sheep, and herds of goats and camels. He had tents for his family members and servants. His bounty was plentiful because of Abram who shared the gifts Pharaoh bestowed upon him. The Everliving blessed Lot because of Abram, but Lot failed to realize this and trouble grew between them.

Their flocks and herds were so numerous that large areas were required to graze them. Herdsmen often traveled considerable distances with their flocks to find good pasture. Abram had commanded his herdsmen to avoid fields belonging to the Canaanites. Lot, however, allowed his flocks to violate these fields. The Canaanites watched this violation and came almost daily to quarrel with Abram about it.

Abram instructed Lot to respect the fields owned by the people of the land, but Lot did not obey. One day Abram took Lot to task.

"What is this you are doing to me? You make me despicable to the inhabitants of the land? You order your herdsmen to graze cattle in the fields of other people. You must know that you place us in jeopardy. Why do you do this to me?"

Lot had become complacent with his wealth and too lazy to comply with Abram's instruction. He was reluctant to confess this, so he looked aside and said nothing.

Day after day the trespassing became common. Abram was caught in the middle. Lot would not comply and Abram would listen to the Canaanites' complaints. Once again Abram confronted Lot, face to face.

"How long will you be a stumbling block to me with the inhabitants of this land?"

Again, Lot turned his face away and said nothing.

"Now hear me, Lot! Let there be no more quarreling between us, for we are kinsmen. You are my nephew, brother to my wife, and I do not wish to lose my love for you.

"My herdsmen complain to me every day about your servants. I have given their complaints just consideration and have observed that your people are always to blame. I now know why your shepherds repeatedly trespass. They are deliberately working to my harm! Your drovers incite bulls and drive them among my heifers. Then your men scatter my sheep that, afterwards, are unable to find their lambs.

"I have found that your wife ordered certain of your herdsmen to arrange these numerous incidents. They have been deliberately intended to provoke me and cause us to separate.

"Your wife has become vain and deceitful. She flaunts your wealth over the other women. She wears it as expensive clothing and jewelry. Still unsatisfied, she seeks more and more vain pleasures.

"You have lost your authority over her, nephew. Ado dominates you with guile, with sweet scents, with her body in unnatural sexual practices. She rules you by manipulating your lust after her flesh.

"I adjure you, my brother's son, establish your authority and control over her or you will lose everything!" Abram finished speaking and stared at Lot, waiting for a response to charges that could not be ignored.

Lot, red-faced with embarrassment, replied at last.

"It is true, uncle, that I have been lax in my authority and control over my wife and herdsmen, but I do not believe...I cannot believe she would dishonor me as you portray her. The women of the tribe are jealous of her beauty and her possessions. They, they pour false tales into your ear like dry tinder on a fire. A...a...a small irritation then becomes enflamed. A...a...spark becomes a large fire," Lot stammered feeble defenses in a desperate effort to convince Abram that his information was faulty, stemming from prejudice and exaggeration.

Inwardly, however, he suspected that every word his uncle said was correct. He did not want to admit it; he just could not. It would be the final blow against his manhood that had already been dissipated on the love couch.

"Enough! Enough!" Abram commanded. "I will hear no more of your whining, twisted tales. Your wife has become a disease to this tribe and must be removed. I will not tolerate this evil in our midst! I regret that we must part company, for I see you have not the will nor the authority to rule your wife."

"It is hard for me to utter such words, son of my brother," Abram continued without waiting for an answer, but I have decided that we shall no longer continue together. It is better to part now, rather than to endure a fester and allow it to grow as a cancer and fill our entire body. Come, walk with me."

Abram led the way up a hill to its crest where they could view the surrounding lands. To the southwest stretched the Negeb, or dry land that they had crossed in coming from Egypt. To the south lay Urusalem among the hills. To the southeast, beyond a range of hills, a low cloud indicated the location of a salt lake lying deep in a valley.

"Behold these lands that you see. Spread out before us lies a fertile land in which no one forbids us to graze our herds. Make a selection and depart from me to the place of your choosing."

Abram's voice sounded resolute and unyielding but his heart longed to forgive Lot. He yearned to embrace him like a wayward son who might confess his disobedience while clinging to his father's feet, begging forgiveness and promising correction. Abram reasoned that his nephew would be alarmed at losing the security of his tribe. He felt certain Lot would promise atonement and ask him to withdraw his decision. Abram underestimated Lot's weakness for his wife's domination and was surprised to hear:

"Let it be as you say, uncle. You choose the way you will go. The first choice is not for me, your servant."

Feeling shaken and defeated by Lot's decision, Abram snapped angrily, "I have said that you shall choose, now choose!"

"Since that is your will, I shall choose," Lot hurriedly agreed. "I would like to settle in the Valley of Siddim, south of the great Salt Lake."

"What is there that makes you decide for such a place?"

Lot grew more confident and described it enthusiastically.

"It is very beautiful, and as fertile as Mizeraim. The grass grows as high as a man's girdle. There are so many trees that it is also called the wooded valley. All around it are hills, and the wind from the desert never penetrates because the hills protect it. The irrigation water flows naturally into canals due to the southward slope of the valley."

"Where does the water flow from?"

"From the Salt Lake. There is a rock formation at the south end that forms some kind of a threshold to the valley that spreads out below it. Through clefts in the rocks, water drips into ponds. In the ponds the salt sinks to the bottom, and the usable water runs into canals.

"There is hardly one spot in the entire valley where it does not reach. And so flowers and crops of all descriptions grow in abundance."

"When did you see this valley?" Abram challenged.

"I have not seen it. A merchant, who travels there every year for bitumen, told my wife about it."

"Ah ha, I understand," Abram remarked with derision. "I am surprised that this valley is uninhabited, if it is so fertile."

"Not so, uncle, a great many people dwell there in five cities! Sodom, Gomorrah, Zoar, Admah, and Zeboim are their names. The largest is Sodom."

"How will you find room for your herds amongst such a dense population?"

"I believe I can purchase a moderate expanse of meadowland that will provide amply, for the grass grows continually. The air is humid. The nights are as warm as the days. The cities are wealthy. Their people live carefree lives. They sing, dance, and watch the games...."

"Just the lifestyle your wife desires!" Abram interrupted. "I understand perfectly."

"Lot's face reddened with guilt, but he said nothing.

They both were silent, looking out over the vast landscape.

"Lot, my brother's son," Abram broke the silence, "why did you not tell me before this that you wanted to leave our tribe? It is clear that your wife has not only convinced you to leave me, but she has also chosen the place for your new home."

"I was afraid of your anger," Lot alibied.

"My anger? Did I prevent Nahor, my brother, from staying in Haran?"

"And I was very sorry at the thought of parting from you, Uncle Abram. You have been like a father to me and a magnificent chief to admire."

"Oh Lot, blood of mine, I too am sorry. But what can I do? I have spoken, and you have chosen your path. The plant does not hold back the seed that has departed and is driven where the wind carries it. Go in peace, since going is your desire. Take with you all that is yours."

"Blessed be all your days, Uncle Abram," Lot spoke affectionately. Turning away he walked down the hill leaving Abram alone.

A depression came over Abram. Sinking to his knees he felt overwhelmed with the disappointment of rejection. After all these years Sarai was still barren. He had thought to make Lot his heir, but now Lot was leaving, and with him went Abram's hopes for progeny to fulfill the covenant of his God. He wept silently feeling a loss more terrible than a severed arm.

"Everliving Yahvah! Do not forsake me!" he cried out with vibrant passion. "Consider your servant, I pray. Remember your promises that brought me to this land. Do not leave me without an heir. Open my wife's womb that she may bear for me. I shall remain separate from those who will not know you and who commit the unclean practices invented by men. Hear me, almighty God...listen to my pleading! Hear me...hear me!" the hills echoed with Abram's imploring cries.

The EVER-LIVING said to Abram, after Lot separated from him:

"LOOK UPWARD FROM THE PLACE WHERE YOU ARE, TAKE A VIEW NORTHWARD, AND SOUTHWARD, AND EASTWARD, AND WESTWARD; FOR ALL THE LAND WHICH YOU SEE, I WILL GIVE TO YOU, AND TO YOUR RACE FOR EVER.

I WILL ALSO MAKE YOUR RACE LIKE THE DUST OF THE EARTH, SO THAT IF A MAN IS ABLE TO COUNT THE DUST OF THE EARTH,

THEN HE CAN NUMBER YOUR RACE. ARISE AND MARCH THROUGH THE LAND, INSPECT BOTH ITS LENGTH AND ITS BREADTH, FOR I WILL GIVE IT TO YOU."

So Abram struck his camp, and came and settled in the Oakwoods of Mamrah which is near Hebron, and there he built an altar to the EVER-LIVING.

Genesis 13:14-18 (Ferrar Fenton Bible)

Chapter 20
The Invasion of Canaan

I

And it came to pass in the days of Amraphel (Nimrod) King of Shinar, Arioch King of Ellasar, Chedorlaomer King of Elam, and Tidal King of Nations;

That these made war with Bera King of Sodom, and with Birsha King of Gommorrah, Shinab King of Admah, and Shemeber King of Zeboiim, and the King of Bela which is Zoar.

All these were joined together in the Vale of Siddim, which is the salt sea.

Twelve years they served Chedorlaomer, and in the thirteenth year they rebelled.

Genesis 14:1-4 (King James Bible)

It was during the fourteenth year of the rebellion that Chedorlaomer, King of Elam, sent envoys to the three kings under his submission. Nimrod, Arioch, and Tidal each heard: "Come up to me and assist me, that we may smite all the towns of the Valley of Siddim and punish their inhabitants, for they have rebelled against me."

"I do not want to join Chedorlaomer with his army in this punitive war." Nimrod complained to his wise men. "It could only further exhaust my forces with little gain to come of it, even if we should win. I would receive little tribute from the cities of Canaan. And if we should lose, my kingdom's military strength would be destroyed. I would have no future opportunity to re-establish my supremacy over Chedorlaomer."

"You cannot refuse to join him, however, my lord," warned a wise man. "Chedorlaomer would simply conquer you first; then blot out your life and your name from the land."

"Your best recourse," advised a conjurer, "is to join Chedorlaomer, defeat the Sodomites, along with their allies, and take as much of the spoils of slaves and goods as is your right."

When the time for assembly came, Chedorlaomer put 150,000 fully armed men into the march. Arioch, his next strongest ally, supplied 100,000 men. Tidal brought 80,000 and Nimrod 70,000 men-at-arms. They gathered in the Plain of Shinar, an army 400,000 strong, and planned their route of invasion. In a few days they pulled up tent stakes and began their long journey of conquest.

Chedorlaomer was Commander-in-chief over all the armies. He ordered that the four kings, in their palanquins, ride abreast of each other in front of their hosts. In this manner they conversed with each other and passed the time during each day's march. Where possible, the columns widened so that fewer commanders would be breathing dust stirred up from the troops ahead.

The route of this huge army paralleled the great Euphrates River as it traveled northwest. They covered approximately ten to fifteen miles each day. Chedorlaomer was in no hurry and the men needed to be strong and ready for battle when the time came. It was early April and the winter rains were over for the most part. A six month dry season of Spring through Fall lay ahead making their travel tolerably easy. By following the Euphrates River, they had plenty of water for men and animals.

The armies had now been marching forty days since they assembled at Shinar. It was a long trek with no cities along the way after they had passed Sippar, thirty-five miles north of Shinar. The river supported many small villages, individual family farms, and tribes of nomads raising small crops and grazing herds. All of this population involuntarily contributed large portions of their food supplies to the king's foragers.

Soldiers swarmed into the habitations taking all manner of food at hand, from grains to animals. None dared to resist; instantaneous death would be their penalty. It was also unfortunate for young women, especially attractive ones, if they were found. Soldiers ordered them to lead animals or carry food to the army. After this was done they were kept, instead of released, as concubines to serve the sexual thirst of the kings and their officers.

On day forty-one of the march, the city/state of Mari appeared ahead on the horizon. The massive twenty-four foot high walls, seen from several miles away, loomed tall and protective. It was there that a group of eight men, seated on asses, met with the four kings.

"Greetings, great kings, I am Bonubar, minister of Zimri-Lim, king of Mari. My lord sends me to greet you as his emissary and offer you the hospility of his fine city in exchange for its safekeeping. He sends this message: 'We Amorites are a peaceful people maintaining this city as a vital trading center for all kingdoms as far west as Cypress, Crete and the isles of the unknown world beyond, to the great kingdoms of the Hatti, Assyrians, Babylonians and Elamites of the north and east. If you bring war upon us you may bring to a halt the flow of world trade to your countries. Why deny yourselves the excitement of spices and fabrics, utensils, inventions, furniture, weapons, beautiful women, incense, perfumes, and oils that pass through our fair city? Continue to enjoy them all, noble kings, through peace with us.

"We are prepared for war, however, if war is your insatiable desire. Our walls are tall, thick, and very strong. We have ample food and water for a long siege and many brave men of war to defend Mari. Let us not talk of war, however, let us talk of hospitality.

My Lord King Zimri-Lim bids me to ask of you: 'What do you require to leave us in peace?'"

Chedorlaomer listened to the entreaty and called for his minister to act as his mouthpiece. It was beneath him to talk directly to an intermediary.

"Tell this Banubar that I, Chedorlaomer, command the armies of four kings, a very numerous host. I can conquer whom I will and great walls will not stop me. Since Zimri-Lim, however, is a wise king who offers hospitality rather than arrows and spears, I accept his offer. Tell your king I shall meet with him at the South Gate of your city tomorrow and discuss the extent of his hospitality. That is all."

The message was communicated between ministers and the party of eight returned to Mari.

Chedorlaomer commanded that his four armies set up camp and prepare the evening meal. He called his three kings to a meeting and they discussed the tribute to be extracted from the Mari king. Also planned was the route they should take with their invasion of Canaan.

"Mari is the jumping off place for journeying west to Canaan, Nimrod reminded. "I sent one of my princes to Canaan many years ago to spy out the land. I recall it is between ten and twelve day's march to the oasis of Tadmor. We have to cross the northern tip of the great Arabian Desert. Our armies will require adequate food and water for twelve or more days to nourish 400,000 men and our many animals."

Having determined an appropriate amount of specific items, Chedorlaomer spoke up.

"Triple the amounts!"

"Triple? What if the Amorite does not agree? Do we war against them?" asked Nimrod?

"Zimri-Lim will agree. I promise you, he will agree."

The next morning, Chedorlaomer met with King Zimri-Lim at the South Gate to the city, as pre-arranged. The high walls provided ample shade for the host king and his guest dignitary. The two kings reclined in their comfortable palanquins and partook of refreshments as they gradually approached a discussion of the items Chedorlaomer would demand.

"My friend, noble King Chedorlaomer, we have been watching your travel toward our land for many days. We have known the numbers and weaponry of the four armies under the three kings and yourself. We are awed by your amazing strength of numbers and we wish to be allied to you. Surely you have not come to Mari as an enemy, for we are friends through trade to all peoples. We have much to offer through an alliance."

"How is it that you know so much about us, as you claim, King Zimri-Lim?"

"We have many eyes and ears friendly to us, because of trade, and they report to us what they deem worthy. Our distant outposts, hundreds of miles down the Euphrates, receive information and observe activities of importance. Reports are transmitted from signal post to signal post, across many miles in sequence, until they are received at my palace."

"And how, wise king, is this transmitting, you speak of, accomplished?"

By means of fire signals."

Fire signals?"

"Yes."

"But how can that be?"

"By day we observe smoke signals. By night we see the light of the flames. We have signaling codes for both methods, which are known only by our trained men. Our coded signals are secret and shall remain so. Beyond our borders there are nomadic tribes that communicate with their members by the same methods. They have their unique code, which we do not understand. We assume that they do not understand our signals either."

"Please allow me to test the accuracy of your 'telling' system, King Zimri-Lim."

"By all means King Chedorlaomer."

225

"According to your information: where did our armies assemble and how many days ago was it that we began our march from that place?"

The King of Mari thought for a moment and then consulted with his minister. They agreed on the information they remembered, and the king answered:

"Mighty king, you assembled your four armies in the Plain of Shinar beyond the city of Shinar, also called Babylon. You began your march forty-two days ago and you rotate your regiments daily."

"Hmm, well it appears that I cannot deny either the efficiency of your spy system nor the accuracy of its information. And so that is how you prepared, well in advance, a defense against us?"

"Yes, well in advance. So much so that our allies have been preparing for your coming as well. The fierce Heberew nomads are out there on the desert's edge awaiting our pre-arranged signal. They are related to us and will fight savagely to preserve this family stronghold, if necessary. They are a proud people who pay no taxes and will not be numbered. They will never be conscripted into an army nor allow themselves to become enslaved.

"These independent thieves steal from the crops of our lands and graze their herds in our fields during very dry months. This is much to my disliking, but my leniency is a form of tribute I pay for their assistance when needed. A less tolerant king would lose this ally and create more serious problems he would rather avoid."

"Hmm, and so this is why you so agreeably revealed to me the secret of your 'telling' system. Is it not so?"

"You are very astute, great king, and I hope, understanding?"

"Understanding about what?"

"Our hospitality, of course. If you will have your minister present a list of your needs to my minister, we may begin negotiations."

"I understand what you mean. Very well, let us see what your hospitality is worth."

The two ministers and their scribes went a short distance away, out of hearing of the kings, and began a bartering process that took several minutes for this initial phase. They returned to their kings and reported the items involved and amounts discussed. The conversations were hushed as each king re-instructed his minister for the next exchange.

King Zimri-Lim knew the needs for food of an army this size and had discussed the problem with his advisers the night before. He also guessed that Chedorlaomer would demand much more than he needed. Each side had an absolute quota; other quotas in mind were for negotiating.

Back and forth the ministers went from the bargaining table to their kings, employing strategy, manipulation of values and enduring patience.

There was no indication of hostility. This non-aggression pact being negotiated, had all the appearances of normal generous eastern hospitality, except...huge armies were on the alert, close by, poised to jump into action if directed by a signal. Refreshments were served and entertainment presented by Zimr-Lim to maintain a pleasant environment.

But, Chedorlaomer had arranged for his own form of entertainment. During the first exchange between ministers, ten companies of charioteers, consisting of 100 chariots each, came pounding in a rush, like the sound of rolling thunder, to within 50 yards of the city walls. Their drivers skillfully reined in the pairs of asses and maneuvered them so they formed a neat line facing the city. It was an effective gesture of strength. The King of Mari jumped out of his palanquin trembling in fear as if to run for the city gate and sanctuary.

A smirk formed on Chedorlaomer's lips; his plan of intimidation began working its effect.

"Ahh, King Zimri-Lim...do not be alarmed. Be assured that no assault is intended. One of my allied kings provides us with a display of military skill to help pass the time. It is merely entertainment, I assure you. Please make yourself comfortable again and let us proceed."

Zimri-Lim had taken a rather hard line in the early round of discussions and his demeanor had radiated confidence and calm. Now, Chedorlaomer detected a slight change in his adversary's bearing.

It was during the second exchange between kings that the earth shook with the pounding hoof beats of another two thousand animals drawing a thousand chariots. They came to a halt abreast of the first contingent, in an even line. The effect was quite distracting to the bartering process.

About fifteen minutes later another thousand chariots came, this time in a column of twos. An opening formed in the standing ranks and the oncoming chariots charged through, splitting into single files turning left and right. To the ends of the ranks they rushed, making a tight circular turn and joining the existing ranks.

The line-up was quite long now and very impressive as three thousand chariots stood poised in a straight line.

Chedorlaomer noticed a softening of King Zimri-Lim's hardened attitude. The unnerving effect of massive chariot drills was taking its toll. Zimri-Lim's minister was beginning to stutter in an attempt to hurry but still resist the huge demands by the city's invaders. His feeble argument was interrupted again by the now familiar, but still terrifying, charge of yet another thousand chariots. The effect was awesome. Zimri-Lim was becoming very nervous and worried.

"Is there no end to their numbers?" he thought. "If this many chariots ever managed to enter the city, all would be lost in an hour. We must not fail to satisfy these hordes lest they tire of our haggling and take what they want by force and put my city to the torch.

The last contingent of one thousand chariots came charging through the ranks. They shouted as they roared by, closer than the others. Zimri-Lim was petrified with fear and desperate to retreat from all this intolerable threat. He agreed to most of Cheorlaomer's demands, politely, but nervously, made an excuse to end their meeting, and commanded his guards to return to the palace.

The ministers were left to carry out the transfer of the tribute as their kings left. Chedorlaomer leaned back against the pillows, gloating over his success.

"What king could withstand such bargaining power as I have?" he asked himself aloud. The question amused him and he laughed. Remembering the look of terror on his opponent's face, Chedorlaomer convulsed with laughter so hearty that defenders on the walls of Mari could hear it. Its evil quality made stouthearted men shiver with fearful doubts. One of them was King Zimri-Lim.

That afternoon the four kings celebrated their good fortune. A very substantial tribute had been exacted from a wealthy kingdom without the loss of a single warrior or animal. His allied kings and their army commanders feted Chedorlaomer. The peaceful victory was experienced by all the soldiers and they, too, shared in the celebration. Morale was very high and every man counted himself fortunate to be a part of such a magnificent conquering army.

II

Two days later, during pre-dawn hours, the four kings headed their armies West across the desert. It was the middle of May. The days were warm and the nights cold. Mid-morning of the twelfth day, the beautiful oasis of Tadmor appeared on the horizon. It was a wealthy city only one mile square, a city luxuriant with greenery and shady from a profusion of date palms growing everywhere. The city's ample springs gurgled to the surface supplying life-giving water to man, beast, and some small amount of agriculture.

Tadmor stood on the crossroads of four trade routes: Mari to the east, Haran to the north, Damascus to the southwest and other lesser cities to the west along the Jordan River. Trade goods of all kinds passed through Tadmor but the most typical were silks, perfumes and jewels from the east on their way to the Mediterranean world. Heavy tolls were taken from the caravans in return for protection from the desert tribes, and duties were levied on all imports and exports.

The city's king, like the King of Mari, was Amorite. He, too, had foreknowledge of the coming of the four armies. King Zimri-Lim had an alliance with him and sent signals warning of their approach. The king had no will to resist such an overwhelming force and he sent his emissary to greet the four kings and arrange a meeting similar to the one at Mari.

Chedorlaomer replied through his minister: "I will meet with your king when and if I feel disposed to do so."

Conferring with his allies, Chedorlaomer expressed a different approach towards extorting tribute from Jokmeam, the King of Tadmor. He also wanted his armies tested before the next step of their journey.

That night, Jokmeam looked out from the highest parapet of his palace. He scanned the territory surrounding the entire city and was astounded by what he saw. Hundreds of thousands of campfires, torches, and oil lamps brightened the black night sufficiently to create an artificial dusk with their glow. Never before had anyone seen such a spectacular display of firelight.

"It is as if the multitude of heaven's stars have descended all around my city!" he exclaimed. "It is truly a sign from Enkidu, God of the Sky! Are the gods displeased with me and my people? The temple priests are always demanding more gifts to the gods. They grow fat and extremely wealthy. But it is never enough; they always want more. Oh my, what is going to happen to us? What do these hordes want?"

On the second night the lamps, torches, and campfires were blazing brightly as on the first night. But this time there was activity all through the night. Movements of troops with torches, hundreds of thousands in one formation after another, kept King Jokmeam awake all night.

Military activity increased on the third night. Wave after wave of chariots, with torches attached, pounded thunderously around the city's walls keeping every man, woman, and child awake and terrified. The days were no different as a seemingly endless number of chariots and foot soldiers inexhaustibly performed maneuvers around the city.

"How long will they keep this going? Are these maneuvers a rehearsal before an attack? Are they ignoring my overture for peaceful settlement?" These and many other questions went unanswered as King Jokmeam waited hour by fearful hour for the night to pass.

On the fourth day, military maneuvers became more fearful than ever. Chedorlaomer's regiments and divisions performed drills with scaling ladders, battering rams, fire catapults and flaming arrows just outside the walls. Inside the city everyone was nerve-wracked and crazed with fear. The suspense of wondering when their city would be invaded weighed upon everyone like a crushing burden. Yet all during this time not one arrow was shot, nor one spear thrown into the city.

The fifth day and night was a repeat of the fourth. The city was totally demoralized and chaotic. A state of anarchy was developing.

On the sixth day King Jokmeam sent Rakem, his minister, out of the city to find and talk to Chedorlaomer. He was guided to the monarch's tent by elite guards. After waiting for some time, Chedorlaomer sent for Nebat, his minister. He, in turn, had servants admit the Amorite.

To Rakem's surprise he found Chedorlaomer relaxing in his tent, bare to the waist. He lay upon soft silk cushions running his fingers through his hair and taking sips from a goblet of beer. Two young women, also naked to the waist, steadily waved fans over his body to stir the heated air.

In spite of the extreme informality of the situation, Rakem followed Jokmeam's orders. He fell prostrate before Chedorlaomer, his face and fine silk robe in the dust.

"Who is this Amorite who intrudes upon my privacy and grovels in the earth at my feet?"

"It is King Jokmeam's minister, my lord." answered Nebat.

"Very well, let him speak and be done with it."

"My king, Jokmeam, sends his compliments to you, mighty king, and urgently desires to please you with his hospitality in a most generous manner."

Chedorlaomer directed his minister to reply: "Tell your king that the Mighty King Chedorlaomer will come very soon with a portion of his huge army and inspect the city. At that time we shall see how generous King Jokmeam's hospitality can be. That is all"

"But your majesty, my king..."

"That is all! You are dismissed. Leave now while you can still walk!" Chedorlaomer bellowed like an angry bear.

Rakem quickly gained his feet and while bowing, backed out of the tent. In his haste he stumbled, fell on his seat, got up again and scurried out, fearing for his life. As he ran back to the city Chedorlaomer's sadistic laughter followed after him.

All during the maneuvers of the past six days, one-half of the huge army rested while the other half was active. Every eight hours the halves changed, affording eight hours of rest after each eight hours of military activity. Each half, composed of 200,000 men, was an extraordinary army of itself capable of taking the city by force.

The small army defending Tadmor was no more than ten thousand men. Their normal occupation was to protect caravans against marauding desert tribes who preyed upon trade routes.
The city's army contingents had always outnumbered their enemy and there was never a question about military superiority...until now. On this occasion their resistance would amount to only a slight pause in the path of half the giant army surrounding them.

"Resistance of any kind is futile and will only incur the wrath of these hordes so that they will utterly destroy us and our fair city," Jokmeam said ruefully. "Therefore I must command that every citizen and soldier in the city give up, without resistance, anything the invaders want: be it food, possessions, slaves, sons, wives or daughters."

Dismissing his minister and wise men to herald the king's proclamation, Jokmeam hung his head in shame, fearful for his life.

The main gate to the city was opened at the sight of the coming invaders, like an invitation to friends. Horns were sounded within the city by sentries alerting the populace.

Outside the city, broad ranks of Chedorlaomer's army approached. Horns blew signaling commands within the great divisions to reform the regiments...then within the regiments to reform the battalions. Voice commands then issued down to company commanders and from company commanders down to platoon commanders. By the time they reached the city, squads of foot soldiers marched abreast through the gateway.

In between each company of five hundred foot soldiers, a company of one hundred chariots came two abreast. On and on they came almost without end as the city filled with soldiers from one extremity to the other.

When the main body had entered and disarmed the defenders, a signal was blown on horns. Now the four kings proceeded to Tadmor's western gate carried on their royal palanquins, guarded by another ten thousand elite guards.

Chedorlaomer was the first of the four kings to enter the city. Every man, woman, and child of the city bowed down before him, their heads touching the ground. Soldiers of the Eastern Armies saluted where they stood guard on the alert.

There were three other gates to the city facing north, south, and east. Since the army of the four kings first encamped surrounding the city, no one had been allowed to leave and no caravans had arrived. The wealth of the entire city was now at the disposal of the invaders.

When Chedorlaomer reached the palace, King Jokmeam and all of his staff and servants bowed down before him.

"King Jokmeam!" bellowed Chedorlaomer.

The King of Tadmor came scurrying and bowed low at Chedorlaomer's feet.

"Listen carefully to what I say and you might live."

"Yes, my lord King Chedorlaomer. You have but to speak and I shall obey," he stuttered through trembling lips.

"This city is mine! All that is in it is mine, every person and every thing! I have the power to take all, or any portion that I choose. Do you agree Jokmeam?"

"Ah, oh yes, of course, my lord, anything...ah, or all, as you desire."

"And if I am displeased, I may ravage the city and blot out your name."

"Please, my lord, take freely, you and all your men. No one will oppose you for I have already commanded that our city is yours. If it will please you, great king, let us live as a city owned by you whereby we may contribute wealth to you continually, all your years. Let us live and we shall be loyal to you in tribute unending. We beg that you let your servants live to serve you," he ended, his voice quivering with anxiety.

"Very well, Jokmeam, issue that declaration to your people again, so that the city may be spared!"

The King of Tadmor hastened to obey this ruthless conquerer and the city was opened to the unbridled lusts of its captors.

For seven days the invaders reveled, pillaged and raped at will. Another three days were spent recuperating from their drunken dissipation. On the eleventh day Tadmor was left intact but poor, except for the treasures people managed to hide by burying them. The huge army, now fully provisioned for many days, headed southwest.

III

Fourteen days ahead, a distance of 140 miles along a well-established trade route, a lush oasis lay waiting. It was located in the center of a plain thirty miles long by ten miles wide 2300 feet above sea level. Snow-capped Mt. Hermon was on its West side. This plateau was bordered by a part of the Anti-Lebanon Mountains on the north. A string of marshes and lakes rimmed the east before the plain dropped to the Arabian Desert. On its southern end, another low range of hills shut off the region.

The plateau and oasis owed their life to the Abana River that rushed from the Anti-Lebanon Mountains, running a course of ten miles through a narrow mountain gorge, then flinging itself into seven streams. These streams further divided into hundreds of smaller waterways, transforming the region into a fruitful orchard and garden. The name of this renowned oasis was, and still is, called Damascus.

Oral tradition names Uz, a grandson of Shem, as the city's

founder. The people of this territory and its kings were Arameans, descendants of Shem. Like the Amorites of Mari, these Shemites were dedicated to trade, not conquest. Damascus was about sixty-five miles east of the Mediterranean Sea coast and the highway junction of three major caravan routes.

Damascus made reciprocal trade treaties with various cities, small and large, near and far. This chief city of Canaan earned its distinction for extensive trade because of its wealth, strategic location and protective alliances with other trading kingdoms.

Damascus had allies throughout the land of Canaan, including the nomadic tribes like that of Abram. The nomads of Canaan were peaceful, pastoral people who normally did not become involved in wars between cities. When their family relations in the city were threatened, or their own security in the country was jeopardized, then they fought...savagely!

King Derazon of Damascus received warning of the huge invasion three days after Tadmor was left raped. He put Damascus and the whole territory on the alert. In addition to mustering the city's garrison, he also sent messengers hastening to solicit the aid of his allies. Within a few days an amalgamated-armed force of 275,000 men had mustered at the city.

Tribal chieftains and commanders of the allied city armies held a council to determine the best means of defense. By the following day, troops were deployed in various strategic defensive positions along the northeast side of the plateau where the invaders were expected to appear. The mountains to the north and the string of marshes and lakes on the east were natural barriers to massive troop assaults. The passages between the barriers were the locations for potential enemy attacks and this is where the Damascan forces set up their first line of defense.

There was feverish activity from the day news of the invaders was received. Thousands upon thousands of workers arrived and joined with those who had come earlier in digging trenches as pitfalls for on-rushing chariots and foot soldiers. Fortifications were raised with dirt and rocks from these trenches, which were about eight feet wide and four feet deep. Sharp sticks protruded from the pit bottom and from the wall of dirt raised in back of the trench that faced the attackers.

After its completion, defenders formed ranks behind the wall; bowmen first and spearmen second. Substantial reserve contingents, stationed fifty yards behind the front line forces, waited to support failing defenders in any area of attack. Spotters were posted on high

Invasion Route of the Eastern Armies

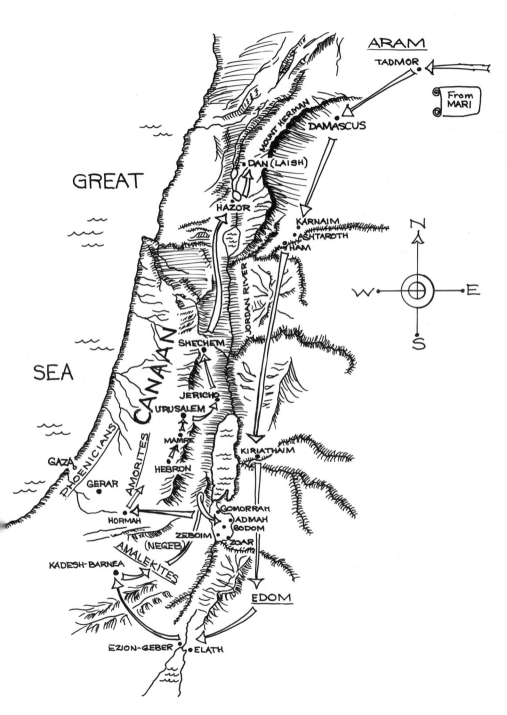

ground locations, prepared to send signals to the command post. The maneuvering of enemy troops, their numbers and types would be observed and reported. This intelligence allowed time for decisive defensive tactics against concentrated attacks.

On the fourteenth day, Chedorlaomer's advance scouts returned with their report on the defenses at Damascus. The information startled their chief commander.

"We spent two days spying out the land around Damascus, my king, and we found the territory well fortified. They have considerable strength in numbers, perhaps 250,000 to 300,000 fighting men. Fortified trenches have been dug to defend every passage around the lakes and marshes on the east and the mountains to the north. A range of hills on the south of their high ground is undoubtedly prepared for defense. I have some men spying out that territory and when they return we shall know for sure what the circumstances are."

"We will set up camp opposite their defenses. Station companies of men all along the northern and eastern approaches," Chedorlaomer ordered his commanders. "They shall know the fear our previous hosts have experienced, and then we shall see how their defenses stand against our invincible army."

The black of a moonless night settled upon Damascus. King Derazon kept a vigil upon the city's wall, looking toward the enemy encampment. What he saw sent chills up his spine. Campfires started up and multiplied by the countless thousands. He knew that as many as ten Warriors might share a fire for cooking and warmth.

"I have never seen nor heard of an army so numerous! I am staggered by its immensity. How can we survive such power?"

King Derazon was witnessing the enemy's night of a million fires to the north and east around the plateau for several miles. His spies had described a similar spectacle as having taken place at Tadmor. The story had been very impressive, but actually witnessing the scene struck fear into the king's heart. He stood in shock, dazed by the threat of so many soldiers poised to attack.

"Will my defenses withstand such a huge army? Did I make the right decision in opposing this awesome invader? Should I have sought a treaty with him without preparing a defense? But now that I am committed, what more can I do to protect the city and its first line of defense along the plateau's perimeter?" A hundred questions nagged at him.

For the next three nights, troops of the four kings flexed their military muscle. Active, noisy maneuvers day and night, kept the defenders sleepless and on edge. On the fourth day Chedorlaomer sent an emissary to arrange a talk with King Derazon. It was agreed that they would meet person to person at the middle of a lake, each in a small boat with only two oarsmen and no weapons.

Chedorlaomer was unhappy with the arrangement. It was a perfectly neutral position. He had no way of intimidating Derazon like he had with the kings of Mari and Tadmor. He had always had the advantage in previous negotiations with kings through their ministers. This time there was no intermediary and he cursed his minister for agreeing to this arrangement.

"I will have to be very clever with King Derazon. It is obvious that he is an astute adversary of some considerable intellect and experience," he admitted unhappily.

The water was fairly calm, with only a mild breeze stirring, when the two kings started out from their opposing shores. The breezes grew stronger and the water more agitated, however, after they met and began their intricate negotiations. The oarsmen in both boats worked continually to maintain position in the middle of the lake and avoid drifting and turning.

The wind created a current pushing the boats westward. Chedorlaomer was preoccupied with delivering his thoughts and maintaining the proper composure of a mighty conquering king. He failed to notice that his boat was drifting closer and closer to the defenders' shoreline. It was only fifty yards away when he looked aside and saw the danger he was in.

A group of men, armed with bows, arrows and spears, ran from concealment towards some boats waiting at the water's edge. Into three boats they scrambled, shoving off in the direction of the kings. Four men pulled mightily on the oars of each boat while a fifth man sat in the front with bow and arrows at the ready.

It was a spontaneous, unplanned exploit launched by King Derazon's commander-in-chief, Anderah-dim, as he carefully watched for the safety of his king. At the most propitious moment, he sent his strongest men and best archers into action. He had boats scattered along the shoreline, ready for use should they be needed to counter any treachery by the invaders.

"The enemy comes for us! We have drifted to them! Turn this boat, you fools, and row for your lives to our shore!" Chedorlaomer screamed at his oarsmen.

His rowers were mighty men of strength. Quickly responding, they dug their paddles into the water and pulled hard, leaving a trail of small whirlpools in their wake. The boat surged through the water as they pulled in coordination. Their speed increased in measure with the increased cadence of heaving grunts.

Realizing there was no other option but to carry out what his commander had initiated, King Derazon saw the opportunity at hand and ordered his rowers to impede Chedorlaomer's boat and hold it. One of them threw an anchor into the invader's boat grappling a side near the rear. It braked the runaways to a virtual stop with the extra boat to tow.

Chedorlaomer screamed an oath at his enemy, drew a short sword and severed the anchor line with one cut.

The lead paddler in King Derazon's boat used his paddle as a weapon to bludgeon the rear oarsman in Chedorlaomer's boat.

Chedorlaomer turned and swung his sword mightily, cutting off the paddle blade.

"Paddle, mighty men of Elam, Paddle!" he shouted.

The boat surged forward again and the two men picked up a rhythmic cadence. Chedorlaomer cursed them to pull faster and stronger. They were bare to the waist exposing their brawn. Perspiration formed into beads glistening in the sun, then ran as streams down their faces and torsos. Thick neck muscles strained, arms and shoulders flexed, chests and stomachs rippled and heaved from the labor.

The Damascans were only about thirty-five yards away and gaining. Their bowmen sat aiming their arrows, waiting for the right moment as the distance narrowed.

Two shields lay under Chedorlaomer's feet. Under them were concealed a bow and quiver of arrows. Quickly he placed the shields over the backs of his rowers, securing them with a length of sash cut from his turban looped around each man's shoulder and chest. Chedorlaomer was an excellent bowman and hunter. He had used this skill to accumulate power and eventually become king in the same fashion as had Nimrod, his ally. Arming his strong bow, he took aim at the bowman in the nearest approaching boat. Taking his time, he gauged the distance, the wind, and the surging strokes of his paddlers. Slowly he pulled the gut taught, holding until the timing was right...then released.

The arrow shot through the air with great velocity in a shrill hiss and found its mark...s s s h h h t t u c k ! " It hit paddler number two, sitting in the middle of the boat, sending him sprawling into the lap of the man in back of him, dead, the arrow protruding out of his back. The boat stopped while men took hold and rolled the corpse overboard. Taking up their paddles they renewed the chase.

Damascan archers were ordered to let fly their arrows at Chedorlaomer, who was already aiming his second arrow at the bowman in the new lead boat. Missiles passed in their trajectories. The archer in the lead chasing boat never knew where his arrow hit. Chedorlaomer's arrow shrieked towards him with extraordinary velocity. Passing clear through the side of his neck it ended its flight in the chest of the first paddler. Both men were out of the fight and their boat was stopped. But the other two kept on pursuing and the gap was closing slightly. Twenty-five yards away the two remaining bowmen let loose their arrows. One arrow stopped in the shield of the back oarsman and the other stopped in Chedorlaomer's armor breast-plate cutting his skin.

The animal hide armor was not detectable under his royal robes. He ignored the arrow and concentrated on his next targets. He continued to let arrows fly at his pursuers without stopping to remove the shaft. It had a startling effect on his would be assassins.

"Look at him!" they cried out to each other, "Is he an immortal who cannot die?

The only answer heard was that of Chedorlaomer's next arrow penetrating its target. A pain-filled shriek emanated from the archer in the nearest boat. The arrowhead protruded out the back of the man's shoulder as he writhed in agony. Oarsmen in that boat stopped their pursuit, yielding to an unreasoning fear of this mighty hunter/king who could not die. As they stared ahead in disbelief, they saw not one but two arrows stuck in his chest...and he was aiming his next arrow at the remaining Damascus archer.

The pursuing archer released his bow a mere instant before the king did and once again trajectories crossed. The rower behind Chedorlaomer could only hear his heart pounding in his ears and his raspy breath sucking desperately for more air. He never heard the arrow hit him at the base of the skull. Feeling little pain, he died instantly. A few inches to either side and Chedorlaomer would have been the recipient.

Chedorlaomer's arrow shot true, finding its mark in the stomach of the last bowman leaving him writhing in an agonizing death. This third and last Damascan boat stopped its chase.

The remaining Elamite paddler kept up his lone cadence, paddling bravely against the weight of the boat and the current against him. It seemed like a long journey, deathly long, but very soon Chedorlaomer was near his shore. The troops stationed there had watched the battle fought by their king with fascination, and cheered him as he stepped ashore, victorious. They bowed down before him as he approached and hailed him: "Chedorlaomer, Almighty God King, The Invincible One."

News of his exploits spread up and down the front lines on both sides. Chedorlaomer paraded before his troops standing proud and god-like in his chariot with the two arrows still protruding from his chest and blood staining his garments. He was an inspirational sight, stirring his armies into a frenzy.

"Prepare to conquer those who would murder your king while they talk of peace. Kill the vile enemy!"

The excitement kept building as Chedorlaomer screamed orders to all his commanders to attack! His usually calm, calculating demeanor was replaced by a reckless compulsion for revenge. He ordered every warrior and every commander to attack at once without regard for preparations, strategy, or consequences. He truly believed the gods were with him and he would defeat the defenders in one great assault.

Nimrod and the other allied kings were not in agreement over the method of attack, but they understood the importance of an army in high spirits, confident of victory. They knew men would be fearless in their invoked frenzy. They also knew this advantage could work against them without proper intelligence and maneuvering of troops.

The invasion was out of control now as the multitude of invaders swarmed all positions of defense at once in a frontal assault. Trenches were soon filled with dead men stuck with arrows, spears, and spikes. Very quickly shrieks of agony replaced war cries as the first wave of seventy thousand men found death, or begged for its release from their excruciating pain.

The defenders' fortifications held for the most part. There was one major exception. Two divisions, commanded by the most zealous of Chedorlaomer's officers, mounted an unremitting attack. A rain of arrows fell upon the defenders. This covering barrage allowed as many as twenty thousand men to overcome the pit of death, and crumble the first line of Damascans. The superior Elamite warriors thrust and hacked their way through less able defenders sending them reeling before the onslaught. Splitting their force in two, they turned on the defender's flanks and began cutting men down like grass before a harvester's scythe.

A sounding of horns was barely discernible above the clanging of weapons, clatter of shields, battle shouts, and screams of pain.

Suddenly a new wave of battle sounds could be heard. It

emanated from the charging Damascans swarming to the aid of the weakened line. The superior force surrounded and counter-attacked the Elamites with a defensive frenzy. The Damascans' combination of fierce fighting and skillful tactics took its toll and the tide of battle began to turn once more in favor of the defenders.

Allied Damascan lancers and swordsmen worked side by side to protect each other with long and short range fighting agility. Bowmen astride camels kept to the outside perimeter and shot arrows over the heads of their comrades and into the vitals of the struggling enemy. It proved to be as efficient as shooting an animal caught in a trap.

The attack lost its momentum and halted. Twenty thousand gallant Elamite warriors were stopped by the counter-attack. Compressed backwards, they buckled and fell in a heavy slaughter. Only a few hundred attackers were able to fight their way back to their own forces as the Damascan line reinforced its strength, closed the breach, and prepared against a possible new assault.

"No! That cannot be; there must be a mistake!" Chedorlaomer railed against his commanders for their disappointing reports. "Our warriors were ready to conquer even the most difficult enemy. I myself instilled in them a greater courage than they ever had before! Verify those numbers! I tell you we could not have lost seventy thousand men and failed to gain strategic passages through the enemy defenses!"

Dusk was descending like a mourner's veil, dark and colorless. The attacking divisions were withdrawn and all commanders called to a strategy conference. Evidence of defeat lay not only on the ground, where bloody bodies stained the earth, but also in the silent aftermath of retreat.

A great price had been paid and nothing gained. This defeat was a bitter bargain and the losers who lived to talk about it felt cheated. They had previously frolicked in victories won too easily, without loss of life. Now, the fearful consequences of war, a losing war, filled every man in the eastern army with dread.

The night of a million lights became a night of darkness where a huge army hid its shame. No order was given to exaggerate cooking fires, torches and lamps to impress the Damascenes; it was another mistake by the wearied and shaken Chedorlaomer.

Secluded in his tent, with ample wine to drown his frustration, he bellowed: "I wanted the glory of conquering this rich city for myself! Every soul in this civilized world would come to know and fear the name Chedorlaomer, 'The Immortal King! Now, my dream of conquest is turning into a nightmare! I must find a way to take this city, I must! I must!

The following night, under the cover of darkness, eight divisions of the eastern army moved quietly, secretly, away from their positions. There was no obvious alarm nor warning sounded by the defenders, but the fire signals, transmitting messages a short distance from the southern end of their army went undetected. They were assumed to be just flickering campfires.

The army marched in a wide arc southward and came up to the foot of the hills bounding the southern end of the defenders' plateau. In the early morning hours before dawn their deployment was complete. Forty thousand men now began their slow advance up the hills.

A gentle, cold breeze wafted across the hills. All was quiet except for the soft 'shsssh' of air and rustle of cautious footsteps in the grass. The four kings believed this sneak attack would succeed. Vengeance for their dead would be sweet when their four divisions surprised the unsuspecting defenders during the night.

Nimrod had conceived this plan and convinced Chedorlaomer it would succeed. The other two monarchs withheld their opinion until Chedorlaomer agreed it was feasible, then they gave their consent to the scheme.

"If my southerly attack is victorious," Nimrod mused, "Once the city is defeated, I will have first choice, if not a very great portion, of the spoils to be shared. Many slaves will be taken and I will claim a lion's share because of my brilliant daring."

Nimrod stood next to his palanquin watching his army advancing with the stealth of hunters. A tingling flush of vanity ran over his flesh, stimulating him. He felt more secure than he had for quite some time. His old self-confidence returned and the anticipation of battle stirred his loins.

The first feature of defense that the army encountered was a barrier of waist-high spikes driven into the ground at different angles to impede attackers in a massive assault. Strangely enough, they pointed uphill as well as down. Ignoring the oddity the officers motioned their warriors forward. After snaking their way slowly and safely through, with careful steps, the invaders came upon a change in the terrain. An abnormal amount of dead grass or chaff from grain lay underfoot. Wild grass and scrub brush was also profuse.

The four divisions were well beyond the line of spiked barriers that stretched for miles along the rump of the hills. They were two-thirds of the way up these grassy mounts when a hardly detectable scent wafted down on the air currents drifting from the northwest. The scent became stronger as they advanced and was finally identified.

"Oil...oil...oil!" The warning was whispered, and leapfrogged from man to man.

They continued their cautious advance, suspicious of what lay ahead.

Somewhere over the top of the hills a Damascan commander lit a torch and waved a signal to his divisions of defenders. After a brief pause, fifty thousand torches came afire and were poised, waiting for the next signal. It came soon and they went immediately into action.

Oil soaked rags were set afire and fastened to arrows that twenty thousand bowmen held ready to shoot.

Five thousand men held throwing sticks with a small bag of oil tied around the shaft next to a barbed head. A few inches up the shafts, oil soaked rags were set ablaze.

Large tumbleweed balls entwined with dried grasses and liberally sprinkled with oil were freed from their restraints and pushed downhill toward the invaders. As they gained rapid momentum, bowmen shot flaming arrows into them, setting them ablaze.

The ranks of spearmen threw their oil-laden missiles, after the fireballs into those spaces in the line not set on fire. The bags burst on impact. Ignited by the flaming rags, fire exploded into fragments starting a hundred small fires. This multitude of splashing incendiaries interconnected to form a continuous wall of flame.

The firewall segments joined with other flaming segments until a fire line was formed. Hungry flames quickly devoured the highly volatile fuel that lay before it. Unfortunately for the invaders, it lay under their feet and all about them. The top and northerly slope of the hills had been cleared of grass and brush for application to the southern side. It was a necessary firebreak for the defenders. The heat was so intense that Damascans had to duck behind the hills for shelter.

The attackers were paralyzed with indecision and fear. The wall of fire soon forced them to retreat downhill in a mad scramble to avoid being burned.

The spikes that awaited them seemed unimportant, even forgotten, as those closest to the fire panicked and ran for their lives, pushing comrades out of the way. Some got through the spikes safely; a great many did not.

Nimrod could not believe his eyes. As he watched, the whole southern landscape as far as he could see lit up with fire. From his position on a rise of ground at the base of the hills he watched with dismay as his great expectations went up in smoke.

As the men swarmed downhill, twelve thousand in the front ranks impaled themselves. Those in the middle ranks, who climbed over the bodies of the dead front runners, escaped. Fifteen thousand men, who were overrun by the balls of fire and engulfed in the wall of flames, died in excruciating agony.

When dawn arrived, it revealed the ghastly remains of twenty-seven thousand horribly charred bodies strewn along eight to ten miles of hillsides. The thirteen thousand surviving attackers retreated to their encampments without weapons and shields, lucky to be alive. Of those that returned, one thousand more died during the following days from the effects of their burns or cuts from the spikes.

This terrible defeat shattered the morale of the entire eastern army. The warriors believed Damascus was protected by the Gods and invaders were punished for attacking it.

The four kings were stunned by this second defeat. Meeting in council for some hours, they reviewed the facts and studied alternative courses of action. Finally, they agreed that all defenses of the Damascans were horribly effective. There were no weak areas to be found. None of the kings wanted to admit defeat, but not one of them wanted the blame for recklessly sending more thousands of men to their deaths.

The defenders watched and prepared for the next invasion attempt, believing it would certainly come, but knowing not where, or when.

Day and night, commanders looked for changes in enemy positions. Information about anything substantial was sent to the higher command and redeployment of reserves was arranged. Signals from their spies, out beyond the enemy, had provided essential information instrumental to every successful defense.

"Five days have passed since our burning victory on the south perimeter," King Derazon noted. "The attackers seem to be taking their time preparing something new. Where will the next attack be? In what strength? Day or night? Signals from my nomad informers have not been received for the past five days, and they do not answer ours. I must find out the reason for all this!"

Derazon ordered patrols of men to venture across battle lines along the perimeter to find answers. By early morning, reports came pouring into defense command confirming the attacking army had moved its forces back, eastward towards Tadmor.

In their departing wake, the four kings left a hideous momento. Almost three hundred Aramean nomads, all those who spied on the attackers, were found. Their hands and feet were tied to poles driven in the ground. They leaned forward, facing Damascus, in a state of collapse. Many were still alive, barely alive. Blood ran down their bodies from empty eye sockets, severed ears, and mouths where tongues were cut out. Their agonizing cries were silenced by the gags in their mouths.

It was a grizzly token of retribution. The defenders freed them from their bonds and brought them into the city. King Derazon ordered them to become his guests and stay at the palace. There he provided necessary care and nursed them back to some measure of health.

In the months and years that followed, survivors of the battles were seen outside the palace wall and gates begging for food, living reminders of the magnificent battles fought in defense of Damascas, against the eastern hordes.

IV

Fifty miles south of Damascus, in a region east of the Sea of Chinnereth (Galilee) lay the sister cities of Karnaim and Ashteroth. This territory rose 2000 feet above sea level and was very rich in grain production. It was the home of a remnant of an ancient race of giants called Rephaims. (In Hebrew it means 'strong') They were the aboriginal people who once lived in Canaan, Edom, Moab and Ammon before the Great Flood of Noah and before the conquests by the descendants of Shem and Ham. The remaining territory later became known as Bashan, ruled by a mighty king named Og.

Karnaim and Ashteroth were city centers for the worship of Ashteroth, the Goddess of Sexual fertility and War. (Anath, Astarte and Asherah were other names given to the same chief diety.) She was represented as a virgin and also a pregnant goddess. Throughout the Land of Canaan her temples were centers of legalized vice where sacred prostitution was practiced as normal ritual.

In front of her temples, in the cities of Karnaim and Ashteroth, there were shrine-houses that showed the earth goddess seated outside a window in a lewd posture holding two doves. Two warring male deities courted her favor. A serpent (the earth) and the lion of power were also represented. It was a glorification of prostitution in the name of religion. Homes and public places displayed plaques with lewd scenes of the goddess. To the Babylonians she was Ishtar; to the Greeks she became Aphrodite; and in later times, she was Venus to the Romans.

Atop the north wall of the fortified city of Karnaim, a watchman detected movement a long distance away. He called a fellow guard to join him in discerning just what type of people were approaching. Could it be an army, a caravan, or nomads?

After some time one of the watchmen said: "It is not an army, that is certain. They are too few in number. There is no great dust cloud following their footsteps."

Finally, they agreed that it was most likely a caravan and a large one at that.

"Perhaps it is on its way south as far as Ezion Geber at the north end of the Gulf of Aqaba...or even the cities along the edge of the Arabian Peninsula facing the Red Sea. This is the main route for those ambitious caravans traveling as far south as Arabia Felix."

"Is that not the southern most point of the great peninsula?"

"Yes."

"I have heard that the landowners grow rich by trading their frankincense and myrrh for talents of gold and other goods."

"Where do they get this frankincense and myrrh from?"

"From the aromatic resins of two kinds of trees that grow only in that area."

"Very rare merchandise. Is that why those aromatics, are more than twice the cost of gold by weight?

"Yes. If only I were there instead of here. I would be a wealthy man.

"Dream on, you poor fool! Only the king, his nobility, and the governing priesthood are allowed to grow and harvest what those trees yield."

"Dreams are all I have at times to give me hope for something better. Curse you for spoiling this one; I could have lived within it for a number of days."

When the caravan came plainly into view, the watchmen alerted the city's inhabitants by blowing on rams' horns: one long bleat and one short. The sound was immediately repeated, followed by a pause.

Along the length of the north wall other watchmen picked up signaling horns and relayed the message to the populace and the military. An arrival of a large caravan was an event of considerable interest and enjoyment for it brought both goods and news.

The caravan stopped outside the gate and its leader asked for permission to enter the city and engage in trade.

A captain of the Karnaim's guards ordered the gates opened. When the bars were thrown, he led a contingent of one hundred fifty men out to inspect the caravan. Satisfying himself that trade was their purpose, the captain accepted a customary bribe and allowed that they be admitted into the city. Guards formed up in front and behind to bring the traders and their servants through the gates and into city. Two hundred men and five hundred camels and asses trudged in with their escort.

After receiving water for their animals and themselves, they were led to a large open marketplace where the captain ordered them to set out their wares.

The traders began an enticing process of revealing their exotic, rare, and longed-for goods. The popularity of the traders grew as news of their generous barter spread. The king's own servants secured objects fit for royalty at a value far below what was expected. King Nisroch summoned before him the traders from whom he purchased items.

"Why is it you are so generous compared to other traders that have come to our city?"

"We merely seek the comforts and protection of your city, my lord king. We desire only some water and provender for our animals, and food and shelter for ourselves at the city's caravanserais. Comfort and security are valuable commodities to wealthy traders, my lord. We can afford to be generous to a gracious host."

Very well then, accept my hospitality for the evening meal and the protection of my city for as long as you stay. I wish to hear the news you bring from your travels."

"As you command, good king."

There was entertainment that night. The friendliness of the visitors encouraged a festive spirit. Food and ample amounts of strong drink were consumed in many parts of the city. Soldiers in particular were treated to fine wines as the traders expressed their desire to remain secure within the city walls.

As the night progressed, gifts of strong drink made their way into the grateful hands of each military contingent posted within the Karnaim's perimeter. Everyone having anything to do with the city's security was encouraged to enjoy themselves and have a rollicking good time, the same as their king.

At every location, guests offered many toasts to the greatness of the city, its king, its military, its warm-hearted, fun-loving people and their goddess. There was not a man who could refuse to drink. To do so would dishonor themselves as well as their guests.

And so the drinking went on until the only sober soldiers were those on guard duty atop the walls. At some time in the dark, early-morning hours, the watchmen were also drunk because officers were too inebriated to perform their duties. Generous traders, considerate of those guards who were unfortunately left out of the festivities, passed wineskins up to them. Later, they even joined them on the ramparts in a spirit of congeniality.

Centered somewhere within the city, a howl could be heard. It seemed to come from a creature part dog and part wolf. It was carried by other responding howls to the four corners of the city. Upon hearing this, the congenial traders suddenly pulled daggers from their girdles and stabbed every sentry, watchman, and guard on duty. The assassins laughed raucously in the face of agonizing screams to disguise the outcries of their victims. Gatekeepers were slaughtered and the gate to the city swung open. Every trader murdered at least one soldier. About three hundred Rephaim died that night before Chedorlaomer's army entered the city.

The four kings had planned this campaign well and the execution was faultless so far. At first, Chedorlaomer had been reluctant to accept suggestions other than his own, but the failures at Damascus were bitter proof that quick decisions by one king could be self-defeating. He never admitted failure, however. That would be a

248

display of weakness and fallibility unbefitting a king, especially a king of kings such as he believed he was.

For three days the four kings had each contributed a fair share to planning, refining and embellishing new invasion plans to the south. On the fourth day a large trade caravan was formed by the command of Chedorlaomer and set out secretly after dark traveling southward. Trailing after the caravan was an army of one hundred thousand foot soldiers.

The Damascans never knew their enemy had secretly moved one-third of its remaining forces directly to the south. That army marched only at night to avoid detection, and on each of the five days traveled, it hid in ravines and wadis during the daylight hours.

There were no signal communications between desert nomads and the Rephaim to reveal this army's presence. The Rephaim had no use for 'Heber-ew pests' who lived freely off other peoples' lands.

At the end of the fourth night of travel the advance army hid itself only four to five miles away from its objective. During the next day the caravan had arrived at Ashteroth to perform their assigned task: murder the city's watchmen.

By the time all sentries were killed and the city gates opened, four of the army's regiments had secretly advanced to within a few hundred yards of the city walls. The howl of the wolf was their signal to come to the city and rush through the gates when opened. On the heels of this segment the remainder of the 100,000 warriors stormed the gates and poured into Karnaim. Led by the infiltrating 'traders,' they quickly found and subdued the bulk of the city's troop garrison.

The sleeping military never knew how it happened, but suddenly they were overwhelmed by a numerous enemy. With their lives threatened at the point of a sharp weapon, every man capitulated, begging for mercy. The first ones attempting to fight were quickly slaughtered and held as an example of what would happen to others that resisted.

Every captive was bound so they could use neither hands nor feet and were left with a token guard force while the main body of invaders moved on to their next objective.

There were signs of stirring by Karnaim's inhabitants. Dogs barked incessantly, passing a canine alarm throughout the city. Their noise woke many who realized this was something more than a usual passing irritation.

The king's palace lay protected by its own fortifications within the walled city. Sentries at the king's palace patrolled their sectors of wall. A squad of eight guards kept their vigil inside a strong gate, the palace's only entrance. To pass the time, some guards gambled while others stood look out for any officer making a sudden inspection. Night duty was boring and something had to be done to stay awake.

"Listen to those dogs will you? They sure are excited about something out there," remarked one of the sentries on the wall to his friend.

"It seemed to start after that wolf call I heard a short time ago. You don't suppose a wild wolf, part dog, is to blame for all that barking and howling?"

"Sure, if he is running wild through the city with a pack at his heels."

"You may be right but we had better keep a sharp eye on the lookout for trouble."

"What was that?"

"What was what?"

"A scream...there another...shouting...more screams...sounds like something serious is happening within the city. You men had better stop that gambling. I am waking the officer of the sentries. I do not like what I hear out there."

Another few minutes passed and the officer of the watch, aroused from his dozing, now listened from atop the wall to the sounds of alarm.

"Hit that alarm gong to alert the palace guard! Keep striking it until the king himself appears. I think we have been invaded! Prepare yourselves for battle!"

The first light of dawn finally brought visibility to sinister scenes below. King Nisroch stood peering across rooftops into the city's streets and saw its population being herded along like cattle towards the palace. His mouth dropped open and he watched with slack-jawed disbelief as men, women, and children were prodded with spears and sword points into the parade ground in front of the palace gate.

"How could this happen?" many asked. "We give hospitality to a caravan and these people turn on us like savages! Is this our proper reward?" The answers they received were brutally insensitive.

Packed in like sheep, they were forced to sit and keep quiet. Those who spoke were bludgeoned with vicious strikes to the head and body with the butts of weapons. Squads of invaders roamed among the massed thousands, sadistically beating people into silence.

The four kings, with the main bulk of their army, had surreptitiously made a wide U-turn from their march to the east and now arrived in Karnaim in the early afternoon of the day the city fell. An honor guard, headed by commanders of the original invasion force, rode out to greet the four kings and give their good report.

"Excellent! Excellent!" harmonized the approvals of four kings. "You say the invasion went just as we planned? And not one of our men was killed?"

"Yes, yes, my lords. It was a masterful plan brilliantly executed. Not one thing went wrong. We have King Nisroch penned up in his palace with his whole population sitting in the court before his gate. Our men have them properly subdued so they cannot resist. The defense forces are disarmed, tied up and under heavy guard in their quarters. They seem passive enough without any desire to rise up against us. All that remains is for your lords to decide about the king."

"Take us to the poor fool and we shall see how he responds to our demands. If he resists, we shall take immense pleasure in looting everything we desire within his city, and palace, and raze everything left so that nothing stands or remains unscorched.

"The entire eastern army entered Karnaim searching and sacking every home and dwelling. Anything of value was brought out into the streets and piled against buildings to collect later.

Marching on to the palace, the army, with four kings at its head, joined its advance troops still holding their position. Chedorlaomer ordered a ram's horn be blown to get King Nisroch to appear.

These were the bargaining conditions Chedorlaomer liked best in dealing with an enemy. He had all the advantages. King Nisroch had nothing but a lump of fear in his throat and, oh, yes...nausea and a terrible headache. This was an awful time for a hangover.

Taking five days to record the loot confiscated, and four more days to refresh themselves, the invaders forced an agreement of future tribute out of King Nisroch in exchange for sparing his life and that of his family. As security to guarantee tribute payments, they also took the king's eldest son hostage.

The 'special caravan' and its advance troops of night invaders left three days preceding the four kings and their portion of the huge army. The commander of the caravan carried with him something equal to a 'key' to Ashtaroth, the next city of conquest. It was a letter of introduction from King Nisroch, with his own personal seal stamped into the clay. If there were any doubts or suspicions about admitting their large caravan into the city, this letter should erase them.

The city of Ashtaroth laid about ten miles southward from Karnaim. It fell as easily as its sister city and was thoroughly plundered and raped.

And in the fourteenth year came Chedorlaomer, and the kings that were with him and smote the Rephaims in Ashteroth, Karnaim and the Zuzims in Ham, and the Emims in Shaveh Keriathaim.

And the Horites in their mount Seir, unto El Paran by the wilderness.

And they returned and came to En-mishpat, which is Kadesh and smote all the country of the Amalekites and also the Amorites that dwelt in Hazazon tamar.

And there went out the King of Sodom and the King of Gomorrah and the king of Admah and the king of Zeboim and the King of Bela (the same is Zoar) and they joined battle with them in the vale of Siddim.

Genesis 14:5-8

Chapter 21
The Valley Of Siddim

When Lot and his family arrived in the Valley of Siddim, more than one year before, his wife Ado chose to live in the city of Sodom. It was the largest and most cosmopolitan of the five cities. She felt she could really shine in that environment and reach the height of her ambitions.

Unlike the Heber-ew women, the women of Sodom were looked upon as being of considerable importance and had a voice in all matters. It was through Ado's enthusiasm and charms that King Bera assigned Lot a substantial stretch of meadow for pasturage and allowed him to buy a house in the city.

Ado never left the city. She immersed herself in its social life, squandering Lot's wealth on an overpriced house and the maintenance of an upper class status.

The temples of Sodom were devoted to the god *Baal-hamon, Lord of Abundance. Within one year Ado began taking her oldest daughter, Lila, to the temple with her. Ado had found that young boys, girls, and beautiful women who go to the priests' couch, in order to show their reverence for the gods, were given valuable gifts, gold, or favors.

Lot avoided the city life much of the time and remained in the fields with his flocks. This particular day was no exception, as he sat in the shade of a tree on a rise of land, listening to the birds and enjoying the view of his garden of paradise.

Mountains lined the valley on three sides: south, east, and west. On the northern side, the water of the Salt Lake showed a dull green/blue. In the hot season a cloud of steamy moisture rose from

---

*The name Baal means lord or master. He was also a chief member of the Canaanite pantheon of gods, an offspring of Dagon, consort of Baalat, and also named Asherah, Astarte or Anath in the Old Testament. The sum total community of Baals make up the Baalim whose worship was Baalism. Baals were gods of fertility and abundance in crops and children.)

the lake's surface. Now, clear of its cloudy mist, the lake's surface was rippled by a gentle breeze out of the north that refreshed the valley. Lot understood why Siddim was also called the Forested Valley. It had an abundance of trees growing everywhere. Groves included oaks, palms, peach, apricot, nut, myrtle and mulberry trees. The air was saturated with salty humidity, naturally favorable to the growth of vegetation. Flowers, beautifully hued and fragrantly scented, grew in profusion within city gardens and rustic fields.

Here and there, in the midst of green grass, were foul smelling, steep-sided holes filled with black ooze. These were the famous slime pits that were the main source of wealth for the valley dwellers. They contained hemar, or earth pitch that was a valuable product for trade with Egypt. Sodom stood in the center of the Valley of Siddim utilizing the matriculating water of the Dead Sea for irrigation. The walls of the city, typical of others in the valley, were poorly made for defense. They had more of a decorative function than a protective one with flowers and vines adding to their charm. News of the invasion of Canaan and the submission of their neighbors, the Amalekites and Amorites, reached the valley and its five kingdoms. A state of emergency was declared and every able-bodied man was armed and pressed into service.

Lot was reluctant to defend a people he disliked. Yet this was now his home and in order to protect his family and defend all he owned he realized it was necessary to fight.

For defense, the combined armies of the five kings numbered as much as three hundred thousand men with more than six thousand chariots. The appearance of the valley army, however, was that of a vast holiday parade with bright, gay colors. Their weapons were also decorated and embellished with ornamentation. Practical battle garb had been abandoned years before in favor of uniforms more appealing to appearances and lusty pursuits. Encamped just west of the mountains ringing Siddim Valley, the four kings organized and sent a special regiment of men and camels to precede the main army by three days. Traversing the mountains through the main pass, they entered the valley. Here they divided into five contingents and dispersed to the five cities situated there: Gomorrah to the north, Zoar to the south, Admah to the east, Zeboim to the west, and Sodom in the center.

The warriors disguised themselves as traders in caravans and entered each city to spy it out. They stayed two nights and left on the third day to rejoin the main army. Before leaving, however, traders visited the temples and left a message for the priests to find readily. They were printed in clay and impressed with Chedorlaomer's seal.

Greatly alarmed by the tablets' messages, priests consulted and devised arguments to persuade their respective kings. In Sodom King Bera heard his scribe read: "I, Chedorlaomer, king of Larsa, have come to war against you for your disobedience and rebellion. Assemble your army on the plain of the valley in the morning two days hence. If you stay in your city I will attack and destroy it utterly!"

The obese King Bera trembled in fear as the words struck him with the effect of a club. The fat on his immense body jiggled and sweat oozed from him forming a glaze. He began moaning like a man who has succumbed to fever.

"We have slain a goat, gutted and examined its entrails, my king. The portents are dark and evil, my lord," instructed the high priest.

"Was there any indication as to how we shall meet our enemy...and fare with him? Should we go out to meet him or stay behind our walls?"

"We read the signs as favoring battle outside the city. Logic also seems to confirm this as the best choice, my lord king. Your forces will be four times greater in strength if you join with your four neighboring cities."

"Yes, yes, you are right of course...yes, I must send messengers right away and make the necessary arrangements."

The forces of Sodom, Gomorrah, Zoar, Admah, and Zeboim assembled the next day near Sodom in the center of the valley. They had not trained together in military maneuvers or strategy for over thirteen years. The men were also soft and dissolute from their excessive pursuits of pleasure. Each city's army presented itself as a colorful pageantry, majestic and precise in their parade. Protective breastplates, body armor and battle helmets had been supplanted with decorative, superficial armor affording comfort rather than protection. The vanity of these people had weakened them long before the present threat of invasion.

The eastern army of the four kings had been sharpened and honed into a precise fighting machine by experience and the best military minds in the world. City after city had fallen before them since their failures at Damascus. Their weaponry and military ranks swelled after each victory. Many thousands of hostages and other slaves were utilized for the hard labor of invasion and transport of spoils.

The Eastern Army arrayed its front lines in a vast arc to contain the enemy and keep him from charging their flanks. Its commanders had chosen the battleground well. During the two days they waited for the defenders to come, battle strategy was rehearsed with precision.

Chedorlaomer had been looking forward to this battle with great relish. It was to be the high point in his invasion of Canaan. The monarch was almost giddy with anticipation, like a dog salivating and shaking while its food is being readied.

The five kings of Siddim Valley, with their royal guards, remained a safe distance at the rear, on a rise of ground, to watch the battle.

The Siddimite Army had a simple plan of attack. They were the first to charge. Broadside into the enemy they came with a single gigantic wave of chariots.

"We shall scatter and destroy their forces with our heavier chariots," exclaimed King Bera to his allies. "Closely following, our foot soldiers must advance on the run. They shall leap upon the disorganized rabble and cut them to ribbons!"

The Siddimite charge was a colorful spectacle of flying banners and streamers on weapons and chariots. Flag bearers had difficulty managing the large fluttering mass of colorful fabrics that were too heavy and awkward for use in battle.

Thousands of speeding chariots, running all out, were close to the front ranks of the enemy.

The foot soldiers facing them remained steadfast, expecting... waiting until the thundering surf of destruction was almost upon them. Eyes widened and throats constricted as the Siddimite charioteers caught a sudden movement in the opposing ranks and faced a terrible new threat. The entire front rank of Elamite soldiers quickly jumped back around a line of strong, chest-high spikes hidden from view. They had been driven into the ground at an angle threatening the racing onslaught.

The charging Siddimites tried to halt but most failed; their momentum carried them into the spikes. Animals, the first to be impaled, thrashed in their agony. Numerous men were thrown out of their chariots with such force that they too were impaled. Other riders, fortunate in missing the spikes, fell hard breaking bones and dazing senses, rendering them vulnerable to the fate that waited for

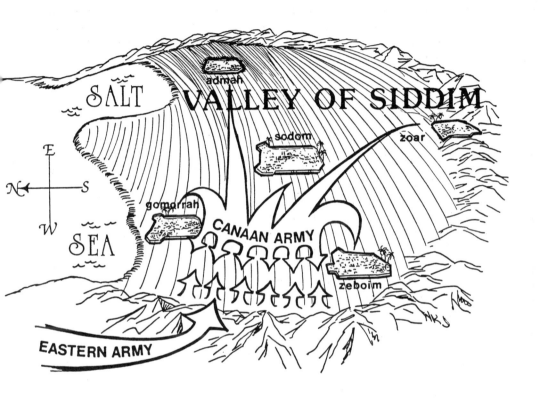

them next. Elamite foot soldiers swarmed over the fallen enemy, spearing and hacking them to death.

The sounds of battle now changed beat, pitch, and volume. Shouts of vigorous annihilation mixed contrapuntally with screams of wounded, dying men.

The debris of fallen chariots and bodies, on and around the line of spikes, afforded the eastern army a bulwark of defense. It was against this that the Siddimite foot soldiers advanced as ordered.

257

Elamite archers stood along side spearmen who held large shields to protect them while they picked off the advancing defenders.

Siddimite bowmen, walking behind the protection of shielded spearmen, armed their bows and let fly overhead as they walked. Vast numbers of arrows passed in the air, finding their marks in the shields and bodies of men on both sides. When the supply of arrows was exhausted, spears and swords were readied.

The Siddimites charged when they should have held their ground.

This was the moment Chedorlaomer had been waiting for. He issued the command, horns were blown, up and down his battle lines, and a great stirring took place at both ends. Climbing atop a boulder to see better, he watched as his chariot divisions went into action.

Chedorlaomer thrilled to see them in battle. Chariots were his favorite weapon of war. He believed that when used correctly they could devastate an enemy and win the battle handily. Now was the time to witness the efficacy of his belief.

Twenty-five hundred Elamite chariots in a column came racing around from behind each end of their battle line and charged along the rear ranks of the Siddimite Army. The two archers in each chariot armed their bows and shot into the enemies' backs while the drivers expertly maneuvered their teams of onagers.

Thousands fell each time they ran the line and turned to run again. Columns of fast rumbling Elamite chariots made their killing runs, turned at the end of the battle line and began a new run in the opposite direction. They passed close by each other in order to keep within shooting range with their bows. There was just enough space between chariots, within the inside column, for the outside returning column to shoot through.

The effectiveness of Chedorlaomer's chariot strategy was devastating. Siddimite men were dropping at the rate of three thousand every few minutes.

Chedorlaomer watched as vast ranks of the enemy crumpled in the wake of each pass of his chariots. It was very much like a farmer cutting down wheat. In just twenty minutes sixty thousand Siddimite men had fallen. The battle excited Chedorlaomer so that he jumped up and down with excitement shouting: "Kill them! Kill the rebels! Fill them full of arrows! Slaughter them all! Revenge is sweet. This sight fulfills my longing for it."

Saliva ran down both sides of his mouth as he spit out the words. His frenzy was like that of a mad dog foaming at the mouth, barking out insults.

258

The sound of a horn was heard over the din of thundering chariots, clanging of metal against metal weaponry, and the shouting of men killing and being killed. The signal came from the direction of the five kings of Siddim and continued its call over and over: Retreat! Retreat! Retreat!

The Siddimite Army began its retreat slowly. Facing warriors on foot to their west, and chariots to the east, they fought with a determination to survive, in spite of the odds against them.

Back to back they moved, beleaguered by a superior enemy. The pursuing chariots, running slower now, still kept hemming in the defenders and the slaughter went on.

Lot and his four herdsmen were armed with bow and arrows because they were expert hunters. Each had slain more invaders than any ten men on their side. Being Heber-ew nomads with keen eyes and quick reflexes, they battled as a team, alert in all directions, ready to pierce an enemy before they were hit by arrow or spear. Precision archers that they were, they selected vital targets.

While the invaders' chariots harassed the retreat and took their awesome toll, they paid a price each time they rumbled by Lot and his men. In several passes the five archers put arrows into a total of twenty-five charioteers, twenty bowmen and twenty-seven animals. It was through these five nomads' valiant efforts that the chariots were at first impeded and then finally disrupted in their process of attack. Several chariots crashed sending occupants sprawling. Others went running off without occupants and stopped, away from the battle scene.

A remnant of the retreating Siddimite Army fought their way through the chariot columns and broke into a headlong dash for some form of sanctuary among the trees. Long-range goals were the mountains on the eastern and southern sides of the valley.

Running from shelter to shelter, men spread out like the fingers of an outstretched hand. Their five kings rode before them desperately urging the beasts to greater speed to avoid being captured or killed.

King Shinab of Admah and King Shemeber of Zeboim were good riders and knew the terrain well. They made it safely to the mountains and hid.

Bela, king of Zoar, made his way through the forest, around the slime pits, and eventually all the way to the mountains south of his city.

King Bera of Sodom and King Bersha of Gommorah fled towards the forest. Yet because of their great obesity and lack of ability in riding, they both fell off into different odorous pits. King Bersha struggled, sank slowly and drowned in the black slime. King Bera, however, was too exhausted to fight the ooze. He simply laid back and floated very buoyantly until enemy soldiers pulled him out.

Lot and his men ran for Sodom. Two of them died trying; pierced with arrows and run down by chariots. Lot and his two remaining servants turned and hurriedly shot arrows first into the two archers and then the driver of a chariot that chased them.

"Quickly," shouted Lot, "cast out the bodies and get on the chariot. This may be our only chance to escape! I will ward off attackers!"

The two servants ran to the slowly moving chariot and pulled off the mortally wounded Elamites. Lot sent as many as four arrows flying at pursuers before he caught up and jumped on the chariot.

"Cover our backs with your shields while I try to drive a chariot for the first time!"

Taking the slack reins in his hands, he slapped them against the flanks of the animals and gave a loud command. The asses sprang into a gallop nearly jerking Lot's servants out of the chariot. Quickly grasping the top edge, they clung desperately, barely managing to stay on board.

Lot was a keen observer and had watched charioteers in Egypt and Sodom as well as today. His life and those of his servants now depended on how well he could remember and apply his observations. Concentrating all his attention on the animals, he somehow grasped the fundamentals of control quickly enough and soon they were racing over meadowlands and through forests.

Lot's skill improved each minute as his instincts with animals surfaced. He gave them freedom to avoid obstacles and pitfalls that they sometimes saw before he did. When Lot saw these dangers first, he took charge; with strong hands he pulled their heads to one side, turning away from disaster.

Unic and Aberanth clung tightly to the chariot top rail with one hand and locked grips, wrist on wrist, in back of Lot securing him against falling between their bodies. On they flew with the wind in their faces out-distancing any pursuers.

"Sodom, I must get to Sodom and remove Ado and the girls to safety in the mountains!" Lot interjected between shouts and the slapping of the reins for unrelenting speed.

Now they were on a smoother path that provided sure footing. The team of asses, now more confident, lunged forward in a unified rhythmic cadence, picking up speed.

Lot's mind raced faster than the team, whose strength he now fully controlled in his hands, and he began issuing orders to his servants.

"Unic! When I stop at the city's gates, you will run to my sheepfolds and drive as many of my flocks as you can up into the foothills to the west. I will join you as soon as I provide an escape for my family." Lot paused for a moment, then continued. "...And Unic...if I should fail to join you...if I am captured or killed...go to Abram, my goel. He will want to know what happened here. He will take care of you and if possible...avenge me...even though I do not deserve it."

"But where would I find him, my lord?" Unic questioned, fearful and confused.

"I am not sure...you will have to make inquiries. He will be known wherever he is, but go first to the plain near Hebron."

"Aberanth!"

"Yes lord?"

"When we arrive at my home, you will water these poor beasts. Hold them ready to ride out again while I prepare to bring out my family. Do not let them be taken from you by anyone! Do you understand?" Lot challenged, gesturing with his eyes at the bow slung over Aberanth's shoulder.

"Yes, my lord...I understand."

Lot pulled back on the reins and the team broke their run, coming to a halt in front of the city's gates.

Unic jumped off, shaken by the reckless dash and grateful to be on his own feet again. He dashed off, his heart pounding in his ears. "I have survived the worst dangers so far, but there is still the risk of being captured or killed!' His mind raced through options as fast as his legs ran through fields and groves. "What are my chances of escaping if I save my master's flocks as he commands? Slim, I think. Why not go to the mountains? I would be safe there. Hear the sounds? The shouts of victory and cries of defeat are getting closer! Why not keep running... away?"

Sweat ran down his face and body while he sprinted towards the sheepfold. Indecision filled his mind. Years of servitude had conditioned him to obey his master.

"What should I do?!" he screamed with anxiety.

"Open the gates and let us pass through! I am Lot, a citizen of Sodom. I bring news of the battle!"

"If you are a citizen of the city," challenged the sentry behind a battlement, "how is it that you possess that chariot? It is not one of ours!"

Lot handed the reins to Aberanth and freed his bow as he spoke.

"We killed Elamite warriors that rode in it; just like my servants and I shot through many others with our bows during the battle. I have risked death on the field and in riding here at a breakneck speed to warn the city's occupants. I warn you, my patience is short and my eye is as keen as ever. If that gate is not opened immediately, my next arrow shall find a home in your throat. That would end your doubts forever!"

"All right, very well, I...I remember you now. You are the Heber-ew who keeps sheep in the south meadow.

"Open the gates for Lot the Heber-ew! And be quick about it!" The sentry turned and shouted down to the other guards. "He is one of our heroes returning from the battle, having slain many of the enemy and taken a chariot to come here with news of the invasion!"

There was a scurry of activity, heavy bars were removed and the gates swung open wide. Without waiting for his master's command, Aberanth slapped the reins and shouted to the onagers as Lot had done. Into the city they drove scattering people out of their path who had swarmed to hear the news.

"We shall leave shortly!" Lot called out to the guards. "Be ready to open the gates for us!"

The officer in charge saluted in reply.

"Say nothing to anyone, Aberanth! You lost your tongue and cannot speak! Your life depends upon the deception. Do you understand?"

Aberanth nodded his head affirmatively although he was not sure at all whether the threat was from Lot or the mob in the streets.

"Faster, Aberanth! Make way! Out of our path or get trampled!" Lot shouted to people converging on them for news.

From Broad Boulevard through winding narrow lanes the chariot raced, bullying women, children and older men out of its path. Skidding around a final corner, Aberanth pulled up hard on the reins.

"There is the water trough. I will run down the block to our house. Meet me there in a few minutes!" Lot declared.

"Yes, master."

Ado was lounging in the shade of the courtyard arcade, sipping on a cool alcoholic drink, when a loud pounding and shouting came from the street entrance.

"See who is making all that disturbance!" she ordered a servant in attendance.

"It is bad enough having this headache without putting up with some rowdy," she complained to her daughters. "Ohh...I probably should not have had so much wine yesterday evening...but, well that foolish husband of mine, telling me he was going off with the soldiers to fight the Elamite invaders...and nothing I could say or do about it...and here we sit, defenseless against intruders like..."

"Ado! My daughters and servants! Hurry, there is no time to lose!" Lot exclaimed and in a rush of words explained and commanded non-stop, spurring his household into action.

"Take only the most valuable things you can carry! We must leave immediately or else be captured and enslaved to the Elamites! Our journey is to the mountains where we will stay until it is safe to return. So prepare yourselves to live in the open once again."

Servants gathered up food, cooking utensils, miscellaneous tools and weapons.

"Hurry!" urged Lot. "Just put everything into cloth spreads and tie the four corners together. Do not fuss about what to take and how to pack it! If we do not leave right away we may not be able to leave at all!"

Aberanth arrived with the chariot and Lot ordered everyone to leave.

Ado whined and complained: "but I cannot leave behind so many fine clothes, vases and objects of value. Surely you and the servants could carry more. What will I look like when I return? We have so little money left. How will I be able to maintain my social position looking like...like a poor nomad?"

Lot turned from Ado, barely able to control his emotions. He had tolerated her vanity for several years, eventually forcing himself to acknowledge how helplessly he was in love with her attractiveness. He allowed himself to be manipulated like a servant, instead of being her lord. When he did not cater to Ado, she held herself from his affections. There were times when he forced her sexually, but afterward he hated himself for it, as much as she hated him.

Lot had self-doubts because of his unending infatuation. He failed, time and time again, to take charge of their marriage, usually accepting the blame for their arguments and acquiescing to her self-indulgence.

"This is one time when I must be the master of this house and resist your spoiled nature," Lot hissed through his teeth, his hands clenched into tight fists.

NO! By the Almighty God, NO! I will not be your servant!" He turned and bellowed. "We will be fortunate if we escape! If you do not move quickly, NOW, you will be wearing a noose of rope around your neck instead of necklaces, with knots of rope on your wrists and ankles instead of bracelets! And at the end of each day's march, if you are still alive, you will be sexual sport for a company of Elamites who will not care if you are pouting or crying with discontent!

A shocked look of disbelief came over Ado's comely features and she froze, unable to move.

Lot, his patience totally dissipated, put his arm around Ado's waist and pulled her with him as he swept through the courtyard, out the gate and lifted her onto the chariot where his two daughters waited. There was no room for him so he took hold of the bridle on one ass and jerked him into a trot.

"Run Aberanth! Run with them to the city's gates; there is no time to lose!"

"The streets are more congested now than when we arrived," Aberanth commented as he held onto the bridle of the ass on the left.

"We are not the only ones leaving the city, nor the first," Lot replied. Look ahead! The streets are filling with carts heavily loaded with possessions. News of the battle's outcome must have spread."

Confusion reigned and panic was increasing throughout the city. Those who were undecided about what to do darted in and out of the traffic of animals, carts, and people flowing like waves toward the city's exit.

"What is happening? Have we lost the war? Why are you leaving? Is it not safe to remain in the city?" people asked.

Lot and Aberanth waved them away, saying nothing that would slow their travel.

The volume of noise in the streets grew as congestion increased. Above the constant din a scream pierced the air now and then, punctuating the chorus of confusion.

"Quickly Aberanth!" Lot commanded, "at this next cross street we will go around those slow moving carts. Now! Run this way!"

The two men yanked the bridles and shouted warnings to people in the way. The onagers broke into a run and scurried around the slow-moving vehicles, drawing shouts and curses for their impatience and audacity.

The way ahead was less congested for a few blocks and people made room to avoid being knocked over. Lot and his servants ignored more questions and insults.

Turning the next corner, Lot headed them towards Grand Avenue, the main thoroughfare out of the city. They were forced to reduce their pace as they entered this busy transportation artery, and walked slowly towards the 'city square' fronting Sodom's main gate.

"Ado!" Lot called out. "Can you see if the city gates are open? Are people leaving?"

Dazed and frightened, Ado looked down at Lot from the chariot with a blank, almost quizzical look and then saying nothing she returned her gaze to the crowds. The knuckles of her hands were white as they clutched the chariot for support.

Lot looked back for a reply but all he saw was the appearance of total fear in Ado's face. He realized she had great difficulty coping with this impending disaster and would be no help at all. Pressing on he held back the panic within him that fought to surface.

"A little bit further and we will be there. Do not be afraid!" Lot shouted back thin encouragement.

The guards at the gate were very uneasy. The officer in command realized that by letting any men of the city leave, the city's defense would be weakened.

Lot watched with dismay as the guards began selecting able men out of the swarming exodus; even separating some from their families.

The press of gathering crowds in the square propelled Lot's chariot towards the gates.

"Aberanth!" Lot called to his servant, getting the man's close attention. "I will have to use deception to get us through. You will obey my original orders! You will slip over the wall and meet me at the stream east of my sheepfold...no matter what I say to the guards! Do you understand?"

"Yes, lord."

"Hail, officer of the guard!" Lot shouted.

"Lot, the Heber-ew, hail to you!" he replied, striding up to him. "I am glad you are here; we need all the men we can find that are capable of fighting to defend our walls. Your keen eye with a bow makes you and your herdsman especially important to us!" He finished his statement of recruitment, watching Lot warily for an adverse reaction, expecting anger and hostility as before.

"Good decision, my lord. My compliments to you for your good judgment. An officer with your ability and good sense is just what we need to save this city," Lot reassured him.

"Why...I am surprised at your agreeableness considering what you have already been through. But I am heartened by your cooperation. What do you intend to do with your wife and children here?"

"Why, I am sending them to the east until we have dealt with these Elamite pigs. My servant Aberanth will protect and provide for them while they hide in the hills; just as an extra precaution, you understand."

"I see...but I need every man who can fight, and it is obvious that he is very capable. Probably worth ten of those fatuous, simpering, weaklings over there," he indicated with a jerking motion of his head to Sodomite men who had avoided going into battle. "I am sorry, Lot, I cannot allow either of you go," he apologized, turning away.

"My lord commander! You are going to need food for a siege, perhaps a long one, are you not?"

"Why, yes that is so but..."

"I have flocks of sheep and cattle out in the meadow that I will give to you and the city, rather than see them fall into the hands of our enemy. The Elamites also need food enough for their large army. If they discover my flocks, and I am sure they will if they are not brought here, you will have helped them conquer Sodom by feeding them. King Bera and all the people will not tolerate that kind of treason, I assure you."

"Sshhh! Be quiet with that kind of talk!"

"I will broadcast it to everyone here with the loudest shouting I can manage if you do not cooperate," Lot challenged.

"Do not threaten me, Heber-ew. I am in charge of this city until the king and his commanders return. My word is law!" he snapped fiercely in retaliation. "I am sending a few of my men to bring your sheep here. You will stay! Is that clear?"

"Very clear commander...but your men will die from arrows, Heber-ew arrows, if I am not with them."

"You would commit treason against Sodomites?"

"Oh no, commander, not me. But if I am not with your soldiers, Unic, my other herdsman will. You may remember, he ran off under my orders, when we arrived. I sent him to guard my flocks until I returned for them. He is a superb hunter...can put an arrow in a lion's eye at seventy-five paces. Ten of your best men would fall before he could be touched. If I do not go, he will believe I am your prisoner. He is a loyal servant...and as I said, a very capable bowman. You would do well to have him here fighting for you rather than against you."

"One man against ten Sodomites? Well...I will not argue with you, but I doubt if..."

"Heed my promise, commander, I will cooperate fully, I assure you. Let my family go now, and I will help your men bring my sheep here."

"I refuse to believe your lies about a herdsman who is an expert bowman. My men do not need your help."

"Oh, but they do. First they have to find them quickly. Secondly, without me along, those that are left alive will never be able to drive the flock back here in time. Elamites will not only capture the sheep but slaughter your remaining men as well," Lot bartered with cunning.

"We have lost much time arguing, Heber-ew. Very well, I will release your family and allow you to go for your sheep, but your herdsman here stays, along with your household servants."

The commander barked out names of five men who came running and listened to their orders: "...and do not come back without Lot, his servant, and their sheep!

"Make way," bellowed the commander, "Out of the way! Make room for Lot and his family to leave!"

Barking orders, the soldiers pushed violently against the crush of escapees, opening a path for the chariot with Lot still at the onager's bridle.

Lot turned briefly to face Aberanth. Their eyes met and focused keenly on an unheard communication.

Aberanth nodded an agreement, turned and slipped away, back into the crowd.

As soon as the chariot cleared the gate into the open, Lot called back to the guards a short distance behind.

"We must hurry if we are to avoid confronting the Elamites!"

He began running with the team before any of the guards could grab hold. Increasing his speed, the onagers quickened their trot in response to Lot's pull on a mouth bit.

The distance between chariot and Sodomites lengthened... more... and more. The soldiers ran short sprints awkwardly with a spear in one hand and a shield in the other. A heavy copper breastplate also weighed them down. Their copper headpieces jostled, tipped and fell.

Humid midday heat bore down upon them. Sweat drenched their bodies, running into their eyes, stinging with salt and the grime of dirty fingers brushing it away.

All five Sodomites called for Lot to slow down. When he continued, unrelenting, they cursed him, gasping for breath. Dropping shields, headpieces and breastplates, they stumbled along, not daring to stop.

Still Lot ran on.

One by one the Sodomites fell to their knees then collapsed and laid on their backs panting. The effects of a dissolute lifestyle had dissipated them.

Lot had been quick to perceive their weakness and knew the burden of arms they carried would surely slow them. But now he also felt the heat, the drenching sweat, and exhaustion. He had been through a series of ordeals this day and his strength was ebbing from him.

With his escort collapsed more than fifty yards behind, Lot halted the team, and mounted the back end of the chariot.

"Get off Lot, you are stepping on my clothes!" Ado screamed her objection. "What are you doing? Wait for the guards, we may need their protection!"

Ignoring Ado's hysterical protests, Lot shoved her aside, grabbed the reins and slapped the flanks of the onagers.

Shaking off the command with a rattle of harness, the stubborn asses refused to move.

"Eeeaa!" Lot shouted and slapped the reins more vigorously than before.

Again the command was shrugged off with a loud whinny of rebellion.

There was a renewed movement among the five guards strewn along the trail. Seeing the chariot stopped they struggled to their feet and began walking unsteadily.

The gap was closing rapidly. Lot glanced back instinctively. What he saw made him realize that in a few moments he would have more trouble than he could handle and all might be lost. His legs seemed weighted, unable to move.

"What can I do to get these beasts moving?" he cried in panic still slapping the reins. The question was no sooner out of his lips when an answer came.

Quickly he dropped the reins, fumbled through Ado's belongings and took hold of two earthen jars, the size of his daughters' fists. Cocking his arm, Lot threw one, then the other in rapid succession at the animals' flanks.

No! Not my precious makeup and body ointments!" Ado screamed with shrill hysteria. "How dare you! Do you have any idea what those cost? When will I be able to replace them? You stop immediately and bring them back!"

Lot ignored Ado's frenzied chatter as the chariot lurched into motion. Grabbing the reins once again he yelled oaths at the onagers and slapped the reins wishing he had the courage to slap some obedience into his wife.

"If that were only her out there," he fantasized.

The thought seemed to inspire him. Shouting and slapping the team for increased speed, Lot felt the animals' power in his hands and arms. The refreshing breeze in his face aided a strong determination to succeed. In danger from both enemy and ally, and nagged by a selfish, witless wife, Lot fought depression and fatigue to concentrate on what lay ahead.

"Has Unic followed my orders? Were the flocks still in the fold or being driven westward by Unic? Was Aberanth still in the city or had he found a way over the wall? He knows where to meet me but will he be able to elude the Sodomites?"

With these questions in mind Lot guided the team by familiar land marks. Soon he would know...soon... and then there it was.

The enclosure entrance was open and the sheep were gone. Lot secured the reins and stepped off the chariot. Walking inside the fold his eyes quickly scanned the ground for a message. At the western edge he saw what he was looking for. Six to eight small stones formed the shape of an arrow pointing west. Scattering the stones with his foot, he walked to the chariot and stepped on.

"Unic was obedient," he remarked to Ado. "He has my sheep. We will head west and look for him."

"The girls and I are thirsty. When can we have something to drink?" Ado whined.

"Soon, my dear, soon," Lot replied, already beginning to fall back into the old habit of subservience.

Glancing left and right, he looked for Aberanth. Turning his head, Lot saw his servant waving his arms then shouting. Pulling back on the reins, Lot halted the team whose backs glistened with sweat.

Aberanth caught up, running with staggering steps, ready to collapse. He held onto the chariot for support gasping for breath.

"Did you have any trouble getting out of the city? Did you encounter any soldiers outside the city?" Lot probed.

To both questions the servant replied with a shake of his head, unable to speak.

"Here, Aberanth, take my place; I will run alongside," Lot ordered and stepped down.

"Must you?" Ado complained. "A servant rides while his master walks? Really Lot, how improper. And look at him, so dirty and sweaty...and he smells."

"He could have deserted us," Lot responded, "but he did not. He ran until exhausted, so he would be obedient to my orders. We need to keep moving, and it is necessary that Aberanth ride, whether you like it or not. If anything happens to me, I have commanded Aberanth to provide for you and the girls, and protect you. If I were you, I would be more considerate, if you know what is good for you," Lot finished, disgusted with Ado's behavior.

Aberanth stepped on, and took the reins while avoiding Ado's haughty look. He tried holding back a smile but after shaking the reins and jerking the chariot into motion, he finally allowed himself the liberty, turning his face away from her. After awhile, they came upon a stream with trees on both sides offering pleasant shade and a measure of privacy. Sheep stood about in contentment, cool and refreshed.

"Unic! Where are you?" Lot shouted as he led the animals to water.

Out of the shadows, from behind some bushes, Unic stood up, waved and came forward.

"Master, how happy I am to see you and your family...and you, too, Aberanth. I have been fearing that you would not come."

"We had some trouble getting out of Sodom but here we are safe, for the moment at least," Lot replied.

"Ado, you and the girls refresh yourselves and take a brief rest."

Walking a short distance up stream, Lot quickly disrobed and laid down in the water. After washing the sweat and grime from his body, he laid back with his elbows supporting him.

"Ohh, how nice. If it were only possible that we could stay here. Ahh, how idyllic it is," he sighed feeling the heat and thirst of his body quenched. "Every part of me calls for rest...I could easily find sleep...just a little sleep...so quiet...so safe...so peaceful...so..."

Lot sank beneath the surface, asleep. Instantly he surfaced, thrashing his arms, sputtering and gasping for breath.

"Fool!" You do not have the time for this luxury! Do you want to get caught?" he chastised himself, choking out the words. Stumbling out of the water he dressed hurriedly. Calling out to Ado, his girls and the servants, they were soon gathered at the chariot where Lot explained that it was necessary to keep moving west into the foothills and locate a good safe place to hide, "A cave if possible," he suggested.

"Why must we move on? This place at least has some comforts. Up in the hills we will be without water and a place to bathe, such as we have here. The girls and I do not want to go from here," Ado asserted.

"We must leave, and leave now!" Lot insisted. "It is not safe to stay here. This whole valley will be searched thoroughly for its residents. If they find us, death will be far more pleasant than captivity, I assure you. Our only chance for safety is up in the hills. The soldiers of the eastern army will be too occupied with rape and rampage in the cities to look for us. Now get on the chariot! Aberanth will drive the chariot!" he finished commanding, a hint of a smile on his lips.

"Frankly, I prefer the company of my servant and sheep," Lot muttered turning away. "Unic and I will drive the sheep and meet you later, Aberanth. If not tonight, certainly by tomorrow. Now go...and may the Everliving, God of Abram, sustain you."

"And be with you, my lord," Aberanth responded.

Hopping on board, the servant took reins in hand, slapped the animals' shanks and howled a command. The chariot lurched forward and crossed the stream slipping on rocks in the streambed like a drunken soldier. Up the opposite bank it lumbered, through the meadowland beyond and out of Lot's sight. Breathing a sigh of relief, he turned his attention to the next task - herding the sheep - still worried that Elamites might catch up to them during the slow drive.

During the next seven days Lot, his family, and two servants hid back in the hills with the sheep. From a high lookout they watched the sacking of Admah during the day. At night fires could be seen where the five cities lay, pillaged and raped.

On the eighth day, Ado complained hysterically about their primitive living conditions and demanded that they return to Sodom.

Lot looked at his wife with sadness in his heart. Ado looked pitifully out of place away from the city. She and her colorful clothes were dirty. Fragile robes were torn and her hair, usually carefully washed, combed and arranged, now hung straight and plain, dingy from dust in the winds that coursed the mountains.

"All right, Ado, all right!" Lot agreed with exasperation. "I shall go down and see if it is safe to return. Unic will come with me. Who knows what we will find; perhaps the Elamites have left? We must be careful, however, they may still be scattered among the five cities. Do not leave this sanctuary before I return! That is my command. Do you understand?"

"Y...Yes," Ado sobbed trying to get control of her emotions.

At dusk Lot and Unic made their way down to the valley on foot and walked cautiously towards Admah. Arriving at the entrance to the city they saw the gates had been battered open. Creeping inside they found the square was deserted except for a few pitiful scroungers looking desperately for something to eat or trade for food.

Entering the city they kept to the shadows in order to be as invisible as possible. The streets were dark, except for the light of a half moon that provided a semi-dark image of rubble and waste.

Keeping to opposite sides of the narrow streets, they walked along carefully, listening for sounds. Now and then Lot saw lamplight projecting out of a doorway into the street like a sentinel.

As quiet as a cat, Lot approached and stole a look inside, wary of possible enemy presence. Inside he saw a few of the city's occupants bartering over scraps. Without making himself known, Lot darted past looking for evidence that any invaders were left in occupation of Admah.

Unic was equally occupied and found nothing so far worth calling Lot's attention to.

Eventually they came upon a large square fronting the temple, warehouse, priests' quarters, and king's palace. Usually crowded with activities of pomp, parade, sacrifice, offering and crowd-pleasing entertainment, this heart of the city no longer pulsed with life. Young children wandering about aimlessly, crying from hunger and the loss of their parents now occupied it. Small knots of elderly men and women huddled here and there, trying to draw companionship in the midst of a calamity.

Lot came forward to ask questions. The people, upon seeing him and his servant armed as they were with bow and arrows, screamed in fear and ran.

"We mean no harm to you! We are Heber-ews, not Elamites!"
he shouted, but his explanation was wasted as everyone scurried off
into their hiding places like rats in the night.

"It appears that the city is left desolate Unic, except for the
old and the very young. There is nothing more for us to see here. Let
us go on to Sodom."

The two men walked along with less caution than before,
having seen Admah no longer occupied by Elamites. Following a
well-traveled road they listened for the enemy but heard only the
familiar sounds of nature's insects and animals, co-mingled with a
slight rustling of a breeze through the grass and trees.

When they arrived at Sodom the gates were smashed in and
hung on hinges in a disheveled array. Lot and Unic looked through
the entrance and scanned the spacious square.

"I do not see anyone but the very young and the elderly just
as it was at Admah," Lot whispered.

"Yes, it appears to be so," Unic agreed.

"Let us go in then," Lot ordered.

Across the square they boldly walked, asking questions of no
one, the young and old hurried out of their path. Many of the
dwellings they walked by were burnt out shells void of life. Building
rubble filled the streets where walls were torn down in the search for
hidden valuables or family hiding places.

Lot's house came in sight and he held his breath in hopes that
it would not be demolished.

"Look, Unic, the door is intact as well as the street wall.
Perhaps they spared my house for some reason, or because we did not
stay and barricade ourselves within. Now I shall see how much
damage has been done inside."

Boldly, without hesitation, Lot pulled the latch, pushed the
door open and walked in, just as he had always done before the
invaders came.

Unic hung back out of respect for the unknown, but also
waiting for his master's orders.

As Lot started across the garden court, he heard voices and
saw lamplight coming from the dining and cooking rooms.

"It appears that some survivors have ideas about living in my
house," he murmured to himself. "I wonder what Ado would think
about that? Well now, let me see who the poor creatures are."

Had he been cautious here as he was at Admah, Lot would
have heard the danger before he saw it. In the few moments it took
him to look around the room, he recognized who these uninvited

guests were. When he realized they were Elamite soldiers it was too late to escape.

They reacted quickly and decisively. First one, two, then three and four savage looking men jumped up from various comfortable postures around the room and surrounded Lot with weapons ready to strike.

Lot's first impulse in seeing his predicament, was to draw the dagger he carried sheathed in his girdle. But even as his hand gripped the handle, his adversaries made loud threats and motions to kill him where he stood if the blade left its scabbard. Lot realized that since he was not killed outright, there might be some hope for his life, at least for the moment.

"But why the delay?" he thought, fear gripping him so he could hardly breath.

It seemed as though an eternity passed while Lot stood motionless, except for a slight turn of the head, his eyes darting around him. He was as tense as a coiled snake waiting for a certain advance, ready to strike out at the most accessible target.

"What are they waiting for?" he hissed through teeth clenched together.

The answer came in the form of a large, surly man, naked to the loin cloth, who staggered into the doorway of the adjoining room with a naked woman under his shoulder trying, not very successfully, to steady him. Holding onto the doorjamb with his free hand he peered at Lot through a drunken haze.

"What is it that disturbs my enjoyment? Who is this that you hold at bay like a beast?" he barked huskily.

"He just walked in here like he owned the house, commander," responded one of the four.

A belch followed a low guttural sound resembling a laugh. "Perhaps he does, perhaps he does."

"Tell me bowman, is this...was this your home?"

"Uh, why no it is not," he lied.

"Who are you then, and what are you doing here?"

'Why, my name is Lot, lord commander. I am only a poor simple Heberew nomad, a keeper of sheep, who lives in the open spaces; a friend to all and enemy to no one," Lot replied, forcing a nervous smile.

"You are a pretty smooth talker for a simple nomad, even though you do smell of sheep. Why did you come here, sheep herder?"

Lot realized that even though drunk, his enemy was no fool. The man stood unsteady but his eyes bore into Lot's eyes trying to fathom the mind of this intruder.

"I came to see my aunt and uncle, "Lot lied again striving not to show it. "I heard about the war and traveled from Canaan to see if they survived it all right. What have you done with them?"

"Who knows where they are? They could be dead, held captive, or still wandering around the city looking for a home, ha, ha, huh."

"Again that dull laugh," Lot thought, "Dangerous, he is very dangerous."

"But what is that to me? I will ask the questions here. Like...who came with you, and where are they now?!" He commanded angrily.

"I came alone, my lord," Lot replied trying to keep his face free of any expression that might betray him.

"You lie, nomad! Only a fool would travel alone such a distance...and through conquered territory. Are you a fool, nomad? Or just lying?"

Other Elamite soldiers appeared, having come from the other rooms in the house after hearing their commander.

"Search outside! See if anyone lingers there!"

Six men drew weapons and staggered out into the night with uncertain steps, dulled and off balance from drinking and whoring. Out in the street one of them saw a figure walking hurriedly, with youthful strides, twenty to thirty paces away.

"There! That is no old man or woman. I'll wager he or she was waiting outside listening. Maybe it is a tender young thing we can have some fun with. Run! The man who catches her will have first turn."

"Hail...You up the street, stop! Do as you are told and things will go well for you!"

Unic looked back, saw his pursuers coming and broke into a run. Even the best Elamite runner was no match for Unic who ran like a cheetah speeding through the streets, leaping over obstacles and avoiding people in the way.

The Elamites ran awkwardly, stumbling, falling, tripping over debris and each other. The last glimpse they had of Unic was when he dashed through the square, out of the gateway, disappearing into the blackness of the night.

Chapter 22
Abram: Ally and Goel

I

Abram had been residing peacefully among Amorite neighbors since Lot settled in Sodom. They came to know Abram as a peaceful and honorable Heberew tribal chief. Distrusting him at first, they watched his people, his flocks and herds daily, taking note of his numbers and his wealth. As the reports came in, it became noticeable that Abram prospered by considerable increases in flocks, herds, and servants. It was deduced that Abram's connection with the "gods of Canaan" was most rewarding.

The Amorite brothers, Mamre, Eschol, and Aner, agreed to seek the friendship of Abram, believing his prosperity and protection would associate to them as well. News of the attacks upon their Amorite tribes to the south by the huge eastern army also filled them with anxiety and anger.

"We need to confederate ourselves with strong allies, even Heberews." ventured Mamre. "Let us discuss among ourselves the procedure we will take to secure a treaty of peace and military alliance with Abram."

That afternoon all three brothers rode up to the Heber-ew encampment and asked to call upon Abram. They were shown to his tent where he was sitting in the shade of its entrance. Abram rose to his feet and greeted his guests graciously, exchanging salutations. He ordered servants to wash their hands and feet, then insisted they have food and drink.

Gratified with the friendliness and hospitality of their host, they accepted with enthusiasm. The men found pleasure in their neighbor's company, talking first about peaceful agrarian pursuits.

"We commend you on your prosperity, Lord Abram. You are a tribal chief of some considerable wealth. Your servants are many, and your flocks and herds seemingly too numerous to count. Yes, how fortunate that the gods favor you," Mamre complimented with humility.

"Only one God, my friends, Yahvah the Everliving who created the heavens, the seas and the earth; the only God with power. He is with me in all that I set my hand to. I have been directed to live here in this land and make his presence known to all the inhabitants. And here you are, looking for prosperity and security also, I venture," Abram finished smiling with understanding.

"Truly your God has given you wisdom in addition to prosperity," Mamre complimented again.

"I am only his servant, my lord," Abram replied with a bow of his head. "Now that you are comfortable, good neighbors, is there a matter of special importance that prompts you to visit me at this time?"

"Stories have reached our ears concerning your past exploits. We beg you, great lord, tell us yourself if they be true experiences or merely the concoctions of storytellers at city gates," Aner explained.

"I will tell you, gladly, how the Everliving saved me from my enemies, so that you may understand his divine providence. He is God over all men, Amorites and Heberews alike. Now hear of his saving power and judge for yourselves if he is not the only true God with powers."

Abram related how he was saved from the fire of Nimrod's furnace and ordered to leave Ur and live in the Land of Canaan. When he finished telling of the Everliving's protection in Egypt for Sarai and his tribe against the evil of Pharoah, all three men prostrated themselves before him.

"Truly your great God is with you, even against mighty kings!" Mamre exclaimed. "Great prince of the Everliving God, surely you are aware of the invasion of Canaan by the armies of the four kings from the east?!"

"Rise good neighbors. Yes, I heard they warred against the Amalekites and defeated them, exacting great tribute."

"True, my lord, and the Amorites as well, our own cousins, who live a few days journey south of here. They too have been overwhelmed in battle." Aner explained.

"We feel certain the great army will sweep up through the entire land of Canaan once they have finished their retribution against the five kingdoms in the Valley of Siddim," Eschol interjected.

"Valley of Siddim?" asked Abram, to be sure he heard correctly.

"Yes, Lord Abram, the Valley of Siddim where lie the five cities Sodom, Gomorrah, Admah, Zeboim and Zoar. The latest news is that their pitiful armies have been decimated by the might of the superior eastern army," Mamre continued.

"What of the fate of the occupants of Sodom?" Abram asked anxiously.

"Of that no one has any knowledge," responded Aner.

Just then a man came running up to the gathering and kneeled down a few paces from Abram. Saying nothing, he waited for permission to speak.

"What is it that is of such importance that you intrude upon the peace of this council?

"Begging your pardon for this intrusion, my lord, but a man called Unic, herdsman for your nephew, Lot, approached us in the fields asking for you. He is so exhausted from his travels that he has collapsed. Yet he insists on reporting to you right away."

"Where is he now?"

"Two of your herdsmen are carrying him here and should arrive shortly."

For three miles the two men took turns carrying Unic on their backs. They were brawny men with strong legs and they came trotting into camp with their burden only ten minutes after their forerunner. Letting him down gently, their ragged, grimy passenger fell prostrate before Abram.

"Great Prince, how fortunate are those that serve you. My master Lot, your nephew, has been captured by some warriors of the eastern army and is doomed to slavery or death."

The words struck Abram like a blow from a club. He rose from his seat and turned his back on the gathering so no one could see the severity of his shock. The thought of Lot being enslaved numbed his senses. He knew the eyes of his guests were watching him and waiting patiently...silently.

Sarai had been a respectful distance away, supervising the preparation of food but also listening to Abram and his guests. Observing the exhausted condition of Lot's servant, Sarah approached Abram and spoke: "I have prepared ample food for our guests that is ready to be served. If it pleases my husband, there is also enough for the servant of your nephew."

"Let Unic be served along with our guests. He has suffered long, hard travel to bring us news," Abram agreed.

"How many days have you traveled from Sodom, Unic?" Abram asked, turning back to the servant.

"I believe it is six, my lord. I had to be careful in avoiding the Elamites and Babylonians who seemed to be everywhere. I have had little to eat or drink, but I managed to barter news of the battle of Siddim for tidbits of food along the way. Many were grateful for the news from a reliable source.

"Perhaps I am the only source from which news of the war comes. The valley was sealed-off by the victorious army. I had considerable difficulty getting through the mountains without being discovered and captured."

"Here, drink some broth first," Sarai advised. "Sip this slowly. After your stomach accepts it you may have heavier food."

"I am most grateful, Princess Sarai."

"It is nothing. Regain your strength quickly."

Abram's guests said nothing while Unic, now able to converse normally, described all the events since the draft of all able bodied men into the Siddim Valley Army, to the capture of Lot.

Abram was patient and gently coaxed the story along allowing Unic to pause for intake of food. He was proud of his nephew, the part he played in the battle and the rescue of his family. But Abram's countenance fell when he heard that Lot and all his possessions were taken captive, except for his flocks. He was crushed by the thought of Lot being lost in a life of slavery to Elamites or Babylonians. Nothing could be worse for a Heberew, especially a nomad. Death was far more desirable.

Unic finished his story and was led away to a tent and a bed of skins where he fell asleep instantly.

Abram was silent for some time, mulling over Lot's fate and what he could do. When Lot separated from Abram he gave up all rights to his uncle's protection. Abram knew very well he was not bound to obtain Lot's release, but the desire to do so took hold of him so completely that he could think of nothing else.

"How can I free him? What can I with my few servants do against such a huge, terrible army that has set out to conquer the whole land of Canaan? Surely they are succeeding, so terrible is their fierceness and countless numbers," Abram spoke bitterly.

Suddenly Abram realized he still had guests, whom he had been ignoring.

"Forgive me for being such a bad host. I have withdrawn mentally from you and now I must beg your leave and withdraw from you entirely. Please understand that my nephew Lot has been enslaved. He...he is very important to me, beyond the description of words. He is more than family. He helped rescue me during a time of personal distress." Pausing for a moment to look at Sarai, he continued. "I must take upon myself the burden of freeing him. I...I am his goel, his protector. I must find a way to free him or die trying. I...I have no heir except him and I will be cut off in my generations if he is lost to me."

Mamre, Eschol, and Aner rose from their seats, expressed sorrow for Abram's misfortune, and excused themselves.

The news spread like a flash fire throughout the Heberew encampment of Abram. Without a word from Abram, weapons were brought out of tents and sharpened. Armor and travel attire were donned. Food and drink were prepared. Every able-bodied male assembled in the center of the encampment facing Abram's tent and waited for him to appear.

"We know Abram will attempt to rescue Lot. He is Lot's goel as much as he is our goel too. He is bound to the code of the Heberews that requires him to seek revenge against any who harm those kin the goel is committed to protect."

Inside his tent Abram paced back and forth talking to himself, hoping to find inspiration for his dilemma.

"Revenge against four powerful kings is an overwhelming task."

"Your men understand this, my husband," Sarai informed, him, "and they have prepared themselves for battle and await your leadership."

They are good men, Sarai; I am heartened by their courage. But they may have a long vigil as I explore possible solutions."

"They would all follow you anywhere into any danger. You must know that," Sarai declared.

"Yes, that I believe, but, sacrificing their lives to rescue one... to rescue even Lot, is a poor exchange. I need a plan that will reduce the odds against us and increase our chances for success."

As time wore on, Abram became frustrated at his failure to conceive a workable strategy. He concentrated hard but this worked against him and he cursed his stupidity. Three hours had passed and he was no closer to a solution than when he first began his deliberations.

Sarai found him out in the fields a few hundred yards from his tent, wandering about. He was arguing with himself and she gauged his frustration to be at a point where it was working against him. By means of carefully calculated questions, Sarai helped Abram become aware that perhaps he should defer the matter until morning when inspiration would surely follow a night's rest.

"Your men, now waiting upon you, will be rested in the morning and ready to go wherever you will lead them."

At first Abram wanted to reject her suggestions as the meddling of a woman who had no place in the affairs of men. But her logic, at this time, was more worthy than his, and being an honest man he submitted to her and came back to his tent. He released his men to their tents promising a decision the next morning about what he would do.

Abram did not fall asleep for some time. When sleep finally came, it was fitful and sporadic. He awoke several times from the anxiety that pressed upon him. When morning came he was sleeping soundly, well after everyone else in the camp had risen and eaten their morning meal.

The sound of animals and men, many of them, infiltrated Abram's tent, slowly penetrating his deep sleep. At first he assumed he was dreaming again; the same frustrating dreams where Lot was taken further and further away until lost from sight amidst a multitude of hostile warriors.

"Lot! Lot!" He called out and woke up in a sweat.

Sarai sat in the entrance of their tent protecting her sleeping husband from intruders. When he awoke with a start, she went to him with refreshment. He drank some water then stood stretching and rubbing the sleep out of his eyes.

"What is all the activity I hear?" he asked Sarai.

Before she could answer he passed by her and went outside.

The brightness of a new day hurt his eyes as he peered into the crowds of men that now looked his way. Abram's vision gradually sharpened. Turning his gaze full circle he recognized his three guests of last night: Mamre, Eschol, and Aner. Each man was dressed for travel and was well armed. Beyond them were almost twice the number of men that served Abram. They too wore travel clothing and bore arms like the three brothers.

"Hail to you, Prince Abram," Mamre shouted. "Forgive us for coming in such a number without notice or invitation. We came not for your hospitality, but for your leadership. Last evening we came to solicit your aid against the enemies of our people. We sought an alliance. Our motives were selfish. We know you are free to move out of harm's way, yet we wanted to obligate you here as an ally, committing you and your people to our aid."

Pausing for an awkward moment with head bowed, Mamre found the words he wanted and continued.

"Last night we left without offering one pledge, or commitment of aid or assistance to you in your time of need. What are we if we turn our backs on a neighbor who is so noble as you? Certainly not an ally, and not friends, ...but...but only devious cowards unworthy of friendship. This title we cannot bear and still lead the people of our tribes. We also cannot live with the shame of it upon our heads. It is for these reasons that we, and all our fighting men have come to help you free your nephew. Perhaps we may also satisfy our revenge at the same time," he added with a bold laugh.

Abram stared at the three men, as their eyes met his, and he knew they were sincere. He bowed before them, dignifying their message, and they bowed in return.

"Before all these men present, witness that I, Abram, son of Terah, do accept and honor the pledge of alliance and friendship offered by the brothers Mamre, Eschol, and Aner. It is with thanksgiving in my heart that I embrace you, my friends."

Abram went to all three tribal chiefs and embraced each one. Amorite and Heberew voices began shouting praises for the new allies and soon a rhythmic chant resounded through the countryside. A thousand men's voices roared louder and louder:

"Mamre, Eschol, Aner...friends of Abram, friend of the Everliving God!

Every man, woman, and child in the Heberew encampment felt tremendous confidence in the alliance and enthusiasm was rampant. Musical and rhythmic instruments suddenly appeared and spirits ran high with song and dance. Amorites and Heberews mingled with one another in mutual feelings of patriotism.

Abram, too, felt like a different man...like the leader of a powerful army full of confidence, thirsting for victory over a hated enemy. The comradeship made him forget his fears of inferiority and the creative part of his brain began to work.

Last night his task seemed hopeless: "A cup of water to put out a plains on fire," he reflected back on his mood.

"Today, my new friends remind me that I am a friend of Yahvah, the almighty Everliving God. He can put out any raging conflagration as well as save his people from it. Perhaps He will save Lot...perhaps He will...."

The next few hours were full ones for Abram. He sat in council with his allies and the men of his tribe who had been appointed captains and advisors. He laid out for them a strategy that required secrecy and daring on their part. A strategy that, if successful, would free the captives, destroy or rout the Eastern Army and return the wealth of Canaan to its people.

Abram's men listened attentively to every word as he spoke. Without question, they accepted his logic and his directions. Their duty was to obey and carry out assigned tasks.

The Amorite brothers, as tribal chiefs, were accustomed to giving orders, not taking them. They were becoming more and more agitated that Abram did not ask them for suggestions. He pressed his plan upon them, with extensive supportive reasoning. It was only after some time, when Abram paused between items, that Aner, the youngest brother, interrupted and blurted out:

"Have we chiefs no say in this matter?"

There was a complete stunned silence for several moments as all heads turned to face him.

Abram, taken back by the remark, said nothing for a moment while reflecting on the question. Finally he said softly: "I meant no disrespect, my friends. Please, tell us what you have in mind. We shall listen until you and your brothers have said all that you wish to say. What plan do you offer?"

Aner looked at his brothers for supporting words.

"Mamre, you are the eldest and therefore the one with the most knowledge. You have a plan do you not?"

Mamre scowled at his brother disapprovingly and replied: "My added years have provided me with a measure of discernment and patience. Using these gifts, I am able to appreciate what is wise and discard what is of no value. If we are to defeat an enemy so terrible as the Eastern Army of four kings, we must be extremely clever and daring. Anything less merely adds our own people to those who have already fallen. The strategy submitted by Lord Abram has great merit. I, and my people, shall support and implement it. I do not believe there is a better way to conquer our enemy and free those who are enslaved. You must have greater wisdom, however, for what other reason would you make such a declaration? Please speak, my brother, and we will listen."

Aner stuttered as he looked at Eschol, hoping this brother would save him from his embarrassment.

Eschol said nothing and turned his head from side to side.

Sweat streamed down Aner's face and in his awkward way he repeated the commitment of Mamre as his own vow.

Abram looked about him at the three brothers, searching his mind for words to mend this crack in their alliance.

"Friends, let us be of one mind and one body for the single purpose at hand. Until this morning when you came I had no strategy, no confidence and no hope for this undertaking. You three lifted me up, however. You gave me confidence. You gave me hope. This strategy is nothing without your leadership in carrying it out. Now, tell me if you will, how each one of you will accomplish the necessary tasks at hand. But before you do, let me say that I have learned a valuable lesson today. It is this: There is a time to talk and a time to listen. Both are necessary to make a man tolerable to his friends."

Abram chuckled as he finished and the whole council, catching the humor, roared with laughter.

There was no further question about Abram's final authority nor his judgement in any matter. The cement that healed the crack in their alliance bound them together stronger than before.

II

The council of patriots first established a signaling code that was understood by a group of men from each tribe's forces. They trained until they were able to communicate detailed messages over several miles by relays during the day or night.

The next phase of communications, taught to all their men, was a set of recognition signals to be used at close contact while near or among the enemy.

The patriots set up a spy network to observe the eastern army day and night. They prepared to report its movements, its strengths, where the captives were, how the plunder was carried and where. They also organized men to spy out the enemy's marching order, camping order, location of the four kings and their commanders, number of guards over captives, and how the captives slept and ate.

These detailed reports would soon come by couriers almost daily and be given to Abram and the three chiefs.

While Abram and his allies counseled and trained in their battle tactics, the four kings and their victorious army plundered the five kingdoms in the Valley of Siddim. All the food and wealth that could be carried or herded was accumulated as spoils of war. All but the elderly women were raped many times by voracious, drunken warriors. Orgiastic feasting went on for several days until the kings grew bored and restless for more conquests, more wealth, and more exhibitions of their power.

Leaving his authority in the hands of Mamre, Abram traveled north to Urusalem. There was someone who was vital to the success of his plan. When Abram arrived in Urusalem, he sought a meeting with Shem.

The two men embraced warmly as they exchanged greetings.

"You look older, my son," smiled Shem the first to speak.

"You age well, my lord. There appears no change in you since I was last here."

"Can white hair become whiter? What are a few more wrinkles among a multitude? Perhaps my back is more stooped from the weight of many years? That you would notice, would you not?"

"Only if I chose to. You live in a vision within my mind, Grandfather."

"Is father Noah still there also?"

"Oh, yes! He lives in my heart as well. The moment I came within these walls, he was with me again."

The two men talked for some time about events that had transpired since they last saw each other. Abram enjoyed listening as Shem reminisced about family events gone by recently and in the dim past. As Abram looked at him he realized Shem was the oldest living Adamic man on earth. His wisdom seemed to be boundless and his health enduring.

"Forgive an old man his prerogative of rambling on about the past. Please, Abram, tell me about yourself. What have you been doing? It has been far too long an absence since I last talked with you."

"I apologize for failing to visit sooner, Grandfather. I also confess that this visit is not just family oriented, but is also of a military nature relating to the invasion of Canaan."

"I understand; reports have come to me. I had hoped you would return and come to my aid, Abram, and here you are just when you are needed."

"Yes, Grandfather, I am involved, not so much in the defense of Canaan but rather in a form of counterattack that I would like to explain."

"By all means do so. I shall hold my tongue until it is appropriate for me to speak," Shem promised.

Abram looked at his advisor with reverence and remarked: "Withhold nothing from me, I pray, for I come in humility seeking your wise council, my lord."

"I so swear, Abram, now continue."

After Abram had finished describing the battle of Siddim Valley and Lot's eventual capture, he paused, then declared: "I am Lot's goel, and I am going to do my best to free him from his captors."

Shem, who had been leaning forward with intense interest, catching every word, now relaxed in a more comfortable position on his couch.

"Abram, Abram, I know what your duty tells you to do, but think carefully of the overwhelming odds against you. Do you really believe you can succeed? I fear that you will merely sacrifice yourself and your tribe for a cause that is hopeless."

"Yes, I know how impossible it may seem, but I think I have a plan that will work in our favor. I would like you to hear me explain it and then find fault with it if you can."

"Very well, you may proceed."

Shem listened carefully as Abram spoke, making mental notes for suggestions he would give afterwards.

"Now what criticism do you have Grandfather?"

"Your strategy is both clever and daring, Abram. It will require the cooperation of most of the kingdoms of Canaan. If that is possible, your plan may succeed. If many oppose the eastern army on their own, out of stupid pride, I have some serious doubts. You have my support and alliance for Urusalem of course. Now, my scribe will write down the details of our alliance, and that which you expect from the other kingdoms of Canaan. If my name and reputation still have authority, you may have the cooperation necessary to be successful."

After Shem's scribe finished writing the treaty on vellum, Shem applied his seal as King of Urusalem.

"Come Abram, let us view the setting of the sun," Shem suggested rising from the couch and stretching his ancient muscles.

Walking up a flight of stairs, they came out onto the top of a tower and gazed out over the vastness of the surrounding countryside.*
Both men absorbed the peaceful beauty and remained quiet for a time before Shem broke the silence and spoke.

"I enjoy coming here at the end of most days to view the panoramic beauty that our God, Yahvah, provides. I feel that I know Him when I am here. As the warm sun travels beyond the edge of our earth and night descends like a dark curtain, I find His presence in the sky.

"The multitude of heavenly bodies sparkle like jewels on His evening robes and rings on His fingers. It is here that I talk to the Everliving and it is here that I find answers to important questions. I am comforted by this. Perhaps you will find inspiration here as well, Abram."

I desire it earnestly, my lord. It has been some time since the Everliving has spoken to me and I yearn for his support."

Then wait and watch with me."

The two men stood and watched another day coming to rest. People finished the day's business and found their way home. Fires were lit and meals prepared. Flocks were herded to their folds and shepherds' fires were seen dotting the hills and valleys. It was a very peaceful pastoral setting and Shem never tired of watching it.

Finally, however, he turned to Abram, placed his arms on the big man's shoulders from the back as if facing him to his God. Looking up, Shem spoke to the great void.

"Yahvah, Everliving God, whom I have known personally... You who art the creator of this earth and all these heavenly bodies we see above... You who have all power of life and death... we come with faith into Your presence. I am Shem, son of Noah, pure in my generations, King of the City of Peace, and inheritor of the title Melchizedek, Your Priest King of Righteousness.

"O, my God, who knows all and sees all...before me You see Abram, whom You know as Your own. You chose him at birth for a special purpose. You saved him from his enemy, King Nimrod. Nimrod ignored Your commission! He turned against You and adopted the pagan customs of Cain for greed and power. Nimrod has

*Located thirty-three miles east of the Mediterranean Sea, and one hundred thirty-eight miles southwest of Damascus, Urusalem was somewhat like an island in the highlands of Canaan. All around the city lay hills and valleys green and gold from the previous season's rains.

allied himself with three other kings as bestial as himself. They murder, rape, and plunder the whole Land of Canaan as they please...and they have taken captive Lot, the righteous nephew of Abram.

"As his goel, Abram is committed to restoring Lot's freedom and possessions. And as Abram's goel I call upon You, my Lord Yahvah, the source of all my power, to clothe Abram with Your protection. Grant him and his confederates success in their battle against these evil men. Weaken Abram's enemies so that their great numbers and skills at war will be useless to them.

"Strengthen, we pray, the arms of Abram's men to be mighty with swords, spears and bows. Let them be Your weapons of revenge against the destroyers and abominators of Your land. This is the land You gave to Abram and his seed. Deliver it for him, we pray, and safeguard him that he may live to fulfill Your covenant."

After this prayer, Shem became silent.

A lengthy pause ensued, and then Abram spoke.

"Yahvah, my Everliving God, Lord of the heavens and this earth, this is Abram your servant. Please let the words of Shem, Your Melchezedek, be my words. Be with me now against my enemies, as You were in Egypt against Pharoah. I hereby pledge to You Lord, a tithe of all the spoils I am able to bring when I return victorious. This will be an example for my people to follow, even after I am dead. It will be payment for the service of their Melchezedek, priest/king of the Everliving God. It will visibly demonstrate the covenant between us as Your holy people, Your weapons of war against Your enemies."

The two patriarchs sat silently looking up into the blue/black sky. As they watched, falling meteors and comets began trailing their dying embers across the heavens. One, two, three, six, twelve.

"The Everliving has heard us, has he not Grandfather?"

"Yes, Abram, I believe he has."

The next morning, Abram embraced Shem and left, traveling south towards Hebron as fast as his camel would take him. Two days later he arrived at his encampment and called a council of the leaders.

When they were assembled Abram showed them the Alliance Agreement on vellum with Shem's seal.

"This, my friends, will make other kings of Canaan believers in the potential success of our campaign," Abram declared."

"Masterfully done, Lord Abram. I bow to your unlimited influence and wisdom," proclaimed Mamre.

The other men also bowed in great respect.

Please, good men, save your bows for one living who is far more wise and righteous than I. This wondrous priest/king prayed to Everliving God to support our cause. His prayers, and mine, were heard. We saw an awesome spectacle of falling heavenly bodies in answer. They seemed to confirm God's commitment to our success.

"Now, brothers and friends, with this understanding of our Lord's blessing upon us, we have nothing to fear. We are from this moment on 'The Strong Arm of the Everliving'! We are His weapons of war! His retribution against evil!

Abram was standing now, his dagger drawn and poised as if to strike. The knuckles of his hand were white, clenching the handle with his powerful strength. His face flushed and his neck muscles distended as a spirit of power and determination filled his entire being. Never before had he experienced such confidence. Abram's emotions soared; his stirring words erupted like fire, enflaming every man around him.

"Fear not our lesser numbers. It is no longer a matter for your concern, for God magnifies us with his might! Knowing this in our minds and hearts, we cannot fail! The captives shall be freed and the spoils returned! Have no doubts! I speak honestly. The four kings of the east shall flee for their lives as we destroy their armies! Now let us go forward as we planned! Victory is ours for the taking! I promise you, victory is assured!"

Every man was up on his feet with daggers clenched, echoing Abram's declarations with fervor.

"Now go tell your men, your women and children!" Abram commanded. "Let them share your dedication! Let them participate with their support. Let them know the Everliving God is blessing us all!" Abram commanded with a booming voice of authority.

The men scattered to their families, as ordered, vibrant with enthusiasm and confident they were going to accomplish a feat that would be remembered for many generations to come.

Four weeks after the battle of Siddim, the eastern army, bloated with debauchery, loaded with plunder and its entourage swollen with captives, left the Siddim Valley. The massive war machine proceeded northward resuming its quest to conquer.

Abram's emotions soared; his stirring words
erupted like fire, enflaming every man around him.

Chapter 23
Counter Attack

Abram, the three Amorite chieftains, and their combined forces of Heberew and Amorite warriors comprised the patriot army. Abram supplied 318 fighting men. Mamre commanded 255 warriors, Eschol 214 and Aner 203. With their commanders the patriot army numbered 994 in all. This small force set out the next morning southward to Hebron. It was the closest city north of the Siddim Valley, only forty miles away. Abram assumed that Hebron would be the next city overrun by the eastern army on its conquering trek through the Land of Canaan. Advance scouts, for the patriots, reported that the eastern army had not come this far north. The joint chieftains agreed it was safe to go to Hebron and negotiate an alliance, if they hurried.

The patriot army arrived after sunset and camped outside the fortress. At the closed city gates, Abram and his chieftains were refused admittance, as was the custom of all cities after dark.

"Fool! The lives of everyone in Hebron may be forfeit because of your ignorance," Aner shouted up to the watchman on the battlements. "We are tribal chiefs, not common traders caught out after dark. We come as allies with an army nearby, ready to oppose the terrible onslaught of the eastern army and save your king and your city. If you delay us unnecessarily I will inform King Aphek, my cousin, in the morning. My messenger will give a full report, on my behalf, of your stupidity. I regret that we will not be here to see your tongue cut out by the king in his anger."

The only sound that could be heard was the fluttering of torch flames and the shuffling of animal hooves. The pause did not last long.

"Open the gates! Admit these dignitaries! They come for a meeting with the king! Form two squads and escort the chieftains to the palace!" the officer commanded after only a slight delay.

"Well done, Aner," Abram complimented with a smile, "there is no time for delay."

Aner beamed a smile in return and looked proudly at his brothers.

Mamre acknowledged Aner's self-satisfaction with a nod. Looking at Abram, Mamre caught a twinkle of amusement in his eyes before he turned away. Mamre had just learned another lesson in how to be a leader among leaders.

Abram and the Amorite brothers were given an immediate audience with the king after showing the credential Shem had provided. Abram presented their strategy for counterattack using every element of persuasion open to him. With the help of his allies, Abram convinced King Aphek an alliance was the best solution with which to bring about a counter attack against the stupendous eastern army.

Desperate for assistance and worried for his life and the life of his city, King Aphek agreed to cooperate.

When Abram was sure that Hebron would fulfill its part in the strategy, he led the Patriot Army off early in the morning towards the next destination.

King Manoah of Shechem reacted in a manner similar to that of King Aphek: reluctant, fearful, desperate, but finally encouraged by the growing list of allies around him. Abram obtained King Manoah's covenant in writing, with his royal seal, to show other kings.

The Amorite brothers could hardly believe the alliance was actually becoming a reality. Never before had the kingdoms of Canaan ever cooperated in such a way. A common front was being prepared for a mutual enemy who had the power to consume these tiny cities as easily as a hungry warrior taking food from a farmer.

Abram stressed the importance of the alliance of Canaan with convincing arguments. He improved his ability to portray graphic realities to the extent that his listeners were soon in his verbal grasp.

It was after securing an alliance with King Naphish of Jericho that Abram was startled by a discovery. He became aware of how much he was like his father in leadership and in ability to sway men, even kings.

Abram realized that somehow he had acquired the ability to speak convincingly, authoritatively. These thoughts gave him mixed feelings of pride and regret. He preferred a simple way of life providing for his tribe, ministering, and teaching.

Now, suddenly, he was catapulted into a position of awesome importance. Abram's natural reluctance for this much responsibility weighed heavily upon him. He felt the stress constantly and slept little.

"No time for personal thoughts. Perhaps after Lot is freed...maybe then I can rest with my reflections," Abram resolved.

By the time the eastern army withdrew from the Valley of Siddim, Abram's patriot army had traveled northward through the land, adding city after city to its alliance.

The Patriots elaborate surveillance system watched and reported all movements of the enemy on its northward march. Up through the land they swept like locusts devouring everything in their path. City after city, and village after village submitted to the four kings without a battle. Every city gave a generous tribute of food, gold, silver, and valuable goods. Slaves and animals were also taken to carry the bounteous wealth.

Hebron, Urusalem, Bethel, Jericho, Shechem, Dothan, and all the way to Hazor they plundered the land...without resistance.

At each city emissaries were sent out to greet the invaders, soliciting peace in the name of their king.

"News of your invincible might in war has preceded you, my lords. Allow us to live and the city is yours for tribute, now and everlasting. Wealth, slaves, power...all yours with increasing abundance. The Land of Canaan is yours! Who will you conquer next? The Hatti? Mizeraim and Nubia? All the ancient nations far east on the other side of the world? No nation on earth can resist you with the terrible power under your command!"

World domination became an extension of the four kings' rabid desire for conquest. In every city that kneeled under submission, lavish feasting was provided to honor the victorious army. Huge volumes of food and strong drink were served amid praises heaped on the illustrious warriors of the east.

This treatment of subservience by Canaanites was a new experience for the victors, who reveled in their vainglories by constant over-indulgence.

In each city there were numerous people serving their enemies food and strong drink; all the strong drink they wanted. The supply seemed inexhaustible.

In each city, a new audience was ready and willing to serve, to listen, even encourage as if to be a part of the conquest in spirit. As the warriors' consumption of wine increased, so also did the tales of their victories become more exaggerated.

At Hazor, once again the invaders were treated to the special hospitality of Canaan. When they left the city and headed toward the city of Dan, Abram's observers again noted carefully the army's condition.

"They march without cadence in a disorderly manner," reported Abram's spies. "They appear to be an army of staggering drunkards. Many are sick along the way. They drag their weapons to lighten the weight. Officers do not watch their companies of men because much of the time they are asleep as they ride their camels. The kings ride asleep in their litters. They too are drunk and weakened."

"What about the captives? How are they treated?" Abram probed.

"The captives are whipped by guards, aggravated by the after effects of strong drink. The captives are roped together by their necks and hobbled at the ankles to prevent them from running for freedom."

"And Lot? Were you able to identify him among the captives?"

"It took quite some time and no little risk to get close enough, my lord, but I, myself, saw him. That is why I am reporting to you on this occasion."

"How did he look? Was he suffering much?" Abram pressed his spy.

"Your nephew seems to be holding up well enough, my lord. I compliment his endurance for he shows stripes from the lash. His garment has been cut by a guard's whip and bloody welts are exposed on his back and shoulders. Yet in spite of his hardship he seems to fare better than most of the others who come under the lash."

"AARRGGHHH!!" Abram bellowed like a wounded bear, feeling Lot's pain as if it were his own. With his neck and facial muscles flexed taut, and eyes flashing, Abram drew a sword from his girdle, raised it, and swore "Soon Nimrod, soon your old dream about me shall come true. I shall chase you with a sword, this sword, and your army will not protect you! My Everliving God and I will have our revenge against you! Very soon, Nimrod, very soon!" Abram shook with rage.

A shiver of fear shook the Heberew spy as he looked at Abram's terrifying countenance. He backed away, grateful to be a servant of this frightening lord rather than his enemy.

Mamre, Eschol, and Aner had never seen Abram this angry. Among them, they had discussed Abram's seeming inexhaustible patience and wisdom, always void of anger. Often they had asked each other: "How would such a passive chieftain lead in battle? Could he inspire his warriors by example? Was this friend of the Living

God only a priest and not a warrior? Never have we seen a man who could be both. What can we expect from him when we counterattack?" Even Mamre, the wisest, had not been able to answer his brothers.

But now they saw a new side of Abram and their anxiety was relieved. The anger he displayed reassured all three that Abram was capable of leading his warriors. They felt a renewed confidence for their success. Drawing their swords also, they cried out:

"Death to the invaders! We shall kill until they are no more!"

"Let death be our gift to them!"

"Yes, let us serve them death until they have had their fill and the earth runs red with a river of their blood!"

The City of Dan (Laish) capitulated to the Eastern Army without a struggle. The king and his administrators treated the enemy as honored guests and abundant food and strong drink were provided. Even the people were solicitous and friendly. Two thousand men and almost as many women kept the flow of food and strong drink coming in constant service.

Jugglers, musicians, dancers, and acrobats entertained the four kings and their officers. This was certainly the best hospitality the invaders had received in all the Land of Canaan. The officers gloated over the ease with which the country had surrendered. They made jokes about Canaanite cowardice and ridiculed every city as being full of old women ready to serve table.

"Where were the men of war? There were none. Because of their cowardice all that remained were weak, timid old women."

The insults became unbearable for some defenders. Those men who dared rebuke any invader's insults, acted alone or in pairs. For their rebuttal, they were promptly jumped on by overwhelming numbers and hacked to pieces in front of their friends and family. The lessons served to instill a dreadful fear, among the city's populace, that the conquerors might utterly destroy them.

Day turned to night. Wine flowed as freely as the current from the headwaters of the Jordan River where it descended from Mount Herman nearby. The proud Eastern Army, the scourge of Canaan, was collapsing, drunk and sick. They had dissipated themselves with so much excess that their bodies were weak. Their minds were full of vanities, put there largely by the people of Canaan.

Guards, less intoxicated than the main army, performed their duties while swearing complaints and struggling to keep awake.

They dared not sleep. To be caught asleep by an officer brought a punishment of public execution.

The hours passed. It was almost midnight and servants were still seen by sentries stopping by soldiers to pour wine or serve food. Even though most were asleep, no one was missed. The servants usually had their backs to the guards and their movements went unquestioned as they kneeled down to serve.

Even as they watched in the dim firelight, the sentries failed to see what the servants were really doing. Hundreds of wine and food servants wound their way in an organized manner among the huge reclining army. They never seemed to deplete their supplies, but the sentries took no notice of that fact. Every sentry was diverted by offers of food and ample conversation by inquisitive, flattering servants.

Abram's patriots had planned and trained well for this crucial tactic and now it was proving successful. Abram watched as each reclining warrior was served; not food or wine but rather a sharp dagger's seven-inch blade. A quick thrusting movement of the hand, and the dagger pierced the body at a point where the neck joins the chin. The narrow two-sided blade severed the vocal chords and then the spinal cords at the base of the skull. Unsuspecting soldiers died quickly and silently. Their jerking death movement went unnoticed in the flickering semi-darkness. Blood ran down the necks of lifeless bodies, mingling with spilled wine as a common stain.

On and on went the silent battle. Here and there the Patriots could be seen pausing for a few minutes between kills. The exertion and sickening effect of murdering sleeping men wrenched their stomachs. But, the fear of discovery and the awakening of this huge army, was a stronger emotion. To survive was to kill. To kill was to plunge the knife...again...again...again...again....

Servants talking to the sentries did their task well, telling jokes and long stories to hold their attention. Now and then, however, a sentry would become suspicious and start to investigate. Before he could raise his voice to challenge or cry an alarm, however, the affable servant drew his dagger and thrust it into the sentry's neck and jerked it out again. The movement was so fast that no cry was uttered. The guard stood on trembling legs ready to collapse, but not before the servant pulled the sentry's arm around his neck to hold him up. It was a very difficult maneuver but the servant laughed with merriment, just as he had earlier, and helped the sentry to a sitting position against a rock or tree. With open eyes and head propped up, the sentry still looked wide-awake. Up close, however, it was a dead man's stare.

At the start of their march out of the valley of Siddim, the Eastern Army carried off as many as ten thousand captives from that war in addition to thirty thousand they had accumulated from previous battles and as payments in tribute. During the trek north through Canaan, fifteen hundred died from hardship and lack of water. Most were women who were raped repeatedly and unable to endure.

Prisoners were tied together, with loops around their necks, in groups of ten. If anyone in their group collapsed or died, the remaining nine had to drag the body until the army was commanded to stop. The dead, or near dead, captive was cut loose and speared to be sure he or she was dead. The body was not buried. It was left for the jackals that followed at a safe distance behind. A grisly trail of skeletons bore evidence of the army's atrocities.

As many as five thousand captives were sold to Hittite slave merchants by the sentries and their officers. The transactions usually took place late at night quietly and secretly. The purchases meant free shekels of silver for the soldiers, and slaves at low prices for the merchants. The four kings had no awareness of this thievery since they were at an opposite end of the vast encampment. The kings always traveled at the head and captives straggled at the rear, often miles away. The poor victims often marched extra hours at day's end to close up the ranks.

Abram, Mamre, Eschol and Aner, posing as slave traders, approached the slave compound late in the evening. Each one had thirty to forty men with him as they approached from different directions. They identified themselves to the officers in charge who readily agreed to a sale.

Pretending to evaluate the quality of merchandise, those of Abram's servants who could recognize Lot, carefully carried torches through the masses of shivering, huddled bodies. The prisoners were unwashed and covered with the dust of hundreds of miles. Their individual features were blended into a common pale look of emaciated hopelessness. They suffered in tormented silence. Moaning, crying, or whimpering only brought more punishment and pain from the guards.

The frigid night breeze sweeping down from Mt. Hermon stiffened the slaves with cold. The wind was a blessing to the guards because it fanned away the horrible stench of unwashed bodies lying in their own filth.

While the sentries cursed the traders for taking so long, the search for Lot went on. Mamre, Eschol, and Aner selected as many male captives as they could find who would have some strength and courage left to fight their captors. The guards knew that the process of selecting slaves in good condition was common and suspected nothing. Those slaves brought the best prices in the slave markets. The guards were busy, calculating their barter and the profits they could have after dividing the money with other guards.

Every guard had to be paid in order to keep the matter a secret, for if the kings discovered them now, every warrior and officer involved would die. Theft of the kings' property deserved such a punishment.

Abram called out to his chief servant farthest away: "Lot, Lot, Lot...what have you found?"

The answer came back: "No one special, my lord."

A few minutes passed and again the question was called out: "Lot, Lot, Lot...what have you found?" Every patriot peered into the darkness looking for a captive to respond to the call by sitting up.

Eventually the technique worked as Lot heard and sat up, disturbing the captive in front and behind him.

"Are you Lot, son of Haran?" Abram's servant asked.

The man nodded his head and through dry, cracked lips uttered "Yes."

The servant turned in the direction of Abram some distance away and called out: "My lord, this is Lot. I have found a worthy slave for your purposes!"

Abram walked over to where Lot sat. Bending over with a torch-light to get a better look he asked: "Lot is it really you?"

"Yes, Uncle Abram, I am your nephew, Lot, a slave to King Chedorlaomer."

"Say no more! We will draw suspicion from the sentries," Abram whispered commandingly.

Abram could not look upon his nephew any longer without displaying affection or even sympathy for him. That emotion would have to wait for some private time. The rage that welled up inside him now was almost at a bursting point. He managed to contain it while Lot and the four to five hundred captive men selected were freed from their former bonds and led away in new bonds.

The barter did not take long. The soldiers were fearful of discovery and were happy to get paid for such a large number of captives.

Abram ordered the prisoners taken to one of the nearby streams descending from Mt. Hermon and washed. They were given warm clothing, sandals, and food. While they ate and gained some strength, their rescuers explained who they really were, and the purpose for buying their freedom.

"And so you are about to be armed with weapons so that you may join the Patriot Army of Canaan. Your first act of revenge upon your captors is to join us in freeing all the remaining captives."

The men began talking excitedly, raising their voices with questions, and grumbling protests. They were unsure of themselves and this strange obligation that was now being thrust upon them.

"Silence!" commanded Aner. "Your freedom is in our hands! Your wretched, ungrateful lives belong to us. We are your lords! Now hear Abram, our commander, and obey all that he says for we will be watching you."

Abram realized the ex-prisoners were confused and fearful of their rapid transition. There was little time to spare but he believed it was necessary to mentally prepare these slaves to become as spirited as warriors, if not warriors in ability. They might otherwise be a hindrance instead a useful company in the patriot army.

"Men...be not fearful. We, who have redeemed you from the slavery of cruel masters, are servants of the all-powerful, Everliving God of the Heberews. The Everliving has set his hand against the army of the east and it is doomed to death for its iniquities. We are the weapons of our Lord's condemnation: His spears and swords, His bows and arrows, His battleaxes and cleansing torches! Our duty is to rid the Land of Canaan of this horrid, destructive, pestilence! God's power is in us! Justice is in our hands! Retribution is ours to administer! We have already killed almost half of the vermin who raped your wives and daughters, took your possessions and enslaved you! Even as I speak to you now, wine sotten warriors are being quietly slaughtered like sheep.

Now, you are being given the opportunity to join with us and share not only our revenge but also our rich returns! And not only our rich returns but also the GLORY OF ACHIEVING THIS MIRACLE FOR A RIGHTEOUS EVERLIVING GOD! In the generations that follow, men, women, and children, over the earth, will tell and retell how you redeemed the land as part of the patriot army of Canaan. Is there any man here who would step forward, look me in the face, and say: "I deny my glory? I cannot believe there is such a coward. Is there such a man among you? If it be so, let him step forward."

Abram paused, silent, starring into the crowd. His gaze pierced men's hearts and destroyed any shred of resistance remaining. They were united to him now; he could see that. Men stirred restlessly, looking around with curiosity, but no one stepped forward. They swore preference to a quick death in battle to a slow agonizing one in bonds.

Abram inspired every man with thoughts and concepts that changed them. Suddenly they drew courage, strength, and inspiration miraculously. Every man became charged with purpose but controlled under authority, listening quietly, attentively to this electrifying prince. Every sentence Abram spoke had the impact of a message from God Himself.

Abram had their complete confidence and attention. He could hear his voice pierce the silence with the effect of thunder before the rush of air and torrent of rain of a coming storm. He knew every man was completely still with concentration. Now the slaves had additional motivation for fighting. Their allegiance to the patriot army was not out of fear, as Aner had threatened. And their loyalty was not only to seek revenge and restitution. They truly believed they would find a measure of immortality, through the history of the storytellers. Every man believed that Abram and his army truly had the invincible power of a mighty God with them. Witnessing such a close relationship between a god and men, especially for justice, was a marvel. Each one believed as he never believed before. And every slave was eager to kill the enemy or die trying.

Abram explained the plan of attack so that every man understood. It was a variation of the plan that had worked so well against the sentries earlier.

"Aner?"

"Yes, Lord Abram?"

"Give the order to arm the captives."

"As you command."

Aner, now captivated by Abram's leadership, proudly and personally saw to the arming of each freed man.

****

"Stop! Who is it that approaches?" a guard at the slave compound called out. "Officer of the guards! Officer of the guards! Men approach!" the alarm went out.

Coming towards the sentry was a torchbearer leading a procession of men laden with food and wine. "We are only your servants, my lord, coming with food and wine to give you comfort during the cold hours before dawn."

Just then a troop of about fifty guards came running up and faced off opposite the procession with weapons poised for defense. Coming up last, the officer in charge shoved his way through the line of his guards and demanded:
"Who are you? What brings you here at this hour?

"Why, my name is Mamre, my lord, "answered the torchbearer, "I am a steward over these servants, from the City of Dan, who have been ordered by a commander of your army to provide you and your men with the sustenance of food and drink. I would assume, my lord, that he wished you and your guards to maintain your alertness."

"You have no right to assume anything, Canaanite coward. Just do as you are ordered and you might live your miserable life a few more years in groveling shame." The troop of guards laughed along with their officer, casting insults of their own at the hapless servants.

Mamre and his men stood still and remained silent with their heads bowed in submission. The abuse was almost intolerable to Mamre and he knew everyone of his men strained against the command he had given them at their start. "No matter what insults are cast at us, we will withhold our revenge until the command is given to permit it."

"Very well," the officer interrupted his men, raising his hand in the air, "you may serve us all. This will be a pleasant relief from the boredom of shivering through the early morning darkness. Now, be quick about it! My men are anxious and deserving!

"Yes, my lord, as you command. You and your men are deserving of this," Mamre agreed submissively. Turning, he gave orders for the servants to walk around the perimeter of the slave compound to serve the guards stationed there. When Mamre's men had finished their service they withdrew from the area the way they came.

The guards all grew tired and very sleepy. The wine they drank had been specially prepared to induce sleep. They struggled to stay awake but the monotony of guard duty, combined with the late hour, proved too much for them. In a half-hour's time most of the guards were deeply asleep. Those left standing were asleep on their feet, propped up against a tree or rock. Their heads bobbed up and down, and their legs bent and straightened as they jerked half-awake, then went back to sleep.

A bird call penetrated the silence. All around the perimeter of the slave camp, dark figures bending low, crept up on every dozing guard and officer. There were a few outcries but they were cut short by the thrust of a blade. Every one of the sentries and officers died almost at the same time without one patriot lost and with no general alarm sounded.

"Secure here, my lord!"

"Secure here!"

"All right here!

"Here, too!"

"And here!"

Around the large perimeter came shouts of confirmation that guards had been killed. When the last report was heard Abram called out: "Have any escaped?"

"No, lord, they are all dead," was the answer Abram needed before proceeding with the next phase of this war.

"Excellent! Now free the captives! Cut their bonds! Hurry! We must make haste! There is much to do before this night is over!"

As the captives were cut loose, their emancipators explained who the patriots were. With Abram's stirring message still fresh in their minds, the captives, who had been purchased earlier, aroused several thousand weakened prisoners. Up they rose in their smelly rags finding new hope. A chance to fight and slay their captors? A mighty Everliving God wills the destruction of this hated enemy? Restitution, revenge, and a chance at immortality? "Yes, yes, by all means yes!" Almost all agreed, their hatred fueling them with miraculous energy and determination.

"My friends," Abram addressed Mamre, Eschol, and Aner, when they returned to his side after inspecting the progress being made, "pass this message along to all the captives. 'By now we have slain half the invaders. The other half lay asleep, unsuspecting of the imminent death approaching at our hands. Rejoice within yourselves for your captors must not know you have been freed from your bonds. Surprise is our greatest weapon, and silence is the way to wield it successfully. Men await you with clothing, food, and weapons they can no longer use. Outfit yourselves as we pass over ground occupied by the many thousands we have slain. Obey the commands of the patriots placed over you. Now, on to total victory!'"

Hearing this news, all the captives found new strength and a renewed will to live and avenge themselves.

"My brothers-in-arms, we are in the presence of a majestic lord whose wisdom must come from his God," Mamre declared. "How else could mortal man conceive a strategy that would raise an army of twenty-five thousand men, ready to fight to the death, at a time when a more numerous enemy was most vulnerable? When we survive this war, it would benefit us greatly to maintain our friendship with Abram, even in the worship of his God."

Eschol, Aner, and the men they talked to, agreed wholly with this logic promising to devote themselves to a close alliance with this friend of the Everliving God.

Abram knew from his spies that the vast encampment of the eastern army began a few hundred yards north of the City of Dan and extended upward as an elongated body for the distance of perhaps four miles. Analyzing the enemy positions, he explained to his commanders:

"The captives are kept nearest the city for three reasons. First, they are visible evidence of the conquering power of the Eastern Army. Second, the captives serve as a bulwark against a surprise attack from the city. Third, they are at the rear of the army in its normal marching order and remain in that position when the march is to resume.

"Eight hundred of our men began their slaughter a short distance north of the captives compound where troop encampment began. I judge that they have been 'serving' death for at least three hours. We have less than four hours of darkness before sunrise reveals our terrible deeds. The Everliving God is with us in all that we have done, for our strategy is working. We cannot relax our efforts, however, for we must use the darkness as our ally until the enemy is destroyed or routed beyond any means to form up against us.

"Now divide our new army of captives among their rescuing patriots. Each patriot is now a commander-in-charge of at least one hundred and fifty men. This is the only way we can control them as an effective army.

"From the time we start our advance from here and join our 'servants of death,' conversations and any other sounds are strictly forbidden. Use only nature's sounds to signal as we have done earlier."

Abram's orders were put into motion. He and his commanders spread out their men, those with weapons in front of those without. They came upon the southern end of the enemy encampment and advanced among the dead soldiers.

The ex-captors stripped the dead bodies of their clothes, sandals, weapons, and money. They consumed all the food and drink they could find. The scene was one of looting on a grand scale.

A remarkable transformation took place within an hour's time. The wretched mass of weakened, ragged captives that had lain helpless and shivering such a brief time ago, had risen and become an army.

For the captives everything good was happening so fast that many kept asking if they were dreaming, having a vision, or had died and gone on to a new life. Up until an hour ago they had lost hope of continuing life. Now, their life was returned and sweet revenge was in their grasp.

Spirits were high and weaknesses forgotten. What thoughts or fears they may have had were now submerged under new purposes. They were revived by an intense loyalty to the brave patriots who had redeemed them. A dedication to the destruction of a common enemy burned in the breast of each man.

Their advance continued northward spreading out the companies to form a 'U' shape that would create a semi-circle around the remainder of the Eastern Army. They were commanded to remain out of sight and hearing range until needed. These were the reserves that would be brought into battle if Abram's 'serving' patriots were discovered and the sleeping army aroused what was left of itself.

The four kings slept within a special compound with a large number of sentries guarding them. These were no ordinary soldiers; they were the biggest and best fighters in the entire army. The kings' guard totaled twelve thousand men. Each night there were three thousand sentries on duty for four-hour watches. They guarded the kings' compound as though it were a fortress within a fortress.

The patriot army was now one-half mile from this destination. The Eastern Army was being killed at a faster rate, now that Abram and his commanders had arrived with additional trained patriots.

And then it was finished. The last of the main body of the invading army was killed quietly and without incident.

A birdcall chirped its sound, remarkably clear and isolated, in the stillness of the night.

From the width of the encampment they came; an army of servants gathered silently before Abram and his Amorite allied commanders. Each man held a blood-smeared dagger in a hand stained red up to his elbow. They reported that their nasty work was accomplished. No one survived their blades.

"An open space of perhaps one hundred paces separates the main army from the kings' compound," Mamre observed.

"The kings' guard will not be so easy to kill," Abram said quietly to his commanders. "They are the pride of the kings' army. Every man is a fierce, dedicated warrior, not easily defeated."

"We have found that their guards are not drunk like their comrades," Eschol reported. "Those that stand sentry duty are sober and awake. They have been forbidden to drink wine while on duty."

"Mmm, then it appears the only way to conquer them is by direct attack, and we must strike very soon," Abram reasoned

"Perhaps one-fourth of their forces are sentries while the remainder sleep heavily at this time of night," Mamre ventured.

"Our patriots, who served there earlier today, gave us knowledge of how the compound is arranged," Eschol continued. "The kings' tents are at the center, perhaps twenty-five paces apart, in a square fashion. The openings of their tents face inwards towards each other. Surrounding them are tents of the high commanders that answer to each king. The tents of subordinate commanders form the next square. Lastly, the warriors of the kings' guard are on the outside."

"How many do you estimate there are?" Abram asked.

"According to our best spies, there are at least twelve thousand guards and eighteen hundred officers," Eschol responded.

"These savages are as numerous as the cedars on Mount Lebenon," Abram observed.

"We have already cut down a forest, my lord. What are a few more thousand to us?" Aner challenged.

"Well said, Aner my friend, well said," Abram complimented.

"Our God is with us, my friends. He has delivered the enemy into our hands. Now that the body of the enemy is killed, we face the heart and mind, which must also be killed if we are to rid ourselves of this scourge for as long as we live. Now, here is what we will do..."

Abram asked his three allies if they agreed with his plan of attack. They all concurred and the enlarged Patriot Army quietly surrounded the kings' compound. When the northern contingent was in position, the bark of a jackal was heard clearly through the campground and beyond. It was a signal for the Patriots to close in. Every man held a bow armed with an arrow. Quivers full of arrows were slung over their shoulders; swords and daggers in their girdles.

Slowly and quietly they moved, hunched low to reduce their visibility. They came to within twenty paces before taking aim at the sentries and sleeping guardsmen.

A bird could be heard warbling. Its mate seemed to answer far away.

The high pitched hiss of almost twenty-six thousand arrows whistled through the black night. They were the prelude to the agonizing screams of nearly three thousand men pierced by the deadly rain.

The patriots armed their bows again as they walked forward, now standing straight and tall. Bowmen took aim at the kings' guards scrambling up from sleep with shocked looks on their faces. In a brief span of time, they managed to reach for their weapons and stand up. Then a second flight of arrows struck. Their victims staggered momentarily - then crumpled like tents without supports.

Activity within the compound grew from excited confusion to total bedlam. Officers managed to muster some groups of men together for organized counterattacks. But the kings' soldiers were no match against the overwhelming onslaught of superior numbers.

"How many are there out there attacking? Where is their flank? What is happening to the south with the main body of our army? What has happened to all the sentries?"

All these questions and more were screamed at commanding officers by the four kings.

No one knew the answers.

The kings were outraged by this turn of events. Chedorlaomer swore at his allies accusing them of betrayal. Insane with bitterness and disappointment, he was slow to accept reason.

Nimrod defended his fellow kings asserting they were all in severe jeopardy and had better band together or face certain death.

Reports began coming in to the commanders who immediately reported the circumstances to the kings. It was quickly surmised that they were surrounded by a superior force who had fully engaged, and somehow defeated, their army to the south. Nimrod reasoned that the only feasible way out of their dilemma was to counterattack to the northwest with all their remaining guards. If they succeeded in getting free they would run up into the mountains and hide.

Chedorlaomer found the plan offensive and refused it.

The other three kings overruled his supreme authority and gave commands to their officers to initiate an escape maneuver.

The sound of horns blown assembled all the remaining guards around the four kings to protect them. Six to seven thousand men formed up in a hurry and prepared to carry out a tactic they had previously only rehearsed. Never had they expected the time would really come when they would have to risk their lives.

The outside ranks held long shields that formed an armored barrier all around the perimeter. The ranks inside held shields over their heads for protection.

A command was shouted and everyone began jogging forward as one body.

Patriot bowmen kept converging towards the remnant of the kings' guard, unleashing their multitude of arrows. Most of them bounced off the protective shields but a portion found and penetrated flesh.

Guards that were critically wounded fell and were left behind. Ranks closed to cover the opening in time to meet the next onslaught of arrows.

Again guards fell and ranks closed. Almost four hundred men fell each time the arrows flew. Their comrades closed ranks and trampled them underfoot as they progressed.

The kings' guard of four thousand men hit the patriots on their north side like harvesters cutting through a wall of wheat. Swords flailed and cut a swath wide enough for the kings' 'battle machine' to pass through. The human square hardly missed a step as the patriot bowmen were cut down like wheat at harvest. The weakened ex-captives were no match for the king's guards in close combat.

As long as the king's guards held together and kept running, they had some protection. The patriots took up a chase, shooting arrows as they ran. In spite of the darkness of the night, the arrows took an uncertain toll and men cried out in pain as they fell.

The four kings, terrified and confused by their plight, whined and panted with exhaustion. In spite of the cold night air, sweat ran into their eyes, stinging and blurring what little vision they had in the darkness. Men, pierced with arrows, fell all around them in constant attrition. Suddenly, Nimrod bellowed out a command and the kings' protectors changed their retreat into a counterattack.

The remnant of the king's men, numbering approximately three thousand, came to a halt. They turned about face and began running back toward their pursuers. The patriots failed to notice the slight opening to the rear of the formation through which the four kings fled.

Guardsmen charged the patriots in a dead run, rushing into and through a hail of arrows. The dedicated warriors who survived that airborne death flailed against the bowmen, and their swords hacked with deadly efficiency. Patriots, who had time, quickly discarded their bows and drew swords to save themselves.

The guards fought well, but they soon realized that this was their last battle. Surrounding them was a force, although weak in fighting skills, certainly devious and vast in numbers. The constant effort required to defend against an innumerable foe wore them down. Without their kings and officers to urge them on, many turned and tried to run away from battle. Surrounded as they were, the remnant guardsmen had to fight their way back out of enemy encirclement. Only the strongest made it through in a charge. Running away from the battle, they did not stop until the distant screaming and agonizing blended into the various sounds created by disturbed animals, birds, and insects. And then only the sound of their panting from exhaustion filled their ears as night surrounded them. The remaining guardsmen were overcome by a swarm of patriots stampeding, trampling, and cutting them down.

The four kings had a head start of about fifteen minutes. They had crept away from the formation when the guards turned to counterattack. On the northeast stood Mount Herman amongst the Anti Lebanon Mountains. It was there that they scrambled and remained in hiding. The headwaters of the Jordan River sustained them until the patriots turned back from their pursuit sometime during mid-morning.

Later that day all four kings stood and looked eastward towards the Euphrates River. Also directly to the east about twenty-five miles away lay Damascus. It was going to be a long hard journey back home on foot, providing they were not murdered along the way. There were no servants to carry them, feed, or protect them. They had only enemies for hundreds of miles. Each king went his own way, traveling alone. They hoped this would help them avoid being identified and captured.

And he [Abram] divided his forces against them by
night, he and his servants, and defeated them, and pursued
them as far as Hobah, which is on the left hand of Damascus.

Genesis 14:15 Lamsa Bible

The City of Hobah

Chapter 24
Return of the Victors

I

And he brought back all the goods, and also brought back Lot, his nephew, and his goods, and the women also, and the people.

And the king of Sodom went out to greet him, after his return from the destruction of the forces of Cardlaamar [Chedorlaomer], and the kings who were with him, at the valley of Shaveh, that is the king's valley.

And Melchizedek king of Salem [Urusalem] brought out bread and wine; he was the priest of the Most High God.

Genesis 14:16-18 Lamsa Translation

Abram established a council to distribute spoils among those deserving of them. All expenses were repaid to the citizens of Dan (Laish) from whom the food and drink came.

The cities of Canaan who had paid tribute had it returned to them.

Every freed captive, alive after the battle now belonged to Abram and his three Amorite friends, as their servants. That was the law of the land. Much to the chagrin of his allies, however, Abram insisted on giving the captives their freedom. In addition, he was firm about giving them a portion of the spoils after tribute was returned to the cities of Canaan.

Eschol and Aner resisted this generosity with arguments as old as the occupation of Canaan. Abram was unmoved.

"Consider yourself in the place of these unfortunates who have lost family, home and possessions. Acting for the Everliving, I have redeemed their liberty and possessions. If you were captive

310

Amorites I would have done the same. Now, how say you about this matter?"

Both men were embarrassed in answering and hung their heads to avoid Abram's penetrating gaze.

"Again we must bow to your wisdom, Lord Abram. All we know are the old ways. Ordain what you deem is wise and fair. Command us and we will obey."

Jubilation reigned as the freed captives and Abram's patriots left the scene of their victory and began the return march home. Abram's men revived the chant that originally bound them together with the three tribes of Amorites:

"Mamre, Eschol, Aner... with Abram, friend of the Everliving God!"

It started as a solo, then it was multiplied by hundreds in a roaring wave of shouting voices. The four leaders were riding camels at the front of the huge caravan. They looked at each other with proud smiles. It was another reward of their victory and they basked in the glory of it.

In a very short time, thirty-eight thousand voices resounded in the chant. The sound was heard for miles as it echoed among the hills. Abram turned side ways, and looked back at the thousands of happy enthusiastic faces. He waved his recognition and pointed to the sky. It was his way of sharing the glory with Yahvah, the provider of their victory.

Groups of freed captives in large and small numbers split off from the main body to wend their way home. As they did so, voices from the main body shouted out the question: "Who restored your freedom and gave you wealth?"

The answer was always: "Mamre, Eschol, Aner... with Abram, friend of the Everliving God."

Whenever the extremely long caravan approached a village or a city, the chant was started up again. And when they left, the question and answer were stated. Over and over the chant was repeated until out of hearing distance.

The fame of the four chieftains spread throughout the Land of Canaan. News of their coming preceded them and cities opened their gates and hearts to the caravan.

When they came to the Valley of Shaveh (Valley of the Kings) near Urusalem, Shem came out and greeted Abram and his allies. The caravan stayed there a few days to rest while Abram visited with his patriarchal grandfather.

Sitting under the shade of a grove of trees, Abram related all the events that had transpired with the realism of a true storyteller. Shem absorbed every word, nodding his head with approval and uttering affirmatives. Abram finished his chronicle and looking Shem straight in the eyes he said: "I thank you, grandfather, and I thank the Everliving for making our victory possible."

"It pleases me to see that your conquest has not made you a vain leader, my son. But why is it that you have given away so much wealth and power? Is it not the law of the land that spoils and captives freed by you now belong to you, the lord of your army?"

"Yes, that is true, my lord."

"Yet you freely provide a redemption for those in bonds; is that not so?"

"Yes, that is true."

"Please tell me why."

"Yahvah the Everliving made a covenant with me. He promised:

'I will make of you a great people, and I will bless you, and make your name great; and you shall be a blessing. And I will bless those who bless you, and curse those who curse you; and in you shall all the families of the earth be blessed.'

"The almighty God has reaffirmed this covenant to me repeatedly. I have no need of power over these people when the Everliving has promised me so much more. I already have more than enough wealth. My only desire is to have a son through which this covenant may be fulfilled."

Shem was quiet for a short time, composing his thoughts. Breaking the silence he ordered his servants to bring bread and wine into his tent.

"Come with me Abram, into my tent."

Abram obeyed, more than just curious about what Shem was arranging as the old man ordered his servants away. Sensing that something profound and private was about to take place Abram stood still waiting for Shem to direct him. Shem gestured for him to sit and took a seat for himself.

"Abram, my son, you have been chosen for a high calling, a great purpose. Your faithfulness to our God has been proven most worthy. But keep in mind, Abram, that the strength of your faith shall improve as it is tested. The same is true of metal. Its strength increases as the heat of the fire it passes through is increased. I tell you this so you will understand why your heart's desire is delayed.

"The Everliving's delay is not His denial. There is a purpose for all things, and a time for them to be fulfilled."

The white haired patriarch paused for reflection on his next thoughts and then continued.

"What I am about to tell you is a great mystery. It has been revealed to me by Yahvah, the One God. This mystery involves fulfillment of His covenant with you, and much more. Abram...you have proven yourself to be a deliverer of your kin, of your friends, and of many others enslaved unjustly. It has been revealed to me that you are the forerunner of an even greater deliverer who shall come from your seed in the future.

"He will be conceived by the power of Yahvah in the womb of a daughter of your race. This man will be called Yahshuah, meaning Yah saves, for Yahvah will personally deliver his people from evil and be an example to them for right living.

"In the midst of his life his human body will be murdered by a corrupted people and their perverted priesthood. He will have the power to prevent it, yet he shall accept the sacrifice to prove his identity. Afterwards, he will raise himself from the grave into life and will eventually judge all nations and peoples at the end time.

"This deliverer will be the High Priest, our God and King over the whole earth forever. His order of priesthood will be the culmination of the Melchizedek Order I now represent."

Shem paused and motioned to the bread and wine, laid out simply on a white linen cloth.

"Now, my son, partake of these simple elements of food and drink with me and remember them as sacraments to be repeated by you and your seed for all generations to come.

Abram's mind was reeling from the prophecy and its wondrous importance. He concentrated on every word in order to remember and understand the message.

"The bread and wine, I am about to serve, represents the body and blood of the Deliverer to be sacrificed for his followers. They signify his victory over all evil. Evil in priesthoods, governments, and corruption by groups and individuals."

Shem took the bread: flat, round like a disc about the thickness of a finger and as broad as the span of a hand. He tore it in half almost reverently and gave one part to Abram.

"Here, Abram, eat this bread that I rend. It represents the body of Yahshua, the Deliverer, passed through a violence of torture and death for the deliverance of his followers."

Abram followed Shem's instruction and both men ate the bread in silence.

Next, Shem poured some wine from a skin into two cups. Giving one to Abram he continued:

"Drink this wine in order to remember that it represents the blood of the Deliverer, to be shed through suffering.

"Never forget Abram, that the purpose of his suffering and sacrifice will be his victory over evil."

Shem looked into Abram's eyes with tenderness, yet with an unwavering intensity that held him, unmoving.

"The very thing you desire most in your life," Shem continued gently, "is that which our God has ordained to be vital to his plan to save this world from destruction. It is through your seed, descended from my seed, that this will come about."

Abram breathed deeply, tilted his head back and let out a deep sigh. His eyes fluttered against moisture and his vision blurred. Taking the rest of the bread and wine, he ate and drank in silence, being unable to speak. Words failed him. To even dare seemed a sacrilege. Any utterance from his lips would profane the magnificence of Shem's words.

The King/Priest saw the effect his instruction had on Abram. He watched tears form and make their way down the cheeks and onto the beard of a man who had just conquered four kings and their huge army.

"You please me beyond words, my lord. I...I simply cannot express..."

"It is not necessary that you say anything, my son. You possess great courage, determination and strength. These are very worthwhile manly qualities. You also demonstrate a submission to the will of your God. What more could a father ask?"

II

On his knees, Abram bowed his head to the ground at the feet of Shem. The king/priest took a small vial of myrrh from the girdle around his robe. Removing the cap he poured the precious perfumed oil over Abram's head.

"Abram, son of Terah, I affirm that our God has consecrated you. He has set you apart, with knowledge, from the peoples of this land, for the fulfillment of his righteous purpose. I, Melchizedek, give you my blessing. I hereby invoke the Everliving's favor upon you. He shall honor, exalt, and protect you as the patriarch of his people."

Lifting his head and looking upward Shem declared: "And let us exalt our Most High God Yahvah, who has delivered our enemies into your hand."

Abram gave praises to Yahvah. When he was finished he went out and divided ten percent from all the remaining spoils. He commanded his servants and they brought the tithe before Melchizedek, and Abram spoke:

"I, Abram, son of Terah, accept gratefully and humbly your blessing, my lord. I also acknowledge my consecration by Yahvah the Most High God. Please accept these gifts as evidence of my gratitude and tribute."

Shem gave thanks for the tithe and embraced Abram like a proud father.

While Abram was at Shaveh, relaxing from his travels, the kings of Sodom and Gommorah arrived. News of the amazing victory had reached them five days previously and they had quickly set out the next day with their servants to meet those who had delivered Canaan from its enemies.

When the kings arrived at the Valley of Shaveh they approached Abram and bowed to him giving praises for his victory. They thanked him for avenging the death of so many countrymen of their valley.

Abram explained that he had warred against the four kings of the east because they had taken his nephew, Lot, captive.

After giving much flattery the kings asked that Abram keep all the spoils taken from them, as was his right. They begged him, however, to return the people of their valley who were taken captive.

And Abram answered the Kings of Sodom [and Gomorrah], saying, as the Lord liveth who created heaven and earth, and who redeemed my soul from all affliction, and who delivered me from my enemies, and gave them unto my hand, I will not take anything belonging to you, that you may

not boast tomorrow, saying, Abram became rich from our property that he saved.

For the Lord my God in whom I trust said unto me, thou shalt lack nothing, for I will bless thee in all the works of thy hands.

And now therefore behold, here is all belonging to you, take it and go; as the Lord liveth I will not take from you a living soul down to a shoe tie or thread, excepting the expense of the food of those who went out with me to battle, as also the portions of the men who went with me, Anar, Aschol, and Mamre, they and their men, as well as those also who remained to watch their baggage, they shall have their portion of the spoils.

And the Kings of Sodom [and Gomorrah] gave Abram according to all that he had said, and they pressed him to take whatever he chose, but he would not.

And he sent away the Kings of Sodom [and Gomorrah] and the remainder of their men, and he gave them orders about Lot, and they went to their respective places.

And Lot, his brother's son, he also sent away with his property, and he went to his home, to Sodom, and Abram and his people returned to their home in the plains of Mamre which is in Hebron.

Jasher 16:14-19

III

Throughout Hebron everyone turned out to welcome home the victors. Wives, sweethearts, and mothers wept with relief and joy as they greeted their loved ones with outstretched arms. Children ran and jumped into warriors' arms that willingly dropped spoils of war in exchange for love and admiration.

The elderly waited their turn, smiling with pride and thankfulness for the safe return of their sons. It was a moment of exaltation for Heberews and Amorites alike. The moment extended into one week, then two as the celebrating and storytelling escalated, reliving and memorializing the events that would become legend if not history.

Travelers came from all regions of Canaan to see this wise and courageous chieftain. Whenever men praised Abram for his daring leadership and wisdom, he gave all credit to "Yahvah the Everliving God."

Sarai was aglow with love for Abram when he returned to her. For a time she had him to herself to fuss over. Cooking the finest delicacies she knew, she fed him with her own hands. He often licked Sarai's fingers seductively, arousing her with this and other affectionate responses.

They loved each other completely and often during those early days of Abram's return. Abram thoroughly enjoyed the new intensity of his relationship with Sarai. It was as though they were just wed, finding a new passionate experience in each other. Sarai giggled like a bride at Abram's new virility.

There was another reason for adoring her husband, equally enjoyable. She was able to bask in the light of his glory. Every woman in the territory knew her to be the wife of the deliverer of Canaan. No woman could be more elevated. Sarai had never been so happy.

"You say that Lot will not be returning to our tribe with his family?" Sarai asked one day.

"No, he will remain at Sodom," Abram replied his eyes downcast.

"I know how fond you are of Lot, but his wife Ado...I... I am glad we will never see her again. You know how she is. She caused Lot to go to Sodom. If it were not for her desires for the despicable city goings on, Lot would never have been there to get captured. He is fortunate his life was spared in the battle. And he is even more fortunate you were able to rescue him. He..."

Abram glared at Sarai and broke in on her prattle.

"My soul weeps for Lot!" he exclaimed. "I had not realized I was so fond of him. At one time I thought he would have a son who I would make my heir."

"She did not want to have any more children, my husband. She did not want to have children ...." Sarai repeated, her voice trailing the words, dazed by the thought that any woman would refuse having children. She, being barren, had yearned for so many

317

years to bear a child. Sarai reviled Ado for discarding so marvelous a privilege.

"I thought that might be so," Abram responded. "Once I threatened to bring Lot to judgment but let the matter pass. It was not because I had forgotten it, but...."

He stopped, unwilling to add that it would have been awkward for him to judge his nephew when he himself had a barren wife and did not take another woman.

Sarai guessed what he was thinking; her face clouded and she turned from him, ashamed.

After a few moments Abram continued.

"And yet my God has promised that this entire land that we have compassed shall be given to my seed. Surely He is not jesting, but I am afflicted with disappointment and confusion. I know not who shall become my heir, unless it be the son of my steward, Eliezer, who is faithful."

Sarai could not face him. The words penetrated her like arrows. Tears of remorse streamed down her face; but this was not the first time. The pain in her heart had come many times. She could say nothing as solace for either of them. It was a horrible impediment that, like a defect from birth, they accepted, painfully.

Chapter 25
Vision and Covenant

Peace reigned in the land and families of men lived in relative harmony enjoying the rewards of fruitful reproduction at home and in the fields. It was during this season of productivity that the Everliving came to Abram in a vision. During the very early morning hours when Abram had been sleeping soundly, suddenly, a light as bright as the summer sun intruded upon him, enveloping his mind and body.

Abram, fully aware of the Everliving's presence, peered into the light in an attempt to fathom its depth and discover the appearance of God at its source. But an image of brightness was all that he could see. When the image spoke it was a voice composed of many voices speaking in unison as if from a distance and yet...also as close as an arm's length...undulating...promising:

"BE NOT AFRAID, ABRAM, 1 AM YOUR SHIELD, YOUR ABUNDANT REWARD. 1 WILL GREATLY ENRICH YOU!"

"Mighty God, how can you enrich me when I go childless and the inheritor of my estate will be Eliezer, my servant? Look at me; you have not given me offspring as you promised. And so the steward of my house will become my heir."

The utterance of many voices replied: "THAT MAN SHALL NOT BE YOUR HEIR; BUT RATHER IT WILL BE ONE WHO SHALL OWE HIS BIRTH TO YOURSELF, WHO SHALL BECOME YOUR HEIR. NOW GET YOURSELF UP AND OUT OF YOUR TENT."

Abram obeyed and watched as the supernatural light ascended up into the sky joining the multitude of nighttime heavenly bodies. The voice of this aberration remained and spoke:

"LOOK UP AND COUNT THE STARS, IF YOU ARE ABLE TO, FROM THE FARTHEST CORNERS OF MY HEAVEN. THUS SHALL YOUR RACE BECOME. HAVE NO DOUBTS NOR FEARS FOR 1, THE EVERLIVING, HAVE SPOKEN THIS COVENANT AND IT WILL BE FULFILLED. BE FAITHFUL ABRAM, BE FAITHFUL. 1 AM

319

YAHVAH THE EVERLIVING GOD WHO BROUGHT YOU FROM UR TO GIVE YOU THIS LAND AS AN INHERITANCE."

"But Mighty Lord, how am I to know that I shall inherit it? What proof is there of this promise? Will you give me a sign?"

Silence bore down upon Abram heavily as the cold night air chilled his body and he shivered thinking of his insignificance relative to such a weighty covenant.

"Perhaps my Lord God tires of my inadequacy, as a father loses patience with a son who is... who is inept and incapable of producing offspring?"

"SELECT FOR ME A THREE-YEAR OLD HEIFER, A THREE-YEAR OLD GOAT, A THREE-YEAR OLD RAM, A TURTLE DOVE, AND A YOUNG PIGEON AS A SACRIFICE FOR ME. I WILL COME AND CONSUME THEM WITH A FIRE BEFORE YOU AND YOUR TRIBE. THIS WILL BE YOUR SIGN FOR ALL TO SEE AND BELIEVE THE COVENANT MADE BETWEEN US."

"My Lord, I give thanks...."

As he spoke, Abram sensed he was alone, talking to himself, sounding empty and of no effect without a listener.

Making his way back to bed, he laid awake thinking, hoping, planning until the cozy warmth relaxed him sufficiently, and sleep finally returned.

When he awoke, later than usual, he ate little of the morning meal Sarah had prepared for him, explaining that he had much to do that was of great importance.

Abram ordered servants to select a flawless three-year old heifer, goat, and ram. Other servants were ordered to select a pigeon and a turtledove without blemish.

Choosing an appropriate site for this sacrifice, Abram ordered a bed of dried grass be prepared. Next he took his short sword and slew each animal, splitting their underbellies down the middle, the length of each body. Servants spread their halves on the grass one after another in a straight line. The birds were killed but not split apart. They too were laid in the line.

Washing the blood from his body and clothing, Abram and his servants changed garments.

Returning to the scene with all the men of his tribe, they stood within the shade of trees nearby to wait. This was a good observation point, up a slight rise in a valley where they could watch and wait in some measure of comfort. The heat of mid-day was now too intense to stand for long in open.

Flies collected on the carcasses so Abram ordered that two men cut branches from a tree and brush them away. The dead animals had to be defended from more than flies. The odor of animal flesh baking in the hot sun attracted vultures. They began to circle high in the sky gradually descending lower and lower.

Time passed so slowly it seemed to stand still as the sun roasted men and beasts with its fire.

Men shot arrows at the vultures both to drive them off as well as to relieve the burning monotony of waiting.

Women brought their men food in dishes, but they ate little. Water bags were passed around. Men drank their fill and again waited.

Men on duty with the branches were relieved when they began staggering from heat exhaustion and the putrefying stench of spoiled flesh.

The sky was white with heat as Abram looked up in anticipation. He stood there for a considerable time holding the mantle of his cloak over head until his arms grew tired. He did not know from which direction the Everliving's fire would come. His legs were weary and he grew fatigued. Worse than that was the fear that his God might not come at all.

"Was the Almighty offended by my doubts?" Abram pondered. "Perhaps He will not come! My people grow weary with waiting. They doubt He will come. I can see it in their eyes as they turn away from me with downcast looks.

"Everliving is God and I am but a man. Is it appropriate or possible for a man to have a covenant with the one God? And then challenge God for proof? Have I become unbalanced that I should ask for proof? My own people were astonished, and for good reason, in as much as covenants are normally made between equals like king with king, warrior with warrior, and shepherd with shepherd. Has ever a covenant been made between God and a man since Adam and Noah? Why? Why did I dare to ask for proof...for a sign?!"

The long wait in oppressive heat seemed to block out reasonable answers to all his self-doubts.

Time wore on and the air was still sultry and hot. Now and then an afternoon breeze sprang up sending columns of dust swirling, encouraging thoughts of relief among those holding vigil. But then, disappointingly, burning stillness descended again intensifying their discomfort.

Exhausted by the waiting, men continued to be relieved from duty in brushing birds of prey and flies away from the sacrifice. The carcasses had turned black and swollen from the heat. Now and then one or more free men came to Abram questioning, looking for reassurance or permission to withdraw, hoping that Abram would agree that there was no further reason to wait.

"Keep the vigil! Our God tests us to see if we are worthy of His covenant. I will not fail to keep the watch and neither should you. Keep your faith strong! Yahvah will come! The Everliving will come!"

Abram's word was absolute and irrevocable. With the force and meaning of his message echoing in their heads, the free men bowed and withdrew. Abram's word was indisputable, both in law and fact in his tribe. They returned to their vigil, suffering the same discomfort as Abram's servants.

There was a battle going on in Abram's head, however. His reason cried out: "The Almighty will not come! Stop deceiving yourself and your people!"

But another voice within him repeated: "Have confidence, do not weaken. Your Lord will not come if you weaken. With your faith you compel Him to come!"

And so Abram strengthened his resolve, wary that his fatigue eroded it. His faith had to overcome the weariness of his body. Ceasing to think of disappointment or what people said or thought, he yielded himself entirely into a condition of trust. Calm and empty of all impatience, he leaned upon his staff and stood peacefully in continued watchfulness.

Dusk descended like a heavy veil over a sky that displayed sporadic flashes of lightning. Thunder, rumbling in the distance, approached closer and closer.

"It is the Everliving walking across the heavens with thunderous strides," Abram imagined, his confidence building as he watched with anticipation.

The sky was lit up by lightning flashes coming closer and closer, followed by the crackle of thunder.

A cooling breeze picked up, fanning relief upon the valley and its inhabitants.

Darkness arrived and with it the Everliving heralded his presence. A series of brilliant flashes made the night like day once again and clapping thunder shook the ground beneath Abram's feet.

Deafening explosions awoke the drowsing tribe, bringing them to their feet. They looked up to Abram and saw him standing with feet apart and arms outstretched, reaching as if to welcome with an embrace, a loved one who had been away for some time.

Abram's white robe caught the brilliant flashes and his people saw him illuminated as a beacon fire, only brighter. No longer ·did he lean on a staff. New life seemed to pour into him and he radiated energy.

Vultures flew off and flies dispersed. Abram's servants began retreating from the carcasses, anticipating the coming of Yahvah with some unknown heavenly power and glory. Then fear gripped the heart of every Heberew as they saw a pillar of fire descending towards them. Hurriedly backing away from the sacrifices, servants tried to run, stumbled, fell, scrambled to their feet again and ran as fast as they could to get out of the way.

Other men of the tribe, a safer distance away, removed themselves further and prostrated themselves. Every man there shivered with fright as they watched the approach of Everliving God with His magnificent sign.

The earth shook from a stupendous explosion of thunder, and the fiery column slowly passed over the carcasses. Its whirlwind of flames consumed the entire sacrifice leaving only a scorched path of gray ashes and black stubble of nearby grass.

The column slowly burned a path up the rise towards Abram where he stood transfixed. It stopped, as if to acknowledge Abram's presence. Abram collapsed to his knees, struck with fear and awe, bowing his head to the ground.

A voice amidst the fire spoke with the magnitude of many voices: "ABRAM, KNOW THIS...I AM WITH YOU. I WILL GIVE THIS COUNTRY TO YOUR RACE. FROM THE RIVER OF EGYPT TO THE RIVER EUPHRATES: THE LAND OF THE KENITES, KENNIZZITES, KADMONITES, HITTITES, PERIZZITES, REFAIM, AMORITES, CANAANITES, GERGASHITES AND JEBUSITES...ALL WILL BELONG TO YOUR SEED.

"KNOW ALSO, THAT YOUR DESCENDANTS SHALL BECOME STRANGERS IN A LAND THAT IS NOT THEIRS. THEY SHALL BE AFFLICTED IN SERVITUDE FOR A TIME OF FOUR HUNDRED YEARS. BUT I WILL JUDGE THE NATION WHICH THEY SHALL SERVE, AND AFTERWARD YOUR PEOPLE SHALL COME OUT WITH GREAT WEALTH.

"AND AFTER FOUR CENTURIES YOUR SEED WILL RETURN HERE; FOR THE CUP OF AMORITE INIQUITIES IS FULL AND THE LAND MUST BE CLEANSED.

"YOU, ABRAM, SHALL IN TIME DEPART FROM THIS LIFE AND JOIN YOUR FATHERS IN PEACE. YOU SHALL BE BURIED AT A GOOD OLD AGE."

The voice stopped and the column began to slowly rise. Hovering over the valley of sacrifice for a minute, as if to examine the scene, it then rapidly withdrew northward until it vanished into a broad sky full of distant tiny lights.

II

During the following year spring rains were abundant, as if to make up for the previous year's drought. The land all around Hebron was green with grass and flowers decorated the fields with their festive colors.

In spite of this blessing, Abram's face carried a frown and Sarai's showed only serious thought. There were long periods during each day when not a word was passed between them. Being absorbed in his own anxieties, Abram never paused to consider the reason for Sarai's unusual silence.

Sarai was wrestling with a possible solution to their dilemma about an heir. She repeated the last conversation she had with Abram to Abdi, her maid and confidant, who in turn repeated it to Eliezer. The chief steward was deeply moved by what he heard and came to his mistress.

"I am not worthy! And my son is not worthy to be heir to Lord Abram. We are overwhelmed by just the thought of it. I am a servant, and my son is like me, without qualities of leadership. My boy has no instruction. He is a simple lad. He is not an appropriate heir to lead your people. If you please, my lady, listen to this advice from your servant.

"I suggest you give my lord Abram another wife. He is no longer young, but he is healthy and strong. Perhaps he can quicken many sons with another woman. Select a wife for him and bring her to your tent. No wrong is done to the first wife when the husband acquires another. The congregation will pray for blessings upon your head for your good deed.

"A proper heir, a strong leader, a...a goel is a guardian over his people. Abram is our shepherd, our lord, and only the fruit of his loins will provide the same security. This belief is not mine alone. It is shared by every man here."

On and on he explained while Sarai listened with troubled patience; her obvious distaste for the suggestions were displayed on her face. Finally Sarai dismissed him, promising to think and weigh his counsel. She was plunged into a disturbing inward conflict.

"Eliezer is correct in his opinions, but the thought of another woman sharing Abram is...is revolting!" Sarai cringed. "The woman would be young. She would have his children.

"Abram's heart would turn away from me and cling to the mother of his children. He would play with them, caress and carry them. He would rejoice over them with his new wife and then I would be cast off, unwanted, merely waiting to die! No! No! No!" she declared emphatically, "no other woman will come to this tent as his wife!"

The burden of her dilemma weighed upon Sarai more and more each day. Passersby noticed her preoccupation with some problem that she seemed to wrestle with verbally day after day. Looking at the ground, or off into the distance, Sarai could be heard arguing with herself in muted sentences.

"The God of Abram has promised him the Land of Canaan as the heritage of his seed. Abram's family line would be ennobled above all others to rule the entire land. But how could this come about when I, who have no children, refuse to allow another woman...?"

When others spoke she failed to hear. Her sleepless nights were filled with tossing and turning.

Finally, very early one morning, Sarai called Abram to wake up. She could not wait for daybreak. The solution, a happy one, came upon her suddenly and she could not restrain her enthusiasm.

"Who called me?" he asked drowsily, sitting up on the couch.

"It is I, Sarai, my husband, I called you awake."

"Oh, Sarai, what is it?" he asked disappointed that it was not a communication from his God.

"I know what can be done that will give you offspring!"

"Oh? And what is that?"

"Is it not true that according to Babylonian law, if a barren wife brings a slave to her husband's bed and says: 'Conceive a son from her that I may have him,' it is hers? When the woman delivers a son, they take the child from her and give it to the wife, that he will be their son, the true heir of the husband and wife. Is that not so?"

"Well...perhaps it is, under Babylonian law; but I am not sure it is right," Abram said thoughtfully.

"I want the prophecy of our God fulfilled as much as you. Since the fault for our lack of an heir is mine, I am willing to accept your conceiving a son with another woman, only...let him be my son."

"Woman, did you have to wake me well before dawn just to speak of such things? You could have waited for an appropriate time. Be still now and go to sleep. We will talk about it later."

"Yes, my husband," she agreed pressing up to him, finding warmth against the night's chill.

When Abram was fully awake, with the sun risen, he listened once more to Sarai's proposal.

"My answer is no! I will not agree to your suggestion. You refer to Babylonian law that permits such a thing. We are free of Babylonian law and I want no part of it ever again."

Taking Sarai's hands in his, Abram continued.

"Our God will establish His law in this land. I have been called to wait upon Him and plant His law so that my seed will have a proper guide. I must be patient... and you must be patient, too, Sarai."

Time wore on and there was no communication from Abram's God. Abram's disappointment grew into a depression. His faith slipped away as the weeks and months bore on relentlessly. Doubts filled his mind, providing fertile ground for thoughts that Abram's God had forgotten His promise of the immense inheritance.

Sarai took advantage of Abram's depression. She never gave up on her solution, and she repeatedly re-introduced it to him. Her persistence had the force of drops of water dripping incessantly on his head. His resistance weakened finally, and one day she heard him say:

"Who knows whether you may not be right? Instead of making Eliezer's boy my heir, I would have my own son. Yes, my own son."

The words rolled off his tongue like myrrh in anointing oil: precious, fragrant, and delightful.

"Then you will permit it, my lord husband?"

"Just the thought of producing my own heir, this late in life, excites both my heart and loins. Whether or not I am capable of it is another matter, however. But, to answer your question...yes, yes I will permit it."

As Chief of his tribe, Abram would not allow himself to take part in the women's meetings. He eavesdropped now, however, without his normal reluctance. His curiosity was keen on the selection process.

"Ketura is a strong girl with broad hips. She could bring forth many babies without difficulty. She is meek and obedient, too. She would give up her babies to you without controversy," some friends advised.

"All that you say is true, but she lacks greatly in comely features and in intelligence. Hagar, as another possibility, is both pretty and intelligent. She has the blood and brains of Egypt's Pharoah. Her male children will become rulers," others said.

"Abram must have the quality of leadership in his sons," Sarai asserted. "No, the son of a meek servant, as comely as a cow, will not measure up as a leader of our tribe."

The women giggled and then remembered the seriousness of their business. This conversation was held in the privacy of Abram's tent; yet, somehow, the news leaked and in a short time every eligible woman, slave or free, found reason to parade by Abram's tent. They were well groomed and wearing their finest clothing at all times. It had no effect for the selection had been made.

At the setting of the sun, Sarai ordered Hagar to a separate tent to await her master Abram. The entire proposition was explained to her and there was no reluctance on the maid's part.

Had Sarai bothered to listen to Hagar's voice and look carefully at Hagar's face, she might have detected something very unexpected. Sarai was too involved, however, in finding the right words of explanation and posturing in their delivery.

After the evening meal, Sarai led her husband to the tent where Hagar waited. She raised the flap and went inside, followed by Abram.

She was struck by the pungent aroma of myrrh and resin burning. The scent was so strong it was intoxicating.

Hagar was seated in the middle of the sleeping couch. It was covered with fine silk, beautiful to look at and slippery to the touch. Long black hair flowed over her shoulders and down her breasts. She wore only transparent muslin that hardly passed for a covering. It was a typical garment of Egyptian nobility. Hagar's head was bowed when Sarai spoke the message she had rehearsed in her mind.

"My husband, my lord, I have provided this maid, a slave, for you to go to. Quicken within her a son for me. The son that she bears will be yours and mine, not hers.

"Hagar, do you hear my words?"

327

Hagar bowed prostrate on the couch and only an unintelligible sound was heard.

"I will leave you with her, my husband, but please hurry back to me," she whispered in his ear. Turning, she left feeling some regret for having chosen Hagar.

Hagar slowly raised herself on the couch. Her head lifted until her eyes met Abram's and locked there in a sultry gaze. The lines of her eyelashes and eyebrows were emphasized and extended with black, creating an effect that gave her a seductive cat-like quality. Hagar stood with her back arched and breathed deeply, heaving her ample young breasts towards Abram.

Abram's eyes lowered to watch the movement of her body. When he raised his eyes again, her eyes were there peering into and penetrating his thoughts.

The look of her began to excite him and he was surprised. He had thought he might be repulsed by her.

"Egyptian women, especially those of noble cast, seem to learn many things about how to please a man," he said softly.

Hagar opened her mouth slightly and sighed heavily with each rise and fall of her chest. Seductively she ran her tongue over her full lips in a circular motion.

Abram had never seen anything like this before and just stood transfixed, staring at Hagar's ever increasing erotic gestures.

To Abram it felt warm in the tent, too warm for a cool desert night. But there he was, sweating nevertheless. The heart rapidly pounding in his chest signaled his brain that he was too warm, not the environment of the tent. He removed his mantle but perspiration continued to trickle down his face.

"If it would please my lord, remove your tunic and be refreshed. May I pour you a little wine to quench your thirst?" Hagar asked in response to a small dry cough from Abram.

In the time he took to think about her suggestions and act, she had poured the wine into a silver goblet and held it in her outstretched hand over the couch of skins.

"Here I am being led to the love couch by a woman instead of doing the leading myself," Abram confessed inwardly. What is happening to me? I feel like I am unable to resist her."

Stripping down to his loin covering, he reclined on the couch. The silk was smooth and luxurious against his skin.

Hagar placed the edge of the goblet to Abram's lips very gently and tipped it for him to drink.

He sipped an amount larger than normal and he felt the pleasant bite of alcohol in his throat as he swallowed. It felt good in his stomach and it helped his dry throat.

"More," he whispered to her face only inches from his. Any regrets he may have had in coming here were completely forgotten. "Drink," he ordered her softly.

"Only from your lips, my lord, that is sufficient for me," she whispered. Leaning to him she kissed and licked his lips lightly.

"The goblet is empty. I shall refill it," she mumbled against his lips.

"Yes, do it," Abram agreed, enjoying her more each minute that passed.

He reclined, comfortably watching Hagar's stealthy, feline movements. The transparent garment was more seductive than no garment at all. Abram wanted it removed and he knew that all he had to do was order it, but the suspense, the mystery aroused him more than a complete revealing, and he placed himself entirely in her hands.

The wine made Abram relax to the point where almost anything Hagar did was both acceptable and deliciously sensuous.

Hagar seemed to have an exciting solution for any contingency.

"I am hot," Abram sighed.

"Oh, master, I shall cool you in a moment," she declared.

With swift dexterity Hagar slid from the couch and poured water into a clay bowl. She dipped an absorbent cloth into the water and squeezing a portion of it out, applied the wet cloth to his body in soft caressing strokes.

Abram was wet from head to foot when she produced a fan, conveniently handy, and proceeded to fan him with evaporative cooling.

"How refreshing and pleasant it is, lovely maid," Abram heard himself say. His previous bias forgotten, he put his hands behind his head and laid back, enjoying this new allurement.

"Just how many favors do you have stored away, my young Hagar?" Abram questioned, amused as well as stimulated.

"Ah, that is for you to find out, my lord...from experience."

Abram laughed loudly at her reply and re-discovered a sense of humor he had lost, long, long ago.

Hagar found other ways to make him laugh and their mirth was heard by Sarai who grew more resentful with each outburst of her husband's enjoyment.

Sarai stayed awake, torturing herself with every eavesdropped word or sound. When it was silent in Hagar's tent, Sarai also imagined what was going on and her jealousy grew.

A scream of unabashed delight from Hagar made Sarai shudder.

"The Egyptian bitch; she yelps like a dog in heat! Some men enjoy that I suppose. I wonder if Abram is embarrassed by that girlishness. Why does he linger there? I wish he would get it over with and return here to me. What can he find so entertaining in a young maid who has not lain with a man before tonight?"

The next morning Sarai, unable to wait any longer went and called to Abram from outside the closed entrance to Hagar's tent.

"Abram...Abram...?"

There was no answer from inside, so she called again, louder.

"Abram...Abram...?

Inside the tent Sarai heard stirrings and sounds of voices so she called a third time.

"ABRAM...ABRAM!"

The tent flap flew open and Sarai was confronted with an angry husband wearing only a loincloth.

"What is it woman? Why do you wake me out of a sound sleep by calling my name for the whole tribe to hear?"

"I...I am sorry I woke you my husband, but I thought...that is...I hoped you would return to my couch and warm me against the chill. I..."

"It was not that cold during the night!" Abram snapped. "You have plenty of warmth."

"But I am anxious for you, now, my lord. It is my wish to wait upon you...to prepare a delicious meal for you. Will you come with me now?"

Before Abram could answer, Hagar came up behind him. She was completely naked. She wrapped her arms around his torso and pressed up tightly against him.

Abram was irritated and embarrassed by this confrontation between two possessive women. Looking at Sarai sternly he asked: "Who am I that you should call out to me as a person under your authority? I am the lord of my house and chief of this tribe, not a servant! Now go and order your servants if you wish, but leave me in peace!" Closing the tent flap he turned to face his next challenge.

He had become young again. Overnight, a youthful interest had overcome him and changed his current outlook. Captivated by Hagar's youth and her lusty attentions, Abram felt an impetuosity of youth that he had never experienced before. It was delicious refreshment from the rigors of self-disciplined leadership. He was not sure how long he could remain at this oasis of love and youth, but for now it was growing into an all consuming passion.

III

The tenth year of Abram's residence in the Land of Canaan was drawing to a close when Hagar conceived a child. During her early pregnancy Hagar held Sarai in contempt, partly because she was barren. The most important reason, however, was Abram's affection. Neither woman wanted to share him with the other. The situation had become unbearable for Sarai who had essentially lost her husband to this younger woman who was also her servant.

The present quarrel raging between the two women started over a trifle. The cause was unimportant but it gave them the opportunity to express openly the hatred they felt for each other.

Standing apart at arms length they measured each other with eyes aflame, jaws set, and fists clenched, ready to spring.

"You disrespectful slave!" Sarai derided. "If you were not with child I would have you put in shackles!"

"I am not your slave, old woman!"

"Yes, you are!"

"I am not, for I am bearing a son to my lord Abram."

"A son? You will bring forth a blind, deformed daughter!"

"Bitter old hag, I shall bear a magnificent son, an heir. And I shall nurse him and care for him!"

"The son will be mine, if you bear one!" Sarai snapped.

"You covet my son, you worthless old woman? You have not given birth even to a blind hunchback, and you want my son!? HA!"

Sarai flushed red with temper and lashed back.

"You Egyptian flea bag! You rat's nest! As soon as you have delivered your child I shall whip you and put a brand on your forehead!"

"You just try!" Hagar set her fists on her hips daring the fight to start.

Eliezer, fearing the worst, had run to find Abram. Fortunately he was not far away. They came running and arrived just in time to prevent a brawl.

"What is happening here?" he commanded sharply. "Have you both been out in the sun too long? Has the heat addled your brains?"

The two women were so consumed with anger that they were deaf to their lord's questioning. Both continued shouting vile oaths at each other until Abram stepped in between. He grabbed them at the shoulder with his big hands and shook violently.

"Enough of this vile wrangling! Stop at once!" He shouted contemptuously. "Now, what is this about?"

They did not answer. What was the point of answering such a question? Abram knew as well as they, what it was all about.

Making an exaggerated display, Hagar, held her stomach and fell to her knees.

Sarai stood straight and arrogant as she returned her husband's furious stare.

Abram knew he was at the center of this dispute and he could not help but feel embarrassed by it. He decided now was the time to settle the matter.

"Your bitter wrangling cannot be endured. I do not wish to see with my eyes nor hear with my ears your fighting or squabbling. From this time on you will not see each other.

This was not to be, however, for the arguing continued, behind his back and away from his hearing.

Finally, one day Sarai came to Abram and protested.

"My wrong be upon you. I gave my maid to you as a concubine to bring forth an heir as if the child were mine. Now that she has conceived, she despises me. Her insolence is unbearable! You have also put me aside because of her. I can endure her no longer. Let the Everliving God decide between you and me as to who is right!"

Abram blushed from the confrontation and turned away from her. As he pondered her words he was convicted by her charges.

"Sarai is right. She is my wife, my first love. I cannot forget that. I have an obligation to her, even though Hagar is lusty and exciting with her youthfulness."

He turned and faced her with a decision.

"Hagar is your maid. She is under your authority. Do to her whatever you consider right. But remember that she is with child. Deal gently with her."

Sarai, now armed with her husband's authority, lost no time in making demands upon Hagar.

"I am your mistress and you are my slave. My husband returned to me my authority over you."

"No! He would not do that to me. You lie! I shall prove you wrong!" Hagar protested hotly.

"There is our lord walking this way; ask him now if it is not true!"

Unexpectedly, Hagar turned an about face and started to walk away.

"Stop! Where are you going?" Sarai raised her voice.

Hagar ignored the command and kept on walking. She did not go more than a few more steps, however, before Sarai ran and blocked her way.

"Oh no! You are not going to change his mind by lusting after him in private. You are going to ask him now!" Sarai demanded.

Hagar felt trapped.

"Abram, my husband!" Sarai called out to get his attention.

Abram came striding over quickly, hoping to prevent a fight from starting.

"Is it not true that you gave Hagar over to my authority as my handmaid?" Sarai questioned.

"Yes, yes that is true," Abram admitted reluctantly.

"No! No! It cannot be so. I am the servant of my Lord Abram!" Hagar began to sob desperately. "I am not Sarai's servant. My lord will not take my son from me! How could you after what I have been to you?"

Abram was silent under the accusation. His authority was being challenged and he knew his answer must reflect a just decision. He found himself pressured by the necessity of deciding between two wrangling women. One, lusty and demanding, while the other had right on her side.

"Your maid, Hagar, is in your hands Sarai," he forced himself to say at last. "I have ordered that you are not to see each other until Hagar's delivery is past. Then I shall decide as I will about my child."

"I will not give my child over to anyone!" Hagar screamed hysterically.

"She has gone too far in her rebellion," Abram determined to himself. "I cannot yield at all. If I give in to her my power over affairs within the tribe will be diminished. I must do what is right no matter what Hagar feels."

Looking at Hagar he saw fear and resentment in her eyes. "You are a servant to my wife, Hagar. You will do as I command you!" Abram demanded tightly.

A crazed look came over Hagar's face as she realized that all her scheming had come to no avail.

"Am I now forced to remain a slave, persecuted the rest of my life by a vengeful mistress? A mistress who will take my son as her own? It is a life too miserable for an Egyptian princess, a daughter of Pharoah!"

Hagar said nothing more. Avoiding the hostile eyes of her masters, she turned and stomped off.

Sarai gave her husband a grateful look, fully satisfied by her victory over Hagar.

Abram thrust her off with an angry glance and walked away.

Later, after Abram had calmed himself, he ordered Eliezer to be sure Hagar was secure in her tent and provide what ever she needed.

Abram found privacy for his thoughts out in the open fields. As he walked along he suffered from the decision he had been forced to make. Realizing that the youth he had regained with Hagar was lost, disappointment covered him like the death of a loved one.

"Lord Abram! Lord Abram!" Eliezer called out as he ran through the fields.

"Yes? What is it Eliezer?" Abram responded, irritated by the intrusion.

"Hagar is not in her tent, my lord! I have looked about the camp and failed to see her! I suspect that she may have left!"

"Curses! I recall she said faintly something about her life here as a servant being too miserable to endure."

Hurrying back towards camp, Abram sounded the call to assemble on his ram's horn. Within moments everyone within hearing was gathered around, curious and anxious for an explanation.

"Does anyone know where Hagar is?" Abram inquired.

"I saw her put her possessions on one of your camels and ride off, my lord."

"In what direction did she go?"

"There...towards Egypt, I believe."

Greatly agitated, Abram organized a search party and off they rode to the south towards Hebron almost ten miles away.

Abram expected they would find Hagar there, looking for a caravan to take her back home to Egypt.

Night fell before the party arrived at their destination. When they inquired at the caravanserai, she was not found.

The next morning they rose early and traveled on towards the settlement of Hormah, at least thirty miles away. During the trip they saw no sign of her. At the caravanserai, in Hormah, no one had seen her. Abram asked merchants if they had seen a young Egyptian woman alone riding a camel.

"Yes, I saw her. I even sold her water," answered a water merchant. "She purchased food from my friends over there and then left the city. I thought it was odd for a woman that young and attractive to be alone. I mentioned it to her and she said her husband and his servants were nearby, purchasing other supplies."

"I am her husband...er...that is... her master. She has run away," Abram explained.

Abram and his servants stayed the night at the caravanserai. It was too late to leave the city. He thought about the search for some time before he finally went to sleep.

In the morning Abram made a decision. Addressing his servants he explained

"It is clear that Hagar does not want to be found and is deliberately hiding... only The Everliving knows where. A person can easily hide and avoid detection out there in the wilderness. We could be gone a long time and still not find her." Sighing heavily Abram ordered his men to prepare for the ride home. "Let us return to camp. She is in the hands of my Lord Yahvah. May He provide for her and protect her."

And so it was that Abram returned with a heavy heart. The memory of Hagar's youthful, erotic body and his child in her womb consumed all his thoughts. He was silent and brooded over his loss all the way back to his camp.

IV

Out of sight of the encampment of Abram, Hagar rode and rode hard, switching the poor beast when he complained. Venting her wrath as if upon Sarai, her persecutor, and Abram, her betrayer, she cursed and ranted until her mouth was too dry to continue reviling.

Hagar gave no thought about the recklessness of her running away until the sun hung low in the west. Finally she began to contemplate her situation.

"I have too little water and food to take me back to Egypt. I could purchase lodging and supplies in Hebron...but Abram would be sure to find me there, if he is looking. Mmm, yes, I think he will come after me. It is best that I find a place to rest somewhere along the inland trade route. Perhaps if I am not found, Abram will give up his search."

With this resolve in mind, Hagar stopped outside the city gate of Hebron only long enough to purchase water and some food.

It was a long day's trip to Hormah from Hebron and Hagar knew she would have to stop someplace off the trail to rest for the night. When darkness descended she had found a suitable place and bedded down near her camel.

The next morning Hagar was very tired from the previous day's travel and the emotional upheaval that had caused her to run away. She ate very little before continuing her journey. Her stomach was upset and she had no desire for food.

"Hormah cannot be too far ahead," she mumbled trying to mentally ease her discomfort. "When I get there I will purchase some food and water for myself, and provender for my four-legged friend."

With her supplies purchased at Hormah and a fairly contented camel, Hagar lost little time in the town before moving on. The memory of Egypt and the Pharoah's palace gardens with its cooling pools and shading arbors was on Hagar's mind, inspiring and motivating her.

"No more a servant to Heber-ews, no more a servant to anyone!" She spat out contemptuously. "In Egypt I will rid myself of this child within me and marry the son of a nobleman. Oh, but it is hot today," Hagar complained.

"Kadesh-barnea is almost two day's journey from Beersheba.

The entire Sinai Penninsula lay in the shape of an arrow-head as a sun scorched barrier between different civilizations. The Negeb was only the beginning of this vast wilderness stretching between southern Canaan and Egypt. The fingers of two long gulfs, extending northward from the Red Sea in a "V", gave the Sinai its pointed shape. It is through this desolate territory that the seed of Abraham would eventually wander in their Exodus from Egypt.

"You knew it was hotter in the Negeb. Why complain now?" she chastised herself.

"I can stand the heat," Hagar argued aloud with her conscience, "but this sickness in my stomach still plagues me."

"You must eat and drink water to survive out here."

"I know that, but to do so is to feel worse. I will simply ignore the sickness and it will go away."

"Do you really believe what you are saying?"

"I must believe it. What else can I do?"

"Maybe you are a fool to go on. Why not return to Abram?"

"Return to Sarai, you mean? Never! Never! I will die out here first!"

That night Hagar again found a place to sleep, well away from the trail and hidden from sight.

The next morning she could barely drink a little water and eat a few dates. It was more difficult than ever for her to climb onto the camel and endure the rocking/dipping motion.

When the sun's heat descended, Hagar's resolve was tested again. She was weaker than ever today. If her bitterness had not been so extreme, she might have changed her mind about going on. Somehow her misery only seemed to intensify her determination to reach Egypt.

"Home...freedom...comfort...servants...water to bath in...food that delights the taste...parties...wine, beer and liquors..." her mind wandered away from the present, escaping into sweet memories of the way life used to be for her.

The reins slackened in her hand and eventually dropped as Hagar dozed off.

With free rein the camel sniffed the air on several occasions for a hint of something. Ambling along he caught a scent and left the trail. For some time he meandered along changing directions, drawn invisibly to some unknown place. Encouraged now by what his senses detected, the direction he took became more definite and his pace quickened. Arriving at his destination the camel stopped to enjoy his discovery.

Hagar awoke when the camel bent forward to drink from the spring. The sudden pitch threw her off balance, too sleepy and weak to prevent what happened next.

Tumbling from her perch, Hagar rolled off the camel's back and landed in a heap on her back and side. The fall sent her sprawling in the dirt. Her head struck a rock and she lay on her back unconscious.

When Hagar came to, the blackness of night was closing in fast. Her head throbbed with pain and her mouth was parched from thirst. The sickness in her stomach was worse and her body ached all over.

Groaning from her ailments, she laid still trying to get her mind to function clearly. The sound of water gurgling to the surface reached her ears, penetrating the noise in her head.

Mustering all her strength, Hagar found only enough energy to crawl over to the spring and drink. The cool water tasted delicious and refreshing as she cupped one hand and splashed it into her mouth. Pausing only slightly for breath, she continued until something forced her to stop.

A wave of nausea enveloped her and Hagar erupted, losing everything. Her stomach continued heaving dryly until all strength left her. Hagar had never felt so miserable. The cool night air turned the perspiration on her body icy cold, and she shivered uncontrollably.

Too weak to rise and get warm skins from the camel's pack, she pulled the mantle tightly around her body, curled up in the fetal position and tried to sleep.

Sleep became impossible. Hagar lay there too sick to think about anything. Her mind wandered in delirium for hours before sleep mercifully came.

It was warm when Hagar awoke. The bright sunlight stabbed at her eyes, but its heat warmed her so graciously she sighed with appreciation. Her whole body ached terribly, but the throbbing in her head was equal to all other pains.

Fighting the pain and fog in her head, she struggled to think clearly.

"I must drink...and eat...get stronger...or...or death will find me."

Gathering all her remaining strength, Hagar dragged herself to the spring's edge and dipped her face into the water. The cold wetness helped awaken her, but the taste was unpleasant. She was reluctant to drink for fear of becoming nauseated again. She lay there weak, frustrated and mentally aware that she would never rise from this place.

"I will never make it to Egypt...home. All those comforts I yearn for...impossible to reach. All is...lost. Death ...is at the door, she resigned herself.

Uncontrollably she wept for the first time, washing the anger and bitterness out of her heart.

When there were no more tears, Hagar resigned herself to a final sleep. Her thoughts turned to Abram, their times together and his heir couched in her womb.

"What kind of a man would he have become? Patriarch of a kingdom? Wealthy? Fierce? Proud?

"HAGAR!" A voice interrupted. "HAGAR...OPEN YOUR EARS AND LISTEN TO MY WORDS!" spoke the voice again, louder and with awesome authority.

Hagar lifted her head to see who was commanding her attention. The only sight to meet her gaze was a human figure surrounded with bright light.

"Wh...what...who is it that calls me? Is it the demon of death? I am not ready yet...you come too soon!"

"I am not a messenger of death. I am a messenger of life! Hagar, servant of Sarai, where are you going and what are you weeping for?"

"I am fleeing from the spiteful wife of my master."

"Return to your mistress, Hagar, and submit yourself to her. I will restore your life and your strength.

"You are now with child and you will give birth to a son. When he is delivered you will call his name Ishmael, meaning God hears, for God has heard your sorrow.

"Now, hear me, Hagar, for I will greatly increase your descendants. They will become so many it will be impossible to number them. Such will be their multitude.

"Your son will be like a wild ass among men, with his hand against every man and every man's hand against him. And he shall dwell on the borders of all his brethren."

No sooner had the figure stopped speaking, than Hagar noticed an improvement in her health. Vitality was being restored. She could feel her strength increasing and she grew thirsty and hungry.

Putting her mouth to the spring she tasted cautiously at first.

"It is delicious!" she sighed with delight.

Gulping more and more water, she felt a surge of energy and moaned with satisfaction.

Excitedly, Hagar washed her face, hands and arms. The more she washed, the better she felt.

Giggling with delight, Hagar disrobed, knelt and washed her entire body. Energy seemed to flow through every fiber of every part as she did so. Traveling in a wave down her throat, through her chest, stomach, loins, arms and legs, hands and feet, she sighed ecstatically as her strength returned.

Hagar sat up marveling at the life that returned to her.

"It is thrilling to be alive again! I feel...I feel as though I have come back a great distance... from the valley of death! I have failed...to realize my life could be so precious... until I almost lost it, Lord. I long to...to... return to life... in whatever way the giver of it demands!"

For the first time Hagar spoke with gratefulness in her heart. With humility and respect she searched her mind for the proper words.

"Behold...I have seen a vision.... You...my Lord must be the...the Everliving God of my master Abram. You are the God he speaks to, and I ...even now I see your presence. And...I...I am saved by you, even after you found me...rebellious...wretched...and...and near death. I...I am undeserving, Lord...but...I shall do as you command."

"So be it," the voice declared and the bright figure disappeared as Hagar watched.

Hagar's camel, who had been off a distance grazing, returned to the spring.

"Ahh, my friend the camel, what a fine animal you are to have brought me here to this well of life. Did you find this spring with your senses? Or did the God of Abram lead you? Was the well here before you came? Or did the Almighty create it...to save me from my foolishness?"

Hagar ate food and drank more water until her intense hunger was satisfied.

Filling her water skin, she packed it away and mounted the camel. Rising to its feet the camel stood waiting for Hagar's directions.

Looking at the landscape around her, Hagar had no idea where she was or the way to go. After a few minutes of indecision she decided to trust the camel's instincts better than her own poor judgment.

Holding the reins slack Hagar spoke to him encouragingly: "Home, you handsome beast, home...home...home to Abram!"

At least a week had passed since Hagar's flight from Abram and Sarai. Each day Abram could be seen alone sitting by his tent or walking in the fields, a solitary, lonely figure.

Since Hagar left, he had little ambition and preferred his privacy. Sarai was concerned about his dark mood and tried to console him with her opinions about Hagar.

This only fired his resentment towards her, so she kept quiet. Desperate to win back Abram's affection, Sarai waited on him constantly with her attentions. After more than one rebuff about how she was smothering him...Sarai withdrew to her normal occupations.

On this particular afternoon Abram was sitting in the shade of his tent opening, gazing without purpose at the industry of his people, and listening to their verbal chatter. Above the gabble, a shrill young voice sent a message hurtling over towards Abram's ears.

The first time Abram heard it he misunderstood its meaning and remained unmoved.

A young boy came into view and his message was heralded with the same high-pitched cry.

"Hagar has returned! Hagar has returned!" he repeated.

"Hagar has returned!" The news raced throughout the Heberew camp, from tongue to tongue, reaching every ear.

Abram scrambled to his feet so quickly he felt dizzy. He staggered towards the boy who ran up to him and bowed.

"She is coming, Lord Abram! She is coming! Hagar has returned! There! See?"

Abram looked where the boy pointed and saw a figure approaching on a camel. The mantle covered the person's face within its shadows and Abram squinted against the haze of heat to see better.

The camel's pace quickened as the animal seemed to sense the end of its journey. A reward of grass and water...and perhaps some fruit for faithful service, would be waiting!?

Hagar's mantle slipped back from the sudden movement, exposing her suntanned face and dark hair.

"Hagar!" Abram heard himself cry out her name. "Hagar! Yahvah has brought you and my son back safely to me!"

"Yes, my lord! Yes! But how did you know?"

"How else could you have returned?" He replied with a question while helping her off the camel.

"By no other way, Lord. By no other way, for I was wrong to leave. An angry demon filled my being, so that I became bitterly angry beyond reason and had to leave. I traveled for days towards Kadesh-barnea and took ill for my rebellion.

"I was close to death and had released myself to it when a vision came to me. I thought I had crossed over the river of no return into the land after death.

"A voice spoke out of an image of light brighter than the sun. He said I was with a male child who is to be named Ishmael.

"He is to have many in his tribe, and generations afterwards; so many that they cannot be numbered!

"The Divine One ordered me to return to my Lord Abram and Mistress Sarai...in...in humility," Hagar struggled with the word.

"My good health was restored in moments, and I was astonished.

"I was completely lost, so I talked to the camel and asked him to go home...to you, my lord. The good demons must have been responsible, for the beast saved my life."

"No, Hagar, demons did not save your life," The Everliving sent a heavenly messenger to save you and restore your life. He also guided the camel in your going out and your returning. The Everliving provided the water where there was none before, and He protected you against all harm."

"It is as you say, my lord. Let the well be a witness to my vision of your God and His saving mercies. Let it be called 'the Well of the Vision of Life'," she finished, then bowed down on her knees to kiss Abram's feet.

"Yes," replied Abram, "thus shall it be written!"

"Now beat me, lord, for I have rebelled against you and my mistress."

Abram looked down at this young woman who had been a queen of love to him, love given with authority, and now he had pity on her.

"Who am I to punish a servant who has run away, suffered, and returned...all under authority of my God? I dare not chastise you with even a word for fear of disturbing His will concerning you in this matter.

"Now go to your tent and rest. I will sacrifice two sheep to celebrate your safe return and that of Ishmael my son to be born. All my people will celebrate with me, for you have returned with my heir and they will not be without a chieftain of my blood when I go to my fathers."

Chapter 26
Son of a Bondwoman

And Hagar at that time returned to her master's house, and at the end of days Hagar bare a son to Abram, and Abram called his name Ishmael; and Abram was eighty-six years old when he begat him.

Jasher 16:36

I

A shrill scream pierced the stillness of the night! It was followed by moans of pain as Hagar suffered with the child-bearing labor she had endured for hours. Her strength ebbed with each surging wave of pain. Hagar's earlier composure of lusty vigor was now reduced to one of frailty. Her stamina was almost gone. Each convulsive push to relieve the agony of parturition brought on even worse excruciating pain that racked her body with a shudder. Perspiration welled up on her skin during each effort; it formed streams, and rolled down her contours to soak the bedding underneath.

Ophni, the midwife in attendance, placed her skilled hands on Hagar's huge, swollen abdomen and gently felt for the life within. She pushed here and there trying again and again to help the fetus turn.

"She will have to deliver soon or it will kill her, the poor girl." Ophni spoke softly to her assistant, a buxom, heavy set, mother of five children, who was well experienced in having children.

The woman nodded her head in agreement.

"She is too tired to cry, and only lies there moaning a pitiful wimper between attempts of the child to escape the womb," Ophni frowned with a slight shake of her head. I must keep trying to turn the fetus..." she murmured.

"Ahh, behold! There it moves...the head is...down," Ophni reported each movement. Oh ho! A kick! Another...yes again...and a shift...downward? Yes? Yes! Perhaps now...?"

Hagar inhaled a great breath, clenched her teeth on a piece of raw hide and grasped the sides of the raised mound of hides supporting her back as she squatted.

Grunting, straining noises issued from her throat, interspersed with cries of pain that stabbed the quiet night around the camp.

"Yes, Hagar, yes...the child is ready, now push! Push down...take a breath...push again...soon the pain will be gone...push!"

Hagar emitted a deep guttural response as she strained at her task.

"Yes! Yes, that is it...good...good! The head is in my hands! Now breath...and push again," Ophni encouraged and directed.

Hagar gathered strength from unknown reserves and pushed down again and again, panting, screaming and agonizing as shoulders, torso, hips and legs were finally delivered.

"It is a boy! A big-chested, long bodied boy!" Ophni exclaimed as she caught the baby.

"Hagar has fainted from the ordeal!" Ophni's assistant declared.

"I am not surprised," Ophni sighed with relief. It is wondrous that the baby had the strength to survive."

"He is fortunate his mother was so determined to live through this ordeal. A weaker woman, might have died from the hardship."

"It is good he was as determined as his mother," Ophni countered. "He kicked and fought to come into this world, unable to find the doorway."

Ophni cleaned his face, nose and mouth, then gave him a slight smack on his back with her hand. The limp little body came to life with a jerk, pawing and kicking, screaming and gasping for breath.

"My, but is he not a lively one? Such strength he has, even after struggling for so long."

Hagar came to and managed a smile watching her son kicking, bellowing, and struggling in Ophni's hands.

"My baby...give him to me," she gasped to have possession. "It really is a male-child is it not?"

"Yes, Hagar, he is that, as you can see.

"He is yours just as soon as we finish our cleanup, little mother; be patient," Ophni soothed.

"Hand me my clean knife," Ophni ordered her assistant. After a few minutes pause, she cut the umbilical cord. "Here, take the baby and clean him with warm salted water while I finish tending to his mother."

Comfortably settled on clean bedding after being washed and robed, Hagar fought off the much needed sleep her mind and body begged for. She struggled to obey her will that demanded the baby. With eyes half open and arms hardly able to rise, she called out: "My baby! Give him to me!"

"Why Hagar... well, if you wish, Yes, here he is."

The babe stopped crying on the warm comfort of his mother's body. Hagar put her hands around his chest and pulled him up to her left breast. His mouth found the nipple and eagerly gave suck. In this security he quickly fell asleep, followed immediately by Hagar, exhausted but proud.

A new day's early morning light silhouetted the figures of Ophni and her assistant as they came out of Hagar's tent and went towards their own. On the way they met a sentry and told him the news of Abram's heir.

"Our lord Abram has a male heir? That is wonderful news! I feel like waking the whole camp," the sentry responded excitedly.

"No, do not do that," Ophni warned. "Lord Abram has yet to find out. When he rises he will be told."

Abram arose from his bed later than usual. He had not been able to sleep well. He was awake much of the night listening to Hagar's screams of pain and frustration. Her agony worried him terribly. He feared that death might claim her and the child. Blinking sleep out of his eyes, he put on sandals and a robe. Stretching his limbs and emitting a yawn, he walked over to Hagar's tent.

"It is a boy, my lord Abram," declared a servant girl. "A big, husky, healthy male-child."

Abram smiled proudly and held back an urge to shout praises as loud as his voice could stand. He clasped his hands together instead and raising them to the sky uttered: "You have not forgotten your servant, my Lord. You have given me an heir at last!"

Turning to the servant girl, Abram asked: "How is Hagar? Tell me the truth, for I heard her agony during the night."

"Ophni, the midwife said Hagar was close to death before giving birth, my lord. I fed her a little honey and warm milk after the babe was put to her breast. She was too weak to feed herself."

"And how is she now?"

"Hagar is still asleep, my lord. I have wrapped the babe in swaddling clothes and laid him down against his mother's breast, where even now he sleeps."

"Although my heart bursts with desire to see my son, I will wait for word that Hagar has awakened; then I shall return," Abram finished and walked away.

It was late afternoon when the servant girl came to Abram as he was sitting at the entrance to his tent with Sarai.

"Hagar and the child are awake and presentable, my lord."

"Ah, good! Come Sarai, let us see my heir."

Abram was in high spirits, happier than he had been in many months.

"At last, at last," he muttered to himself as he walked hurriedly, disregarding Sarai who scurried behind, almost running to keep up with her husband's long strides. When Abram reached the entrance he stopped momentarily, spoke Hagar's name and walked in slowly.

Hagar was reclining, in a half-sitting position against some animal skins, with the baby nestled in the hollow of her left arm. She was still very weak but full of determination to make the most of her success. A look and posture of fierce pride overcame her and she was once again a proud daughter of Pharaoh.

Abram came to her side, and with a smile of great anticipation he knelt down to get a better look. Even so it was not enough to satisfy Abram. He reached out his hands to take the baby and examine him.

A look of uncertainty, bordering on fear, appeared on Hagar's face. She made a confused and feeble effort at holding onto the baby but Abram ignored it and swept him up to his face.

"By my father's name, look at the size of him! These shoulders will draw a great bow and let fly an arrow as far as the eye can see! No game or enemy will be safe from him. And his chest and legs...look at his legs move! He will run like the wind with the freedom of a wild ass!"

Abram gloried in the feel of his son's strength as the baby pedaled and kicked the air.

"Ah, Hagar, you have done well, very well! He is marvelous!"

"I am pleased that you are happy, my lord," Hagar said faintly.

"Happy? I am filled to overflowing with delight! Nothing could make me happier! Ishmael! Ishmael! Ishmael...!" Abram began chanting.

Disturbed and frightened, the baby began to cry.

"Oh, ho! Listen to the voice of the new lord of my people. Already he commands with authority. Very well, little Ishmael, since you are the new lord of the Heberews I bend to obedience and kneel at your feet," Abram laughed.

Kneeling, he reluctantly returned Ishmael to his mother's anxious arms.

Only when Ishmael was in her possession did Hagar relax and resume her air of haughty pride.

Still on his knees, Abram bent to kiss his son. The baby's scent was so pleasing he lingered on, not wanting to leave.

Hagar reached out and grabbed the front of Abram's robe, preventing him from backing away. She held on with remarkable tenacity for a woman so weak. Pulling Abram to her, Hagar tilted her face upwards waiting for him to kiss her. It was impossible for him to refuse, so he pressed his lips to hers. Hagar reached an arm around his neck and held him to her mouth with a passion that startled him and awoke memories.

"Ishmael is hungry, like his father. Stay while I feed him, my lord husband."

Without waiting for a reply, Hagar bared her breasts, large and full, with milk oozing from her nipples. She placed Ishmael's mouth on one and he began sucking eagerly.

Abram was surprised by Hagar's unabashed directness but was pleased at what he saw. He quickly lost his awkward feeling as memories of days and nights of pleasure flooded his senses.

Sitting there next to Hagar, he watched Ishmael's every movement. He was touched in the heart with great affection for mother and son, and nodded his head with approval.

Sarai had been standing just inside the tent opening observing all but saying nothing, except to herself.

"I want to take the baby but I know Abram will not allow it. The baby needs his mother's milk also. But when the child is weaned, there will be a celebration and I shall have him; he will be my son. I will have to wait but Oh! it is terrible watching her expose herself and flaunt her lust at Abram. I must be patient. I must be patient!" She kept telling herself.

It was impossible for Sarai to say anything complimentary so she turned and left saying nothing, knowing she would not be missed.

Hagar looked around Abram's shoulder and saw Sarai withdraw. She smiled smugly and returned her gaze to Abram. He never knew Sarai left.

During the ensuing weeks and months, Abram was drawn to spend more and more time with Ishmael and his mother. Hagar regained her youthful strength week by week in step with that of the baby. Each day Abram ordered servants to prepare a lavish meal. Each afternoon he visited Hagar and Ishmael, followed by a procession of servants who served them. In returning from each occasion he boasted to anyone asking: "My heir is getting stronger every day. I am seeing to it that Ishmael's mother's milk is good and plentiful. And, yes, Hagar is recovering nicely. Yes, that is good, very good!"

Ten months went by before Ishmael was weaned from his mother's breasts. When the day arrived Abram caused a feast to be prepared in celebration and the whole tribe turned out to give praise. There was much eating and drinking, music and dancing. Everyone was happy, even Sarai who had been waiting so patiently, enduring the loss of her husband's affection for all these months.

"I will not take Ishmael just now," she quietly plotted. "Hagar might resist and embarrass Abram before his people. But tomorrow...tomorrow I will claim him as is my right."

And so the festivities lasted late into the night with Hagar reveling in the gentle flood of tributes paid to her.

Early the next morning, Sarai arose in the dawn's first light and softly walked to Hagar's tent. Without any hesitation, she quietly drew aside the flap and stepped inside. It was dark within and she could see nothing at first. Turning her head slightly, she cocked an ear for sounds that would lead her to her objective.

Time dragged by. It seemed like forever. She heard Hagar's heavy breathing and inched forward in that direction. When she got close she stopped and listened again. Her eyes strained to pierce the darkness, waiting...waiting...and then a different sound barely caught her ears...a higher pitched resonance.

Ishmael moved, sighed a long breath, and found his mouth with a thumb.

Sarai's ears guided her toward the sucking, breathing intonation, groping for the little shape. On her knees, she found her objective, encircled him with her arms and slowly lifted him from his bed next to Hagar. Placing him against her flesh, Sarai pulled her robe together, adjusted her mantle for warmth, and rose to her feet.

Ishmael made only a small sigh of adjustment in his new environment. The warm breast against his cheek conveyed security and comfort for his continued sleep.

Quietly Sarai left Hagar's tent and returned to her own compartment, silently slipping into bed. It was a welcome warmth from the cold night air. It also helped calm her shivering from an anxiety over what she had just done.

Sleepless, she laid there relishing the experience of a baby against her breast. The feel of his little mouth sucking for milk that was not there. It sent a thrill into her body from head to toe that tingled her whole being.

"So this is what it feels like to be a mother. I believed I would never know...until now."

Sarai heard the screams in her sleep. A sleep that seemed only seconds long.

"My baby is gone! Ishmael is gone!" Hagar's outcry stirred the camp and people came running to see what was the matter.

Abram came out of his compartment with a deep worried look and made Hagar tell him exactly what happened.

"I awoke a short time ago and found Ishmael missing from his bed. I looked inside and outside the tent thinking he may have crawled away...but he is not around! I heard nothing during the night to indicate someone came and took him. The baby never cried out or made a fuss. I would have heard it if he did!"

"We will find Ishmael, Hagar, now be calm," Abram tried to sooth her fears. "I will have all my servants..."

The muffled sound of a baby starting to cry caught Hagar's ears.

"There! Hear that? It is Ishmael! I know it is him! He is in your tent, my lord!"

Startled, yet relieved, Abram turned and went inside. Throwing aside the curtain to Sarai's compartment, he marched in and saw his wife holding Ishmael to her breast, attempting to hush him with a rocking motion.

"Sarai! Why have you taken Ishmael?"

Sarai said nothing in response to his interruption and returned her full attention to the baby.

"Why have you taken Ishmael like a sneak-thief in the night?!" he demanded in a loud voice.

"He...he is my child now. It was for this purpose that I gave Hagar to you for a concubine. I have waited a long time for this moment, even until Ishmael was weaned. Now he is mine to nurture, for you my husband."

"But...he is Hagar's flesh, blood, and bone...and you stole him without warning did you not?"

"I took what is rightfully mine, and in a way that would prevent her from resisting. I did not want her to be another embarrassment to us."

"Embarrassment? What do you mean?"

"Hagar ran away, stealing one of your camels. She traveled towards Egypt and nearly died on the way with your unborn son in her womb. If a messenger of your God had not saved her, Ishmael would not be here," Sarai calmly explained.

Just then Hagar burst into the tent compartment. Unable to contain herself she screamed at Sarai with indignation:

"My baby! You stole my baby! Give him back to me!"

"He is no longer yours. Ishmael is now mine to nurture for my husband. You have fulfilled your part as I arranged it. Do not forget your place! You are still my servant, my property to do with as I see fit! Beware of your Egyptian tongue! I will not tolerate disrespect from my handmaid. As for Ishmael, he is my property as well, and I choose to have him with me. There is no other choice for you, so leave my presence, now!"

"No! No! I am Ishmael's mother. He is of my body, not yours!" Hagar cried her defiance.

"That is of no importance," Sarai proclaimed with confidence. Ishmael must be raised as a Heberew, not as a Hamite! I will tell him all about his heritage. I will prepare him for the time when his father will train him to become prince over this tribe. You cannot do these things properly."

"But I..."

"There is nothing more to say. If you withdraw peacefully, I may allow you to have some time with Ishmael now and then. If you continue to bother me with your demands, however, I will send you away...alone!" Sarai repeated one more time.

Hagar cringed at the thought of losing her baby to Sarai or never seeing her baby again. She felt a terrible depression of defeat. Throwing herself at Abram's feet she clutched at his hands and looked up into his eyes imploring him to intervene.

"My lord...surely you will not allow this...?"

Abram turned his head aside and said nothing. He could not, for Sarai had right on her side. All parties had agreed to the baby's conception on Sarai's behalf. The child was hers by right of Abram establishing it to be so. He was ruler of this tribe; his word was law and he would not violate it.

"You may be sent away alone!" Sarai repeated one final time.

Sarai relished her victory over Hagar during the weeks and months that followed. Each day Hagar asked to hold or care for Ishmael, and each day Sarai refused her. Sarai remembered the pain she felt when Abram spent many nights with Hagar. The flaunted youth and erotic sex that enticed Abram was still vivid in Sarai's memory.

"Revenge is sweet, oh so sweet," she murmured to herself.

Hagar became a changed person. Hovering around Ishmael at every opportunity, she was obedient and solicitous to Sarai's needs and, of course, those of Ishmael.

Abram now enjoyed the peace and harmony that existed between Sarai and Hagar. He finally admitted to himself that Sarai was wiser then he realized, and allowed her freedom to care for Ishmael as she saw fit.

Sarai saw her relationship with Abram improve. Even though she had been barren for so many years, Abram found his wife to be a caring mother, enjoying Ishmael almost as much as he. Together they laughed, played and cooed over the child.

Their marriage, grown cold and menial over the years of disappointment, blossomed once again. More often than not they could be found each evening, lying next to each other with Ishmael between them, asleep.

During these months of happiness Abram remembered the part Sarai played in providing an heir for him. The memory of her guilt and shame at being barren tugged at his heart.

He recalled how he replaced her in his affections and attentions with Hagar, a concubine, who encouraged a lusty, more youthful relationship. It was an exciting interlude in his life that would continue to be substance for an old man's dreams of the past. But Abram accepted Sarai as his only wife, his one true love and princess of his tribe.

The tribe held Sarai in respect and admiration for the way she brought about her husband's heir. At last they had a son of

Abram to be their new Goel one day. He would assuredly continue to bring them security and providence as Abram had done all these years, or so the people thought as Ishmael grew.

Little by little Hagar was permitted opportunities to hold and care for her son. Sarai accepted suggestions of help when Ishmael became too active or demanding. Hagar was always eager to assist but tried not to show it, for fear that Sarai would call upon another servant just to spite her.

The years rolled by and Ishmael, at age twelve, had become spoiled, callous and brutish towards other children and servants of his father. He roamed hill and vale around the encampment, practicing the hunting skills his father taught him.

Ishmael had respect for only two people: Abram and Hagar. All others he held in contempt, unless it suited his devious purposes to do otherwise.

Hagar had very carefully and methodically won Ishmael to her and poisoned his mind against Sarai. Whenever Sarai tried to train Ishmael with discipline, he ran off, finding comfort and words of encouragement for rebellion from Hagar.

"I am your real mother, my proud prince. I understand you like no one else, and I care for you better. So ignore what Sarai tells you. I will give you what ever you want.

"Respect your father, Lord Abram, for he will give you all his wealth one day when he takes his last breath. When that day comes you will be able to have or do whatever your heart desires with your authority. You could provide for me, your only mother, and raise me from slave to princess. Then if the nagging Sarai upsets us with her self-righteousness or other nonsense to correct you...well, you would know what to do about it."

Chapter 27
The Sins of Sodom and Gomorrah

During the years following the war in Canaan, occupants of Siddim Valley were ignorant of the lesson of chastisement shown in their losses. Their priesthood failed to change any of their corrupt practices nor understand and communicate a message of repentance from inhumane conduct. Only intimidation and extortion was practiced. Whatever the judges and the people did to bring a continuous flow of wealth to the temples and palace was condoned as proper.

Sexual perversion and unnatural copulation were commonly accepted as alternate and legitimate forms of social behavior. This debasement often constituted accepted religious forms or practices.

The people grew vain and restless for more and different forms of social diversion. They regained their wealth and had need of little. Yet they stole from strangers - assaulted, raped and murdered them.

Corrupted law was enforced in the valley by four judges. Serak was the judge in the city of Sodom. His form of justice was contrived to favor the citizens of Sodom without pity to any strangers.

In the course of time Abram sent Eliezer and his son Jashub to Sodom. Their mission was to visit Lot and see if he was well and restored to his previous living standard.

They had stayed in the city only long enough for a short visit with Lot. On their way out of the city, while walking through the streets, Eliezer saw a man of Sodom fighting with a stranger who was weaker than he. The Sodomite stripped the man of all his clothes and money and walked away.

The poor man cried to Eliezer for help against this robber.

"After him, Jashub!" Eliezer commanded.

The strong young man responded instantly and ran to stop the Sodomite.

"Stop! my father wants to have words with you!" Jashub snapped at the man, barring his way.

The Sodomite turned to face Eliezer as he came walking up with the naked stranger at his heels.

"Why are you interfering in something that does not concern you?"

"Why have you treated this stranger so harshly, taking all that he has?" Eliezer replied with a question of his own.

"Is this man your brother?" asked the Sodomite.

"No, he is not, but..."

"Have the people of Sodom made you a judge this day so that you have authority to speak about this matter?"

"No, but there is an obvious injustice being done here and..."

"What do you know of Sodomite justice? You admitted you were not a judge!"

"Yes, but right is right and wrong is wrong in the eyes of God."

"And so now you are a priest, I suppose."

"Well, no but..."

"Then you have no authority to tell me right from wrong. Be gone you fool and stop bothering me!"

"I can see it is futile to argue further with you, but I will not allow you to rob this man, leaving him without clothes and the means to sustain himself."

Eliezer grabbed at the stranger's belongings and pulled.

The robber resisted at first, then let go suddenly, dropping everything.

The sudden release took Eliezer by surprise and he stumbled backwards, falling on his backside. He struggled to get up on his feet but when he did another surprise awaited him.

The Sodomite reached down, picked up a stone and hit Eliezer in the forehead sending him staggering into the arms of his son. Blood flowed copiously down his face from the wound and became matted in his beard. Eliezer expected the thief to run, but he did not. What happened next was the third surprise he faced.

"Give me my fee for having rid you of this bad blood that was in your forehead!" the Sodomite demanded tightly. "This is the custom of our land. The law says you must pay me!"

Eliezer stood there blinking in amazement as well as to keep the blood out of his eyes.

"You wound me out of hostility, and now you demand payment for this injury? This is utter nonsense! You must take me for a fool."

The Sodomite called out to other Sodomites nearby to assist him, and together they brought Eliezer before Shakra, the judge. He was an immensely obese man, highly regarded by the populace for his size, his booming voice of authority and his biased judgments authorizing corruption.

"Who interrupts me in the midst of my meal? What is the cause that brings you here?"

"I am Baalab, honored judge, a citizen of Sodom. These others are strangers to our city, ignorant of our laws and disobedient to them," answered the thief. "I hit this stranger with this stone so that bad blood would flow from his head. It can be seen that I was successful, yet he refuses to pay me for my service."

"It is plain to see that this man speaks the truth," the judge declared issuing a loud belch as an exclamation point. "Give him his fee, for this is the custom of our land."

Eliezer heard the judgment with disbelief. His first impulse was to shout his objections to such obvious bias. He quickly realized, however, that he was surrounded by hostile people without any consideration for fairness, including the judge. His mind raced to construct a debatable defense against such collusion. Thinking of what his master Abram might do in such a circumstance, he decided upon a bold action.

"May I see the rock that my accuser used as evidence?" Eliezer asked mildly.

The Sodomite gave the rock to the judge who glanced at it casually.

"Is there blood on it?" Eliezer asked.

The judge examined it carefully and replied," Yes, there is a spot, which proves the accusation is correct."

"Let me see the proof, if you please," Eliezer requested as he calmly approached the judge to view the evidence.

The judge held out the rock in one hand, condescendingly, as Eliezer came close and bent to see the spot.

Swiftly and without warning, Eliezer snatched the rock out of Shakra's hand, cocked his arm, swung and smashed the rock against the judge's forehead.

The blow caught him completely by surprise. He fell back into his chair, barely conscious. Blood oozed from the wound and trickled down his face.

"If this then is the custom in your land," Eliezer spoke loud enough for all to hear, "you have my permission, O noble judge, to pay this man with the money you now owe me!"

Eliezer then fixed his gaze upon the Sodomite instigator. Approaching him with the stone held menacingly he asked: "Do you agree with this arrangement?"

The man tried to run but Eliezer's son restrained him.

Eliezer raised the stone, ready to bring it crashing down on the man's head.

"And you will return the clothes and money you stole from the stranger?!"

"Here, take them! They are yours! See, I give them up willingly," he squeaked, trembling with fear.

"But if I draw your bad blood you will owe me a fee, and I see that you do have bad blood!"

"Here take my money, but do not strike me. I will forego the treatment," he stuttered.

"Very well, I accept your offer," Eliezer frowned. "Give those things to my son and tell this rabble that my son and I go from this place in peace, and with your blessing."

"But I..."

"Tell them now! Or by the Everliving God I will smash in your skull with this stone and rid the earth of a thieving scoundrel!" Eliezer spit the words out in a threatening snarl.

The Sodomite saw that his life was in the hands of this powerfully determined nomad. Any further trickery on his part could end his life.

"Tell them you are escorting us to the gates of the city as friends, now that our dispute is resolved," Eliezer hissed.

The man did as he was ordered, assuring the threatening mob that all differences had been resolved peacefully.

Eliezer looked back at the judge still collapsed in his chair, just beginning to stir himself back into consciousness.

"Let us hurry. Move faster! Now!," he commanded.

Eliezer's son bulled a path through the spectators for his father with the Sodomite sandwiched between them. Out in the open they walked fast toward the place where the thievery began. Sitting there in the sun, attempting to keep warm without his clothes, was the stranger. Eliezer came up to him and returned his possessions.

"Oh thank you, my lord! You are a brave and kind hearted nobleman for taking up my poor cause for me."

"Be thankful to Yahvah, the Everliving God, who has returned your clothes and your money. It is He who saves us."

Pointing to the Sodomite, Eliezer continued: "and this scoundrel's money is given to you also, because the Everliving is a generous God as well as a merciful God. Forsake all other gods for Him, for he is jealous as well. Now, let us leave this city. The stench of its depravity suffocates me."

The stranger clothed himself and looking into Eliezer's blood-streaked face, he fell before him and kissed his feet.

"You are surely a priest of Yahvah the Everliving God you speak of. Let me come with you and learn at your feet. I would have died here if you had not come to my defense. You have given me my life. Let me now give it to you in service."

"Oh, no. I am but a servant myself, sent here on an errand by my master who is both prince of the land and priest of the Everliving God. Travel with us, if you will. Righteousness reigns in our tribe and you are welcome to stay among us."

"Righteousness? What is that?" the stranger asked as they began walking hurriedly.

"Come, let us hurry from this place. I will tell you as we travel!" Eliezer urged.

Chapter 28
Covenant and Circumcision

"ABRAM...ABRAM," A VOICE CALLED OUT AS THE FIRST GLOW OF A NEW DAY PENETRATED THE BLACK PASTORAL NIGHT.

"What...? Who calls? Is someone there?"

"YES, ABRAM, IT IS THE EVERLIVING. GET YOU OUT TO THE HILL NEARBY!"

Abram was ninety-nine years of age and he moved much slower now than he did several years before when his God called upon him last. But hurry he did; it would not do to keep his God waiting. Slipping into his sandals and outer robe, he shuffled sleepily out into the cool air.

Blinking away the sleep from his eyes, he gave a shiver and walked eastward. Hurrying his steps, Abram warmed sufficiently to stop his shivers. By the time he reached a crest of the nearest small hill, Abram could see a fair distance in the increasing light.

The sunrise seemed especially beautiful to Abram this morning. From his vantage-point, objects far and near turned from dark silhouettes to highlighted forms, their tips sparkling from low angled-rays.

Abram waited, appreciating the pause to catch his breath and take in the surrounding beauty.

"Abram!"

The voice came from behind him and he turned to see a figure dressed in white robes with a mantle covering a portion of his head. A dazzling ray of light glanced off his head and shoulders hurting Abram's eyes with its brilliance.

Abram tried to see the divine messenger's face but most of it was in shadow as his mouth, the only part visible, spoke.

"I AM YAHVAH THE ALMIGHTY GOD! LIVE ACCORDING TO MY LAW OF RIGHTEOUSNESS AND I WILL RE-AFFIRM THE COVENANT BETWEEN US. I WILL ALSO INCREASE YOU VERY GREATLY."

Abram went to his knees out of respect and bowed his head to shield his eyes from the glory before him.

"Yes, Lord, I am your obedient servant."

"HEAR THIS, ABRAM. YOUR NAME SHALL NOW BE CALLED ABRAHAM, FOR YOU SHALL BECOME THE FATHER OF MANY NATIONS, DESCENDED FROM THE CHILDREN OF YOUR LOINS. YOU SHALL BE VERY FRUITFUL IN YOUR OLD AGE.

"THIS COVENANT I ESTABLISH IS WITH YOU, AND YOUR DESCENDANTS AFTER YOU, FROM GENERATION TO GENERATION, FOREVER. I WILL BE YOUR ONLY GOD AND THE GOD OF YOUR RACE AFTER YOU.

"I WILL GIVE TO YOU AND YOUR RACE THIS COUNTRY WHERE YOU ARE A FOREIGNER, AND THE WHOLE LAND OF CANAAN WILL BE THEIRS FOR A POSSESSION FOREVER AND I WILL CONTINUE TO BE THEIR GOD.

"SARAI, YOUR WIFE SHALL ALSO HAVE A NEW NAME. SARAH SHALL NOW BE HER NAME. I WILL BLESS AND RESTORE HER SO THAT SHE WILL HAVE A SON BY YOU. SHE SHALL BE GREATLY HONORED IN BECOMING THE MOTHER OF MANY NATIONS. KINGS OVER MANY PEOPLES SHALL COME THROUGH THE SON SHE WILL BEAR IN HER OLD AGE."

Abraham fell upon his face and laughed through tears of confusion and doubt. He uttered from the depths of his heart: "When I am a hundred years old? And Sarah...when she is ninety...she, she shall have a child from her womb?"

"DO YOU DOUBT THAT I HAVE THE POWER TO GIVE LIFE OR TAKE IT BY ANY MEASURE I PLEASE?"

"Oh Lord...my head is dazed by the thought of your gift. We are so old! I...we...that is, ah...our present limitations make it impossible...."

"NOTHING IS IMPOSSIBLE FOR THE EVERLIVING GOD, ABRAHAM. I SHALL RESTORE FEEBLE SARAH. HER YOUTHFULNESS SHALL BE RETURNED TO HER AND YOU SHALL HAVE YOUR VITALITY. SHE WILL GIVE YOU A SON AND YOU SHALL NAME HIM ISAAC, MEANING LAUGHTER. I WILL ALSO FIX MY COVENANT WITH HIM AS AN EVERLASTING PROMISE TO HIS RACE AFTER HIM."

With anxiety in his heart Abraham offered: "If it please you, Lord, I wish that Ishmael might live in your favor."

"AS FOR ISHMAEL, I HEAR YOUR PLEA. HAVE NO FEAR, MY BLESSING WILL BE UPON HIM. I WILL CAUSE HIM TO PROSPER AND EXTEND HIMSELF VERY GREATLY. HE SHALL BEGET TWELVE PRINCES AND I WILL GRANT HIM TO BECOME A GREAT NATION.

"MY COVENANT WITH YOU, ABRAHAM, IS FOR ISAAC, WHO SARAH, YOUR WIFE, SHALL BEAR NEAR THIS SEASON NEXT YEAR.

"NOW THIS IS THE COVENANT WHICH YOU SHALL KEEP BETWEEN MYSELF AND YOU. EVERY MALE IN YOUR TRIBE, SLAVE OR FREE, MUST BE CIRCUMCISED! YOU WILL CIRCUMCISE THEM IN THE FORESKIN OF THEIR BODY AS A PROOF OF THE VOW AND AGREEMENT TO THIS COVENANT BETWEEN ME AND THEM. ON THE EIGHTH DAY AFTER BIRTH, EVERY MALE BABY SHALL BE CIRCUMCISED. THIS SHALL BE MY COVENANT SIGN ON YOUR BODY AS AN EVERLASTING BOND.

"THE DEGRADED MALE WHO HAS NOT BEEN CIRCUMCISED SHALL BECOME SEPARATED FROM MY PEOPLE BECAUSE HE HAS BROKEN THE COVENANT.

"UPHOLD THE LAW OF THE PATRIARCHS I GAVE YOU SO THAT YOUR PEOPLE MAY KNOW RIGHTEOUSNESS, AND BE AN EXAMPLE TO THE WORLD."

The divine messenger ceased speaking and rose in the air, uniting with the sun's brilliance now pouring down upon the hilltop.

Abraham tried to follow him with his eyes, but was forced to cower from the heavenly light.

Ecstatic from his communication with divinity, Abraham rolled onto his back and looked straight up into the high reaches of the Everliving's home. He concentrated on remembering the exact words.

"My new name is Abraham – Father of many nations... Sarah, mother of nations and kings...Yahvah the Almighty God will bless and restore her youthfulness... and my vitality... a son... his name Isaac... Ishmael a great nation... but the covenant is for Isaac... whom Sarah shall bear this season next year... circumcise every male... a sign of the covenant to my race forever... uphold the law... know righteousness... be an example to the world."

How long he laid there Abraham could not tell. The sun had chased away all traces of the cold night, bringing comforting warmth, and then discomforting heat.

"...every male shall be circumcised!" He sat bolt upright, struck by the immensity of this assignment. "Do not delay! There is much you have to do!" he chided himself.

Struggling to his feet, he started walking with uneven steps, almost stumbling. But soon he was covering the distance back to camp with long, even, vigorous strides.

Sarah stood away from the tents, scanning the countryside for the sight of him. When she saw Abraham, she knew that he was returning with a purpose that would have considerable impact on the tribe. She had seen him like this on few occasions but the results were always profound.

Now as she watched him approach, his strides seemed like those of a vibrant young man, confident, sure-footed, and strong. Seeing her, he waved excitedly as though they were separated lovers about to reunite.

When Abraham came close enough to see Sarah's face clearly, he saw a look of bewilderment and smiled even more broadly.

"Sarai! Sarai! I have been with Yahvah the Everliving God! After so long...and the things he promised.... Oh, Sarai, He has changed your name to Sarah!"

"What? Why?"

Picking her up in his arms, that were suddenly stronger, "You shall have your youthfulness restored!" he shouted excitedly. "We shall conceive a son by this season next year! His name...his name shall be Isaac! Isaac! Isaac for laughter, Ha, ha, ha!" Abraham laughed with a joy he had kept suppressed for a great many years.

He swung Sarai around until she cried for him to stop. Putting her down he kissed her with a passion she could not remember experiencing before.

"Abram!"

"Abraham, my love, Abraham! This is my new name. Come, I will tell you and my people all about the Covenant the Everliving swore to me...about you...about Isaac, and our race!"

He took her hand and swept her along towards their tent. There he took a knife of flint, and stuck it in the girdle wrapped around his waist. He found the ram's horn, took it in hand and marched out to the center of the encampment where he gave the call to assemble.

The tribe hurriedly scampered over and gathered around their goel, anxious about his reason for calling them.

Finally he silenced their muttering voices with a raised hand, and spoke. **"The Everliving God, came to me at the break of day through his divine messenger. He made a Covenant with me..."**

Abraham gave a complete description, detail by detail, of his experience on the hilltop. At last he came to the difficult part that would test his headship over the tribe.

'"...Every male in your tribe must be circumcised! You will circumcise them in the foreskin of their body for a vow and agreement to this covenant between me and them..."'

A rush of shock ran through the camp like a sudden wind through the oak trees.

'"...Every male, whether born of your family or purchased shall be circumcised..."' The rush of breath developed into a roiling of murmurs and exclamations.

'"...The degraded male who has not been circumcised shall become separated from My People and My Blessings because he has broken the Covenant..."'

Gasps of astonishment quieted the tribe and they listened intently as Abraham, full of power, finished speaking.

'"...Circumcision is My Covenant sign in your body as an everlasting bond between us. Your race must uphold the Law of Righteousness so that my people will be an example to the world.'

'Thus saith our almighty Everliving God! You all are his people through me. Dare any of you refuse me? Those whom I do not own, step forward! Now those among you who will refuse me, step forward so that I may cast you out!"

An oppressive silence descended while every male cast glances around him, curious about others and apprehensive about himself.

Abraham waited patiently, and watched, carefully. Not one man approached to resign his place in the tribe.

'Loyal to a man; just what I expected," Abraham admitted confidently. "Now, to the task."

Abraham instructed Eliezer who took note of each family of males, recording each name after Abram administered the rite. Those who came first, the bravest and most loyal, suffered somewhat more from the operation than those who followed, for Abraham's skill improved with experience. The male population all bore their suffering with dignity, regarding the mark as an honorable distinction and guarantee of divine protection.

Abraham worked inexhaustibly, happily, sealing the covenant. The joy of that day was marred for him only by Ishmael who was unwilling to submit.

Unmoved by the example of his youthful companions who obediently, though trepidly submitted, he ran off and hid.

A search was made and when Ishmael was found, he fought, hitting and screaming until he was overpowered. Four men brought him at last, kicking and screaming in mock pain, to his father.

"Ishmael, silence!" Abraham roared.

The hysteria continued worse than before.

Abraham was finishing with a young lad, whose lips trembled and tears streamed down his face, but nary a loud cry escaped. He complemented the boy for his bravery in enduring the pain, then Abraham sent him away.

Ishmael was a disgrace that Abraham could no longer forebear. Not waiting to wash, he stood up and went to Ishmael who screamed and struggled anew.

Putting his left hand over Ishmael's mouth, he swung his right arm with considerable force. An open hand, wet with blood, caught Ishmael's face with a loud "smack"!

The force of the blow squelched all resistance in the boy, rendering him semi-conscious.

"Hold him securely!" Abraham commanded.

Exposing Ishmael, he proceeded to circumcise him.

The pain brought Ishmael to consciousness. Again he screamed and struggled hysterically against the cutting pain...then fainted. This allowed Abraham to finish the rite, although he was sweating profusely and his hands were trembling.

Hagar tried to intrude on Abraham during the rite, but was prevented from doing so by men posted at the tent's entrance. Ishmael's cries from within drove her wild. Like a mad woman, she screamed curses and ran around the tent looking for a way inside. Finding none, she remained at the entrance and shouted: "He is only thirteen! Wait until he is a man!"

Ishmael was soon brought out, supported under each arm, looking pale and weak. He took refuge in Hagar's embrace and together they shuffled off weeping and vilifying Abraham.

The remaining families of males, in attendance for the rite, behaved as though they had seen nothing, so Abraham would not be shamed. They saw that their lord was already deeply afflicted by his son's conduct.

Sarah followed Abraham's instructions and prepared a banquet. She ordered servants to give olive oil for treating surgeries, as much as was desired.

Wine was served abundantly and myrrh added since it helped drug the pain. Most partakers, however, preferred to drink wine without the bitter herb. Living in the wilds as they did, many were often stepped on, kicked by herd animals, or attacked by wild beasts. Pain and discomfort was something nomadic men adjusted themselves to.

Lastly, Abraham circumcised Eliezer, his sons, and then himself. After washing and applying to himself the oil, he joined the tribal banquet where he sat content and cheerful.

Sarah waited upon him like a servant and ordered away anyone who would interfere.

Turning to her at his side Abraham smiled with a look of extreme confidence about him and declared: **"Let the heavily armed kings and their powerful priesthoods raise massive temples to false gods in Ur, Babylon, Mari, Ninevah, and Egypt. Some new conqueror will build a vast army and destroy them, or set new gods up in their place. The one true Everliving God has founded His indestructible habitation here in my people, forever!**

"Do you realize what that means, Sarah? For all time, long after you and I are at rest with our ancestors, our descendants will continue in what we have begun. We have good reasons to be happier than ever before!"

The food and wine satisfied and sedated Abraham. He dozed off with his head in Sarah's lap, her happy countenance smiling down at him.

"You have had a busy day, my lord husband. A very busy day, now sleep."

And Abraham was ninety-nine years old when he was circumcised in the foreskin of the body.

Ishmael also was thirteen years of age when he was circumcised in the foreskin of his body.

On the very same day Abraham and his son Ishmael were circumcised. All the men born in his house, or bought with his money, and foreigners, were circumcised with him.

Genesis 17:24-26 Ferrar Fenton Bible

Chapter 29
Cleansing the Valley of Siddim

This particular summer was different from others in the Valley of Siddim. Unprecedented phenomena were occurring. Violent storms and burning winds swept through the valley. There were times when the ground trembled. Trees were uprooted, unexpectedly, and fell when there was no wind at all. Waters boiled and rippled at the southern end of the Dead Sea and inhabitants of Sodom and Gomorrah came in crowds, with their priests, to watch and wonder.

"The waters are disturbed by the anger of the gods!" exclaimed the priests.

Thereafter, numerous sacrifices of children, slaves and cattle were conducted to appease the gods and demons.

There was a few days' pause in between tremors. According to the priests, the demons were resting before starting their disruption of the earth again.

Throughout the valley, slime pits of bitumen boiled and emitted a horrible stench, as underground gasses were released.

Lot was very concerned about these strange conditions but felt helpless to do anything. He talked to Ado about leaving the valley but she refused to even consider it.

"All my friends are here and I have finally gained the social status I deserve. The king and all the priests know me, and provide favors. We have never lived better since we returned after the war! These conditions you worry about will not last long. I am surprised that you should fear them. Do not be a fool and cast your fears about like a little boy, who fears a storm with its thunder and lightning," Ado chided her husband as though he were a child to be manipulated.

Lot finally gave up trying to convince her the valley was a dangerous place in which to stay. Nothing seemed to be reason enough to uproot her, so Lot resigned himself to endure it all. He kept a watchful eye for additional signs of impending disaster, however, hoping to prepare even stronger arguments for leaving.

Amidst a grove of oak trees on the Plain of Mamre, Abraham and his tribe had no awareness of these ominous happenings. On this day, as he was accustomed on most days, Abraham stood outside his tent and swept his gaze all around the valley. His heart was filled with contentment. God had been good to his tribe. The sheep that multiplied abundantly could be seen as dull-white spots against the green grass on the far slopes.

A stream flowing through the meadowland sparkled like polished silver from the bright summer sun. Overhead a large oak tree reached out its gnarled branches. Sunlight, filtering through the leaves, cast dancing lights upon tents, people, and the ground itself. This part of the world was beautiful to Abraham and life was good.

As he stood gazing out into the expanse of the valley, his eyes caught sight of three figures in the distance. At first Abraham thought they were his servants caring for the flocks. But the way they walked, straight towards him three abreast, soon proved he was wrong. Now he was curious as to who these strangers might be, and he continued to watch their approach.

Rays from the hot sun glanced brilliantly off their white cloaks. They were much too far away to identify, yet Abraham had a curious compulsion to go and greet them.

Leaving the shade of oak trees behind, he walked in the direction of the visitors. His compulsion turned to anxiety as he walked. The anxiety then became an unexplainable yearning, and he walked faster and faster.

The sunlight intensified as it reflected off the figures. But then as he grew closer to them the dazzling light seemed to emanate from them rather than reflect off them. As the distance between them lessened, the light grew in intensity. Abraham shielded his eyes with his hand, peering through spaces between his fingers. Yet, even then the light was too bright. His eyes hurt, then watered. Blinking in half blindness Abraham realized these were no ordinary men. They must be divine messengers.

Falling down on his knees, Abraham bowed his head to the ground and waited as they walked up to him. Afraid to look up into their faces he fixed his line of sight at their sandaled feet and addressed them:

"My Lords, will you not come unto your servant? Allow me to wash your feet while you rest in the pleasant shade near my tent. I will serve a little bread also to refresh you. Perhaps it was for this that you passed near your servant?"

"Do as you have said," one of the three replied.

Abraham rose to his feet and hurried to his tent calling out to his wife.

"Sarah! Sarah! Quickly! Take three measures of fine flour that is kneaded and make cakes for our illustrious guests, messengers of our God!"

He then ran to the fold and selected a fine, fat calf and gave it to a young male servant who killed and prepared it for cooking. The meat was cut into pieces and boiled over the fire. When cooked it was served with cheese, cakes, butter and honey. The dishes were placed on a fine linen cloth spread over a ground covering.

Abraham's guests reclined on pillows under the oaks that cast their speckled shadows on those they sheltered. Abraham kneeled in the shade facing the divine ones while they ate.

When the messengers finished eating, one of the three asked him, "Where is Sarah, your wife?"

"She is in the tent," Abraham replied.

"Now hear me, Abraham, you shall know your wife Sarah and there shall come forth a son as I promised you."

Although Abraham believed in the Covenant that promised him an heir through Sarah, he questioned the process.

"How is it possible for a man my age? Sarah's monthly cycles stopped many years ago. She is too old to bear."

Sarah had been listening and she laughed softly at the prospect of conceiving a child and breast feeding it. "After I am old and unable to produce children, will there be the bliss of motherhood for me? And with my husband old and unable on the love couch, how is this possible?" She laughed again.

When Sarah returned with water and cloths to wash their hands, a messenger said to Abraham, "Why did Sarah laugh and say: 'Shall I give suck to a baby when I am old?' Is it an impossible thing for the Everliving God to say: 'At such a time I will return to you the period of youth and give a son to Sarah'?"

"Sarah?" Abraham looked at his wife sternly. "Answer the lord."

"Did I laugh? I do not recall," she answered blushing and afraid.

"Yes, you did laugh, Sarah. Your time is near, however, and the son you will bear shall bring tears of joy and thanksgiving. At that time you will remember how you denied laughing. Then you shall laugh at yourself."

The three messengers then stood up to leave and gave compliments to their host for his hospitality. They left the encampment looking towards the Valley of Siddim. Abraham walked along with them, not wanting to leave their divine presence.

One of the messengers mused: "Shall I hide from Abraham what I am going to do? I think not." Turning to Abraham he revealed this message. "The seed of your loins, Abraham, will become a large and powerful nation. They must avoid abominations and keep to the path of righteousness established on high. Every nation of the earth will have the opportunity for blessings through my law. I have instructed you in order that you may command the sons of your house after you. They must respect justice and the law of right living. All this is so I may bring upon you all that I have promised.

"Loud is the outcry against Sodom and Gomorrah and the cities of Siddim Valley, Abraham. Their crimes are wicked and depraved. We are going down to see if there is any reason to spare the valley from destruction."

Two of the three turned away and went towards Sodom, while Abraham remained in the presence of the third messenger.
Worried for the safety of Lot, Abraham sought to barter his rescue.

"Will you destroy the just along with the wicked my Lord? If there are fifty just persons within the city, will you destroy it, and not forgive it for the sake of the fifty just persons that are within it? Far be it from you to slay good and bad together.
This would make the good and the wicked to be alike. This must be far from you, Lord. Will not the judge of the whole earth serve only justice?"

"If I find fifty just men in the whole City of Sodom, I will forgive the whole place for their sake," replied the divine messenger.

"Look at me! Although I am but dust and ashes I speak to the divine messenger of the Everliving God. But, my lord, if there should be five less than fifty just persons, will you sweep away the whole city for want of five?"

"I will not sweep it away if I find there forty-five just persons."

"Perhaps forty may be found in the city," Abraham suggested.

"I will spare it, for the sake of the forty", he said abruptly.

"Oh, please, do not be angry master, let me say a word further. Suppose thirty are found in the City of Sodom who are just?"

"I will spare it if I can find thirty just persons!"

"Here I am daring to speak to my master as if I were in the market place. But if there are found twenty in the city who are just?"

"I will not destroy it, for the sake of the twenty."

Abraham bowed low and pressed on with more humility than before. "If my master will listen to one more appeal from his servant without being angry... what if ten are found there?"

"Rise, Abraham. Your concern for the righteous few in Sodom is understood, and commendable. I will not destroy the city for the sake of only ten, but ask no more."

Turning away he walked off toward the Valley of Siddim.

Abraham stood, looking after the messenger of the Lord until he walked out of sight in the distance. A feeling of anxiety and suspense enveloped him as he pondered the fate of Sodom and Lot.

"Oh, Lot, why did you leave my protection in favor of that valley of iniquity? Here I have dared to anger my God's messenger in order to preserve your life. What more can a goel do for his nephew? I pray that you demonstrate an honest heart before these divine messengers. I pray for your life!"

The two divine messengers arrived at Sodom in the early evening. Lot was sitting at the gate to the city when they walked up. When he saw them he rose to his feet. His spirit identified with theirs and he went forward to greet them. Bowing his face to the ground he offered:

"If you please, my lords, come over to this your servant's house to pass the night. I will provide water to wash your feet and food to refresh yourselves. In the morning you may rise early and go on your way."

"No, generous sir, but thank you for your kindness. We will pass the night in the open."

Knowing full well the hostilities shown to strangers by Sodomites, Lot was fearful for their safety. He pressed them strongly with urgency in his voice that they recognized. They agreed to accompany him to his home, understanding it was necessary for their own safety.

"It is good to know we shall be safe in the house of a just man."

"Let us hurry, lords; already people look this way and I can see the evil intent in their eyes!"

They hurried through the streets as darkness canopied the city. Lot ushered the guests into his home and bolted the door securely. Providing the men with seats, Lot washed their hands and feet personally.

Ado took her husband aside and chided him about doing a servant's task. "Why do you act like a slave? We are not lower class servants to wait upon any stranger that comes wandering by. We are of the noble class of Sodom. You demean us by your humility. And for whom? We do not even know who they are! I intend to act like a noblewoman. I will not grovel for them. I suggest you do the same."

"It does not matter who they are; they need our protection and I will provide it in order to preserve what little honor I have left," Lot declared quietly.

Lot ordered food prepared for his guests and they sat down for the evening meal.

Afterwards, when it was time to retire for the night, they heard a commotion outside. Lot heard the shouting voices of many men...then a pounding on the door. What he feared would happen had come to pass. He went to the door, slid aside a little panel and revealed a small opening only large enough to talk through.

"What do you want?" Lot shouted to the mob in the street.

"Where are the men who came to your house tonight? Bring them out to us so that we may enjoy them in ways pleasurable to us all!" A spokesman answered, accompanied by disgusting noises and jeering from the crowd.

Lot heard the demand and knew full well what it would mean to his guests. They would be used and abused unmercifully to satisfy the insatiable wantonness of a depraved people. Successive waves of shame and anxiety washed over him. The awful reality of his mistake in leaving Abraham was more immense than ever before. He and his guests were in a terrible predicament.

Sliding the panel closed he stood with his head sagged to his chest, full of grief and confusion.

"What little righteousness I have, my very life, as useless as it is, I owe to Abram and his God. I know not whom these men are that I have sheltered. I sense they are righteous, however, sent by Abram, perhaps, to see about my welfare. I cannot give them up to the mob. Anything I have is worth sacrificing to save them. Anything!"

Lot threw the bolt and slipped out the door, closing it behind him. Quickly he drew an angry looking dagger from his girdle and held it up for all to see.

Those nearest the door backed away, pushing and stumbling against the press of drunken bodies.

"Look out! He has a dagger!" came a warning. "He knows how to use it well!"

"Listen to me! I have two daughters who have never bedded with a man. Let me bring them out to you, to do what you like with them; only do nothing to these men in as much as they have come under the shelter of my roof and my protection."

"Your daughters never bedded a man? Ha, ha, ha, that is a laugh! We know otherwise. You are a fool, Heberew, who knows not what goes on in his own house. Now get out of the way! This Heberew came to our city as stranger and now he would make himself a judge over us! Here, we will treat you worse than your precious guests!"

The lusting mob pushed forward to assault Lot and gain entrance. Lot stood firm, prepared to battle until he fell.

Just then the door opened, the two messengers reached out and pulled him inside, shutting the door and throwing the bolt.

Saying nothing to Lot, one of the divine ones raised his arms and closed his eyes in concentration.

"Let blindness come upon those that plague this house!" he commanded with a voice of awesome authority.

Lot could not believe his eyes and ears. He stood in dumb silence as he heard the mob outside shrieking in pain and stumbling around in confusion.

Opening the door panel Lot watched with amazement as every man groped in utter darkness. Some still searched in vain for the entrance to the house. Eventually they all wandered off after a fruitless endeavor.

"Is there anyone else here in the city who is righteous like you Lot? Sons-in-law, sons, daughters, or anyone at all? If so, go tell them now! They must leave this place by the morning's light!"

"Who are you, my lords"? Lot questioned. "Why did you come to this awful place?"

"We are messengers of Yahvah the Everliving God. We are about to destroy this city. The outcry against its abominations and those of the other cities of Siddim is so loud and numerous that the most high God has sent us to destroy this valley. Now go, make haste in your preparations! Do not delay with questions!"

Lot left his house and went to the homes of his married daughters. Pleading with his Sodomite sons-in-law he warned: "Leave this place at the break of day for the Most High God is about to destroy the city! I have been instructed by his divine messengers to tell you...to plead with you to come out! Prepare now what you want to take. I will look for you at first light at our house!"

Lot finished his task of warning and went home to direct his family's preparations and then get some rest.

When the early light of dawn shone its rosy hue above the horizon, the divine messengers urged Lot to take his family and leave.

"Get your family together, your wife and two daughters that are at hand, and go before it is too late. You must hurry now and run or you will be swept away in the punishment of the city."

Lot hesitated, stalling, in hope that his married daughters and their families would come.

Ado and her daughters cried their objections to leaving, adding to Lot's indecision.

"They are not coming," one of the messengers declared.

"It is true," added the other messenger, "they did not take you seriously. They have rejected your God in favor of the abominable practices of the priests."

The messengers, seeing Lot's hesitation felt pity for him. They seized the hands of Lot, his wife and two daughters and pulled them along hurriedly through the city until they were outside the gate. Releasing them they exclaimed:

"Run for your lives! Do not look behind you nor stop anywhere in the valley! Fly to the hills, lest you be swept away!"

Just then the ground moved under them with a series of jolts sending Ado to her knees.

"Oh, but gracious lords, your servant has indeed found favor with you. Great is the kindness that you have done me and my family, lords," Lot declared. "You have saved our lives but...but we cannot possibly run to the hills before the disaster overtakes us and we perish. There is, however, a town to the south called Zoar. It is near enough to reach, where we can find shelter. Let us fly there, masters, to save our lives!"

"Very well. See, I grant you this request as well," replied one of the divine ones." We will not overthrow the town of which you speak. Hurry and run, for we can do nothing until you reach there! Remember, do not look back!"

Lot's wife, Ado, spoiled by a life of physical and sexual dissipation, doubted the disaster would even take place. She whined and complained constantly as Lot pulled her along.

She stopped a number of times to catch her breath, swearing at Lot that she could not move another step. Each time she voiced her regrets at having left Sodom.

"What will life be like without those things that give me the little pleasure I enjoy?"

She pleaded, cajoled and threatened Lot to stop 'this silly escape from a danger that simply did not exist.'

Just as the sun rose full upon the earth the smell of natural gas and sulfur drifted towards them from the north, pushed by a slight breeze off the Salt Sea.

"Phew," Lot sniffed, that must be the odor from the slime pits. It is filling the valley! We must hurry Ado! It is dangerous to breathe!"

"Nonsense! We have endured that smell for several years. Why should there be a danger now? Must you be a fool any longer?" she spat out insultingly.

"I am returning! I do not care what you say or do!" Ado fended off Lot's grasp and started walking back towards Sodom.

Shocked and helpless to do anything about his wife's rebellion, Lot stood still and called out to her, pleading for her to come with him.

Ado had heard him plead with her before. This was nothing new or exceptional. She felt relieved to be free of him. "Good riddance," she thought.

His voice was far away when it happened.

The ground jolted and jumped more drastically than before. A crack appeared across her path opening wider with each convulsion. Trees fell with a crash here and there around Ado, threatening her and adding their impact to the earthquake's terrifying crescendo.

Ado reeled back in fright clutching her chest, as the pain near her heart became overwhelming. She went rigid, petrified with fear. With neck muscles distended, eyes bulging, mouth open, gasping but not able to breath, Ado teetered off balance and staggered forward. She managed to turn back towards Lot and see him for a fading moment. He and the girls were a blur of shaking motion...a final unbearable pain...then darkness, total void.

Lot and his daughters glanced back only long enough to see Ado stiffen and fall into the chasm. They did not have time to stay and do anything for her. The ground was coming apart and the air more foul smelling than ever.

On Lot ran, pulling his daughters along, holding them up when they stumbled, choking and coughing. The land heaved up and down in irregular seizures. Trees fell blocking their way. Over and around obstacles they climbed, moving relentlessly onward.

Zoar appeared in the distance, tiny and almost unreachable in the hills.

"A little further!" Lot gasped. "Only a little further," he encouraged the girls. "Keep moving...do not stop...and do not look back!"

Staggering up the last rise, Lot and his daughters reached the hills near the city of Zoar and collapsed. A fresh breeze from the south pushed the smoke and stench northward and they breathed some decent air for the first time in hours. Almost unconscious from exhaustion they lay panting and moaning.

Suddenly it happened. Lot sat bolt upright and stared in shock, back towards Sodom.

Lightning showered down from the heavens thousands of white barbs. It crackled, hissed, and snapped its whip of death, exploding gasses and igniting fires in a rushing firestorm. Asphalt pits continued to erupt as burning geysers, scattering flaming fuel around them. Pillars of dark gray smoke shot upward, pushing through the billows of white smoke roiling through the valley as though it were a giant cauldron in a stir.

Outside of the cities there was fire everywhere. All plant life was ablaze, from grass to trees. Most animal life had felt disturbances in the earth before the great upheaval started and had left the valley for other parts. They could be seen swarming up the hills on every side, escaping to higher more stable ground.

Throughout the Cities of Sodom, Gomorrah, Admah, and Zeboim, buildings shook into pieces, tumbling down on sleeping bodies. Fires broke out in every house as oil lamps and embers from cooking fires were upset. Gasses issued from fissures asphyxiating and burning to death countless victims.

City gates were choked with crowds trampling upon each other to escape. Those who managed to stagger out of the cities were welcomed by fire, gas, and burning asphalt.

The floor of the Siddim Valley depressed into a bowl during the valley's day-long orgasmic convulsions. Now as the sun left this part of the world and removed its light, another calamity struck.

The Salt Sea's threshold to the valley, along the southern shoreline, gave way like an earthen dam. Great heaving waters, heavy with salt, oil, and asphalt slime came like a tidal wave. Down they swept into a huge depression thirty to fifty feet deep. Rolling and swirling, the sea swept over everything in its way, tumbling debris and bodies along in a gigantic, long wave.

Raging fires were extinguished with a tremendous "hissss" as they were submerged in the rush of waters. Here and there unrelenting geysers of gas and steam burst through the surface displaying their deadly presence.

On the waters rushed, conquering and smothering all life on the valley floor. Giant waves crashed up slopes of the low hills around Zoar bringing trees, bodies and flotsam with it. Settling back to find a level depth, the waters left grotesque remains in its path.

Totally inundated by the Salt Sea, the Siddim Valley became a huge watery grave. A swirling and bubbling could be seen in hundreds of places as the hot, angry earth was cooled and put to rest.

Lot gazed out over the water for hours waiting for the steam to clear away so he could spy its expanse. His exhaustion defeated his determination to look for signs of life. He fell into a deep sleep and awoke long after sunrise the next day. After resuming his vigil the fog showed some sign of lessening its intensity. By late afternoon it had lifted and thinned enough for Lot to see the length of where the valley used to be. Of the five cities, only a portion of Zoar survived.

Chapter 30
Restoration: Birth of Isaac

S ometime after the destruction of the four cities of Siddim Valley, Abraham left the Plain of Mamre and moved his tribe westward. They traveled over coastal mountains to the maritime plain that centuries later became known as Philistia, or the land of the Philistines.

Grass was good there during the warm season, pampered by the mists of the Great Sea. The rich fertile land was watered from rains as well as streams coming down the mountains.

Close by was the ancient city of Gerar, located inland fifteen to twenty miles from the sea coast. It lay on the south side of Wadi Ghazzeh near the border of Egypt. Gerar was situated on an inland trade route more protected than the coastal route used through the centuries by warring armies.

It was during their stay in this new land near Gerar that Abraham and Sarah were restored to a youthful state of being. Sarah's skin lost its wrinkles of old age. A golden luster replaced the gray of her hair. She regained her vitality, lost many years before. The miracle that astounded her most was the return of her monthly cycle.

When Sarah informed Abraham of this latest miracle he built an altar and sacrificed an ox to the Everliving as a sign of his thanksgiving. Abram then groomed himself properly and began a new courtship of Sarah.

Abraham noticed remarkable changes in himself, as well as in Sarah. He also had lost some wrinkles. His hair was regaining its youthful color and his beard was growing dark instead of gray. The strength he had enjoyed in his prime was returning, and he looked upon Sarah as he did early in their marriage.

They fell in love with each other as it had been in the beginning. Every night they slept in each other's arms, exploring with the curiosity and wonder of young lovers. They made love, first delicately and tenderly, but their passions soon overwhelmed this initial sensitivity.

Simple sighs became moans and groans of delightful passion. This, their first union in several years, produced an explosion of ecstasy that racked their bodies. An electrical sensation surged from fingertips to toes. In complete union and harmony of emotion, Sarah's climax raised her high on the crest of a wave that made her float over and down, down, down. She was left panting with exhaustion as she collapsed on Abraham's chest.

She lay there, relishing the aftereffects, and then cried softly, tears of joy and amazement.

Abraham smoothed the hair away from her beautiful pink face with both his big hands and looked into her tear-filled eyes.

"What is it, sweet Sarah?"

"I cry tears of thankfulness, my husband, just tears of thankfulness."

The months that followed were full of happiness for Abraham and Sarah. She had conceived and was cradling a child in her womb. Sarah was more radiant each new day that dawned. She waited upon Abraham's every desire, delighting in their renewed intimacies. Sarah confessed she could never be as brash and seductive as Hagar could, but she would please him. Yes, she would please him.

Abraham responded with renewed affection and attention to Sarah's comfort and pleasure.

Their marriage was renewed to a high point neither one had believed possible. It was as though each day, packed with happiness and enrichment of soul, made up for each year of heartache and disappointment in the past. They had each been given a new life, and now they were in turn producing a new life.

Each new day Abraham woke up, he looked at Sarah and felt the baby crouched within her. And each day at this time he smiled and said to Sarah: "Yahvah's delay was not his denial".

Late in the Spring Sarah went into labor and gave birth to a healthy, pink-skinned baby boy. Abraham was giddy with joy, praising Sarah and the Everliving. When he heard the good news from the midwife, he called for immediate feasting in celebration of his miraculous good fortune. While the music played and his people clapped a rhythm, Abraham danced like a proud young father for his heir.

Sarah's labor was short and the delivery mercifully brief without any difficulties. Surprisingly, Sarah made a brief appearance before the tribe during the celebration.

Abraham ran to Sarah as she stood in the opening of her tent.

"Sarah...Sarah you are up so soon? Are you strong enough? Is this proper for a new mother having delivered so recently? Is it safe? What is the reason you honor us with your presence, O mother of kings?" He smiled and bowed before her, his heart full of humility.

"Yahvah, our God has given us an heir in our old age to prove His power over life as well as death. There is nothing that escapes his control. I, too, want to rejoice with my people. The gift of a goel, He has now provided, will grow to lead and safeguard them. Let me see your happiness as you can see mine."

"Let it be as you request, my love," Abraham declared. "You are the light of my life. Ask anything of me and I will proclaim it as a covenant."

"For now, I would appreciate a comfortable place to sit down and hold Isaac for all to see."

"Oh...yes, of course. A seat for Sarah! A throne for my queen!" Abraham exclaimed and within moments a varied assortment of packs and furs were arranged into the semblance of a large throne-like seat.

Sarah was led to it and seated with considerable reverence. Isaac was placed in her arms by a handmaid and the tribal procession filed by to give praises. Everyone bowed in obeisance as they approached. Everyone, that is, except Hagar and Ishmael.

Off a short distance, they stood together, murmuring against Sarah, Isaac, and even Abraham. Hagar was careful to avoid letting anyone hear her. No one had to, the look on her face expressed bitterness and resentment for all to see.

On the eighth day of Isaac's life Abraham circumcised him. He declared to his tribe: "I hereby make the mark upon my son's body in fulfillment of the covenant made with our God. And I declare his name to be Isaac, as he was forenamed by Yahvah the Everliving, before the miracle of his conception. Let this birth be a witness to the favor and power of our God, who rewards those who have faith in Him."

Abraham was one hundred years old and Sarah ninety when Isaac was born to them.

Sarah rarely left the child to the care of anyone else. Isaac was the most precious thing on earth to her. She was no longer embarrassed at having no children. She had a son, a gift from Yahvah. And the Everliving elevated her among all women by changing her name. Sarah means "Princess among women."

"Isaac, Isaac," she said softly, looking tenderly at him as he suckled from her breast. She laughed softly as she remembered the origin of his name. "His name means laughter. He will laugh and be happy. I pray that he will have many sons...whose descendants will be called 'Sons of Laughter'...Isaacsons."

EPILOGUE – Food for thought

"The evidence on which a family relation has been established among these nations is that of language. Between **Sanskrit** (the mother of the modern Hindu dialects of Hindustan), **Zend** (the language of the ancient Persians), **Greek** (which is yet the language of Greece), **Latin** (the language of the Romans and the mother of the modern romantic languages – i.e. Italian, French, Spanish, Portuguese, Rumanian), **Celtic** (once the language of a great part of Europe) now confined to Wales and parts of France, Ireland, and Scotland), **Gothic** (which may be taken as the ancient type of the Teutonic or German languages – including English – and of the Scandinavian), and **Slavonic** (spoken in a variety of dialects all over European Russia and a great part of Austria), the researches of philology have within the 19th century established such affinities as can be accounted for only by supposing that the nations who originally spoke them had a common origin."

Chambers Encyclopedia: *Aryan Race and Languages*